FOOTPRINTS

A JOURNEY THROUGH DREAMTIME

DAVID ENGLISH

Copyright © 2023 by David English

All rights reserved.

No part of this book may be reproduced in any form or by any electronic or mechanical means, including information storage and retrieval systems, without written permission from the author, except for the use of brief quotations in a book review.

This is a work of creative nonfiction. The events are portrayed to the best of David English's memory. While all the stories in this book are true, some names and identifying details have been changed to protect the privacy of the people involved.

The conversations in the book all come from the author's recollections, though they are not written to represent word-for-word transcripts. Rather, the author has retold them in a way that evokes the feeling and meaning what was said and in all instances, the essence of the dialogue is accurate.

For all those who love adventure in their life…
happy reading x

PART I
THE EARLY YEARS

1

This is where it all starts. A beginning that leads to a labyrinth of events and adventures which, as I write, are still unfolding before me – albeit at a somewhat reduced rate.

So, where do I start? If I think back to those very early years, it is at my grandmother's house in London; Clapham to be precise. I lived there with my gran, my mother, and my father as well as three sisters: Delia, the eldest, then Dinah, and finally the youngest sister, Jo, who was three years older than me.

The nearest tube station was Clapham South and you had to walk through the Common to Clapham Common West Side to get to Broomwood Road. It was a very rural part of London and great for us kids to have the Common at the bottom of the road. However, you could say this story really starts earlier, in Australia, where the family had moved when I was three.

I have vivid memories of Australia, which I shall recall shortly, but I'd like to start when I was seven years old, living at 185 Broomwood Road. This terraced Victorian house was my first truly strong recollection of a home. My gran had been renting it for years, well before the last world war. Looking recently online, the cost to purchase one of these now, on the same road, is a minimum of £1.5million – stunning, for this quiet, suburban London area.

My cosy cave was in an attic room at the top of my gran's house. It was a typical Victorian terrace with three floors and a cellar. My bedroom was at the pinnacle of this design – the topmost room in the gable of the house. There was a small landing at the top of the stairs with a bathroom on the left just outside my bedroom door.

The bedroom itself was quite small but in a comfortable way. There was one window facing the door that looked out over the rooftops of the houses at the back, giving a brief glimpse to the gardens far below if I pushed my face up close to the window and stood on tiptoe. My bed was central to the left-hand wall and opposite this was a fire that, on cold nights, Dad would build up and light; he was the master of the fire grates.

An object that stands out in my memory of this room and those days, stood atop a white chest of drawers to the right of the door as you entered the room, was a small, plastic gondolier in the middle of which sat a perfect, midnight blue, square bottle of perfume. This was 'Soir de Paris' by Bourjois, the smell of which, to my seven-year-old senses was magical and heavenly and always reminded me of my mother.

I was not one for staying inside a great deal, so the bedroom was not a place I hung about in to any extent. In fact, during colder weather, it was a race against the clock to get dressed before frostbite set in. Jeans were a luxury I cannot recall – it was grey flannel shorts, long, grey woollen socks, a grey flannel shirt and a tank top, also grey, with a blue and maroon stripe around the V neck. Chucking these things on in haste, I'd leg it out the door and hurtle down the stairs to the top landing, which was where my mum and dad's bedroom was.

Further along this landing was another room and then a few steps down was the next small landing where the main bathroom was. The door to this had patterned, frosted glass with the edging pieces having red and blue coloured glass. A long set of steep stairs then led down to the ground floor and the front door. These stairs were the longest run and had a great mahogany banister that was the best mode of transport to the lower level – leaning over it and sliding down, crashing into the tall knob at the bottom.

From end-to-end, our street was filled with similar houses on both sides. Outside our large, glossy, black front door, there was a small porch and the typical black and white ceramic tiled path leading to two red brick pillars and a wrought iron gate. Just beyond the front step (a red waxed and highly polished affair that my mum used to keep that way) was the circular, black metal coal hole. It was down this that the coalman, on his monthly visit, used to dump his four sacks of tarry-smelling coal. The coal was delivered by dray horse and cart that we chased up the street, pinching the coal that fell off!

The coal hole outside the house led to the cellar, which was accessed from within the house by a small door under the stairs. Cellars are wonderful places to explore, and I was no exception in my efforts to do this, not only in our house but also those of my mates in the street. In one, we found an old Webley .45 calibre pistol, complete with officer's brown leather holster. The pistol proved quite a find and we took turns in playing with it in our hunt for German spies up and down the street. Alas, we never did find the ammo for it – or the German spies – although we did tie up fat, Tom Wolkowyski in his cellar and interrogate him for being an agent of the Gestapo. Fortunately for Tommy, they didn't have 'water boarding' in those days or we would have used it...!

My first primary school was Bellview Road School in Webbs Road. Being educated was never uppermost on my list of priorities at this time and what little I can remember of it was of falling hopelessly in love with our form tutor Miss Austin – a blonde English Rose who entranced me for hours. The impact she had on me was long lasting, with her delicate hands and gentle voice which – when aimed at me – left me in a daze. Other than that, I don't recall anything that made an impact.

This may have been, in part, due to the fact that I needed glasses.

However, everyone around me was blissfully unaware of this rather neglected matter. Sitting at the back of the classroom didn't help but this was the best place to be; one could write secret intelligence reports and plan further forays for after school all whilst looking studious and innocent.

I hadn't been at Bellview long when, one day, it got a little too much for me and I legged it out of the place with the intention of heading home. Getting hopelessly lost, I had visions of wandering around the streets of Clapham well into the early hours. Sitting outside a particular house on one of the many look-alike streets I started to cry (not something I was particularly proud of). This must have aroused the attention of the occupant, an elderly lady with masses of grey hair and wire framed glasses that gave her the impression of being very strict. However, this assumption turned out to be totally incorrect. She, in fact, was softly spoken and gentle as she helped me up and into her house where I was plied with tea and custard cream biscuits. This time it was me who was on the receiving end of the interrogation, albeit in a rather more gentle manner! When I told her my name, she immediately knew who I belonged to and proceeded to walk me through the streets back to Broomwood Road. Assuming she knew of me from the misadventures I had been up to with the lads, I thought my game was up and that, master spy catcher that I was, I had met my match in the shape of an elderly lady with glasses – I would have difficulty living this one down and decided that she'd have to be assassinated! However, it turned out that she knew my family from her efforts to teach my eldest sister; my secret life was safe, for the moment.

What this episode did achieve was that it brought it home to my mum that I needed glasses and an appointment with an optician on the Northcote Road was arranged.

I can't recall a lot about that appointment, but I do remember a rather fat Indian ophthalmologist trying various lenses in those strange frames where they drop in different lenses and rotate them. He had the largest 'pigeon's-egg' ruby in a gold ring that I had ever seen! And that is how I ended up wearing glasses. The bane of my life. At least, in those early days. Later, they came to be quite useful, but I never got out of the habit of wearing them in swimming pools and this often caused comments from others.

Another thing I had in my earlier years – apart from poor eyesight – was an abundance of uncles with tales of 'daring-do' in faraway exotic places. Like most boys, I hung on every word. Their tales of exploits in places with strange sounding names like Kuala Lumpur, Bombay, Changi, Bangkok, Rangoon were a veritable feast of excitement that, in my minds-eye, conjured visions of the sights and smells these places would introduce me to. Little did I know then what a profound effect these stories were to have on me and how they were to shape my life. Earlier than all of this, however, when I was three, my family took off for Australia.

2

Moving to Australia was probably a monumental mistake on the part of my parents. I guess Dad must have painted a rosy picture of Oz to Mum because he had previously spent some time there when he was in the Merchant Navy. However, it was most damaging for my two elder sisters. Delia was very good at art and had won a scholarship to the London College of Art in Camberwell and I believe that, at the time, my other sister Dinah was on the verge of taking exams which would have gotten her into grammar school. So, it seems not a lot of 'forward thinking' went on between my mother and father. I know that Mum saw education as a means of getting us kids out from under her feet and, it is sad to say, not a great deal of interest in our education was shown by either of my parents.

The call of a new life, away from a war-torn London, must have been a driving factor in my parents applying for the 'ten-quid tourists' gig that had us en route to the land of Oz.[1]

In the UK, the country was struggling to get back on its feet and, with all the remnants of the black market and the influx of so many people returning from the war, jobs must have been hard to come by. I don't really know why my parents decided to make such a monumental decision and, to be honest, I can't recall any of the preparation for this journey. I sort of 'came to' when we were rolling around the Bay of Biscay, gripping Mum's hand, terrified that she was going to take a dive overboard and take me with her!

The ship we were on was an old troop carrier – the *Astorius*. The scrubbed wooden decking and the lumpy, black caulking between the planking gave off a tarry smell that, to this day, reminds me of that moment of realisation that I was on a boat, heading into an adventure. That little glimpse of memory coupled with coils of very large rope at various locations on the decking is the only thing I can recall of the journey. I've seen pictures of my Uncle Joe holding me up on his shoulder in the port of Colombo, where he was stationed with the RAF, but have absolutely no recollection of it.

What I do remember is where we lived in Australia. We were split up as a family as, apparently, accommodation for all six of us could not be found. This was yet another blow to the two girls; Delia and Dinah went to live with a family called Mr and Mrs Tull, about twenty minutes away from where Mum and Dad, Jo and I were living in a suburb of Melbourne, Pasco Vale. Our street was called Waverly Parade and our house was a large corner house belonging to two doctors, the Elders, who were husband and wife. They had six children and Mum secured a job as their housekeeper.

Meanwhile, Dad was off somewhere doing something, I don't know what, but rarely seemed to make an appearance. We lived in an annexe on the Elders' property, and I didn't go to school. So, this is where I started to develop my earliest memories. As for the two girls, Dinah went to a local school which she didn't enjoy and had difficulty being accepted, while Delia ended up working in a large department store called *Myers* doing odd jobs. I now look back at these events with horror. My personal belief is that none of this should have happened, and that we should have stayed in England. I fully blame my parents for a total lack of vision and interest in their children's education; our futures are often shaped by such things.

Being almost four, I guess it was because I was not very big that everything seemed so large where we were living. I remember a massive Magnolia tree in the back garden, which was often a place of refuge us kids used to climb, and a fig tree that we pinched the fresh figs from – usually ending up with a dose of the trots. There was also a large pond which had Koi Carp in it, but the whole thing was covered in wire so we couldn't fall in.

What little I can remember of Australia comes in snatches: sticking my finger in the tin of Nestle's condensed milk; eating fresh baked bread and jam that Mum had made; Mum chasing tarantulas around the kitchen with a broom and beating the things to death with it; Dad climbing onto the porch roof to get the wire rat trap down, usually containing several rats. (He would then proceed to drown them in a forty-gallon oil drum that served as a water butt, much to our delight, as we yelled and cheered.)

I spent most of my time at this age running around with the Elders' kids – Nairn, Jamie, and Margy – and spent most of those hot, sunny days in bare feet and shorts.

One of our neighbours was an elderly lady who lived in another enormous house just up the road. The only trouble was that she was a witch! We used to raid her garden for cumquats and one day on a 'dare raid' we could smell hot toffee. The others thought she was making a witch's brew and legged it, while my curiosity overpowered me and I crept up the back garden to open patio doors that led into her kitchen.

There stood this horrific witch, crouched over her 'cauldron' on the stove, slowly stirring and cackling away. I was about to discreetly leg it myself when, without looking up, she said, "You can have some if you like."

I was caught like a rabbit in headlights, but she came towards me with a tray of buttered toffee, still soft from cooking and smelling like heaven. My stomach got the better of me and, being a sucker for a soft voice, a tray of toffee, and the street-cred I'd get from confronting a witch and coming away with such a bounty, I couldn't resist.

After offering me the toffee, the witch invited me in, showed me pictures of her family, including a son who was killed in the war, and made me an iced lemonade. By the time I left, I had made a good friend and gained a bag full of toffee. It turns out she had known about our 'secret cumquat raids' for a while and, in the end, we all would turn up in her garden regularly for toffee, cakes and lemonade.

On the rare occasions that I recall my dad, it was usually him telling me off for not lifting my feet up as we walked along. The problem was, I couldn't keep up with his lengthy strides so ended up, on several occasions, tripping which was something of an embarrassment to Dad. He did, however, manage to be a great storyteller.

His 'thing' was game hunting in the wilds of Africa, and he would go to great lengths to explain how he used to capture wild animals and bring them back alive for circuses and zoos. Many times, us kids used to sit around in a circle, thrilled in terror whilst Dad described the hunt.

One time, from continuing prompting from us, he decided to get us to re-enact a lion hunt. Our front garden in Waverly Parade was huge, even to an adult. To a five-year old's eyes, it was a Zulu game reserve and safari hunting territory. How we got away with it, I have no idea, but Mum was washing clothes inside, so we were relatively safe.

To recreate the right circumstances, Dad got a large spade and began to dig a pit in the lawn about ten metres from the back porch. While he worked, we all stood round in a circle keeping an eye out for wild animals, park rangers and Mum, and trying to shield Dad from being seen. What eventually looked like a massive pit was nearing completion. A couple of us had gathered stout sticks and, using my trusty scout knife, were whittling vicious points at one end. At this stage, Dad hadn't noticed our efforts. He eventually finished and went back to the house to get some newspaper and pinch a small joint of meat from the cooler. A couple of the kids collected grass cuttings, weeds, and sticks. Nairn and I jumped into the pit and pushed the pointed staves into the earth at the bottom of the pit. Climbing out, we then started laying a criss-cross of sticks across the top of the pit.

Dad came back with a stack of old newspapers that he then proceeded to lay across the mesh of sticks. He hadn't noticed the five-pointed staves at the bottom of the pit. We laid the grasses, weeds, and sticks over the newspaper and Dad finished it off very professionally.

To our eyes, you couldn't see that there was a pit there at all.

He then placed the piece of raw meat gently in the centre of the covering. This was the moment. He told us to go and hide nearby.

Now, I should perhaps point out that we had a silver-haired terrier called Timmy that was a total maniac but quite a loving little beast. At this time, we had shut him in one of the garden sheds where he had a doggy bed, at the back of the house. Jeanie went round the back and released the latch on the shed and came back to hide with us. Dad said the time was right to call him. Mum was still out of sight, and we were in a high state of excitement.

"Timmy, Timmy, Timmy," we called and yelled, and then waited.

Within a few minutes, a mad streak of grey fur came hurtling around the side of the house looking for us. He skidded to a halt just before the pit and sniffed, distracted by the smell of the meat (now festering nicely in the heat of the sun). He obviously sensed that something was not quite right, or at least, different. Then, in single leap, the dumb mutt leaped onto the meat. At first it held his weight then Jeanie screamed in excitement, the dog spun around, and the sticks, grass and weeds gave way.

Timmy disappeared and then let out a dreadful screeching howling sound.

We all jumped out of hiding, shouting, and cheering, all expecting to see an impaled Lion (Timmy) in a mess of blood and fur at the bottom of the pit. Fortunately for Timmy, he had fallen between two of the staves and was at the bottom, looking up at us, howling and barking. Dad was pleased but pissed off about the staves.

"I said we wouldn't put the spear points in the pit – who did that?" he barked, immediately looking at me as I was the only one who had a scout knife.

But we were laughing so much that his protestations fell on deaf ears.

Jeanie then got frightened and started crying. Timmy was still howling at this point, and then Mum came out to see what all the noise was about. Ooops! We scattered to the four safari park African winds, leaving Dad to take the hit. And boy did he get it when Mum looked in the pit and saw Timmy. Actually, she was more angry about the damage to the lawn and the loss of the joint. But it had worked, and our faith and belief in Dad and his jungle stories knew no bounds. Of course, as punishment, he was banned from African safari stories for a few weeks and had the onerous task of filling the hole in and making the lawn look good again.

Another strong memory I have of our time in Oz, was a holiday we took to a coastal place on the edge of the Bush. I remember the prefab-type bungalow we stayed in, the mozzies and the mozzie nets we had to have over our beds.

This place was the start of a big adventure for me that, in hindsight, may have been what took me down a totally unexpected path; a path my life was destined to take.

It was certainly the moment my life took a new turn.

I was around six years old. One afternoon whilst on holiday here, always looking for adventure, I wandered off into the interior of what was, to me, a forest of humongous proportions – the Aussie 'Outback'. This was an adventure that beat the beach, anytime. I had shorts and a t-shirt on and bare feet. At first, I followed a narrow trail leading through tall stands of eucalyptus and a tangle of vine and fern. I had found a stave a few days prior, which made a great walking stick and sword. Thus equipped, I felt invincible.

The shrill of parrots and budgies gave way to the laughing chatter of kookaburras, echoing through the forest as I made my way along what was, for me, secret sandy trails. The dappled sunlight turned shadows of leaves and branches into mythical creatures and elves that taunted me. I had no fear of any such being and loved the sounds of the place. Even the kookaburra stilled as the clicking song of the cicadas became more frequent and shadows lengthened down through these ancient stands.

As it got later, I started to tire and get hungry but, by this time, I was well and truly lost. One trail crossed another, and everything was shadow and flickering light. At last, I sat beneath a tree and leaned back against the smooth trunk, thinking I'd rest for a bit.

I must have fallen asleep because when I woke it was darker and stood in front of me was this strange person, about my size, with ebony skin and white lines painted across his chest and face.

"Hey mate, what you doing out here, boy?" he asked me.

In response, I burst into tears and murmured something about being lost.

"Naw, you ain't lost. I'm Jon-Bud, you follow me."

I stood, picked up my stave, cuffed my tears away and followed him. This strange boy knew me. He said he'd been following me for some time and asked if I knew I was in the dreamtime land with him.

"You're on Walkabout, man, just like me. Our ancestors live here in this place. I been on me walkabout for thirteen moons now. You can walk a ways with me if ya wanting, but you need to get back to your folks."

I seem to remember just nodding and thinking I was really in the shit and that Mum was gonna kill me when I got home.

"I got a little wookie hole up ahead you hungry?"

I was bloody starving but just nodded.

We came across a massive, smooth boulder. Just around the side of it was a shallow cave in an outcrop of rock. It was more of a depression in the rock face and the floor was sandy. There were the remains of a fire to one side and Jon-Bud started chucking some dried eucalyptus sticks on the ash. I was expecting him to start rubbing some sticks together but, no, he pulled out a box of *Bryant & May* from his torn trousers, cupped his hands around the struck match and lit some dried leaves. It took a few goes but he got the fire going and soon we had a small blaze that had a sweet, pungent aroma from the wood.

Jon-Bud had an old tin can and a billy. From the back wall of this shelter there was a wet patch running down the rock wall, which dribbled off the rock onto large fronds that lined a small pit sunk into the sandy floor. The water was crystal clear; this was Jon-Bud's water supply.

To this day, I couldn't tell you what it was we ate. Some of it was a root he had dug up and the meat was something that looked like a cross between a rabbit and a small cat. At some point, as dusk fell, we both could hear a faint 'coo-ee-ing' quite some way away. Jon-Bud reckoned it was a stockman out looking for me, but it was too far away to do anything about it tonight.

As darkness fell, Pandora's box of stars opened up in the night's sky. The food was good, and I felt great. This was the adventure I had been looking for, the consequences of which I hadn't given a thought to.

We lay on our backs looking up at the stars and Jon-Bud told me about the Dreamtime and how all his ancestors were there, in the stars, watching us. He said I had a good aborigine spirit with me that stayed with me at all times.

"You lucky, man, you got a Numakulla spirit that wanted you to see this place. This ancestor of the Dreamtime is gonna take you on a journey for many years. You been touched by this ancient one, but you have to be careful too, they sometimes like to play games with you. But they will always keep you safe. He showed me where you were 'cause the tree spirit told him."

"How did the tree spirit know?" I asked.

"Cause you was sitting beneath him and your eye-water touched his roots. You on walkabout. Numakulla called you to come into these forests."

"How long will I have to be on this walkabout? Me mum's gonna kill me!" I asked.

"Naw, you be okay. Jon-Bud will get you on the home path at sunrise. I'll show you how to call the stockmen, they'll find you pretty damn quick. Besides, I have to go on me walkabout." He started singing a strange song that had a sleepy, hypnotic effect.

As I listened, I guess I must have drifted off to sleep.

Jon-Bud woke me the next morning with a hot billy of tea and the sounds of kookaburra echoing around the forest. Shards of early morning light speared through the trees, and everything felt damp and cool. The smoke from the fire was drifting lazily and caught in the light streaming through the trees.

We had some porridge-like stuff made from roots and he squeezed several honey ants on it for me. After we'd eaten, he took me along a trail that looked quite new to me and pointed out where the sun was and to keep it on my back.

Cupping his hands in front of his mouth he made the 'coo-ee-ing' sound we'd heard yesterday evening. I told him it seemed really loud, and he said the trees pass the sound on from their trunks, which was why the rangers and stockmen use it in the bush. After several attempts, I got the hang of it.

"I have to leave you now, David-man. You'll be okay. Just keep to the trail and call out every few minutes, they will find you."

"Will I see you again Jon-Bud?" I asked him.

"Of course – in Dreamtime. We both have long journeys to make."

"I see you David," he said.

I took my sword stick and gave it to him. "You can keep that. I see you, Jon-Bud."

I don't know how long I walked that morning, but I kept 'coo-ee-ing' like he showed me. Then, what seemed like hours later, I heard an answering 'coo-ee'. Before I knew it, a stockman on his horse came out of the trees. He jumped down out of the saddle.

"You must be David, right? Your folks are gonna be real glad to see you, my lad. Come on, I'll get you aboard, you can ride in front of me."

On the way back, I tried to tell the stockman about Jon-Bud, but it was obvious he didn't believe me. When I returned home, Mum was fine, although I thought she was going to smother me. She cried a bit and hugged me. I didn't mention Jon-Bud this time, but I overheard the stockman saying to my dad that I was bloody lucky because there were poisonous snakes in the bush, and I was barefoot. He also told him what I'd said about Jon-Bud and then laughed said I must have overheard someone talking about Jon-Bud.

When Dad asked him why, he replied that Jon-Bud was an old Aborigine character from their ancient Dreamtime myths. The handed-down story could be well over a thousand years old.

As I listened to this, I thought, *Well, I bloody-well saw him and now he's got me sword-stick!*

No one ever asked me what had happened to it, nor did I ever mention it; I said I just fell asleep at the foot of a big tree when I thought I was lost, and it started to get dark. Let's face it, they wouldn't have believed me if I did tell them…

The author at six years old

I guess this infamous incident helped to make Mum's mind up about leaving Australia.

Those were heady days in Oz, and I didn't go to school until we arrived back in the UK, by which time I was seven. Despite my feelings about my parents' decision to take us there, Australia was a magical place for a young lad with an imagination and my memories really started in earnest at that time. For example, I remember I had a model Holden car in maroon plastic with a beige plastic seat interior. When you moved the steering wheel, the front wheels moved. I also had a green, plastic model, of a Douglas Dakota. Underneath, it was hollow and, for some reason, if I put my tongue in the fuselage groove the plastic made my tongue tingle. If I kept it there, it would actually burn!

I was an avid collector of Dinky cars and trucks and would play for hours with these, often on my own, in the sandpit and grass, creating imaginary worlds. Sadly, I guess all those toys got left behind when we returned to the UK.

Like most boys, I was always fascinated with cars and aircraft. I had a three-wheel trike that had a boot at the back, which was my greatest joy out there in Australia. Putting toys and bits in the back was great, and I used to pedal this trike just about everywhere I could. When on paved areas I would go like a maniac, the intention being to go as fast as I was able; it was all about the speed and the thrill. However, there turned out to be a down-side to this. About three months before we were due to head back home, I developed a lump about the size of an egg at the back of my left knee. When the Australian doctor saw it, he told my mum she had two options – we could leave it, in which case it would get bigger and cripple me, or we could have it removed surgically. Either way, I would in all likelihood have a limp.

Mum was horrified but as we were due to leave, she said that she would get it dealt with back in the UK. Eventually, when the doc in London saw it, he just laughed and said it was only a cyst and that as long as I kept off trikes for a while it would disappear, which is exactly what happened; six months later, there was no sign of it. So much for the GP in Melbourne – a lucky escape!

I recall very little about the trip home to the UK, except that the ship was called the *SS Orontes* and she was of the Orient line. I do remember that they had a children's fancy dress competition. I dressed up as a pirate complete with eye-patch and a brass dagger. I also remember my sister Dinah taking me on deck for the competition. I won it, which is why it probably sticks in my memory, but I can remember little else of that trip with the exception of the smell of tar and the ropes on deck.

Mum had hated it in Oz ever since we arrived, especially as the girls were separated from us. She stuck it out for three years but we didn't have a lot of money. Dad had managed to get work away at the Lambert Sheep Mills, but we didn't get to see him too often and as 'ten-quid tourists' it would have taken years to get accepted into society in those days. I think the heat got to Mum as well and she missed the more temperate climate of the UK.

In the end, I guess it was one of Dad's schemes that he never quite pulled off. I'd had a great time, but school was looming and all my energy and fun would soon have to be channelled into education.

Well, that was the intention…

3

Having three sisters who were of an age when girlish fantasy was the order of the day may seem like a bit of a drawback for a boy like me. Well, to some extent, it was – because my father had been quite involved in the cinema industry, as had my mum's sisters and cousins, it was not unusual for there to be a family outing to the cinema from time to time. Thanks to my sisters, this often entailed me being dragged along as an afterthought, and the romances of the late 50's usually consisted of musicals like *Oklahoma*, *Carousel*, and *Seven Brides for Seven Brothers*.

It was the age of the American musicals and Rogers and Hammerstein were knocking them out like Harry Potter movies. Now and again, I got to see a Glenn Ford Western but there were also plenty of 'weepies' that I was dragged to like *Little Women*! Not really my cup of tea. However, it was the musicals that gave me my love of music, something that we had an abundance of in our house. We were now living with my gran in the Victorian terraced house in Clapham South. Broomwood Road was your typical suburban London street. As mentioned earlier, this house and my room at the top held particularly strong memories for me.

A benefit of having sisters, apart from my reluctant indoctrination to the virtues of musicals, was that we grew up with lots of books in our house as we were all avid readers. Despite that, however, I avoided too much close contact with the girls.

I never really remember a lot about my sister Delia who, at this time, was around nineteen years old. I know she had a job in the Northcote Road working in a clothes store, but on a daily basis our paths rarely crossed. Dinah was fifteen and was at Battersea County Secondary School because she had not taken her 11^+ exams due to us being in Oz. Josephine, however, who had just turned eleven, did take the exam, passed and was at Battersea County High Grammar School which was located at the top of Broomwood Road. At seven years old, I was attending my first Primary School – the aforementioned Bellview Road Primary.

Although we were living with Gran, Mum was on the waiting list for a council house but, as there were six of us, it was going to take a while. While staying with Gran, I know that my dad worked in the Strand as manager of the Tivoli Bar, but I don't remember him a lot at this house.

It was whilst living here that myself, Michael Stadden and John Bayford set up the 'Greenstick Gang'. This was one of many forays into the world of adventure and the symbol for our gang was a green stick of the plane tree in John's garden – we all carried one.

After school, we usually ended up at Michael's house for a plate of Welsh Rarebit. His mum was always obliging. Mike's dad was a mounted policeman, but John's folks were a bit more reserved. If we ever ate at John's house it was usually ham salad with lashings of Heinz Salad Cream.

Of course, girls were not allowed in the Greenstick Gang until one evening when, whilst playing in the street, we met the 'new girl on the block'. She was as tough as we were and after some serious debate – that took all of five minutes – we decided to let her join. The proviso was that she had to undertake an 'initiation ceremony'; she had to climb to the highest point on John's plane tree and bring a suitable stick down. This she did without hesitation whilst the three of us stood beneath, shamelessly looking up her skirt as she did it!

When she came down, we were all falling about laughing. When she asked why, we told her that we wanted to see what colour her knickers were. At this, she got really mad, lifted her school skirt up and said, "If you'd have asked, I'd have shown you."

It was at this point that my youngest sister Jo came up the street calling me in for tea. We all four ducked down behind the wall of John's front garden and waited until she had gone in. Meanwhile, we decided that Sally had passed the initiation test and was now a fully-fledged member of the gang. Despite our antics, she was really pleased, and we arranged to meet the following day at school and discuss our next foray.

At the bottom of our street there were four old air raid shelters set amongst the start of Clapham Common West Side across from Broomwood. There were two shelters on each side of this little expanse of green. The tops were tarmacked, and it was on here that I learned to ride Sally's two-wheel bike and tried out her roller skates. Once I had mastered the bike, I knew that a whole new world was now opened up to me. The roller skating was easier because I got a pair for my birthday. Unfortunately, they weren't the 'classy' Jacko skates that had hardened rubber wheels. Instead, I was given a pair with metal wheels which were noisier and allowed you to slide a lot easier. But these skates played a significant role a little later – in my survival – and gave me a worldly lesson.

At this age, school and education never figured high on my list of priorities. The only things in that line that interested me were drawing and English. I loved to read, and I guess that helped enormously with my homework. Enid Blyton's *Famous Five* and the adventures of Tom Sawyer and Huckleberry Finn were the corner stones of my life at that time.

The *Famous Five* stories were about the never-ending adventures that Julian, Dick, Anne, and George had on their constantly sunny, summer holidays. And as for Huck Finn, well him and Tom were the way I saw myself at that time; looking for adventure, ready to tackle anything, and prepared to take chances!

Every winter I always had either tonsillitis or a cold and so would be up in my attic room, a fire in the grate which reflected shadows across the room, reading *The Adventures of Tom Sawyer* with the smell of friar's balsam permeating everything. Dad had put a small, red, oval-shaped, Bakelite radio in my room, made by Pilot. So, when I wasn't reading, I would lie in the dark, with the glow from the flames dancing across the walls, listening to stories of King Arthur or the goings on in the court of Henry VIII. The clash of swords, the jangle of horses' bridles, and the creak of a longbow being drawn all added to the magic of those wintry nights with the wind howling and rattling the attic window in its frame.

Sadly, though, leaving that attic room had to happen in the end and a new journey was about to start.

4

As well as putting our name on the list for a council house, Mum had, as an added measure, written to the Minister of Housing explaining our plight. As the girls were all in their teens and I was the only boy, we had a certain amount of priority to move up the list. As much as we loved living in Broomwood Road, my uncle Bert was never happy about the arrangement and had made it pretty uncomfortable for my mother even though my gran never minded much.

Uncle Bert was the oldest of all my mum's brothers and had served during the First World War as a horse handler in the artillery. The war must have had an impact on him because, for some reason, he became a Communist. His 'leftist' views were never popular around the house and, because of this, he was not very popular with all of the family. He was always good to me, though, and I came to enjoy his company in the pub, at times, when I was a bit older. He was great to chat to and never once mentioned any of his Socialist ideology to me on these occasions.

Eventually, our move came through and we 'upped sticks'. Mum had managed to secure a brand new, four bedroomed flat in Stockwell.

I don't recall much about the move except that I was sad about leaving the boys, Sally, and the Greenstick Gang.

The place we moved to was called Enfield House – an 'L' shaped, four-storey block that had only just been completed. It was set in the middle of a complex of other similar blocks, many of which were still under construction. This was the Stockwell Road Estate and, in those days, it was a reasonable place to live.

We had a top floor flat in the middle of the block which had a balcony outside the front that ran the length of the block. There were apartments on either side of us and at the far end, under the enclosure of the stairwell, was another. At the opposite end from the stairs was a lift that went down to the main entrance to the block and a stairwell.

I remember that if you looked over the balcony outside our front door, you looked down onto a playground. And that, to the right of this, was the boiler house where there was a laundry in the basement as well as the main central boilers that supplied the central heating to all the flats. Above the boiler house was a residents' hall where dancing classes were held, family do's if you wanted to hire the place, and other study classes.

Living in this flat was a gigantic move from the Victorian elegance of Broomwood Road. Not that, at eight years old, I was aware of the significance. To me, it meant new places to investigate, new friends, and a new school.

Little did I know that we'd end up living here for fourteen years and in that time, life would significantly change for me.

When Mum secured the flat, both my parents must have been over the moon to get this large, four-bedroomed place and to be able to decorate it their own way. Access to public transport was premium and we were surrounded by all the public services. Brixton was a stone's throw away and the number forty-five bus stop was just across from the entrance to the estate.

Stockwell underground station was nearby, too, and sitting on the Northern Line which gave good access to central London. Seen through eight-year-old eyes, the flat was big and I certainly didn't miss not having a garden.

The view out of the rear windows was good and being under the flight path into Heathrow enhanced my interest in all things aeronautical; I was fanatical about aircraft. Mum had given me an old pair of theatrical binoculars and I would lean on the back of the sofa in the lounge watching the aircraft fly over and trying to get their numbers. Much like the trainspotters, I would jot down as much info about the plane as I could, including the time it passed overhead, direction, cloud formation at that time and the general weather conditions. In other words, I was becoming a bit of an anorak!

In those days, the planes were mostly Vickers Viscounts, four-engined turboprops belonging to British European Airways, DH Comets of BOAC, and Super Constellations with their tell-tale triple fins at the rear. Boeings and Douglas were the occasional 'gift'.

The high-pitched whine of the Viscounts was noticeable as they flew over every three minutes but, in the end, you didn't notice them; rather like a clock ticking. To us, they became part of the background noise that was London.

What I did learn from my plane-watching days was weather patterns. I had a book with all the different cloud formations in and spent some time learning them all and identifying them outside. It was something that I loved to do, and I would jot down as much info as I could. It was about this time that I also started becoming interested in model cars and model aeroplanes. Both of which coincided with another new interest... girls.

My new school was St Andrews Primary in Lingham Street, just at the back of our flats. The smell of chalk, dusty old classrooms and smelly kids still lingers in my mind. This is the first school that I have any real memories of. It was a mixed school and corporal punishment was still well in vogue. The classrooms were of around twenty-five pupils and the teachers were definitely 'old school'. We lived for playtimes and all the teaching bits in-between were a necessary evil.

There were two girls that I had my eye on – a certain Linda

Holloway and Barbara Morris. Linda was the school beauty, a slim, blonde girl who was shy and well-spoken whilst Barbara was the more 'earthy' type brunette that was also attractive. I'd had a few attempts at getting to go with Linda but with little effect until, one day, my persistence paid off. I walked her home to where she lived in Stockwell Green, just adjacent to Lingham Street. I was invited in for tea and met her parents. They were all very well spoken, and I must have appeared as a 'bit of rough'. It was nearing the Christmas of '55. Going to school the next few weeks I was subjected to taunts of, "Linda Holloway loves David English," in the playground. I didn't give a toss but to Linda, who was really quite shy, it was too much. It didn't last and by New Year, it was over. However, we were in the same class, so we still remained friends.

The protagonist of this was a developing bully called Barry Fidgett. He lived up the road in the prefabs opposite our estate. We were mates of a sort and I think I even went to his prefab one lunchtime. It was getting towards my last year at St Andrews. We were in Mr Cheeseman's class. I was approaching eleven and I knew we were going to be doing our 11^+ exam this year. This was to decide whether we went to a grammar school or a secondary school. However, by this stage, my attentions were more focussed on my next love, Barbara Morris.

The earthiness of Barbara's character meant she was tougher and less affected by all the taunting of Barry and his cohorts. I think Barbara was my first 'love' and on occasion she came home and had tea with us. She was allowed in my bedroom as long as I left the door wide open. She was amazed at my collection of model aircraft but was not that interested in the subject itself. Luckily, there were plenty of places around the estate where we could cuddle without being seen. In fact, in one such place, in a stairwell, we stole our first kisses on the lips.

One morning in the school playground before the first bell rang, it came to a scrap between Barry and me. The chorus of, "David English loves Barbara Morris," was the thing that tipped the scale. I think I told Barry and his mates to fuck off which resulted in a pushing contest that got a little out of hand. With arms locked around each other's heads, we were rolling around the ground. Someone must have shouted that a teacher was coming because we broke up and stood. It was at this point that I was pushed hard by Barry and hit the school wall with my head. They all legged it and muggins here was left leaning against the wall with blood trickling down my face.

I actually did see the proverbial stars and was dazed. I must have had a mild concussion, the fact of which escaped the teacher on playground duty who came over and accused me of fighting and using bad language. I was sent to the school nurse and thence to sit on 'the box' outside the headmaster's office. This box was a long, grey, low wooden container that housed the school cricket gear. If you were told to sit on it, it meant only one thing; you were guilty of a misdemeanour which, in turn, meant you were guilty beyond any shadow of a doubt. The only thing to be discussed was not what type of punishment would be meted out to you but how many strokes of the cane you were to receive.

I remember the Head's door opening. Like the box, this character was grey too – from receding hair, complexion, and suit to his shirt.

"You again English?" he snapped. "You're never going to make anything of your life the way you behave. Fighting, eh? Well, I'm afraid we don't tolerate that sort of thing here."

"But Sir, he started it, I was—"

"I don't want any of your excuses," he interrupted my eloquent show of innocence. "Where do you want it – hand or bottom?"

Surprisingly, the whack of the cane on the palm of the hand hurt more than the sting it gave you on the bum. I pointed to the rear of my grey shorts. He walked over to the rack of canes standing in the corner, took one of medium thickness, swished it in the air a couple of times and then told me to bend over his desk.

As I touched my nose to his green blotter, I noticed the smell of chalk dust and old men. I screwed my eyes tight, took a deep breath and held it. The first one was the worst and by the sixth and last one I could feel the pain radiating down my legs. Fuck, that hurt. I stood up, keeping my eyes wide so as not to let the tear sneak out.

"Now get out and back to your class and let that be a lesson to you."

Fuck you, Sir, I whispered in my head – which was aching almost as bad as my arse. I practiced walking straight, without a limp, as I went back to my classroom. The kids had already started the first lesson. Mr Cheeseman then poked the fire with a, "You again, English." This became something of a stock phrase – something that seemed to follow me around in my loosely academic career.

To this day, the smell of chalk dust and old sweat reminds me of that awful Head's office with the rack of canes in the corner. These Victorian attitudes, held by many of the schools at that time, were carried through to secondary and comprehensive schools in a lot of areas. I don't think it was just confined to London either, but I do think I was unfortunate as there was a change in the air and attitudes were being forced to change. Just not at the schools I attended! So, the caning continued.

One particularly hot summer, whilst still at my primary school, we were having a lesson with an English teacher who we used call 'The Moustache' behind her back. She was an extremely overweight, middle aged, frumpily dressed, short woman who sprayed saliva over whoever was sitting in the front rank of desks. Not a pretty sight with her tousled, greying hair and long flowing dresses. She didn't smell too bright either. Fortunately, us boys sat at the back of the class leaving the front desks to the weak n' weeny (mostly girls).

This particularly lesson was during an afternoon session and the temperature in the classroom must have been well into the seventies. After the hour-long lunch break, most of which had been spent in a queue for the one, single drinking fountain in the playground, many of us were suffering from thirst. In those days we were still using the school issued wooden handled pens with the removable nib that you stuck in the small, round, china inkwell which sat in the left-hand corner at the top of each sloping desk. The ink was made up from a dark blue powder dye that had to be mixed with water and used to top up these inkwells at the start of the day.

Now, half-way through this lesson it was obvious that we were all suffering from thirst as many of us hadn't had the time to reach our turn at the fountain before the bell went and we were ushered inside, back to classes. One particular lad sitting in front of me put his hand up and asked if he could get a drink from the fountain in the playground. This was vehemently denied. A few minutes later he asked again with the same result. A few of us tried to explain to The Moustache that the queue had been too long and we didn't get a chance at our turn. She ignored this and carried on at the blackboard, pointing with a cane at words and sentences we had to form. In the end, the lad in front of me took the inkwell out of the desk and drank the contents. I shall never forget the state of his mouth and lips as he turned around and we all gasped and fell about laughing. The Moustache went ballistic, called him out front, caned him on his hands and sent him to sit on the box. He didn't. He went into the playground and used the fountain then absconded home. The outcome of this was that The Moustache was suspended following a complaint from the parents and we never did see her again.

One of the things that was quite fashionable at this time was roller skating. I still had a pair of old metal-wheeled Jacko's and after Saturday morning pictures at the Odeon, Brixton, with mates, it was always a discussion on what we were going to do for the rest of the day. One particular morning it was decided that, as we all had skates, we ought to see how far around London we could roller skate. So, setting off from Stockwell, we made our way into town.

The thing about metal-wheeled skates was that they worked exceedingly well on fresh, smooth tarmac. But in general, the pavements around London were the standard paving slabs, concrete, and often uneven. If you had the hard, black rubber wheels, you were really cool, as these were a lot smoother. It did cross my mind that I would update my cranky, metal wheels one day because one thing about the metal ones was that if you had to stop, at speed, you were at a distinct disadvantage; they skidded and slipped, and you had to be a pretty nifty skater to come to a stop with ease. That being said, on that particular day I never gave it much thought and was enjoying myself being with the lads and skating through London's busy streets.

After a few hours we had made it as far as Old Billingsgate and our minds were on where we should stop and get something to eat. There was a side street that led down to a busy main road that ran along the bottom of the road where we were stood. Looking down from the top of this street, I noticed that the pavement here was the nice smooth tarmac, one that was a joy to skate on. We had all stopped and were looking down this narrow but smooth pavement. What was concerning us was that it was very steep, so we knew we could get up quite a speed.

Of course, muggins here thought he would be the hero – with the smooth tarmac I felt confident I could handle this one.

"I'll go first," I said, feeling a little tingle of fear.

"I think it's too steep," my mate Steve said.

I ignored him. I thought that if it was too much, I'd just stop halfway down and tell them not to bother. Now bear in mind that I was not a particularly religious person. I hadn't stepped inside a church since I don't know when and, to me, if there was a God it was an old very tall man with long flowing white hair and a long white beard. This person was definitely not on my mind as I was about to undertake this excursion down the steeply sloping street. But perhaps he should have been…

From where I was, I could see that the main road at the bottom was very busy with cars and vans in a more or less constant stream. The lads were all waiting for me to go. The pavement was clear of people. So, despite my nerves I thought, *Right, let's do it, I can't back out now.*

Off I went, lined up nicely with the centre of the tarmac. Within a matter of seconds, I was gaining speed, knees slightly bent, akin to downhill skiing but without the ski poles. About half-way down I knew I was in trouble. My braking skills weren't bad but at this speed I had no hope, and I was still accelerating. My only chance would have been to grab the traffic light pole I could see at the bottom. The buildings on my right had no doorways I could have steered myself into and, by now, they were just a blur as I hurtled down, totally out of control.

I was approaching the busy road and was keenly aware that if I couldn't grab the traffic light pole on my way past, I would burst out into the path of moving vehicles.

It was at this point that I knew I'd had it. In those final split seconds as I hurtled toward the traffic, I think my mind just sort of went numb. Although I do remember thinking that I hoped none of the others were coming down behind me.

Then... in that final flash of a second, when I was no more than two feet from the end of the pavement, I felt a very strong pressure on my chest – as if a very powerful hand was pushing against me. It was so powerful that I couldn't breathe, and it was enough to stop me almost instantly.

I felt a wind coming from my right but nothing that could have stopped me at the speed I was travelling. My first thought was for the others, and I quickly turned around and waved like mad, yelling at them not to come down. I then sat on the pavement and took off my skates with shaking fingers. I never wore them again. Even at that age I knew I had been saved by a force more powerful than any I could have imagined.

I have since looked back at that episode on many occasions and each time have come to the same conclusion; I had a guardian angel. Someone was looking after me. It didn't make me any more religious or rush to a church to seek forgiveness for my sins, but it gave me the sure knowledge that there are forces around us that we know very little about. As a much later famous Jedi Knight saying goes: 'May the Force be with you.' Well, it certainly was on that day.

5

As a kid, summer holidays were the best thing that happened and, to be honest, every day at school was spent simply working towards the holidays. For some reason, at nine years old, they seemed to go on forever and I can remember breaking up in July knowing that I had the whole summer stretching before me, which meant that there were a host of adventures to go on.

I loved books of adventure stories like Henty's *The Treasure of the Incas* and Rider Haggard's Allan Quartermain stories. Enid Blyton's *Famous Five* books were also a particular favourite, but perhaps the one that started me on my journey to seek adventure was *The Adventures of Tom Sawyer* and Thor Heyerdahl's *The Kon-Tiki Expedition*, these books, and a movie. We used to go to Saturday morning pictures at the Odeon at the top of Stockwell Road and two of my favourite films were *Smiley* and *Smiley Gets a Gun* – an Australian series starring Colin Peterson as Smiley and Chips Rafferty as the Sergeant. These two films had a big influence on me as far as adventure went and add to that Alan Ladd, Audi Murphy, and John Wayne Westerns and I was an adventure junkie!

The *Smiley* movies I could relate to; being out in Oz at about the same age, running around the place in bare feet getting up to all sorts of things with my mates. And it was not long after seeing those movies that I decided to run away from home with a lad who I was quite pally with called Lenny. This had absolutely nothing to do with being unhappy at home or anything like that. It was about the adventure of it and the excitement of the journey.

I managed to get hold of a small suitcase and over about a week, I snuck things into it that I would likely need on my journey. You know, notebook, scout knife, my Uncle Jo's book on Scouting, a ball of string, some chewy sweets, a flashlight, pocket money, a pair of socks and underpants, t-shirt, shorts, and a favourite cap. I hid my case under the bed, right at the back.

The object of the journey was to make our way to Southampton and stow away on a Union Castle ship that was going to Australia. We'd pretend we were with families going on board and then, once on, move about the ship, pinch food, and find a place to bunk-down. Seemed easy at the time. Once we got to Oz, we would sneak off at the first opportunity, make our way to the bush and find some Aborigines to hook up with. Sounded like a plan to me! However, Lenny blew it because his mum found his packed suitcase and wanted to know what the hell was going on. Daft bugger went and told her it was my idea, and she came to see my mum about it. Mum wasn't so much angry as perplexed. Was I that unhappy at home? In the end I confessed that it was just an adventure thing. Then she was angry. Goodness knows what she told my dad, but he wouldn't talk to me for a week!

Dad was a bit of a mystery to me when I look back to those years at Enfield House. He only seemed to be there intermittently. Yet he always seemed to be around on Sundays when we had Sunday lunch. *Forces Favourites* was always put on the radio (a massive freestanding Decca unit with a gramophone player and, below, a forward opening cabinet that held all our LPs and Singles) and the girls loved to hear it. Roast beef and Yorkshire pud was nearly always the dinner with lots of gravy and chrain – a Jewish sauce of horseradish and beetroot. Funny, but we only ever had roast chicken about twice a year as it was a bit of a luxury. After dinner, Dad would sit in the Ercol rocking chair reading the Sunday press (back pages – horse form) smoking a Havana Cuban cigar on occasion. Quite often he would fall asleep with the newspaper over his face.

Dad's work at that time was as manager of the Tivoli Bar in the Strand. This place was well known in London social circles and famous for actors and actresses that would frequent it. It also had an Australian corner and a New Zealand corner. You went down plush carpeted stairs to the main bar, which must have been well over twenty feet long, made of oak with a red vinyl top inset, and the proverbial brass foot rail running the length of the bar.

There was the usual array of pumps that pulled the beer, which at the time was Barclays Best bitter and Worthington's. At the back of the bar was a mirror that ran the full length of it and here were the optics with a dazzling assortment of spirits. Above the front of the bar was a large glass beaker, three feet long, with a bulb at one end and a fluted lip at the other. This was the proverbial 'yard of ale', and many had unsuccessfully spilled most of it down their front in an attempt to get their name added to the 'Hall of Fame' plaque that sat at the back of the bar.

Behind the bar, on the oak floor, were two large trap doors that led down to the cellar. This was a whole different world, and it was down here that the massive wooden barrels of beer were stood on trestles with the thick, clear plastic beer-lines that fed the pumps, twisting their snake-like way up through the ceiling to the bar above. The cellar was an enormous cavern with brick arches at intervals along both sides. Fresh barrels sat on more trestles with wooden bungs in, waiting to be connected to the pumps. The place had that sour, musty smell of centuries of beer, wine, and hops. Here was also where the plastic pipes were washed in a large china sink. It later transpired, many years after the Tivoli was no more, that this cellar was originally Roman built. It has been preserved to this day.

On Sunday mornings, Dad would do his bookkeeping in a small office on the right as you came down the stairs into the bar. Quite often, I would accompany him on his trip into town and play around in the bar whilst he balanced the books. This often meant sampling the beers and spirits and playing 'flicker cards' with the beer mats. This was then followed by a visit to 'Arthur's', an electrical wholesale outlet on Charing Cross Road. Arthur was an enormous fat Jewish man who always wore a shiny, grey suit and was a dead-ringer for an old, English actor – Sidney Greenstreet of *The Maltese Falcon* fame.

Arthur's store was a magical mystery tour of just about everything electrical on the planet. Dad was always doing some kind of dodgy dealing with him, and they would spend a lot of time in deep conversation. His main reason to visit him, however, was to sit under a UV lamp with a special pair of glasses on and a piece of card over his nose. This gave my dad a sun-tanned look as we went about all pale and anaemic looking.

Whilst this was going on, I was roaming the miles of shelving looking for anything worth nicking. It was during one of these forays that I came across a roll of bundled-up one-pound notes, hidden behind a cardboard box of fuses. Dad was, at this particular time, under the sunlamp chatting to Arthur. I slipped the bundle into my pocket, feeling as excited as ever and thought of all I could do with it. I never did tell my dad but gave the money to my mum who gave me some back to get some Dinky cars with. She was well pleased, if angry at me at first.

The culmination of our Sunday mornings was a trip to Petticoat Lane and 'Ginger Kit's' stall that sold rollmop herrings in wooden barrels and pickled cucumbers the size of your arm. Next to her stall was another selling jellied eels and I was always treated to a tub. These stallholders were Yiddish friends of Dad's. There were occasions when we would go to the Tivoli with my sister Jo and her friend Mavis, who lived in the flat below us. One time, Jo and Mavis sampled so many spirits that they were totally out of it by the time Dad had finished his work. He was really angry, and we went home in a taxi – the girls giggling and laughing all the way. He never took them again.

One evening, Dad took Mum to the Tivoli to a special do at the theatre above. I couldn't stay at home alone, so I went and sat in his office in the bar, reading, until he came back with Mum. That evening, I was introduced to Richard Burton and Elizabeth Taylor in Dad's office. I was stunned. Elizabeth Taylor was so beautiful and larger than life. Mum and Dad had been with them in the bar, earlier.

The Tivoli has sadly gone now. It was originally built as a theatre that played host to Marie Lloyd and many other Vaudeville entertainers. It was hit quite badly in the Blitz and then restored to become a cinema. The whole building was then sold to become Peter Robinson's department store then taken over by the Australian Government as New South Wales House. This has now also gone and today it is a row of nondescript offices and shops. A sad end to a place that held so many memories for so many people.

Dad's love of horses and horse racing was something Mum never approved of. Over the years, he must have spent a small fortune on betting, but he was never in your face with it and kept it all rather low key. In his travels he had met a lot of people, including Scobie Breasley and his trainer Sir Gordon Richards. Being Jewish, he knew lots of people in that business and many of them were quite wealthy. One such friend of his lived in Hove, near Brighton, and when Brighton Race Week was on, Dad would up sticks there for the week. On a couple of occasions, I went with him.

We would stay in an hotel in Hove and Dad would always get me up early so that we could walk to the front and watch the catch of the day being brought in by the local fishermen. After breakfast we would meet up with his wealthy businessman friend who would take us in his Rolls Royce Cabriolet to the races. Dad would then also have access to what is called the 'saddling-in enclosure', brushing shoulders with the wealthy elite of the racing fraternity.

On one of these visits, I was introduced to a rather large man wearing a Crombie overcoat, a hat, and smoking a very large cigar. He looked down at me and shook my hand – it was Sir Winston Churchill.

Once Dad had placed his bet with the 'tic-tac' man, we would go up to the Members' Lounge and watch the race from behind the long, glass windows. I never knew if he won much but he always came away in a good mood, so I guess he must have done.

In my final year at St Andrews, the 11⁺ exams were imminent. These were the nationwide decider on your competence that would decide the path your future education was to take. Passing the 11⁺ meant your ticket to a grammar school and thence, if your parents could afford it, on to one of the established universities. Failing it meant you were never likely to get to a university. Going to university in those days, more often than not, meant your family was quite well off. So, even had I passed, I may never have gone as we didn't have the finances; my sister Jo passed hers and went to grammar school, but she never went on to further education.

Although English was by far my best subject, Maths was my nemesis. Whilst I clearly understood the basics of addition, multiplication, and division it was fractions and mental arithmetic that always floored me. My sister Di spent hours helping me to understand fractions but to no avail. Had we gone metric in those times, I think I would have had a better chance. Alas, my lack of maths was a hindrance. Despite this, I felt I could make my way without worrying about fractions. Needless to say, I didn't do too well in the exams, which was enough to condemn me to go to a secondary school. One of the questions in English was to describe the meaning of the word 'optimistic'. I remember seeing an advert in Rayner's, my opticians along Stockwell Road. It said: *You can't be optimistic with a misty optic*. I remember thinking that was a really clever use of words so, like an idiot, I put it as my answer to this particular question in the exam. No wonder I bloody failed!

Unfortunately, caning was to remain in vogue for all of my scholarly career and I'm sure that many a sadistic bastard 'got it off' by caning. My last caning at St Andrews was following the results of our 11⁺ exams. It was in summer during our final week at the school before we went our separate ways. We were in Mr Cheeseman's class – he was our form master, and it was just after lunch. We were all milling around our desks waiting for the first period of the afternoon to start. Mr Cheeseman was not in evidence and as we were discussing what we were going to do in the holidays when a 'Toni Bell' ice cream van came along the street with his well-known musical chimes. I looked down from the first-floor window of our classroom and saw him stop just up the street. Being that hot an afternoon I suddenly had a flash of inspiration – why not get some cones for me and my two mates? Checking my pocket money, I had enough. I dashed out the classroom, down the stairs and ran to the van. I came back quickly, knowing I was going to beat Cheeseman's return. I gave my mates one each and was chatting away when my ice fell out the cone onto the seat of my desk. We all fell about laughing but, as luck would have it, whilst I was cleaning it up, Mr Cheeseman arrived back in the classroom.

"Who is that with the dirty laugh?" he shouted as his eye immediately fell upon yours truly. This long, lanky piece of dog excrement then pointed at me and called out in front of the class, "How dare you joke about in my class?! Get out of here and on the box."

"But Sir, I was only laughing," I said, dreading the obvious.

"Get out!" He pointed to the door.

I looked back at the class for a bit of sympathy and support, but they were all silent and looking down at their desks. Now here I was, back on the bloody box, thoroughly dejected. About twenty minutes later, the Head opened his door and there I sat.

"Get in – what is it for this time, English?"

"Mr Cheeseman said I had a dirty laugh, Sir."

"Did he indeed? Well, I won't tolerate that in this school and on your final term you should know better. Now get over my desk."

The usual ritual took place, and I came out of there thinking how much I hated school. When Mum found out she was angry at me but furious at the school and sent a letter to the London County Council about it. I never did find out what happened about that, but I believe there was action taken.

Thankfully, the summer holidays had now arrived, and I had what seemed to be an endless amount of time in front of me before I started my new school on Hackford Road. The summer was destined to be a good one and this year I was going to spend some time with my Uncle Joe and Auntie Martha. They lived on a farm in Brentwood, Essex and Uncle Joe was the manager.

I look at these times now with a degree of nostalgia because we were at a point of great change in the UK. Although I wasn't aware of it, we were losing the war years mentality that had held us in check for so long.; people were starting to think outside the box and that meant fashions, music, and the arts, were slowly changing. Even food was a part of this. The burger joint suddenly appeared and every major High Street had a Wimpy's burger bar. Coffee shops became the forerunner of the internet café. Mind you, the coffee was still crap and there wasn't a Starbucks or Costa in sight yet. I won't even go into the taste of the Wimpy burger (a couple of thin onion rings on an even thinner piece of meat, no lettuce, gherkin, mayo, or any butter on the roll – you needed a gallon of coke to wash the bloody thing down). I digress – now where was I? Ah, the farm.

I went by train to Brentwood, on my own. Uncle Joe met me at the station, and we took a taxi to the farm. The taxi was a brown Vauxhall Velox with a column change and bench seating. Heaven knows why I remember that, but it was about then that my love of motors started to get into gear. I had been an avid collector of Dinky cars and most of my money went on those, every week. I was building up a good collection that at today's prices would be worth a small fortune.

Staying at the farm, my German aunt Martha introduced me to her fantastic cooking. I also had an attic room with a creaky old floor and no electricity. The lamps in the kitchen and the front room were gas mantles. I had never come across these and was fascinated by them. They provided a comforting atmosphere and the light they gave was literally a warm glow. There was a background noise as well, but you hardly noticed it.

Uncle Joe had a large, beige Alsatian called Silver and he was the best pet I had ever been with. Up until then, apart from Timmy, the nearest thing to a pet we'd had in London was our budgie called Billy.

I soon made friends with a lad from a neighbouring farm and during the day, when I wasn't with Uncle Joe helping around the place, I was with him exploring the fields and woods.

Uncle Joe taught me fieldcraft, the love of birds, how to whittle a stick with my scout knife, how to throw the knife so that it would always stick in a piece of wood or a tree. He showed me trails of different animals like foxes, rabbits, and badgers and what their prints were like in the dirt or mud. He taught me how to tell how old an animal's tracks were, when rain was due, and one of the finest things in a wood – seeing with my ears and not my eyes. One day, we were following a fox's trail in a wood, and he asked me to stop, not to make a noise, and to close my eyes and listen. I stood still in the dappled shade of some tall oaks and beech trees and focused on what I could hear.

Joe had taught me the different songs the birds made and today he wanted to test me. Keeping my eyes shut, he asked how many different birds I could hear. With my eyes closed, suddenly I could hear so many that I hadn't noticed with my eyes open. I started reeling them off: "Blackbird, thrush, sparrow, greenfinch, starling and, what seems like a long distance away, a skylark." He then asked me to point where I thought each bird was. Still with my eyes closed, I listened carefully and shut out all other sounds except the one bird I was listening for. I managed to get four out of six correct. The skylark threw me though. When I opened my eyes, Joe pointed up through the trees. It was singing on the wing, way above the trees.

Joe taught me lots of other things too like how moss always grows on the north of the tree trunks, where animals had slept, and the different types of trees and how important they were. For me, I was thrilled by the adventure of it all and I knew that none of the kids back at school in London would know any of this.

There was a railway line that ran at the back of one of the fields and, many a time, I would sit nearby and watch the big diesels thunder by with a long string of freight cars that seemed to go on forever.

Tommy wasn't as interested in the trains as I was but not far from the tracks was a linesman's hut and in here were old bits of railway ties, some tools, a rickety old chair, and a small bench. The lad's party trick was to pull out an old tobacco tin he hid in the shed and when he opened it there was a heap of old smoked tobacco that he had filched from dog-ends. With this was a pack of Rizla green papers and a box of matches. He taught me how to roll your own and we would sit in the shed and puff away on these things. I couldn't inhale the bloody smoke but pretended to. Tommy was a master, though, inhaling and blowing smoke rings.

It felt good to do it, except that when I heard the rumble of a train coming, I'd beat it out the hut and watch the train pass by. The relationship with this lad was short lived, especially when I got back to the farmhouse. Aunt Martha could smell the smoke on my clothes and asked me if I had been smoking. I told her it was Tommy's house; it stank of smoking and his father always had a cigarette in his mouth. In the end I didn't feel it was worth the risk, so I concentrated on helping Uncle Joe around the place. In the evenings he would tell me stories of when he was in Burma and India during the war. The noise and smell of the gas lamp in the front room, to this day, is so evocative of those times and a very comfortable experience.

Aunt Martha was always cooking cheesecake or making German salads. She used to laugh at Uncle Joe's stories sometimes and I found it a very happy experience. What I didn't know was that Aunt Martha had her own story to tell of the dying days of the last war, in Berlin, hiding in the bunkers with the injured German soldiers as the Russians advanced on the city. I was not to learn of the horror of her experience as a nurse during those times until many years later. She was a very special woman.

6

There was no thrill or excitement of going to my new school; I was dreading it. I suppose it was the fear of the unknown and the fact that we had to wear a school uniform. Long grey trousers, white shirt, striped tie, and a black blazer with a badge on the pocket that was the LCC (London County Council) badge for the area. It was the next stage in my educational career, and I wasn't looking forward to it.

My mum was a very practical person and as long as we could read and write that was the only requirement in that regard. Hence, we were never pushed to study or encouraged to get good grades with a view to going to college or university. Any other talents that we may have had never really mattered. In my case, as long as I was out from under her feet, she could get on with the running of the household.

Dad was of a similar mind and, in my case, he would try to use his influence as a Freemason to get me a job when the time came – regardless of my educational standing. His main dream was for me to be a jockey. He knew all the right people and I was the right size and weight. I also loved horses. However, Mum saw it as a complete waste of time and thought it was probably one of Dad's moves to keep in with the horseracing community and – by default – gambling. So, she put her foot down and after a few rows, Dad acquiesced.

Not being pushed to study but rather to get on the job ladder was our parents' main aim. In fact, as I mentioned earlier, before we had moved out to Australia, my eldest sister Delia had won an arts scholarship as she was extremely good at design and art. She never got the chance to take advantage of this, which I think was quite sad, but I suppose the 'fates' dictated that this was not to be.

This Victorian attitude that my parents had, which was generally the case among the working classes, was not uncommon. If we had not gone to Oz, I'm sure Delia's life would have taken a completely different turn. It may have also turned my own life in a similar direction to Delia's. But all that is water under the proverbial bridge as fate led us elsewhere.

Kennington Secondary School, Hackford Road, was an imposing Victorian structure. Built in 1888 as a boys' school, it later became mixed sex in 1908. This school has really stood the test of time and is now known as The Durand Academy.

I walked to school along Clapham Road and into Durand Gardens where the school stood on the corner with Hackford Road. It took about fifteen minutes and we all carried satchels. In my first year, at twelve years old, my voice hadn't broken. Every morning we had assembly and were made to sit in the large hall in front of which were two gigantic hymn sheets that we had to sing from. It was found out (I can't remember how) that I had a soprano voice and, as the school sat in front of these sheets singing the hymns, I had to stand up and sing every other verse *solo*. I didn't mind and, in fact, enjoyed singing.

Following the songs, the Deputy Head would stand in front, say prayers, and mention any school issues that were relevant at the time. Then, one day, it happened... I stood up to sing the solo and couldn't. As hard as I tried, it just came out croaky. The other kids thought it was a huge joke and laughter disrupted the morning's assembly. I was to report to the Head later that day – he was convinced that I was messing about, especially as all the lads from my form were falling about laughing. This was my first introduction to Mr Fawcett and his cane. Of course, it later transpired that my voice had broken. Needless to say, however, it wasn't to be my last encounter with the cane. Trying to turn over a new leaf had failed at the first hurdle.

I never really get to grips with the idea that I needed to learn something, but I didn't do too badly and excelled in English and Art. History was interesting, but lessons had focused in the main on Roman Britain. French was an awful struggle, Maths was torturous, and Geography was intensely boring – focusing a lot on wheat production and the GNP. Science was a good laugh, though, usually involving trying to blow things up, playing with copper sulphate, growing crystals, and leaning how batteries worked. The smell of freshly brewed coffee always permeated the lab as the tutor had his own brewing pot at the end of the lab and constantly had it ticking over.

French was a nightmare and about the only phrase I learned was to 'open the door'. The French master, a Mr Smith, had a rubber face and pulled these really exaggerated mouth formations to get us to use the right sound for the pronunciations. We always used to play up in his class and one day, for a laugh, it was decided to play a joke on him. When he disappeared out of the classroom, we were to play the bucket-of-water-falling-off-the-door trick on him. We'd all seen it in *The Beano*, often played out by Dennis the Menace; a T-square was placed above a partially opened door and a fire bucket of water was precariously balanced atop it. The big drawback to this (which didn't occur to any of us watching) was that the fire bucket was metal and was very heavy. When Mr Smith returned and strode through the door, pushing it open, the bucket plummeted down perfectly without tipping. It gave him a glancing blow but rendered him somewhat dazed and soaked. Of course, there was hell to pay for that, but no one got done for it as, for some reason, none of us could remember who had perpetrated the act. The whole class got detention and Mr Smith got a ride in an ambulance to A&E and a week off school.

There was always a class bully and at that time it happened to be one Frank Cawley. I had my own group of friends, of which I was the weeniest. At 5'6", and weighing in at around seven stone, I was one of the lightest in the school for my age. – Frank had found his target and whenever an opportunity arose would wade in.

Most times I just walked away or ignored him. Eventually, though, it came to a head. It had started during a particularly interesting history lesson. I was sitting at a desk about two from the front. Frank was immediately behind me. During the lesson, the master, Josh Haley, was going through a battle scene of Roman soldiers marching to meet Boadicea. He was particularly animated about the telling of this and you could almost hear the beat of marching feet, the jangle of harnesses, spear and sword, and the chanting of the legions.

While this was happening, this jerk behind me – Frank – thought it would be great fun to stab me in the back of my ear with the nib of his pen. At first, I ignored it but after repeated stabbings (unnoticed by Mr Haley) I knew I had to do something. With as much force as I could muster, I swung my arm around and clocked him one in the side of the head. Most of the lads behind me saw it and knew why I had done it. They also knew I was in deep shit.

All Mr Haley saw was me swinging at Cawley and, of course, he had a go at me about it. In an undisguised aggressive whisper, Cawley said, "You're dead, English, I'm gonna kill you at lunchtime."

"Yeah, whatever," I murmured back. Meanwhile, in my head, I was running through all the possible scenarios like legging it as soon as the end of lesson bell went, going home feigning sickness, running away back to Oz, or – as it was becoming increasingly obvious from all the murmurings around me – stay and fight. I had no confidence in my ability to do this; although I was a 'street kid' and had a lot of mates who were always getting into scraps, I had always managed to keep out of it. I was an extremely good runner – short distance and long – but that was of no use in this situation.

I knew my only option was a fight during the lunch break and that it would be in our form classroom across the hall. Our form master, Mr Goldsmith, was very strict but at lunch he always went to the staff room.

Word quickly spread a fight was in the offing and all the class went to our classroom in anticipation. One of our class prefects closed the door and stood guard, looking out through the window in the door in case Goldsmith came back. The rest moved several desks out the way to make room.

One of my friends took my blazer and glasses. Meanwhile, Frank was down to his rolled-up shirtsleeves pulling aggressive faces and shadow boxing, saying out loud, "I'm gonna kill you, you've had it English."

I slowly rolled up my shirt sleeves and then stood there. I wasn't going to make a prat of myself with all this shadow boxing bollocks. Someone said, "Come on Frank, get on with it." He came over to me and said loudly, pulling an ugly, aggressive face, "I'll give you one last chance English, you can go." This wasn't a friendly gesture by any means and, in fact, if I took him up on his offer it would make me a future target for all and sundry.

Frankly, at this point, I'd had enough of this guy. It was make or break time. Some of the lads were saying, "Come on, Dave. Don't fight, let it go." Others were saying, "Fight, fight!" I said nothing, just looked at him thinking, *Oh man, I'm really in the shit now.*

"No," I said, "let's just get this over with."

I brought my fists up in the classic boxer's stance and Frank came towards me in a similar fashion. Then all of a sudden, he tried to head-butt me. It was as if it was happening in slow motion. I saw it coming, so I had time to slightly turn my head and the bony side of my forehead caught him smack in his eye. Within seconds I saw the skin just above his eye split and his eye start to close up. I didn't waste a minute and jabbed him as hard as I could with a right hook (I'm a Southpaw) in the same spot as the split above his eye. There was blood everywhere and his now-swollen eye had fully closed. One of the prefects stopped any further fighting. I wiped my hand on my hanky and someone gave me my glasses back.

I picked up my blazer and put it on. There was a stunned silence in the classroom. I don't believe anyone noticed that his head-butt had caused his split eye. All they saw was me punch him in it and the damage was done. I didn't say anything and walked towards the door. The prefect moved aside and, calm as anything, I opened the door and went out to get some lunch. No one followed me.

I quickly went downstairs and out of the school. I didn't want to talk to anyone, so I hopped a bus to Brixton and went to the Pie Mash shop in Atlantic Road for lunch. I felt good and couldn't believe my luck. The idiot thought he was being smart using a head-butt. But because I was so skinny and bony it did me well. Walking away like that made me feel like Mr Cool. I'd seen something like that in a movie and knew I was on a winner. I never did have any more problems from Frank Cawley and some months later we became quite good friends.

For me, these were not the heady days of school that so many people look back to wax lyrical about. I enjoyed English and History, but the rest didn't arouse my interest in any way. Actually, I hated school. I know it seems easy to sit here and look back at those days wishing I had put a little more effort in. But honestly, I couldn't wait for the day I left school and don't even remember it.

The South London Horse Auctions used to take place near the school every now and then and they interested me more. Horses would be paraded for potential buyers to observe. In the lunch breaks I would go outside the back of the school gates, chat to the horse owners and sometimes hold the horses' reins and walk them up and down the road after they took them out of the horse boxes. I loved horses, their big doe-eyes, beautiful smooth chestnut brown hides, their smell, and the general feeling of their strength, power, and intelligence. Maybe being a Sagittarian had something to do with it, but I found a great affinity with these animals.

At this time, London was still recovering from the war. Unlike the German cities, London still had its fair share of bomb sites. The

Elephant and Castle was one in question. Weekends were often spent exploring these sites and looking for anything that might have been hidden in the old underground shelters. The Elephant had a massive one and, as yet nothing had been done to it. Wandering around the tunnels and corridors was an adventure albeit a smelly, damp one. There was a maze of concrete bunkers underground here and, at one point, we found a bolted steel door deep in the bowels of this place. We struggled to get it opened but that might have been because it was locked from the other side. What we needed was a crowbar – something not readily to hand. One of the lads, Micky, knew of a building site where he could most likely get one, so we arranged to meet back at the door the next day – Sunday.

I made a terrible excuse to Mum about going over my mate's house to play and off I went. Gaining entrance to the shelter was not difficult but you had to dodge the traffic and try to appear nonchalant as you made your way across the weed-covered rubble. When I got there none of the others had arrived. I made my way down into the bowels of this place and soon the noise of traffic was swapped for the echoing drip of water and an odd, sustained rumble and vibration from beneath my feet. I called out but no answer. I got my flashlight out and felt the comfort of my scout knife on my belt, under my jacket, though God knows what I thought I could do with it. I followed chalk marks we had made on the walls leading down to this old, rusted metal door. No one had arrived yet. I looked at my luminescent Timex and sat down in a dry spot, leaned against the wall, and waited.

The minutes dragged by and after ten-or-so I was hearing all sorts of noises that were starting to freak me out. Maybe this wasn't such a good idea, I mean, I could be attacked by some ghost from the war that had died down here.

I carefully undid the small stud that held my knife in place, wishing I had a sword or, better still, an S&W Colt 45 with a holster full of rounds – something along the lines of John Wayne in *The Searchers* movie. That was when I heard it. A long, drawn-out scraping noise and a sort of moaning that was getting nearer. I stood and backed into the recess of where the steel door was and knew that I was well hidden unless they were practically on top of me. I slipped my knife out and tried to breathe shallowly. The moaning became a load whisper as whatever it was got nearer.

"Dave, Dave, where the fuck are you?"

I jumped out of my hiding place, making a loud scream, facing the oncoming voice. Another answering high-pitched yell, the crash of metal on concrete and the patter of feet running full tilt in the opposite direction. I realised it was Mick with the crowbar, only he was now headed back the way he came.

"Hey, Mick, it's me, Dave, come back you daft bugger!"

Slowly he came back to where I was standing. "You fucking turd, you frightened the shit out of me!"

I explained I had been there for ages and that he was late. "Do you think any of the others are coming?" I asked.

"Naw, they're too bloody chicken, probably gone to church most likely." He picked up the crowbar. "Come on, let's have a go at this door."

I re-sheathed my knife and took out my flashlight. Focussing on the door, we looked for an edge and about halfway down the opening side found a crack large enough to force the end of the crowbar in. It took about ten minutes of waggling the bar until we both heard a short screech and felt movement on the door. That gave us the encouragement we needed to both put our combined weight behind it and force the bar further over. We were rewarded with a gap large enough to get our hands in and start to pull.

We dropped the bar and started to pull at the door. It screeched and groaned at the hinges but started to move. After a few minutes we had it wide enough to squeeze through. "Hang on a minute, let me shine the light in, just in case there's a drop or something," I said.

I poked my head in and used the light. There were two small steps down leading to a dusty concrete floor. In the middle of the floor were a set of railway tracks, rusty from lack of use. Looking left and right there turned out to be a long tunnel in either direction, disappearing into darkness. I squeezed in, went down the steps, and looked to either end. This was what we'd dreamed of exploring – a hidden tunnel under

London with who knew what waiting to be found. "Come on," I said, "let's investigate." Mick picked up the crowbar and squeezed through to join me. "Mind the steps," I said, shining the light on them. As I was the one with the flashlight, I led the way. It was decided to go right, so we carefully set off, trying to see what was ahead. The light didn't penetrate far. We began walking carefully along the side of the rail lines.

"What if a train comes?" Mick asked.

"We flatten against the wall. We'd hear it long before it got here. But I doubt there will be one coming – these tracks haven't been used in years by the look of them." Then I remembered a scene from a John Wayne movie. I bent down and put my ear to the track.

"What the fuck are you doing?" Mick hissed.

"Shush, I'm listening. Sound travels through the steel of the track."

Mick waited, I listened, then I heard it. A deep rumbling like an eerie wail in a thunderstorm. I quickly stood up. The noise stopped.

"What did you hear?" Mick asked, eyes wide.

"I dunno, sounded like a long rumble."

We debated the need to continue and decided it was too good an opportunity to give up. Mick knelt down and marked the rusty line with two lines across it. "So's we know where the door is." Fuck, the lad was thinking.

"Good idea – come on let's continue."

7

The musty air was starting to get to me. Our footsteps echoed off the tunnel walls and, once we felt a little more confident, we started to chat. I mean, what the heck was this place? It could only have been a spur line from some other more main line but what was it for? After about ten minutes my flashlight picked out something ahead.

It was a flatbed trolley with 'bogey' wheels sitting on what turned out to be the end of the track. A set of buffers just beyond it. There was nothing on it but dust. However, in the side wall was a wooden door. In fading letters were the words 'Keep Out' and the War Department symbol. We tried the Bakelite doorknob – it was locked.

"What say we use the bar and force it? It doesn't look like anyone has been down here for years," Mick said.

I agreed. Jamming the bar in the side next to the knob, we both gently eased against the end of the bar. There was a loud crack and hey-ho, it was open. The door squeaked loudly as we opened it and stepped over the threshold.

Behind the door, we found an office with an old grey metal desk in the far-left corner. There was a chart on the wall showing listings of railway stores and dates of delivery – most were in the August of 1941.

The last entry on it was dated 16th August 1941. Blimey, that was spooky; the date on that very day we were standing there was also 16th August but fifteen years later. I pointed this out to Mick and we both shivered and groaned.

There was a light switch close to the door near where he was standing.

"Try the light switch, you never know," I told him.

Click – shit, it worked! A dull yellow glare filled the room. I turned the flashlight off and looked around. There were two shelves with three old mugs on them, dirty and unwashed. The only drawer in the desk housed an old writing pad and a chewed pencil, a bulldog clip, a chipped ruler, and a set of three keys on a rusty keyring. I took the keys and pocketed them. There were two metal chairs and we both sat down.

"What do we do now?" Mick asked.

"Well, we could consider this place as a club-house," I said.

We thought about that for a moment and then decided against it. When we both got a good look at each other, we were filthy. I had a brown, rusty streak across the side of my face and ear where I had listened at the rail and Mick had black smudges across his cheeks. We both laughed. In all honesty, it was more of a nervous giggle. Then we both went quiet. Mick had heard something. I quickly ran over to the light switch and turned it off. We both stood by the door and listened. Then we heard it – a low rumble and a screeching at the same time. It was getting closer.

Trouble was, it seemed to be coming from the other side of the blanked-off wall. I looked at my watch. The glowing hands, now brighter because of the light in the office, said it was 02.20 p.m., we had been down there over an hour.

Going out of the office, I pulled the door shut. The damage had been minimal and at a casual glance the door looked much like it had before we broke in.

The rumbling and screeching were now getting very loud and both of us could feel a significant vibration. Turning the flashlight on we both looked at the flatbed rail cart.

"Why don't we get on that and push it with our feet down the line?" said Mick.

This seemed like a good idea to me. It was tied with a rope to the buffers, but it snapped easily as I pulled it. We stood by the side of it and moved it on the tracks. It was a bit stiff and noisy at first but seemed to run smoothly. Then the rumble noise got to the point where we were having to shout to hear each other. The vibration in the tunnel was bad and, no matter where we stood, it felt like an earthquake. Bits of dust and rubble were dropping everywhere, and we just sat on the flatbed waiting for the end. Eventually, it eased off along with the rumbling and screeching which seemed to disappear ahead of us, back the way we had come. Then it came to me – it was the bloody tube trains. I mentioned this to Mick who agreed. This tunnel must run parallel to a tube train tunnel and there was only one line in this area that I knew of – the Northern Line.

My fear was lessening by the minute. "Ok, let's get this thing rolling and see where this line ends. It can't be in use because the lines are rusty," I said, not convinced I believed what I was saying.

Mick laid the crowbar on the wooden platform of the truck. We both got behind it and started to push. It was slow and hard to get it rolling but then it started to pick up a little momentum and we both jumped on, one on each side with a leg hanging over the edge, just above the side of the track. As it started to slow, we both pushed with our legs along the ground. This way we kept up a steady speed.

It was slow and hard work but quicker than walking. My flashlight was on all the time, and we passed the metal door where we first entered the tunnel. Then the light dimmed to a yellow glow before going out altogether.

"Shit, now what?" I said.

Mick got out a cigarette lighter but couldn't keep it alight. So, we just carried on in the dark. Neither of us had noticed that we were slowly picking up speed until we realised that we didn't have to use our feet anymore.

"Mick, how do we stop this if we want to get off?" I asked, a little panicked.

"We can't... we'll just have to jump off, I guess!" Both of us were straining to see ahead into the dark but there wasn't a lot to see. "Er, what is that little light ahead?" Mick asked. "Am I imagining it?"

We both tried to stop the cart with our feet. It slowed some for a moment but continued on. I strained my eyes to see if I could see what he was talking about. There was certainly a darker patch a long way ahead... and then I saw it. There was a light in the distance, but it seemed to come straight down from above. "It's daylight, there must be a grate or something in the ceiling," I said and then noticed I was shouting.

We were picking up speed again. What bothered me was that we were moving further away from the metal door we had entered by. Then I had an idea. I picked up the crowbar and started to use it as a sort of anchor, digging it into the ground as we went by, trying to slow us down. It was nearly ripped out of my hands, but it helped; I could feel the cart slowing. The beam of light was getting nearer. It soon became clear that a patch of darkness was right in front of us on the track.

"Christ, it's a bloody tube train," Mick shouted.

I dug the crowbar in as hard as I could.

"We have to jump off," he said. "On the count of three – one, two, three, jump!"

We did, me going to the left and Mick going to the right. I tried to keep my momentum going but tripped over a sleeper, grazing both arms and getting a mouthful of dust and debris.

The cart continued for what seemed ages then, with an almighty crash, hit the front buffer of the tube train. The noise seemed deafening and then there was utter silence. I sat up and leaned my back against the curved wall of the tunnel.

"Mick, are you okay?"

It was quiet for a moment, then I heard him coughing. He was just across the track from me. "Fucking hell, I hit me bloody head on the wall."

We sat in silence for a moment. I stood and made my way across to him, stumbling into his leg.

"Watch it!" he yelled.

"Are you ok? Can you stand?" I said.

"Yeah, I'm fine just got a bit of a headache."

We waited to see if anyone had heard the noise but there was nothing. I spat out to the side. "I've got a mouthful of shit." I took out my flashlight out and tried it. For a moment it came on, bright, but quickly dimmed to a glow. It was enough to see each other by though. We looked like miners coming off shift and we both burst out laughing.

"Come on, let's go and see the damage. The train obviously isn't moving." Mick led off and we made our way up the track towards the light and the train. The cart had hit a buffer on the train and had jumped the track. We hauled it back on and, with the daylight coming from a long way up, we saw what was an old single carriage of a tube train. It must have been one of the first they'd ever built.

All the doors were closed. We couldn't get into the driver's cab. The darkness continued behind the train, so goodness knows how far the line went on. For a moment, we heard the rumble and steady increasing thunder and vibration from another train somewhere on the other side of our tunnel. We waited until it had passed and, in the dim light coming from the grate, we looked at each other.

"We better make our way back to the door and get out of here, we don't want to be still here after dark," I said.

Mick agreed and we crossed over the track to the side where the door would be and started the long trek back. It wasn't long before I tripped over the crowbar and, picking it up, handed it back to Mick.

As we trudged back, he used it to scrape along the wall to our right. After what seemed like hours, we suddenly found the metal door. I'd never been so relieved in my life. I'd had enough exploration for one day. We wearily made our way through the door and heaved it closed from the other side. Then we brushed ourselves off as best we could and made our way out.

In the daylight we must have looked grim. Mick said he had to get the crowbar back and in the evening light I knew I would have to sneak into the bathroom at home and hope I wouldn't meet my mum on the way. We agreed to meet up the next day – we had a cricket match to play on the Common with the some of the lads so that would make a welcome change.

I had made it in and managed to get to the bathroom and clean up some. However, my sister Jo saw me coming out and pointed at my jeans and tank top. "Look at the state of you, where have you been?" she snapped.

I asked her to shush and not to mention anything to Mum. She just laughed and went on to the bathroom. I shut myself in my room and took stock – she was right, I was a mess. I quickly changed and stuffed my dirty clothes in the washing basket. When I next saw Mick, we agreed not to mention our little adventure and that it was too risky to use the office as a club house. I think that was the last time we ever went back there but I did often wonder what the train carriage was doing there.

8

There were often times when I look back at those days and wonder what on earth I was thinking about when I did things. Like the times I would collect empty Bryant & May wooden match boxes, find snails on waste ground, and squeeze them into the boxes. When we—usually Mick and I—had amassed about three boxes each, we would find a main road, usually Brixton Road, wait until the road was clear, and line the boxes up spaced out across the road. We would then wait for the traffic to pass by and watch as the wheels crunched and splattered the contents on the tarmac. The winner was the one whose boxes lasted the longest. We would then take the winning snail out and set it free! Jesus, hope I don't come back as a snail!!

Apart from making mischief, my big passion at this age was aircraft; I was absolutely nuts about them. By the time I was at secondary school I could name ninety percent of most WWII aircraft, most current passenger aircraft, and the latest fighters of the RAF. In those days, the Gloucester Javelin was replacing the Hawker Hunter, the Vickers Vulcan, and Valiant were the 'V' bombers, and Swifts were the other fighters. Canberras were Navy aircraft, often used on photo-reconnaissance, and Shackletons were flying with the Fleet Air Arm.

I had created a photo album of cut-outs of aircraft from all over the world and was amassing an enormous knowledge of them from types, engines, sounds of engines, and all the other trivia that went with it. It was at this point that I joined the ATC – Air Training Corps, 343 Sqdn, Camberwell. I'll come back to this later because it was to keep me on the straight and narrow following a bout of being a bit of a 'bad lad'. A phase that started half-way through my time at Hackford Road School.

I can't remember how it actually started but I know that as 'street kids' we used to hang around various places in Stockwell well after dark. One such night, when I was about fourteen, Mick showed us how easy it was to break into cars. In fact, there was no 'breaking in' at all. We just used to walk along a line of cars and discreetly flick the door handle to see if it was unlocked. I didn't like doing it around our own area, so we would go to Central London and then down obscure side streets, knowing that seeing a policeman would be rare.

It was surprising how many cars we would find unlocked. There was no such thing as the sophisticated car alarms they have today and a lot of people obviously didn't bother locking their cars, so it was no problem getting in. Then it was a case of looking for anything worth pinching. To this day, I don't know why I did this – it was only a few times and I think it was done for the thrill of it. It didn't help that Micky was a bad lad. The other lad with us was Steven H, who lived in the same block of flats as me, around the other side. Like me, Steven was in it for the thrill.

Mick lived in Walworth Road, another favourite haunt of ours as there was a corner shop where you could get Sarsaparilla drinks and liquorice wood, great for chewing. I always had some in my pocket. One night, we decided to go over to Kennington. I went to bed at home at around ten and, once all was quiet, I climbed out my bedroom window, pushed it to, and legged it downstairs. Folks at home didn't even know I was out.

This particular night we decided to see if we could nick a motor bike. I had learned to ride on another mate's bike and had always wanted to have a go again.

So, it was decided we would each steal one. Outside Shepherd's

Bush television studios there was a bike park and about a dozen bikes parked there. I picked a Triumph Tiger Cub, turned the ignition on (no key was required), backed it out, and bum-started it down the road. Mick and Steve did the same to two other bikes.

In those days people rarely locked bikes either, so off we went. We rode all over London and were having a great time. We'd been on the road for well over an hour and the other two were ahead of me. We were heading down Knightsbridge and the road was empty of other traffic – I was loving it. Then ahead, walking along the pavement towards me, was a policeman and policewoman on the beat. They pointed at me and stepped out into the road. One of them put their hand up to tell me to stop – a stupid thing to do as I was doing around 40mph.

A car came past on the other side of the road so I couldn't turn that way. To avoid running the two of them over, I turned towards the pavement instead, jamming the brake on as I went. The front wheel hit the curb and the bike took off. I jumped clear and rolled over on the pavement. The bike continued and hit the large shop window of what I believe was Harvey Nichols.

I should add that at the time of this all happening, I was wearing a duffle coat that I'd nicked out of a car and a flat cap, also nicked. The coat saved me from getting hurt and I just sat on the pavement, stunned. The policeman got the bike and turned the engine off. The policewoman helped me up and asked me if I was okay. They told me I had been riding the bike without any lights on which was why they flagged me down. However, when I couldn't provide a licence or tell them what the licence plate number was, they deduced I had stolen it. They called it in on their radio and we waited for a police van to come pick us up. I was hustled into the back and was taken to Bow Street Police Station.

There, they phoned home and told my mum where I was and what I had done. They said for her to come down in the morning to collect me.

This was my one and only night in a police cell; not good. I never told them about Mick or Steve, although they had guessed I had been with the other two as they had passed them ahead of me.

Mum came down the following morning, stunned at what I had done. She said Dad had gone ballistic and refused to come. As far as he was concerned, I could spend the week there. When I got home, he took a belt and was going to give me a thrashing, but Mum stopped him. Instead, he refused to speak to me. This lasted for almost a month. Meanwhile, I was not allowed out until I had been sentenced at the Courts.

I told Mum about Mick and Steve and never did go out with Mick again. Steven's parents wouldn't let me see him again, so that was it. I was on my own. I appeared at Bow Street Magistrates' Court and Lady Isabel Barnet was the judge. Mum came with me. I was given a fourteen pound fine and put on probation for three weeks. Mum was not allowed to pay the money for me, and I was told by the judge to get weekend work and pay it off myself. Thankfully, I managed to get work with the milkman from Jenkins, the dairy at the back of where we lived in Lingham Street.

The worse part of all this was that the headmaster of my school, Mr Fawcett, was informed. Although, to this day I have no idea how he found out. As a result, I was made to stand up in assembly and my crime was told to all the other kids in the school – a public humiliation. Of course, some of the lads cheered and clapped although most remained silent. It was a wake-up call for me and things moved in a slightly different direction as a result.

Thus ended my journey into the 'dark side'. Truth be told, it shook me up. I was not cut out to be a bad lad – I loved my freedom too much.

It was at this stage that I decided to join the ATC – Air Training Corps. I had previously joined the Scouts in Clapham as it was the 'boyish' thing to do. I never really enjoyed it much and my tenure with them was brief. In fact, it lasted just one summer camp. We went to the

New Forest in Hampshire and camped under canvas in a field at the edge of some woods. Here we were shown how to cook over a campfire, woodsmanship, and various skills to gain our badges. Swimming in a local river was great fun and one of the parts of the trip that I enjoyed.

I remember, though, having to wash up all the cooking pots and wondering what bloody badge I was earning to do that. Later, being put onto spud peeling for swearing at one of the scout leaders, I decided to wander off to the edge of the woods and pretend I had seen a snake. I came running back into the camp shouting there was a snake and it nearly attacked me. A scout master clearly didn't believe me and took me back with some of the others, asking me to show him where. As we walked into the woods, there, just by some bushes, was a three-foot-long grass snake. I was vindicated but remember thinking, *Christ, that was a stroke of bloody luck!*

In the next field was a Girl Guides camp and we were warned that this was strictly off limits to us. Of course, we would go up to the wire fence separating the two fields and watch the girls – sometimes waving to them. One night, a group of us decided to raid the girls' camp. Needless to say, I instigated it but thought that it would be just a bit of fun. There were four of us and we made a stealthy approach across the field, over the fence, and viewed the area.

We all chickened out of actually going into one of the tents, so one of our lot had the bright idea of pulling the pegs from the guy ropes that held the tents up. I was more for getting into the tents – there were some good-looking girls there and I knew which tent to go for. But before I could voice my objection, one of the lads ran over to a tent, crouching low, and waved us over. Like sheep to the slaughter, we went. We started pulling the pegs out, but it proved more difficult than we thought. Just as we got the last peg out, one of the girls from another tent spotted us and screamed. All hell broke loose. The tent collapsed and we ran for the wire fence with a horde of night-dressed guides chasing us.

I cleared the fence in one but one of the lads didn't make it and got hooked up on it with an elderly guide hanging on to his leg. We quickly made it back to our tents – just as our lot started coming out to see what all the fuss was about. We pretended to be sleepy-eyed and asked what was going on. It later transpired, however, that the lad who was caught spilled the beans. In the morning we were hauled before the Scoutmaster.

We were confined to permanent spud peeling and washing dirty pots for the rest of the time at camp but had a good laugh about it. In the end, we met up with some of the girls later on and they all thought it was good fun. But when we got back to London the Scoutmaster sent a letter to my mother about my behaviour and said that they didn't want such reckless characters – with no regard for manners – in their troop. Mum thought it was funny. So, my Scouting life was very short; about six months in total. I never did like the bloody hats anyway…!

Joining the ATC was much more serious than joining the Scouts and I loved every minute of it. This was a precursor to joining the RAF and I guess that deep down there was no other option I even considered. My love of aircraft was second to none and the fact that I liked the thought behind a disciplined way of life meant that the RAF was the way to go.

The ATC was my first sortie into this military environment. I loved it. We all had to do what they classed as basic training which included learning how to march, form ranks, open and close order ranks, and how to dress and look after our kit. This was also where I learned how to spit and polish the toe caps of my boots.

When I first joined, our boots had leather soles which meant that when we marched – and it was all in step – the sound of the leather clapping the ground was amazing. However, we later changed to what were known as DMS boots and these had rubber soles. I was quite disappointed.

Being in the ATC, we all had to pick a trade and, as pilot was not an option because of my glasses, the next best thing seemed to be the role of navigator. So, I started to learn navigation, course plotting, and radio operating which included Morse Code. I studied it all avidly, soaking up the knowledge. Although it was only one night a week, we often had weekend parades and that involved a lot of marching and inspections. I decided to join the band and became a side drummer. This way, we didn't have quite so many inspections as we were learning our instruments and practicing. I quickly became very adept at the side drum and playing it on the march. The sound was great, and I really enjoyed it.

We also had basic weapons training and I learned to shoot. In those days, it was the Lee-Enfield 303 rifle. A really heavy old thing with a bolt-action and a small magazine of ten rounds. It had a kick like a mule, and I suffered many a bruised shoulder. But once I was on the firing line, it was a thing of beauty. It was here that I realized I was left-handed at many things and shooting was one of them. So, when we were lying down on the firing range, I was always on the right-hand end as my legs would be lying opposite to all the others. Pulling the stock hard into my shoulder and regulating my breathing, I didn't get the bruising and felt I could hit any target. And I did. I quickly became very good at it and impressed my instructor, unlike with navigation which I was struggling with.

Maths was not my forte and there were a lot of math calculations in navigation. But my drumming was good, my kit was always well maintained, and my aircraft recognition was the best in the group. Once a year we went away on camp and most often it was to an airfield somewhere. My first flight in an aircraft came at RAF Northolt in a De-Havilland Chipmunk. It was breathtaking and I loved every minute. Doing things like a 'Barrel-Roll' – when the aircraft banked hard whilst at the same time doing a large loop, flying upside down. It was important to keep the engine revs up so that you didn't stall but as these were trainer aircraft, the pilot was always in the cockpit seat behind you and guiding you. It was simply stunning. I went up as a passenger in many different types of aircraft whilst in the ATC, all prop engines. Many years later, I was also fortunate enough to fly in a Jet Provost fighter version when we attacked a group of Arab gun runners in the desert; I even got to fly it hands-on for a short while. But that is in another, much later, story…!

My love affair with aircraft continued and by this time I had built up a fair collection of Airfix models. They were all over my bedroom, the largest being a Lancaster Bomber. At night or on dark days I would create an airfield and put torches and lights at various locations around the bedroom. I raided Dresden and Berlin many times.

With my collection of Dinky cars, I had a mass of things to use my imagination on and would often play for hours, in my room, on my own. At times I remember being made to play with my sister Jo and her friend Mavis from the flat directly below us. I would be forced to drink concoctions made by Jo and Mavis, pretending I was a patient of theirs. I had a secret crush on Mavis that lasted for many years and at a later date we got to know each other in a more intimate manner but at the time I wasn't a fan of playing their games.

My bedroom was my sanctuary, and I had some great items in it. One was a metal Art Nouveau bookcase in black and white. On it I had a fish tank with cold water fish and sticklebacks. My bed was a double and my side tables were two orange crates side-by-side. Here I kept all my aircraft books and my stamp collection. I had a built-in wardrobe that I kept my model making bits in.

Although I never minded winter, I was always managing to get either tonsillitis or mumps and on one occasion I even had pneumonia. This of course meant that I had to spend days in bed which I put to good use.

I had quite a large collection of the Matchbox series of cars and would often play with these. I also developed my drawing and progressed to art and painting. I would often paint a scene from a Christmas card. Of course, a lot of this time was also spent reading. As well as my favourites – the *Famous Five*, *Tom Sawyer* and the Rider Haggard books – I had my collection of Eagle magazines that came weekly. Marvel comics were another favourite and there were also the Battler Britton comics that I had swapped at school.

Now fifteen years old, on my headboard, I had a collection of female film stars – my favourites being Sophia Loren from *El Cid* and

Elizabeth Taylor. On my orange box I had an old WWII tank radio that I had swapped with one of the lads from school as well as the Pilot radio. The tank radio could pick up all police comms, aircraft comms, and many other interesting comms on shortwave.

As my secondary school life progressed it became more obvious that I was not going to stay at school. The school didn't exactly promote academic learning and, as I wasn't pushed too hard, I never got the chance to pound the hallowed halls of serious learning.

To be honest, I hated Hackford Road School and could think of nothing more than moving on. The sad thing about this, as I've already mentioned, is that Mum (and Dad) were not into the 'academic' thing. I think Mum just wanted me settled in a job and away from school. She was a great provider and home maker but did not push us at all on the education front. Not that I'm sure it would have made any difference anyway. The area was a tough London working-class area. In those days, only the better-off kids went on to university.

Dad was not into education either and I think if you'd have asked him the name of my school, he wouldn't have known. However, he was very loving and a good laugh on many occasions. His party trick was tap dancing. He would roll back the carpet corner by the lounge door and as we had Marley tiles underneath, they were ideal to tap on. A bit of music would come on the radio and Dad would be away, tap dancing in his trousers and braces – and he was very good at it. He'd continue for a good five minutes until Mave's mum, Mrs Chiles, in the flat below, banged on the ceiling with a broom handle. We used to fall about laughing.

Dinah was probably the only one who would have pushed me into better education but by this stage I had my eyes set on the RAF.

Another thing I remember about the winter is that Mum used to move the dining table into the lounge, as it was warmer, and that we would have our meals there. For Mum, it was always a very serious time – cooking our meals, cleaning the flat, getting the shopping in.

My memories of her in those days are that she was very serious and strict. I think with hindsight, life was quite difficult for her with my dad. He was always gambling on the horses and knew a lot about their form, jockeys, and trainers. He probably spent a lot of money on them, and I should think there were weeks when she struggled with the housekeeping.

By now, Dad was working as a manager of The Londoner hotel which probably didn't pay a lot. For a while, my mother did early morning office cleaning with Mrs Chiles from downstairs. In the evenings she worked as an usherette at the Gaumont in Streatham, and one of the things I always remember is that around midnight I would hear the lift go at the end of our block, mentally counting off the floors as it ascended, then wait to hear her distinctive walk along the balcony in her high heels. She always used to bring me an Orange Maid ice lolly.

I can rarely remember my mum smiling or laughing, though. She was always so serious. I also think my dad was a bit of a ladies' man and I wouldn't have been surprised if he had been playing around some. I'm sure, too, that this had a bearing on Mum's behaviour.

I remember an incident one winter's morning as the girls were getting ready to go to work and I was getting ready to go to school. We were going to have breakfast in the lounge where the dining table was, and Dinah had laid the table. She had inadvertently forgotten the dessert spoon that I was to use for my cereal. Mum came out with the steaming plate of Ready-Brek, and I sat there looking at it. She went back to the kitchen, and I called to her, "Mum, I can't eat this." She came storming in and started getting on at me to eat it. I tried to speak out the punchline, but she gave me a clip round the head.

"Why can't you eat it?" she shouted at me.

"Because I haven't got a spoon," I said, in a high-pitched squeal, rubbing the side of my head. She just looked at me whilst Dinah turned away, trying not to laugh.

At that, Mum marched into the kitchen, got a spoon out the drawer, marched back, and slammed it down on the table snapping at me to, "Eat!"

My attempt at humour had backfired badly; Mum didn't take prisoners in those days.

I vividly remember the smog that we used to get in London before it became a smokeless zone. It was awful and, if you had to go out in it, you had to wear a face mask and carry a torch. The visibility was around two yards on a really bad night. This was nearly always in the winter as the low cloud cover kept the smoke from the chimneys from rising at a time when most houses had coal fires. The smog was a grey/yellow in colour and I remember looking over our balcony at Enfield House and not being able to see the ground below even though we were only four floors high. No wonder so many people suffered from lung conditions and bronchitis!

My love of all things military meant that I would often pay a visit to an Army & Navy store at Coldharbour Lane, near Brixton. They would sell all sorts of paraphernalia from old uniforms, ex-army knives, bayonets, and gadgets. One that caught my eye was an Aldis Signalling Lamp. It was a portable type in a metal and canvass box. In the lid was a morse key linked to a battery and the lamp. The light itself was quite large with a powerful lamp and a concave mirror reflector. I forget how much I paid for it, but I loved it. It was possible to use it on mains or battery. When I got it home, I connected it up and tried it out. It was as good as a search light. The beam was powerful and on top of the lamp was an aiming sight with cross hairs. If aimed up at the night sky, the beam was as good as anything I had ever seen – it appeared to go for miles.

The reason I mention this is because one night I had the bright idea to see if I could light up the underside of a passenger plane as it flew over us at home. We were directly under the flight path for Heathrow, and I thought this would be a challenge.

The aircraft came at a rate of about one every three minutes, so it wasn't long before I could see one approaching – he had just turned his front set of lights on. As he got nearer, I rested the lamp on the balcony edge and lined up the sight with the nose of the airliner. I flicked the switch on, and the beam shot out, right on target. As the aircraft came nearer, I followed him with the lamp, clearly illuminating the nose landing gear.

All of a sudden, the pilot must have switched on a set of landing lights from under each wing as the whole block was illuminated in these gigantic spotlights which virtually turned the night to day. He flashed them a couple of times as he went over and frightened the shit out of me. I then had visions of the Old Bill coming out, bells ringing, screeching into the estate, and arresting me – if they knew where the light came from. I was hoping the pilot wasn't that good at knowing exactly where I was. Still, I quickly dismantled the lamp and packed it away. Close call. I didn't tell anyone until a couple of days later when, as I hadn't been arrested, I guessed I'd got away with it!

One of the things that did happen to me, however, was that I had developed a stutter. I can't remember when it started but I think it was sometime after we moved to Stockwell. I was fine when I was talking normally but as soon as I got enthusiastic or had a lot to say about something, it would start. Again, it was Dinah who helped me gradually overcome it by getting me to talk slower and take deep breaths. Thankfully, I think it just gradually faded away in the end.

Despite whatever financial difficulties Mum and Dad might have experienced, we did manage to go on holiday once a year – often to the Isle of Wight. We would rent a caravan on a park at Bembridge, near the downs. We nearly always went with Mavis and her parents, and it was great fun. I would get excited the week before going and was always packed and ready to go well in advance.

The cosiness of the caravan was great and even if it rained it didn't matter too much. We would play board games or cards and listen to the rain drumming on the caravan roof. Jo would be with Mave in their caravan, hatching plots for the boys they might see at the caravan club and bar in the evening. If the weather was good, we would go to the beach, walking along the cliff top and finding the winding path that went down the cliff face to the beach. Mum would carry the 'grub bag' and Dad would hoist the chairs down. I was a sight to see in my Speedo's, looking something akin to a stick insect! Meanwhile, Mave and Jo would be in their one-piece costumes, and I would sneak glances at Mave's developing figure, enjoying the sight!

Swimming was not on the list of sports I particularly enjoyed but I liked it more in the sea than in a pool. I'd learnt to swim in the local pool at the back of the main road towards the Oval. My problem, as always, was that I hated taking my glasses off as I couldn't see a bloody thing without them, so most times I would keep them on.

I remember one of my early forays into the mysterious world of girls and sex, happened in this pool. There were two girls that were often at the pool and me and a couple of the lads got to know them. I was always a bit self-conscious of my skinny physique but in the pool, it didn't matter so much.

I really liked swimming underwater and would practice holding my breath as long as I could. One particular day we were swimming around with these girls and one of them decided to see how long we could stay underwater together. Up to the deep end we went, and then we went under. We swam around together and then she decided to swim through my legs. We came up for air, looked at each other and dived again. This time, as she went through my legs, her fingers brushed my todger. I was a bit shocked but decided to see what happened next…

Coming up for air, she just looked at me and dived again. I stayed on the surface and this time she put her hand there and started rubbing. Obviously, she could tell I was enjoying it, which encouraged her even more! When she came up for the final time, she grinned, and I laughed. We kissed on the lips and then swam to the shallow end. Her friends were calling for her to get out and make tracks. I was disappointed, of course, but realized she was just playing around.

Meanwhile, my mates had been busy jumping in and hadn't seen what we'd been up to at the other end. I suggested we get out, but they disagreed. As the girls disappeared into the changing area, gradually my 'stiffy' went and I felt more comfortable. Thinking back, it was probably best we stayed in the pool a while!

Sadly, I never did see the girls again despite looking out for them every time we went swimming.

Another bonus of going to the pool, however, was that once out and changed we always went to the chip shop – a large bag of chips for a tanner (sixpence/6d) and a large, pickled onion for tuppence/2d.

Sadly, in the sea, on holiday, nothing as raunchy as what happened in the pool occurred with Mave, although I did hang around her in the water, just in case!

Mostly, we played cricket whilst Dad and Mum sat in their deck chairs reading. If we weren't on the beach, we used to go walking and it was always good fun. Eating hotdogs or sandwiches Mum had made, the day soon filled up. Sometimes we would go for a walk to the town of Bembridge and look around the shops, buying gifts for people at home or just browsing. In the evenings we would all go to the Club House and sit listening to jukebox music whilst the girls made eyes and whispered about the boys they saw. It was always an enjoyable time for me, being on holiday, and made the summer break from school stretch out the summer.

9

Looking back, school was never going to be high on my radar in those days, probably because mine was a typical London secondary school and didn't do anything inspirational. It was a machine that did the basics necessary to get you in one door and through the next with a minimum of fuss. Fodder for the London machine.

English and Art were my best subjects but the only constructive artwork I did was to carve my name into the top of my desk, for which I was caned and had to unscrew the desktop and take it to woodwork classes to sand it down and revarnish it. I made a hash of that, and it actually would have looked better leaving it with my name cut into the top. English was always enjoyable, though, writing essays, reading good stories, and trying to get a handle on grammar and literature. I really did like that.

As my final year was drawing ever closer, I was starting to look toward what I would do when it came time to leave. The earliest age you could leave school back then was fifteen and I knew that if I joined the RAF, I would be able to hopefully learn a skill that would serve me once I had finished my time and still continue with my education.

However, Dad had other ideas. He was a pacifist at heart and was dead against anything that smacked of military and uniforms. He wouldn't even discuss it. His idea was that he would try to get me an apprenticeship in 'the print'. In those days, this was one of the higher earning environments, involving anything from proofreading to typesetting for newspapers, books, and magazines. A compositor could earn as much sixty thousand pounds a year, which in those days was practically off the scale.

Dad was a Freemason and had been the head of his Lodge, so he planned to use this as a lever to get me in the door of the printing industry. My objective, however, was just to get out of school and join the RAF.

Mum and I chatted about me leaving as the time drew nearer. I could have stayed on at school until I was sixteen and taken my GCE's but, as I had said to Mum, I could do that in the RAF. Sadly, she couldn't convince my dad, so she decided to let him try and get me the print job.

I was nearly fifteen when I left school – it was the autumn of '59. Dad decided to take me to a number of printers in and around South London. I would be introduced to the boss/owner whilst Dad did the old Masonic handshake. He would not let me leave home without the drawings and sketches that I had done. Mostly copied from the *Battler Britten* comics, these generally consisted of German soldiers with voice bubbles saying things like, "*Achtung, Englande,*" and, "*Achtung Spitfeuer.*" Lots of aircraft sketches, mostly Spitfires and Messerschmitts in dog fights.

Dad never really took on board what I had drawn, he just knew I had done a lot of sketches. His thinking being that the printing boss could see that I had an artistic skill which he, Dad, equated with the print.

Well, the boss must have thought I was some maladjusted lunatic with a war and aircraft fetish! Dad didn't see it in that light, however, even though the Masonic bit wasn't working. Clearly, they just weren't that desperate – either that or Dad's Masonic shake was the Antipodean one and wasn't recognised back in England!

Eventually, after being dragged around several such places and getting nowhere, he threw the towel in. "Well, I don't know what you are going to do but you are not going into the military," he said passionately after coming out of yet another printing company with a negative response. This last one was somewhere in Lambeth. It was a cold, wet, dark winter's day and we were both demoralised.

"I want to join the Airforce," I said resolutely, at which point Dad obviously made the decision that he couldn't do anything else to help me and reluctantly acquiesced.

Despite no longer trying to stop me signing up, I knew Dad wouldn't sign the papers to allow me to do this. So, Mum said she would sign them when the time came.

To tide me over, I got a job at Freeman's, a large mail order distribution centre at 139 Clapham Road, on the way to the Oval. Actually, I enjoyed it once I knew the ropes. My job was to pick up a batch of orders, take a large hand cart, and collect various items from massive warehouse racks. The place was enormous and a lot of the items in the section I was working in were female underwear. Needless to say, I got a lot of ribbing from the majority of the female workers. But it was good fun and it paid well.

However, as a working future went, this was not the job I was after. Whilst there, I applied to join the RAF hoping that my service in the Air Training Corps, of which I was still a member, would help. Within a few weeks of my application, I received a letter with an order to go to RAF Cardington in Bedfordshire for the recruitment assessment which would include fitness and a medical. It was an all-day job and Mum was to accompany me. I had just turned fifteen.

Getting to RAF Cardington was a blur. On the train I was thinking about what life would be like in the RAF. I imagined being up close and personal with the aircraft, sitting in the engineer's seat as part of the aircrew, feeling that elation as she took off and working in hot, tropical countries.

My dream was coming true, and I was a little nearer to it.

We were bussed in and met by an airman who asked us to go over to an assortment of white, block buildings. There were other parents there too, with their sons. Most of the parents were dads and I felt a momentary twinge of regret that my dad couldn't be there too.

Mum looked a little bewildered by it all and I detected a sadness in her eyes as we were ushered into a waiting area.

Eventually, my name was called out and I was directed to a door. I turned and looked back at Mum, and she gave me a wistful smile and nodded. What followed was a lot of doors, different people checking and prodding, and then a basic education test. I thought I had done okay at this.

For the medical checks, I had to strip to my underwear and have a full check done. I was conscious of my size because I was a very skinny fifteen-year-old and, stood alongside other lads of a similar age, I must have looked like a stick insect or a much younger brother. Once dressed, we moved on to an eye test. I had to sit down and point out numbers in a book of coloured dots for colour blindness. The next test was to look at a Snellen chart in a corner of the room about six feet away. I started to read it with my glasses on but was asked to take them off. I think I manged about two rows and the second row was more from what I had just seen with my glasses on. I certainly couldn't read any of the letters from the third line down. I said this to the man in his white coat who made a note on his board he held in his hand. He smiled briefly and told me to wait outside. A few minutes later he came out and told me to get dressed and go back to the waiting area.

I sat with Mum, and she asked me how I got on. I explained all the tests I'd been given and that I now had to await the results. Other lads were also joining their parents. They were then being called up, one by one, to a room down a short corridor. They seemed to be in this room for ages and once they came out, exited the building through a side door.

Eventually, my turn came and, with Mum holding my jacket over her arm, we went to the room. Inside, it was the Wing Commander's office. He sat behind a large mahogany desk, in uniform, with his hat to one side on the desktop. We were asked to sit down on the two chairs in front of his desk.

He sat quiet for a moment, looking at me. Then, after looking at Mum, said, "I'm afraid I have some rather bad news. You've failed the medical and I'm going to have to turn down your application to join the Airforce. You failed on the eye-sight test."

I turned towards Mum and we both looked at each other. No words were necessary. My eyes watered up and she looked down and put her hand on my arm.

"I am so sorry," the Wing Commander said. "Perhaps you can try again in a few years."

I didn't want to blub out in front of this guy, so I stood up and pushed the chair back. Mum looked at the man across the desk for a moment and he just said, "I'm sorry," again.

We walked out and, to be honest, I don't remember much about the trip back home to London. I do remember thinking on the train, *What the fuck am I going to do now?*

My entire life for the past few years had really been geared up to joining the RAF, even before Dad's escapades with the printers. For the moment, I couldn't think beyond that. Mum was reassuring and kept telling me not to worry; that I would find something. But I knew that in her heart she was as devastated for me as I was.

10

While all this was going on I did manage to find a half decent running club. If there was one thing that I was confident with, enjoyed doing, and was good at, it was running. I was a loner for the most part and this form of sport suited me.

Any sport that involved a ball, I was pretty useless at. I enjoyed football, as in a kick-about, but tennis, table-tennis, badminton – any of the competitive ball games – forget it. I could run very well, though.

I'd tried ice skating and found it was also something I enjoyed and was reasonable at, so I soon had my own figure skates. Streatham Ice Rink was nearest to me, and it became my regular weekend activity. I had a mate who lived in Brixton and we both made it our thing to do. Eventually, I joined the Streatham Junior Ice Hockey Club and, borrowing a friend's ice hockey boots, gave it a shot. I enjoyed the speed but was soon bruised and bored.

Figure skating was more enjoyable and there were plenty of the opposite sex to chat to. One girl I met lived in Richmond and was also a member of a local running club… and that was my breakthrough to joining the Ranelagh Harriers.

The good thing about this club was that its running and training area was Richmond Park, which was just across the road from the Club House. Richmond Park is a great place to run and pretty large, so I soon got into running on the various routes around the park. As a club, we entered several competitions, and I worked my way up to become one of their 'promising juniors'. I managed to win a club silver medal, which helped my self-esteem a lot. My best distance was a half-marathon, road or grass, and running helped me to overcome my intense disappointment at not getting into the RAF. At that point, I had no clue what I was going to do with my life now that the RAF wasn't an option for me. Aircraft were still my all-consuming passion but where I went from here was anyone's guess.

If Dad was relieved that I wasn't accepted into the RAF, he never said much about it to me and, after about a week, life went back to normal at Enfield House. I was moping around for a while, still a bit stunned. I had thought about the Navy but, for some reason, it didn't appeal.

On a visit to the local job centre (or Employment Exchange, as it was known) I saw an ad for a proofreader for a small printing works in West Norwood. It looked interesting so I gave it a shot. I managed to get an interview and got the job.

The salary wasn't brilliant, certainly not by printing standards, but it was my first real job. I was working in a small room with three other people. These three were two elderly men and one in his thirties. I was fifteen-and-a-half, streetwise and had a lot to say for myself but I fitted in perfectly. The two old boys smoked pipes and the other man cigarettes. A permanent fog hung over the room, but the Sobrani Balkan pipe tobacco smelled great.

I was sat at a corner worktop with a dumb-waiter next to my right elbow. The work was to proofread, amongst other material, the sheets of the Fatstock & Marketing Corporation monthly journal. The proofs would come down in the dumb waiter from the compositors upstairs. I would proofread them, marking off any spelling mistakes or letters/words put in incorrectly and using a printer's code to mark the offending item. Once completed, the periodical would then be sent back up to the print room where the compositors would make the necessary changes before going to print.

Truslove & Bray (T&B) were also government printers and the year I started working there (1960) was the year the Queen was making an official tour of Australia. I was tasked with proofreading all of her public speeches. Another job I remember was to proofread a classified document for the Royal Navy: *Cryogenic Liquids for Rockets*.

I began to enjoy it and at least my work meant I was doing something useful. I started to get into a routine. There was a greasy spoon diner two doors down the hill that made fantastic bacon rolls with HP sauce. I used to get four every morning on my way in for the lads. This was a post-breakfast treat, and we would eat our rolls with a large mug of strong tea before the pipe smoke descended in clouds.

I used to take a packed lunch in a plastic Tupperware container and eat it in Streatham Cemetery whose gates were opposite T&B's. As it was summer, it was a good place to have lunch because as soon as you walked through the back entrance, the noise of the traffic disappeared. After a few minutes' walk, there was a small monument of an angel with her wings spread. This was above the grave of a young girl in her early twenties. I can't remember her name, but it was a good place to sit on the grass and lean against the base of the grave to eat my sandwiches. We became good friends.

Sometimes I was sent up town to Fleet Street and the offices of the Daily Mirror. This was usually to deliver some documents or to pick something up. It was following one of these trips that I had a chat with one of the old boys I was sitting next to at T&B. He asked me if I was going to make a career of this and I said I wasn't sure. I went on to explain about my disastrous attempt to join the RAF. He was ex-RAF, and we had a long conversation about his work in the war.

I mentioned that I really wanted to travel and see foreign lands. He then said that this place was no job for me, stuck in a small office with three old boys! He was right and I agreed with him. I told him I didn't fancy the Navy as I didn't like the uniform, so that only left the Army.

That evening, at home, we happened to have my Uncle Doug staying with us. He was the manager of the Dominion Theatre in

Tottenham Court Road. He lived in Brighton, so when the trains up to town were particularly bad, he'd stay with us, which I'm sure suited Mum as it meant a bit of additional income.

As we sat down to our evening meal, I explained about the chat I'd had that afternoon at T&B's. Dad was away for a week on some management thing as he was the manager of The Londoner hotel at this time. Uncle Doug asked me what I really wanted to do, and I explained about joining the Army and my wish to travel. He said I needed to get a trade in something that was useful when I came out of the services. I agreed as I knew that that was what Dad would want too.

I explained that Dad would not sign my papers, but Uncle Doug said that he would sign on Dad's behalf. I told him that I could finish my education in the Army as I had been going through the brochures.

My nearest recruiting place was in Whitehall at the Central Recruiting Office. My elder sister Dinah was living with us at the time and said she would come with me to 'sign on', something that had to be done before Dad got home as we all knew he would go ballistic. Over the next week Mum, with the collaboration of Dinah and Uncle Doug, contacted the Army recruiting centre and arranged for me to attend a signing-on session at the Whitehall office where I would undergo a physical, an academic exam, and discuss my career options. Uncle Doug had signed the necessary documents that had come earlier in the week, these had been sent off, and we had received a date for me to attend the Central Office.

The morning of the visit I awoke early. The sun was streaming into my room, and I knew it was going to be a hot day. We had agreed that Di would accompany me to Whitehall because she was Dad's favourite, and it would be less traumatic for Mum if she kept out of the way on this one.

Sitting down to breakfast we all discussed the coming event. I was nervous in my stomach but tried to keep it hidden. Uncle Doug explained that it was now up to me and wished me luck. Mum didn't say a lot.

Di left the table to put her makeup on and I kept pretty quiet too.

This all sounds as though I was setting the scene for a disaster but, the fact was, I didn't know what I wanted to do or even could do.

The rest of the family was getting ready to throw the towel in regarding me so I knew that this would be a serious move and that, once undertaken, it would set the seal in place for the next few years. I couldn't back out of it as I had too much pride and, besides, I really did want to get away from home. Joining the Army would mean a fresh change, new people, new places, and perhaps the opportunity to go abroad at last.

The tightening knot in my stomach didn't help but, whatever I decided to do, I was always going to get that. Best get it over with.

I don't remember much about the trip up town, but I do recall the drab interiors of the Central Recruiting Office. The distinctive cream and green of the corridors and rooms were true to what I imagined an 'establishment' building would be like. We were checked in and then told to take a seat in a waiting room. It was far worse than being in the dentist's.

I was not the only one. There were about a dozen others of similar age to me with their parents, looking as nervous as I was. Eventually, I was called to a room for some written tests. This was because when I completed the documents to send in, having gone through the glossy brochures, I had settled on a Marine Engineering Apprenticeship at the Military Army Apprentice College in Chepstow, Monmouthshire.

In some ways this was to appease Dad as it, at least, fell in with some of his wishes. The test I was about to undertake was basically a Maths, English, and general knowledge test as well as a psychiatric evaluation. If I flunked this, I would really be in the shit.

As it turned out, I flew through the tests and was then sent for a medical. This was much like the RAF one and I stripped down to my underwear. The usual poking and prodding were carried out – I weighed in at seven-and-a-half stone. There were murmurs and mutters and when I asked what the issue was, they said that I was the lightest recruit that had ever passed through their portals!

My eyesight test with this lot didn't require me to remove my glasses, so I whizzed through the Snellen test chart. They must have been desperate, was all I could think; they'd lost a lot of cannon fodder after the last war.

It is true to say that I didn't have a particularly high opinion of the Army, but I was a bit beyond caring at this point. By the time I had been fully processed it was late afternoon and my hopes were not high. I was prepared for a rejection – probably because I was either too light or thick as a plank. I then started thinking about what else in life I could do. I didn't fancy staying at T&B for the rest of my life. So, I was thinking that maybe I could get to join the Navy after all. I would certainly give it a try. If that failed too then I really was up a creek without a bloody paddle!

I had been there for over two hours. Di and I were ushered into an office where a Major sat behind a large desk.

"Well, young man, looks like you'll be going to Chepstow."

I nearly fell off my chair. I looked at Di and I'm sure I detected watery eyes. She didn't exactly stand up and punch the air with a resounding, *"Yes!"* but I could almost hear her sigh of relief.

We were both directed to a side room where the Major came in and a civilian stood next to an enormous Union flag, holding a bible. Di was asked to take a seat and I was ushered forwards to take the oath of allegiance to the Queen, the flag, and my country. *Jesus*, I thought, *that's done it, I've actually managed to get in! Sorry Dad!*

The next stage of my life was about to kick off and I wasn't really prepared for it. But hey, I was eager to see what life could come up with next. I was a great one for diving in and saying *Sod it, let's just go for it!*

It was something along those lines that I was thinking as Di and I made our way home. In my mind, I don't think I was expecting Mum to burst into tears and clutch me to her pinnie; I just thought she may be a bit shocked that it had happened all so quickly. I didn't dare think what Dad would say and this did concern me a bit. As it turned out, I had got that wrong too. Once again, he went into a kind of sulk and didn't talk to me for the next few days.

I had to wait for a little over two weeks before I received my marching orders.

I was sent a letter telling me that in three weeks' time, I was to report to the Junior Leaders Regiment in Yeovil, Somerset, my new designation being: JDvr English – Army No 23874505.

I was surprised – no one had mentioned Junior Leaders to me and what was this Yeovil place?

Mum thought it was because I had done well in the education test at the Whitehall centre and that they had decided that I was to be a, quote, Junior Leader. Surely, that was better than an apprentice? "But what about my Marine Engineering?" I said.

The letter had also mentioned that following six weeks of basic training I would start driver training in all forms of military vehicles. That sounded great but not what I thought I was supposed to be doing.

To this day, I cannot think why the penny never dropped, especially with Mum and Di. Dad was no help as he wasn't talking to me but I'm not sure why they didn't question it. Also, I myself should probably have made more of a fuss but I thought that perhaps you first had to learn to drive before starting the apprenticeship. Plus, the thought of being taught to drive those fantastic big army trucks and jeeps overwhelmed my common sense. Stupid boy.

What was to come was not at all pleasant and I was certainly not ready for it...

PART II
A MILITARY APPRENTICESHIP

11

I look back at those times of joining up and do wonder whether the Royal Navy would have been the better choice. Having three sisters was for me, a prompt to leave home. That and the lure of overseas travel were deciding factors.

I knew I'd miss Mum and although Dad wasn't really an inspirational father, he was very loving and fun. Having said that, he also knew my career prospects at this time were zero. I'd been in trouble with the police and my mates were not those your mother would have liked.

So here I was, sitting on a train from London on my way to Yeovil in Somerset to join my unit, looking out of a grimy train window and wondering what the hell I had signed up to. I had no idea that I was being sent to the wrong unit and to be honest, at that time, I wouldn't really have cared even if I had known.

Steam trains were still in use and the smell of smoke, coal, and steam remain evocative to this day. I looked around the carriage to see if any of the other passengers were doing as I was. It was not obvious – everyone looked a little spooked but that could have been for any reason.

I only had a small case with me; we had been told in a letter what we were to bring, and it wasn't much – just washing gear and a change of underwear. At a signal stop, I leaned my head against the window and looked out at the steep, grassy embankment. Looking at the scene I noticed a small, yellow wildflower set amidst a sea of grass and scrub and felt a bit like the flower; adrift, isolated, as if I had always been this way. Sure, I had butterflies in my stomach but it all felt like this was the natural progression of things – like, no matter what I had done in these last fifteen years of being on the planet, it would always come down to this; sitting here on a train heading West with my chin resting on my hand, en route to an army base that I shouldn't have been sent to in the first place.

It was fated to happen this way because, unknown to me at the time, nature was saying, "You need some training, boy, something to strengthen that inner, mental toughness I know you possess."

I was certainly going to get that, but I was totally oblivious to it all. I was embarking on a journey from childhood to the grey misty world of young adulthood. That single yellow flower was like a monument, and it has remained set in stone in my mind ever since. It is still there – even as I sit and write this fifty-five years later.

That train journey was a giant leap for me. As I sat in the smoky carriage on my way to Yeovil, another thing I was not aware of was the passing of an era. The age of the steam train was quietly slipping away. Diesel engines were the next stage, and these massive leviathans were rumbling along the tracks on occasion and were exciting to see.

From Yeovil, we changed to the train that took us on to Taunton. On arrival at Taunton, I realised there were quite a few of us that had signed up and had even been in the same carriage from London. I sort of guessed this was the case during the trip down, but I was so wrapped up in thoughts of what I had done that I hadn't paid much attention. I think on that journey down we were all feeling a little nervous and wondering what the hell we had done.

Outside Taunton station several three-tonners were lined up with green tarpaulin covers over the back. A staff sergeant and a couple of corporals were waiting for us. As we were herded out of the station, we were told to line up in three ranks. There must have been thirty or forty of us in total. It was a grey and overcast day and a light drizzle of rain was beginning to fall. After we settled into a semblance of three ranks all went quiet. The chatting stopped as the sergeant moved in front of us. His look was challenging as he and his two corporals surveyed this motley crew of civilian boys. A couple of the lads were still smoking and were called out in front. I wouldn't have dreamed of lighting up in front of these three, even if I had any. Besides, at that time, I didn't smoke.

"You like smoking do you son?" the sergeant asked one lanky lad who was grinning.

"Yeah, it's okay," he said, shuffling from one foot to the other.

"Put it out now."

The lad dropped it and stepped on it. He then put his hands in his pocket. Even I knew he shouldn't have done that.

"Place your packet of cigarettes on the ground," the sergeant said quietly.

The lad took out a packet of Woodbines and a box of Swan Vestas. The sergeant watched as he placed them in front of him.

"Put the matches on top of the packet," he said.

"They'll get wet... er, Sergeant."

The sergeant said nothing, and the lad did as he was asked. Then the sergeant walked across to them and stood in front of the lad. Slowly and deliberately, he brought his highly polished, toe-capped boot down on this little pile and crushed it. There were sniggers from some of the recruits behind me.

"Get back in the rank," he said disdainfully. Then turned to the rest of us. "Listen up you lot. If I catch any of you smoking, you will be tapping the boards in my office. You will do nothing unless I tell you to. There will be no smoking, no talking, no chewing. Do I make myself clear?"

Quiet, as the wind picked up and a steady rain started to fall.

"I said, do I make myself clear?"

"Yes," we all murmured.

"Yes what?" he continued.

"Yes, Sergeant."

"Louder…"

"Yes, Sergeant."

"I said fucking louder! Are you all deaf?!"

This time, we yelled. "Yes, Sergeant!"

"Good," he said, "now get in the back of the trucks in an orderly fashion." Turning to the corporal he added, "Corporal, sort them out, fifteen to a truck."

We shuffled forward, rank by rank, towards the back of the three-tonners. There were no steps just a toehold and a short rope hanging inside as we struggled up with our cases. Inside, there was bench seating along each side and down the middle. We were all glad to get out of the rain and, despite feeling damp and chilly, I was starting to feel the excitement of what was to come.

Once both trucks were loaded with all of us, we pulled out of the station and set off for Norton Manor Camp.

When I saw the camp for the first time, it reminded me of prison camps I'd read about. Barbed wire fencing, drab single-storey buildings or, rather, wooden structures. The deep orange glow of the sodium street-lights gave the place an eerie atmosphere and showed the rain slanting down in the reflected glare. Water dripped off the wire fencing and puddled in pools behind us as we came to a halt.

It all went quiet in the back of the truck and the darkness that had quickly fallen took on a sombre note. I heard muffled voices coming from the front of the truck, a door slammed, a voice called out, and we lurched forward. Someone mumbled something about having a cigarette and the corporal quickly told them to be quiet.

As we passed the entrance to the camp, I could see that we had been stopped at the guardroom, and as the back of the truck cleared the entrance to the camp, a white bar came down across it. A peaked-cap soldier in a dripping poncho with a rifle slung over his shoulder watched unemotionally as we pulled away. He disappeared back into the lighted doorway of the guardroom.

We drove on for a few minutes and then came to a halt alongside one of the other trucks. The sergeant walked to the back of ours and the corporal jumped out. He undid the latches on each side of the rear gate and dropped the back flap. The sergeant moved forward.

"Right, I'm not going to stand here all night in the rain, so listen up. I want you lot in this truck in the first billet. Wait for me in the corridor."

He turned to the corporal. "Get 'em out with their cases and inside."

"Follow the corporal, come on, make it snappy."

I jumped down, grabbing my small case as I went. The billet structures were black wood barn-like things but looked quite cosy. I followed the others into the entrance. A large corridor space got us out of the rain. I stood a moment and took it all in.

The corridor led off to the left and right and at each end I could see a large room. We were lined up in the same group as we had travelled in the trucks. Both corporals carried out head counts and separated us into the two groups.

"Okay, look up," the sergeant said. He pointed to our group. "You lot are A-Section." Then he pointed at the others. "And you are B-Section… I want A to go along this corridor to the room at the end. B, I want you to go along the other corridor to the room at that end. Find a bed position and I'll be along in a while to explain the rules."

We shuffled off down the corridor with our cases and entered the large billet area. I wasn't too bothered about a bed position. There were eight beds on either side of this large room, facing each other across a centre area. There were large 'A' frames in the ceiling that was open to the slanting roof. I walked halfway down and chose a bed in the centre on the right. Beside each bed was a large green metal double door locker. The bed was a green metal-framed structure with taught springs. At the top end was a folded set of grey blankets and white sheets. I dumped my case on the springs of the bed and sat on the edge of it. A tall, dark-haired lad was on my left and a fair-haired lad on my right.

"Hi, I'm Dave English," I said. I stood up and shook hands with him across his bed.

"Hi, I'm Roger, do you know how to make a bed?" he asked, grinning.

"I haven't a clue," I said, "but I'm sure they'll come and tell us shortly."

There were some keys in the door of the tall locker, and I opened both doors. One side was for hanging clothes, the other had shelves and one drawer. Across the top was a shelf the width of the locker. It all looked new and clean inside. I also noticed that the floors were wooden parquet with a high gloss.

At the far right-hand end of the room was a small corridor with rooms off to one side. I guessed these were the toilets and washrooms. The lighting – down the centre of the room – was tungsten bulbs hanging from long cords with white metal shades. Most of the other guys were exploring and chatting as I was. We all looked a little tired and bewildered by it all.

I opened my case and looked at the neatly packed clothes that Mum had prepared for me. I felt a momentary pang of homesickness but knew I had to get on with it. There were wire hangers in the locker, so I grabbed a handful and put them next to my case. As I was thinking of what to put where, the sergeant and a corporal walked in. They came to the centre of the room and looked around at us all. Some guys were chatting and paying little attention.

"Okay, listen up," the corporal said. It went a bit quieter, but some were still chatting. He banged the side of a metal locker. "I said listen up!"

It went quiet.

"I'm Corporal Hayes and this is your platoon sergeant, Sergeant Campbell."

He turned and looked at the sergeant who put his hands behind his back and walked up to one end of the room, looking at us all, then came back to the centre.

"In future, he said, "when I come into this room you will all stop what you are doing and stand at the ends of your beds. Do I make myself clear?"

There were a few nods and murmurings.

"I'll say it one more time, do I make myself clear?"

A chorus of slightly louder 'Yes, Sergeant' came from us.

"Do you understand?!" he said for the third time.

A much louder, "Yes, Sergeant!" came from us.

We were all told to stand. "There will be no smoking in these rooms at any time. If I so much as get a hint of anyone breaking this rule, you will wish you'd never been born. You can smoke in the NAAFI Club only. You will be shown where that is later. You have all sworn an oath to serve Her Majesty and to become a soldier in the British Army. You are no longer who you were, you no longer belong to your mummies and daddies."

There were a few sniggers around the room.

"You are just a number. You are a private and you belong to me. I am your mummy and your daddy."

This time we all laughed, and the sergeant grinned.

"I see you have all your clothes with you. Say goodbye to them because you will no longer be allowed to wear them. Don't even bother taking them out of your cases. All you will need is your washing gear and underwear, as you were told."

No one spoke and in the quiet the rain could be heard beating against the windows.

"It is in our generous nature to provide you with all you will require. However, it is not in our remit to make your beds for you. After I've finished with you, Corporal Hayes will demonstrate how to make a bed and you will do well to pay attention. Having made one up he will then show you how to 'box' your sheets and blankets and place them at the head of your bed."

He looked around at us all as we stood there like a load of stunned rabbits.

"I expect you to have your bedding boxed every morning. Tomorrow, you will be taken to the Quartermaster where you will be sized and issued with your uniforms. These will consist of your dress uniform, which you will wear on certain occasions, and your fatigues which will be your everyday working dress. You will not be allowed to wear civilian clothes at any time."

There was stunned silence. I looked at my case and thought, *Well, I got that right.*

And so began my career in the military.

12

The early days at Norton Manor were a blur of cold mornings, shouting NCOs, the smell of hot polish burnishing boot toecaps, making beds, learning how to iron impeccable creases in shirts and trousers, learning how to drill, and making friends.

Learning how to heat the handle of a spoon over a candle flame and apply it to the toecaps of your DMS boots was novel. It burnished off the little raised pimples of the taut leather and you ended up with a smooth finish. Opening a tin of Kiwi black boot polish, you used the hot spoon end to burnish the hot lumps of polish onto the toecap. Still using the hot spoon end, this was then rubbed over the toecap. Applying more polish to a yellow duster you then spat on the toecap and started rubbing the polish and spit over the smooth surface (hence the saying 'spit n' polish'). This exercise went on for a few hours. It was whilst doing this that you got to know your room mates. Chatting about where you lived, what home was like and, of course, girls. Looking around the barrack room, it was a hive of activity as guys were spitting and polishing. We had two pairs of these highly polished boots that were to be our parade boots to wear for inspections.

Physical training was an essential part of this as was assault course training. I was pathetic. It was early days yet, but I was struggling with things like 'heaves' – chin-to-beam – push-ups, and weights. However, I excelled at running and my agility was good; I could fly up a rope, balance on a beam, and fly across the wooden horse.

Early morning runs in the icy dead of winter soon got you moving. I loved the long-distance runs and any excuse to go, I would. The other thing I enjoyed was drilling. I loved the parade square and the drilling, left to right, front to back, close, and open order. All of this came under basic training. Up to a point, we never saw a rifle or a handgun. Slogging across wet, muddy heathland in full gear with a backpack was a regular occurrence. The smokers struggled most and if you were at the back, you usually ended up with extra duties. I'd had 'off' days and the extra duties usually consisted of cleaning out the barracks toilets and showers. They even came and inspected them after. But for the most part, I saw it as a challenge and, considering my 105lb size, did well.

We all learned how to keep the wooden barrack room floors highly polished. Room inspections happened regularly with both A and B platoons competing against each other. Saturday mornings were inspection mornings, and this meant most of Friday night was taken up with dusting and polishing.

We had an electric buffing machine for the floor and took it in turns to do our portion. One of us would take a tin of a yellow/orange wax, scoop a handful out with our fingers, and flick it over the floor. This would be allowed to dry once it had been spread thinly with a cloth, on hands and knees, then the electric polisher would be run over the area. The finishing touch was with a 'bumper'. This was a broom-like device with a heavy weight on the end. It had a flat, felt underside over which we would wrap a yellow duster and proceed to 'bump' our own bed areas.

Keeping your locker tidy was essential and this was made apparent quite early on. One Saturday morning, as we were stood by the ends of our beds, the sergeant came round for pre-inspections. Our CO was to inspect later in the morning. He came to the first bed on the left and looked at the recruit who was stood at ease by his bed end. The bed was 'boxed' with the lad's best parade boots sitting on the end of it. The sergeant had his 'swagger stick' with him under his arm. He did not look happy. He looked at the boots and pushed one off the bed onto the floor with his stick. This invariably damaged the toecap, which would then have to be done again. Saying nothing, he walked to the head-end of the bed and pushed the boxed blankets into disarray. Walking around the bed to the locker he told the lad to open it. Once opened, he stared at the poor attempt to tidy it. He then proceeded to pull everything out of the locker onto the floor. By the time he had gone through all our lockers, beds, and boots, the place was a tip.

Throughout all this, the sergeant had said nothing. Nobody escaped his silent devastation. He turned to the corporal and said, "This is your platoon, your bunch of useless privates, your responsibility. Sort it for the CO's inspection. I'll be back in one hour."

Then he stormed out of the room.

We were stunned. For the next five minutes we were told in no uncertain terms, by Corporal Hayes, what would happen if everything was not ready. To top it all, we were confined to the room for the remaining weekend with inspections every couple of hours.

I had to have a little chuckle to myself; this was what I had signed up for. For the life of me, I must have been nuts, seen from an outsider's eye. To me, it was what I had expected. The drills on the square were carried out regardless of whether in freezing rain or on frosty mornings; it made little difference. The shouting, polishing, clumping through the mud of the assault course, the agony of the gym, and the incessant screaming of the PT instructors – the days dragged on into weeks. We had to learn how to iron shirts and put creases into our best dress uniforms. Scrubbing floors, cleaning latrines, making hospital corner beds, how to squeeze all the toothpaste in the tube to one end, stripping the SLR rifle down and putting it back together, writing letters home, and the excitement of getting mail from home. It was the cycle of basic training.

There was another thing, too. Making friends. These guys were from all walks of life and from all over the country. Most of us were failed intellectuals. In other words, we never completed our schooling. This meant that fifty percent of the time was spent in the classrooms. The work was the usual Maths, English, History, and Geography but we could pick a subject of our choice too. Mine was Technical Drawing and I excelled at this. All of this was what was, at the time, to GCE Standard.

About six weeks into training, we started trade training as a taster. We still had to complete basic training which was six months at being a soldier. This meant the start of driver training. The vehicles we started with were the three-tonne Bedfords. This was the standard army workhorse and was great to drive. You climbed up into the cab and you felt you owned the road. The view was excellent. The gearstick was a black plastic knob atop a long stick and a simple clutch system with a handbrake on the driver's side. Key in the ignition and away we went.

The first thing they taught us was to 'double-clutch'. This meant clutch in, shift to neutral, clutch out, slight touch on the gas pedal to get the revs up, clutch in, change gear, and clutch out. The idea was that the clutch plate would rotate at the same speed as the gearbox plate and, thus, the clutch wouldn't snatch as you changed gears. It wasn't difficult to do. In later years, the synchronised gearbox eliminated the need to 'double-clutch'.

It was when we were well into basic training that I began to realise that perhaps I was in the wrong place. When I saw the schedule for trade training for the months ahead, there was no mention of Marine Engineering. When I mentioned it to my instructor, he just laughed. "We don't do that here son. You should have joined the navy."

I wrote this in a letter home and Mum said she would get Dinah to investigate it. To be honest, I was settling in nicely, so I wasn't too worried. I'd made some good friends, I was enjoying all the training, and the food wasn't too bad either. On the rare occasions that we had a free evening or weekend, we went to the NAAFI Club. Here, the favourite was sausage, eggs, chips, and beans with lashings of Daddies brown sauce and toast. Then a few rounds of snooker and a beer made for a good evening. No one was allowed out of the camp until basic training had been completed and that was still some months away.

As it turned out, I never did get to see what life was like outside the camp. One afternoon, following drill training on the square, I was making my way to the classrooms for education when I saw two bowler-hatted civilians heading for the CO's office. It was noticeable because you never saw anyone out of uniform on the camp during the working day. We were well into English composition when an orderly came into the classroom. He spoke quietly to the captain, who was our tutor. The captain looked up and singled me out.

"English, you're wanted in the CO's office. Go with the corporal here."

Everyone in the class was looking at me as I stood up. *Oh, shit*, I thought, *what have I done now?*

I did wonder if it was anything to do with going out on to the parade ground at 11:00 p.m. the previous night. My mate Roger and I had been walking back from the NAAFI having a smoke and chatting. It had been a particularly nice night; clear skies and loads of stars. The best place to see them was in the middle of the parade ground because of the lack of light pollution. We had made our way furtively across to the centre of the square, sat down, and looked up. It was amazing, with thousands upon thousands of stars. Both of us sat there looking up, wondering what was out there. We spoke softly about it, pulling on the roll-ups and hoping that no one spotted us.

I now wondered whether someone had indeed seen us after all. I made my way to the front of the classroom, glancing at Roger who just shrugged. The orderly led me out.

"Any idea what this is about?" I asked.

"None," he said.

I felt the tingling of butterflies as I followed him. We walked outside and along to where all the admin offices were. I'd never been to this section of buildings before and wondered if I was sufficiently dressed for them. I had on what we called 'fatigues' – not ideal for my first meeting with the CO.

I smartened my beret and smoothed down my green jumper. He led me along a few corridors to a room at one end. The corporal knocked on the door, told me to wait where I was, and went in. I looked at the closed door. The CO was a Lt. Colonel, and I felt the nerves as I waited.

A minute later, the corporal opened the door, stood to one side, and said out loud, "Private English, Sir."

I marched over to stand in front of his desk, came to a thumping halt, saluted, and remained at attention, looking at a spot somewhere above his head.

"That will be all, corporal, thank you."

The door closed behind me. The two bowler-hatted men I'd seen earlier were seated in the room with the CO.

"At ease, Private English," the CO said.

I stood at ease, wondering what was coming next.

"How have you been settling in?" he asked.

"Very well, Sir, thank you."

"These two gentlemen are from the War Office in London. I'm afraid there has been a bit of a mix up. It appears that you qualified for an apprenticeship as a marine engineer. Now, obviously, this is not an apprentice school, and we don't teach marine engineering here. You are currently here to carry out your driver training. Your mother sent a letter to the War Office, enquiring as to why you were here. That's when it came to light that an error had been made. Now, I have here your current record and your platoon sergeant is pleased with your progress. You are two months into your basic training and your trade training has yet to start in earnest."

He turned to the two men sitting quietly to one side. One of the men had a file in his lap, turned a page in it and said, "We have a space available for you at the Army Apprentices College at Chepstow, in South Wales. Firstly, we would like to apologise for the mistake that has been made. However, you now have the choice. You can remain here at Norton Manor as a junior leader, and continue with your driver training, or you can relocate to Chepstow where you will continue with your basic training but also start your apprenticeship to become a marine engineer. The choice is yours. Should you decide to go to Chepstow, we will arrange for your travel in one week's time. Alternatively, you can remain here and continue as normal."

He looked across to the CO. The Colonel looked at me and spread his hands.

"Naturally, we'll be sorry to lose you, but I understand fully if you want to continue to Chepstow. Have a think about it and come and see me in two days' time. If you choose to go, we'll make all the necessary arrangements for your move to Chepstow."

He stood up and held his hand out for me to shake. I guessed that meant it was my time to go. I shook his hand and saluted him. "Thank you, Sir," I said. I turned to the two civilians, nodded, and left.

And that was it. A bit of a non-brainer really; I had made some good mates and hated the thought of doing it all over again, but I knew the apprenticeship would serve me a lot better in later life than driving a truck. Looking back, it was a sweet/sour move. An apprentice college was a far cry from a junior leader's regiment. But I knew the training was going to be very good and, I must admit, I did have a somewhat romantic notion of myself serving on a fast patrol boat in somewhere like Hong Kong. The downside to this would be making new friends, who were already established in their own relationships, and I knew I was in for a bit of a difficult time. As it turned out, it would be even worse than I imagined.

13

The relocation to Chepstow was a bit of a blur. I was picked up at Chepstow station and driven in the back of a three-tonner to the camp at Beachley. Dropped off at the guardroom, I felt a bit adrift. A squad of soldiers were being drilled on the parade square and the orders being shouted drifted across it in the wind on a bleak, grey day.

I was met by a sergeant who took me to a company office where I was introduced to the CO of J Company. He had the fanciful name of Capt. De Planta de Wildenburg. He apologised for the mix up and welcomed me to Chepstow. He told the sergeant to take me to the J Company billets where I could set my gear and meet my platoon sergeant and the rest of the platoon.

The billets were black, wooden structures set in a row at the rear of the camp. They were about two grades below that of Norton Manor, from where I'd just come. I had a sinking in the pit of my stomach and a nagging doubt as to whether I had made the right decision.

Chepstow - One of the old billets of J Company

There were about six of these billets in a row, backing onto the sports field. In front of them was a tarmacked assembly area. The billets each had a T-shaped section that formed the toilets and shower areas. The apprentices were allocated to the billets according to their trades. These were engineering, electronics/radio, painters and decorators, bomb disposal and admin. Once basic training was over you would then be redeployed to your various companies of A, B, and C. Eventually, we would be going to C Company. For the moment, however, we were all in J (Junior) Company. The year was broken into three intakes – A, B and C. Ours was the September intake and, the year being 1961, we were group 61C of J Company.

Those early winter months passed quickly but settling in was difficult. Many assumed I had simply 'upgraded' from the Junior Leaders Regt, not knowing that I was sent there by mistake, and therefore thought I believed I was better than the guys at Norton Manor.

I knew it was nothing like that but after several attempts at trying to explain that Whitehall had got it wrong, I just couldn't be bothered anymore. Of course, that meant coming in for some stick, mostly from two guys that were fast becoming the platoon 'alpha males'.

Undaunted, I set about getting into the training. Our Platoon sergeant was an old 'Dads Army' type: Sergeant 'Pop' Westerman, late, of the Gloucester Regt. He was a dear old stick, standing about 5'1" in his boots, rotund with a ruddy glow, and he was totally fixated on drilling us on the square. He also oversaw our behaviour in the barracks, standard of dress, general well-being, and discipline. He was very 'old-school' and could be quite fierce.

As the winter months settled in, I gradually managed to shake off the shadows of friends and life at Norton Manor and started getting used to the routine at Chepstow, along with the others. There were fourteen of us in the billet and my bed was halfway down the room, on the right, much as it had been at Norton Manor. Any other similarity ended there. These billets were old and draughty. At the far end was a set of double doors that opened out to three steps down to a path and then the sports field. In the middle of the room was what was commonly termed 'The Cenotaph'. This was a chimney stack with two large stoves: one facing the main entrance and the other, on the opposite side, facing the double doors to the sports field. They were black, cast-iron stoves with a flat top you could put a kettle on. These were kept black with the use of Zebo, a sort of black metal polish. When these stoves were in use, Zebo had to be applied daily and whoever was duty billet cleaner and polisher, had to do this. You could get into a right mess doing it, too.

Keeping the wooden floors polished was much the same as at Norton Manor. Boxing blankets and keeping the lockers spic n' span was also the same. Sheets were changed weekly but no one objected to the constant bed making. Woe betide anyone whose bed space wasn't neat and tidy. The individual didn't suffer; the whole billet did, so there were no excuses.

My nickname became Hank, after Hank Marvin of The Shadows. My glasses were the thick, black frames similar to his and Buddy Holly's who, along with the Shadows and Cliff Richards, were very popular at that time. My favourite song was Buddy Holly's 'Everyday'. A few mates called me Giggsy – full name Gig Lamps – because of the glasses. He was a character from the Beano and was a cricket fanatic.

We had to get up at 06:00 a.m. and by 06:45 a.m. we were washed, shaved, beds made, and blankets boxed. Our general dress for the day was fatigues. At 06:50 a.m. we lined up outside the front of the billet, mug, and utensils in one hand, were brought to attention and marched off to the cookhouse for breakfast as a platoon. It was freezing and, even though we had green pullovers, the icy winds would blast up the Bristol Channel and assault you.

The food wasn't too bad as long as you didn't mind rubber fried eggs, watery baked beans, thin toast, greasy bacon, and cold plates. The coffee was rubbish but hot and wet. The saving grace was the ubiquitous bottles of tomato and brown sauce. Smothering your breakfast in either was the rule of thumb. You could go back for more except that you only had half an hour to finish and being late for morning muster was not an option. So, you wolfed it down and legged it back to the billet, having rinsed your utensils and mug in a lukewarm trough of greasy water on the way out of the cookhouse. Norton Manor was five-star compared to this place.

I was starting to find many reasons to rue my decision to relocate to Chepstow. But fate obviously had other plans for me!

Once the breakfast utensils were set away, you were back out front, formed up into your platoon and marched off to either drill, sport, the gym, or trade training. A lot of emphasis was put on sport, as you can imagine, and as we were all new recruits in the J wing, we had to be assessed. Our PT kit was blue shorts and red or white T-shirts. Our gym shoes were black pumps and, believe it or not, these had to be kept black which meant using black boot polish on them. Once dressed in the PT kit you were inspected. The PTIs (Physical Training Instructors) were ruthless, and me being the proverbial seven and a half stone weakling, didn't help. If you were found to have dirty kit or pumps, you were punished. This would mean having to do some brutal exercise in the gym and/or running around the sports field in the middle of winter and if that wasn't enough, they gave you extra PT periods in your own time. So, you tried not to mess up too often.

On one of our first gym periods, we were lined up in the gym to be inspected by the chief PTI and his corporals. The chief was a WOII in rank and always carried a pace (swagger) stick. This was a drill sergeant's 'weapon' for measuring out the pace or length of the stride you were supposed to march at. Pop Westerman was never without his and always had it tucked under his left arm. On this particular occasion, we were lined up in the gymnasium in three ranks in what was called 'open order'. This meant that the inspecting PTIs could walk up and down the ranks. On this occasion, I was in the middle of the 2nd rank with a further rank behind me.

As we were stood there, the WOII and two corporals slowly walked along the front rank, inspecting each lad and making the odd comment. One of the PTIs had a clipboard and made notes against a name if something was not to their liking. They came around the front rank and inspected the back of each boy. Names were taken, including haircuts if it was felt necessary. Then they started along my rank. We were all stood at attention, and I was doing a quick mental check, trying to think of anything I might have missed with my PT kit. I felt quite happy that all was well. Slowly they came along the line, then it was my turn. Nothing was said. They looked me up and down and the PTI with the clip board made a note against my name. I wondered what that was about.

Eventually, they came behind us and inspected us from the back. They were slowly working down the line, and I could see them in my peripheral vision. They came to me and stopped. It went silent. I wondered what I had neglected to do. I waited for them to pass on – they didn't. Then the WOII called across to the Sgt PTI, "Hey, Sergeant, come and have a look at this."

I quickly tried to figure out what the fuck I had forgotten to do. My hair was recently cut, my pumps were spotless, and my PT gear was clean, so what the hell were they looking at? I heard someone say, "Hmm." Next minute, a pace stick came through my legs. He flicked it from side to side against my knees.

"What's this space here, boy?" he asked, breathing close into my left ear. I could hear the other two PTIs chuckling behind me.

Thinking quickly, I said, "Horses, Sir, horses".

"Horses? What do you mean, horses?"

I stood a bit straighter. "I've been riding horses since I was three, Sir."

He blew in my ear. "I could drive a London bus through here, lad."

Now the rest of the platoon was starting to chuckle.

"Shut it, you lot," he said. "Hmm, well, we'll see," he continued, "perhaps you should have joined the Cavalry."

It went quiet then they moved on. I breathed a sigh of relief and thought, *well, maybe bullshit really does baffle brains*. Did sitting on the rangers' horses in Oz count? I'd ridden along a bush path and trotted around a paddock a few times. Still, it got them off my back for a while.

I wasn't good at any exercise that required upper body strength. But I was very agile and could shimmy up ropes like a monkey. Pull-ups and push-ups were a killer; I was useless at these. But running, now there was my thing. I could run for miles and do it well. I had spent many a weekend at Richmond Park running for Ranelagh Harriers, which had stood me in good stead. Doing it in earnest for the Army Apprentices College would come a bit later.

One morning in the gym, it was decided that we would all be tried out for boxing. Now, my dad loved boxing, but me? Not a chance. It was my worst nightmare. I hated taking my glasses off to do anything and boxing was all about upper body strength. Plus, it hurt if you got punched in the face – the principal target area!

On the other hand, though, I didn't want to look a wimp in the eyes of the platoon. A couple of the smaller guys did manage to be excused and I just knew that many were expecting me to do the same.

There was no other small guy to be paired with. A mate of mine, Roger Hayward, although he was 5'10", hated the thought of boxing. So, I wandered over to him whilst the others were pairing off.

"Rog, what about me and you pairing up?" I asked, grinning.

"I'm too tall," he said.

"Yeah, but I don't want to come up against any of the others. They are all much bigger and too aggressive."

He agreed but looked doubtful.

"Look, I have an idea. You know how that American boxer, Mohammed Ali fights? He dances all over the ring. So why don't we do a lot of dancing around, you give me a couple of taps," – I emphasised 'taps'– "and I'll go down for the count."

He thought about it for a moment then agreed.

They had set up a boxing ring in the gym and everyone had sorted their boxing partner out. Roger and I were the fifth pair to go. The PTIs gloved us up and explained the rules. We watched the fights begin. When I saw how hard and serious the punching was, I started to get serious butterflies. Roger and I looked at each other.

"Shit," he said, "the PTIs are egging them on."

It was true, they were shouting at them things like, "keep heads up, don't drop your guard, no punching below the belt!" A couple of the guys were taking a beating. The rounds were just one three-minute round each pair. Once the bout was over, they left the ring, and the next pair were told to get in.

When it was our turn, we climbed into the ring and went to opposite corners. I gave my glasses to one of the PTIs.

"Shit, I can't see a bloody thing," I murmured to him.

"Look, just keep your guard up and try to get a few jabs in, you'll be okay. He's taller than you, get in under his guard."

Someone rang the bell and we both sauntered to the centre of the ring. Some of the guys were shouting, "Hank, Hank, he's over here," and laughing. *Fuck you lot*, I thought. It then occurred to me, *well, okay then, I've got an audience, let's have a laugh.*

I started my Mohammed Ali dance. I was going all over the ring and Roger was trying to follow me, every now and again throwing a gloved jab in my direction. But I wasn't there, I'd moved away. Shit, I was beginning to enjoy this! The lads were laughing,

"Come on Roger, get him, take his head off!" they shouted.

Still, I evaded him. I was enjoying it now and getting cocky, doing the 'Ali shuffle', dancing around the ring. Roger was getting frustrated. In the end it had to happen. The crowd were winding him up a treat. One minute I was dancing around grinning then all of a sudden, he came in close and threw a left hook at full force. It caught me on the side of the head. I felt myself falling and hitting the deck. There really were stars and twittering birds. I lay there for a moment and caught the sound of a PTI giving the count.

"...eight, nine, ten. Ok lads, all over."

"Dave, Dave, are you ok?" I glimpsed the shadow of Roger standing over me.

"Yeah! No! What the fuck was that? You were supposed to give me a gentle tap!"

The PTIs stepped into the ring.

"OK you two, come on out. English, you need to get some weight on you. Looks like J Company's got a couple of clowns!"

That was my one and only foray into the world of boxing.

The winter days went slowly and most nights we had to light the stoves. Lights out was 10:30 p.m. without exception and, to be honest, by then we were pretty whacked anyway. It was during these cold, winter nights that I started my storytelling.

My bed was just one bed away from the stove. One night when it was howling a gale outside and the bitter easterly wind was hurtling across the sports field, slamming into the back of the billet, sleet was scratching away at the windows and the whole billet was rattling and moaning, I decided to tell a ghost story. It was gone eleven, but no one could sleep very well with the wind howling. Both stoves were well stoked up and glowed a red hue part way up the chimneys.

"Who wants to hear a ghost story?" I said into the darkness. There were encouraging calls from around the billet for me to continue.

"Okay, this is about a museum in an old part of London that housed Egyptian mummies and artefacts..."

There was silence, so I started.

"One day, on a cold, windy, grey, winter afternoon, a single figure walked the slick, wet pavement to the steps of the museum..."

And so, I went on. Part way through the story, several lads moved their beds closer to the fire. Most of us sat around in our PJs on the ends of our beds to get the heat from the stoves. The guys loved it, and storytelling soon became a ritual. The atmospherics of those billets was certainly conducive to ghost stories.

Slowly, the days drew nearer to our first leave, and we were getting excited.

One particular lad I can remember was called Richard 'Titch' Gething, on account that he was quite a small lad from Cornwall. He had a bad habit of being up last every morning and if we were late on parade, we got extra duties. After several times of this it was decided that action was required. The mornings were freezing and most times foggy with the mists rising off the River Severn that was not too far distant.

On this particular morning we had been warned not to be late on parade. We had to be up by 05:30 a.m., get washed, make our beds, get dressed and booted up, clean the floors, and muster outside. By 05:45 a.m. Titch was still sound asleep in his pit.

One of the guys opened the double doors that backed onto the sports field. It was shrouded in a dense, white fog. You couldn't see more than a few feet. We all crowded around Titch's bed, making sure he was snuggled up tight in it and sound asleep. Then we gently lifted the bed up and slowly manoeuvred it out of the double doors, down the three steps, and onto the grass. We hiked with it right across the sports field to the centre of what was the football pitch. Titch hadn't stirred. Here, we gently set it down and made our way back to the billet. When we went on parade a little later, Pop Westerman asked where Gething was. One of the lads pointed towards the sports field. It was the right moment; emerging from out of the mist was a bedraggled figure with a blanket wrapped around him. Westerman never said a word and we continued off to breakfast. Titch was never late for morning muster again.

My first leave was a blur of a journey back to London, drinking and celebrating on the train. A bottle of vodka was passed around until we arrived at Paddington. I got a taxi from there to Stockwell and home. I guess we were all feeling a bit gung-ho, and I was particularly glad to be home again. There was, however, one big downside to this. Whilst I was away Mum had decided that 'as I was a man now', she would clear out my room.

My many years of Dinky Car collecting that I had saved up all my pocket money for, and we were talking about a substantial collection, she had given away to my cousin Mark. He was my Uncle Jo and Aunt Martha's only child. I was speechless and quite angry about it. When I tried to get them back, it was too late; they were nearly all lost or broken.

I was quite devastated and never forgot. To this day it still makes me angry to think about it. But that was Mum. She had absolutely no sentimentality at all. She had done the same to the girls' collection of fairy story books. Di and Jo had collected the complete set of *Flower Fairies of the Garden* books and Mum had given them to the dustman.

The effect of this many, many years later is that all of us, perhaps with the exception of Jo, never give up anything.

14

Basic training was over, and I was beginning to see things in a different light. Going back to Chepstow after that first leave was never going to be enjoyable. On the Beachley peninsular it was bloody freezing. Trade training had started in earnest and all in our platoon were doing engineering. This entailed hours of classroom work learning about combustion engines and carburation. The practical side of this was bench fitting, which amounted to being given two large square blocks of mild steel that we were to shape so that one fitted seamlessly inside the other. The fit was to be so good that friction would hold it in place without falling through. All of this was to be done with a file once you had cut the square hole in the centre.

Well, I wouldn't like to say how many times I botched it up. By about the fourth attempt I got it right. The key was mastering the art of filing using an assortment of files from really rough ones (known as bastards) to the really fine. The instructors didn't take prisoners and you had to continue for hours, if necessary, to get it right and accepted. Blistered hands from the hours of filing were par for the course. But I did learn how to get the best from a file and how to use it successfully. This stood me in good stead many years later in my hobbies and in work. Education also continued. I still struggled with Maths but also took Technical Drawing as one of my GCEs, which I loved.

Because I weighed only about 112lb and was not very good at most sports, except long distance running, I became the target for the two bullies we had in our platoon. In part, I don't think it helped that I was outspoken by nature. My size never hindered my expression of various things. Add to this a certain amount of arrogance and I was setting myself up nicely. I refused to back away from anything that I saw as an injustice and was also a bit of a joker. Sometimes this didn't work, and it would end in a fight. A few times I was hauled up in front of the platoon commander who tried to be fair. I usually ended up with extra duties, either sweeping the large parade square, cleaning in the guard-room at weekends or, at one point, painting lumps of coal white and putting them around the flower beds.

One of the fights I ended up in was a result of one of the bullies putting broken glass in my bed. There were all manner of things these two buggers got up to. I'd go to the toilet prior to an inspection and find when I got back to my bed that someone had wrecked my highly polished boots or wrapped my nicely blanco'd green belt and brasses around the blackened stove. The result of trying to put it right, before the inspection, was that I'd be either late on parade or get done for dirty kit. It was a bitch, and I would fight against it but still get done. I just refused to give in. There was no point in complaining to the platoon sergeant or the officer in charge; that way you just ended up with a bad reputation and were bullied even more. So, I fought it and often had to write home for Mum to send me new pairs of glasses.

Also, I was beginning to be the one that ended up with the 'trouble-maker' reputation. I suppose it would be untrue if I said I didn't care. I did but couldn't afford to show it.

When I had been at Chepstow about eighteen months, it all finally came to a head. It followed a particularly bad spell of bullying and I'd had enough.

We were sitting on our beds in the evening, cleaning our kit which, for this particular parade the next day, included bayonets for the SLR rifles we used. As usual, it wasn't long before the two 'alphas' started and wandered over to my bed space, intent, I'm sure, to mess up my parade gear. When they started, I threatened them with the bayonet. I knew I shouldn't have done it, but it was all getting a bit too much and, after a week of their incessant harassment, I guess the dam broke.

I went for one of them with the bayonet, faster than he was expecting, and it caught him in the side. It went in quite easily, which surprised me. At this point, all hell broke loose and some of the other lads stopped us.

I was called before the CO and explained what had been happening. I realised then that the bullying had been noticed by the staff, but I think they were just letting it run to see how it panned out. In my opinion, they left it a little too late.

The CO was actually very good about it. I was confined to barracks for two weeks and the boy I'd hurt was strapped up following a short stay in the medical infirmary. I never regretted it and although the bullying eased off for a while, there was a minor resurgence as we neared summer leave. By then, however, it was only words. I think they were all a little wary of me.

It was whilst on leave that I discussed this all with one of my uncles, Hayden, who had been a captain in the services. When he heard all that had happened, he decided to accompany me to Paddington Station on my way back to camp following this particular summer's leave. The major culprit of the bullying used to catch the same train as I did. When we were standing on the platform, I pointed him out to my uncle. And he went along the platform to have a chat with him, telling me to stay where I was. He spent about five minutes talking to him. When he came back, he said, "You won't be having any more trouble from him."

Well, it worked – for the most part – with only a minor resurgence in our final year at Chepstow.

Summer leaves at home were great. Once I had spent a few days at home with Mum and settled back into the routine of being at home, I was soon bored. I had no mates that I knew anymore; we'd all gone our separate ways. I had an uncle, Les, who lived over at Battersea and in between his various jobs as a milkman and van delivery driver for Ravenscroft glasses, he would sing in various pubs in the area in the evenings. I wasn't a particularly big drinker but now that I was in the forces it was sort of expected. So, I gradually became more and more a resident of my Uncle Les's.

Les had an amazing basement flat in a Victorian terrace just off Battersea Rise on Lavender Walk Road. He also had an Alsatian dog called Vicky. She was a fierce guard dog, but we became very close friends. Les had converted part of the basement area to a bar, and he had a fantastic vinyl record collection of all of Bing Crosby's recordings. Bing was Les's idol and quite often he would sing his songs in the pub in the evenings. He also used to dress up as a drunken vagrant when he was 'on stage'. His signature tune was 'Mule Train', and he often took off Jimmy 'Snozzle' Durante with a fantastic rendering, in mime, of 'I'm the guy that found the lost chord'.

The main pub where he sang was The Rifle in Fulham Palace Road. At the time it was run by Alf Mancini the boxer. Les had a great crooner's voice and was well known around the pubs in South London. During the day he worked as a milkman for Express Dairies. I'd been with him before I joined up, helping him deliver milk at weekends, especially at Christmas time. He had a fantastic yodel and when he was delivering, he always used to sing. Sometimes, when entering a block of flats during the Christmas holiday, he would yodel around the estate, and it would echo off the walls and blocks. He was well known.

In later years, when I used to stay with him during my Chepstow leaves, he worked for the Ravenshead glass company delivering glasses to pubs all over London. I often went with him, having a drink in many as we went. It was always amusing and, of course, drinking and driving wasn't such a big issue at that time, thank goodness.

Sometimes my uncle Hayden would come and stay at Les's place, and then it was party time every night. Hayden was a bus driver at the time on the No.88. He was a bit of a ladies' man and there was certainly no shortage of women at Les's place.

Les married an Irish girl, Bridget, and she was great. They eventually separated but every now and again she would come over and stay. Les had a son by Bridget who later went on to become a Catholic priest. I came across him many years later at Addenbrooke's Hospital in Cambridge, where he was the resident Chaplin for a while. I had tried to have a chat with him about Les and his mum and my connection to them but, sadly, he didn't want to know and was quite dismissive of me.

I spent my summer leaves with Les most of the time and only went home a few times. Les taught me to cook and so did Hayden. Hayden missed his military days and later went on to become an officer in a mercenary unit fighting for President Tshombe in what was then the Belgian Congo. He would come back to the UK from time to time, but the authorities were after him for a while for recruiting mercenaries in England. Then he ended up with a price on his head in the Congo and the UN were after him too! He was eventually caught and ended up back in the UK. He later went on to work for the Sultan of Oman's Airforce. I came across him there some years later whilst I was in Aden on active service.

Les drove an old London taxi, one of the black ones that were around in the 1930s. We always had to push it to get it started but it was great fun to ride in.

Les and Hayden didn't always strike it off. I remember one night we were all going out for a drink. Les was in one car with some friends, and I was in another behind him with Hayden. They'd had an argument earlier in the evening and Hayden was still angry. Les, in the car in front, had obviously decided to go somewhere else and turned onto the Northcote Road but then got caught at a red light. Hayden pulled up two cars behind him, got out, left the car, door open, engine running, and ran towards Les's car. The lights changed and Les started off with Hayden in hot pursuit chasing him up the road. I was well pissed off. I moved over to the driver's seat and, because there were a lot of cars behind me, hooting, moved the car over to the side of the road. I was hoping that there were no police in the vicinity, so I switched off and moved back to the passenger's side and waited for Mr Angry to get back. He did, after about fifteen minutes, still fuming and threatening to do all sorts of things to Les.

He managed to cool down enough for me to convince him to go to a chippy, get a takeaway, and go back home, which is what we did. Eventually, all was okay between him and Les. Their relationship was always a bit tricky, and explosive, and their arguments usually involved a woman or money.

One day someone broke into Les's flat and stole his entire Bing Crosby record collection. Hayden and Les both seemed to know who had done it. They eventually found him and chased him into Stockwell underground station, down the escalators, and beat seven bells out of him. Unfortunately, Les never got his record collection back.

They were interesting days with never a dull moment, and I loved my leave time with them. Both Hayden and Les were like big brothers to me, and it remained that way all the time they were alive.

On one of my summers at home, Mum and Dad bought me a Lambretta L1 Series III motor scooter. I absolutely loved this machine and went everywhere on it. It was about this time that the 'Mods and Rockers' thing was taking off and Brighton was the place to be seen. It often made the news headlines when gangs of both met up and had a major punch-up.

One weekend I decided to make the trip to Brighton on the scooter. The ride down was good. It was a warm summers day and, even though it was a Saturday, the roads were only moderately busy. It was not compulsory to wear helmets in those days, but I had an American style one that was silver, and I had painted a blue stripe on it, matching the side panels of my scooter.

The leafy suburbs of Surrey were calm and quiet as I sped towards the coast. Once I started getting near, I could smell the salt in the air. I'd seen quite a few other scooters on the road and many of these were 'Mods' with the scooters decked out with a myriad of lights and aerials, and with the riders' long, flapping green anoraks with fur trimmed hoods.

I wore jeans, a T-shirt, and a light brown suede bomber jacket. The jacket cost the earth, but I loved it and only got to wear it whilst on leave. Arriving at Brighton, I cruised the seafront parades. It was teeming with scooters – I had never seen so many in one place. I drove along the front towards Hove then back again. Dropping down to the paved section of road before the pebbled beach, I had some lunch, sitting alongside the scooter as I watched the 'talent' parading by.

At the other end of town, towards Worthing, there was a whole group of 'Rockers' on big Harleys, Triumph Thunderbirds, and an assortment of Hondas and Suzukis. The big Japanese motorcycles were just starting to make an appearance but Harley, Triumph, BSA, Norton, and Ducati still dominated the scene. I made sure I kept well out of their way as they were cruising for a fight. Judging by the size of the riders it was wise not tangling with them. There were large groups of Hell's Angels in their various chapters and their reputation preceded them. Low profile was the order of the day.

After cruising some more, I tanked up and made my way back to London. The weather was so good that I decided to take it easy and go a slightly longer route home. This way took me past Brands Hatch. It never occurred to me that this was motorcycle country. I had noticed that I hadn't seen any scooter riders. About an hour into the journey, I came along a wooded road. Coming round a curve I noticed a large pull-in on the right-hand side of the road. It was a well-known transport café favoured by truckers and motorcyclists. I slowed down as I neared it and then noticed the parking outside. It was packed with motorcyclists – Rockers and Hell's Angels. There were lots lounging around their bikes, chatting, and drinking.

Most were Hell's Angels, all sporting their various chapter motifs on their jackets. I felt my heart sink and thought, *oh shit*. I immediately opened the throttle but, bearing in mind that I only had a 125cc engine, I wasn't going to get a great turn of speed.

As I went past, I saw heads turn, fingers point, and I'm sure I heard some of them yelling, "A Mod!" There was a mad scramble for the bikes, dropping glasses and bottles en-masse as they climbed aboard their machines. I knew they were coming after me. I was now going flat out but I just knew it would never be enough – I was in the shit. I could hear the roar of engines bursting into life even as I was getting further away.

The roads in this area were winding and curved and I knew I had to get off the one I was on. All around, it was heavily wooded and as I shot around a curving bend, I noticed a small side road to the left. It was signposted to a village two and a half miles away and I immediately turned down it. I could hear the roar of motorcycles getting close, so I drove the scooter off the road and into the trees. Fortunately, it was dry, so I drove into the thicker parts, over the mulch, and came to a stop behind a particularly large tree. I quickly switched off the engine. Leaning the scooter against the tree, I waited. What seemed like seconds later, I heard them go past the turning. They were shouting to each other and the numbers of them went on for quite a time. I reckoned there must have been around fifteen to twenty of them. After the engine noises faded into the distance, I realised I had been holding my breath. My knees were feeling a bit weak. *I can't go back on that road,* I thought, *I'll have to continue to the village along this side road and see if I can find another route.*

Quickly covering the scooter with a few branches of leaves, I sat down and waited for at least fifteen minutes. I made a roll-up and had a smoke. All the time I was listening for the sound of motorcycle engines. After a while I decided to make a move. I started the engine but walked the scooter out of the trees. As soon as I was on the tarmac road, I made my way to the village. I was constantly checking my rear-view mirrors but saw nothing.

I continued through the village and just kept going until I came across a major A road and followed signs to Croydon then home. It was as I was driving along that I realised the importance of speed and having a larger engine. I also realised that scooters were not for me; I needed a motorbike or, indeed, a car, something with a bit more oomph to its engine. It was frustrating turning the throttle grip and not getting the power I really needed. My short-lived year of scooters, I realised, was coming to an end.

15

My Chepstow days were well underway. We all progressed from J Company and the draughty wooden billets to the smart new blocks of C Company accommodation. The rooms were good, if a little institutionalised with green linoleum flooring and magnolia walls. There were about eight of us to a room with the rear windows overlooking the River Severn.

Trade training was settling in, and we had moved on from bench-fitting to capstan and lathe setting and use. It was fascinating work, and I was beginning to enjoy it. I never thought I would.

Following the lathes, we went to sheet metal working. Using tin snips, sheers, and silver solder we made various types of boxes with hinged lids and sliding compartments. Learning to use oxy-acetylene torches was fascinating and demanded a steady hand when it came to welding metal sheet together. The most trying was arc welding but once you got the hang of it, it was good fun and quite satisfying.

But by far the most enjoyable for me was blacksmithing. I absolutely loved it. Learning the temper colours of the hot metals, the smell and heat of the coke fires, pumping the bellows to get the heat drawing to the metal and watching the colours creep up the metal. It was fascinating. We were fortunate enough to work on a project to make new wrought iron gates for the college entrance. Bending, hammering, and twisting the metal bars across an anvil with a short handled 4lb ball hammer was very satisfying. Quenching the hot metal in a bucket of oil, the smell of this made me realise what this sort of work could be like for the professional blacksmith. I loved it. I did enjoy dismantling and reassembling vehicle engines also but wasn't too hot on the fault-finding.

About this time my superiors realised that, although I wasn't much good at ball games like football and rugby, I could run. So, whilst winter was spent in training, the spring and autumn were spent going to different army apprentice colleges as well as RAF and RN bases to run competitively against them as part of Beachley Harriers.

Chepstow - Sunday Church - I'm on the left with my hat under my arm

In March of '63 we attended the English National Cross-Country Championships in Leicester. Four of us went to represent Chepstow Army Apprentice College. We came back as winners of the Western Command Cup for the Army. We were well pleased. Several further tournaments followed, one of which found us staying overnight at a WRAF barracks. We didn't win anything, but we had a great night with the girls in their rooms. They could drink us all under the table and a lasting memory for me was sitting on one of the girls' beds, all of us in our underwear, drinking from bottles of vodka which somehow seemed to keep appearing.

Meanwhile, the education system was continuing, and we sat exams which were the Army equivalent of GCE 'O' Level. I didn't excel in any except English and Engineering Drawing. However, there was one subject that I immediately got the hang of and that was Orienteering – map reading to most people. We were handed out Ordnance Survey maps and taught to read them accurately. This included what all the symbols meant, how to position a compass accurately, and how to measure distance with a compass point and a piece of card. There was a practical side to this, and it was to be tested when our platoon went on annual camp, usually in the Brecon Beacons.

Ever since I was a young lad I had been fascinated by maps. During camp we would carry out many map reading exercises which I never found difficult, although many of the others – who also saw very little point in it – did. I was often the one who ended up with the map and led the charge around various hillsides and valleys to get to trig points indicated by our platoon sergeant.

On one such camp outing we had been instructed to pitch tents at the foot of a particularly large hill in the Brecons. We were on a small plateau that was quite flat, and at a distance of around twenty metres in front of our tents was a fast-flowing river. The water came down from the many ranges of hills and the odd mountain and was, therefore, quite drinkable. This was where we drew our water for cooking and drinking.

Latrines were dug, privacy windbreaks put around them, fire pits established along with the cook's tent. The only problem was that, on this camp, the platoon sergeants we had were the PTIs. This meant that they were fanatical about keeping fit, exercising, and team building. At 06:00 a.m. every morning we were 'encouraged' out of our two-man tents (*bivvies* as they were known) in PT shorts and vests. An elaborate system of warming up exercises began for about ten minutes, culminating in a mad dash up the bloody hill behind us.

Early morning in the Brecons, in late September, was not pleasant. It was fucking freezing and my poor old knees were knocking together like a woodpecker tapping at a tree. But off we went like a bunch of demented lemmings, yelling as we charged up the hill. We were told that the last few back were on cookhouse duties and latrine cleaning for the morning.

On these sorts of occasions, there were always the sickeningly fit few who tore up the hill and made it look easy. I was not one of them. Given their due, though, the PTIs always ran with us and would be halfway up the hill encouraging us on.

Like a bunch of half-baked, semi-clad, demented tribesmen, we made it to the top and then it was the mad dash down again. Once we had made it back and stood there, bent over, hands on knees, panting to get our breath back we were told to strip off our PT gear and jump in the ice-cold, bloody freezing mountain water of the river. Like I really needed this shit!

But I knew that if I didn't do it, the other lads – who had – would throw me in. It just wasn't worth the agony or the loss of face. So, in I jumped, a lamb to the slaughter. After that, we crawled out and up the muddy bank, having now turned blue and being unable to speak because our teeth were chattering so much. Then we stumbled our way back to the tents, fell in, grabbed our towels, and sat there shivering and trying to dry ourselves.

I bloody hated it the first time we did it but, in the end, it became a challenge. Because I was a good runner, towards the end of the two-week camp, I was even in amongst the leaders up the hill and often amongst the first back.

There was a good side to these camps in that I loved the orienteering exercises we went on and the route marches. One such exercise took a group of us along rivers, through little used pathways and forests, and through a disused railway tunnel that still had the rails in place. We ended up at a place called Symonds Yat, an extremely beautiful spot with great commanding views. I always carried a pack of Players Weights cigarettes with me in the little flat cream and blue pack and my trusty Zippo lighter. On this particular day, I remember smoking one cigarette after another. I was so hungry, and this seemed to alleviate that. I'd never enjoyed a cigarette so much.

It was during our last camp, in our third year, that it was decided to send us on a three-day map reading exercise in the Brecons. When we were briefed in the main tent about the exercise, the importance of this was stressed. This was to be our last big exercise before we left AAS to join our units later in the year. It didn't impress most of us who just saw it as a bit of PTI and Army bullshit.

The weather had turned atrocious. It had been raining most days with icy winds and was freezing at night. We were to be split up into two groups of six men per group. We would be taken at night, sealed in the back of a three-tonner to a point in the Brecon range and dropped off. There would be five trig points that we had to make for. These would be marked on our maps and at each one there would be a message that we had to copy and a question to answer. We were to leave our answers in place.

We were given rations for the three days which consisted of the usual army rations: tins of processed cheese; pork and beans; and, of course, hard tack – a cracker similar to a Jacob's cream cracker, hard as iron and looking a lot like compressed sawdust. We were divided into the two teams, given rucksacks, told to 'kit-up' and that we would be moving out that night.

We had loaded up our rucksacks and packed our rations and were sitting, huddled up, in the back of the truck as it rattled and bumped across the wet, windswept moorlands of the Brecons. This was supposed to be a National Park but who the hell would want to come here, in these conditions, at this time of night, I could not imagine. Only bloody mad HM Forces.

It was 04:30 a.m. and I don't think any of us were really awake, although I did feel a little excited at the prospect of the map reading side of this as it was something I felt quite confident about. Each of us was lost in our own thoughts as the truck drove through the darkness and the rain hammered on the canvas top and sides. Our military parkas were great for this sort of thing, and I hunched down into the comfortable warmth, as it seemed the wind too had picked up and was howling. Someone mumbled, "Fucking great lads, this is, we're gonna have a nice country stroll... shit."

No one answered.

After about an hour and a half, the vehicle must have gone 'off road' as we were thrown around some in the back. Then we came to a halt. It went very quiet, and no one moved or said anything. I think we were all hoping that maybe they would cancel it due to the weather. Then two doors slammed and the next moment the sergeant was banging on the back of the truck.

"Ok you lot, here we are, let's be having you. Come on, let's go."

We grabbed our rucksacks as he opened the back. It was pitch black. The rain was horizontal, blown by a gale. I pulled my zip up to the top and my parka hood over my beret. I jumped down and, shrugging my backpack firmly on my back, I stood there, stunned by the conditions. We were all numbed to silence.

"Right, you all know what you have to do," the sergeant shouted against the wind. "I know it's a rotten start but hang together, good luck, and try not to get lost," he grinned.

We waited until the sergeant climbed back into the cab with the corporal. The engine started, the truck turned around and disappeared into the driving rain and darkness.

"Yeah, and fuck you too," someone mumbled.

There was a line of grey appearing in the east.

"Let's find somewhere to shelter," one of the lads shouted.

We looked around us. Hummocks, rocks, and hills began to take form as our eyes adjusted to the dawn light. I couldn't see a bloody thing; my glasses were splattered with rain. Someone shouted, "Over here!" and we trudged over.

Just over a small rise, the ground started to drop away, and we could make out a large overhang from the cliff that we were standing on top of. It was dry and sheltered from the wind and driving rain. We made our way down a few feet then turned almost back on ourselves. It was a minor triumph. We dropped our packs and sat around. I leaned against a rock and lit up as most of us did. If anything, the wind had picked up, but I was okay with that as it would blow the rain away that much sooner. Nobody said anything for a while – we just sat there smoking, looking out into the darkness.

"I'm fucking starving," one of the guys said after a while and proceeded to open his pack and pull out a small tin of processed cheese and some hard tack. The tin had a small opener attached to it. He opened his tin, stuck a knife in and started cutting out lumps of cheese. It must have taken all of thirty seconds and we were all doing the same. Some of us opened the tins of pork and beans. It was heaven.

As we ate, we lightened up some and started laughing and chatting. The food was making us feel better.

Before long, the rain eased off and it started to get lighter. I took a swig from my water bottle and got my OS map and compass out. I could just about see the map and, wiping my glasses, looked closely for a location I could recognise. After a while I roughly knew the area, we were in and identified the hill and lee we were sheltered under. I set the compass on the ground and waited for the needle to settle. It finally stopped swinging, so I rotated it to show North. Turning the map the same way I started to look for obvious points I might recognise once it was lighter. I managed to identify the hill we were sheltering under as it was about the only main one in the immediate area. The rest were either mountains or moorland. I knew we'd risen a bit on the ride here. It was certainly a mountain road and most of these hills and mountains didn't have roads.

The lads were sitting around chatting and smoking and the wind was still howling in thirty to forty knot gusts. I grabbed the map, stood up, and looked out. It was bleak. I turned almost a full circle looking for anything else I could recognise that would be on the map. I wasn't feeling too confident but knew that we had to travel in the opposite direction to the truck. It was agreed that that was what we would do.

We all had maps but only two of us were looking at them. The sky was grey and heavy, but the wind was pushing the clouds fast. All the trig points we were to find were indicated on the maps. I'd circled them with a pen back at base. We decided to head Northwest, following what looked like a small animal trail, aiming for what we agreed to be the nearest trig point. All of us were looking out for some recognisable feature.

After about an hour of making our way across the narrow path, around the side of a hill, fighting the wind, we'd all ceased talking and just trudged on. One of the lads called out that he could hear a dog barking, so we stopped and listened. Sure enough, every now and again I could hear it, but it sounded a long way off.

We looked at the maps which showed a small cluster of what looked like farm houses about twenty miles in the direction we were going. If we could identify these by sight, we could get a bearing on the nearest trig point we were aiming for, which seemed to be about fifteen miles from the farm. The others weren't too sure where we were on the map, but I had a good idea.

We trudged on in what was a more leisurely stroll – much to my irritation. I wanted to get on, do this properly, and get at least two of the trig points done this first day. But it was useless trying to say anything; a couple were horsing around as we walked, and the rations were going down at an alarming rate. I still had quite a reasonable amount of mine left, as did a couple of the other lads, and it was looking like we'd have to share these out in the end. It started to occur to me that we were not going to achieve our targets and, in all likelihood, would be bested by the other group who had a much more serious bunch of guys with them. They were headed in the opposite direction so there was little chance that our paths would cross unless we really screwed up – anything was possible with this lot. We were the 'cowboys' and I was beginning to think it had been arranged this way, possibly to show us up. This just made me more determined to do better. We trudged on.

It was full light now, but the wind hadn't eased off. As we came to the crest of a small hill, I could see sheep grazing in the distance on the side of a hill. There was no farmhouse in sight or anyone else. The wind had gradually dropped, and the lads had quietened as we continued on, lost in our own thoughts. After a while one of the guys started limping so we called a halt while he sorted his boots out. Off to the right, in the distance, I noticed a coppice of trees. Looking closely at the map it wasn't long before I felt I had identified them. Judging from the hills around us and the lines on the OS map, I felt pretty certain.

"Ok lads, I know where we are," I said, feeling hesitantly confident. They gathered around and I pointed out the features on the map. "We're here. If we walk in this direction a few more miles, we should see the farmhouse from the top of this rise. It will still be some distance but it's in the right direction for the first trig point. If we stop at the farmhouse, we can get our water bottles filled, have a rest, and move on to the first trig. What do you think?"

The general consensus was that we do as I suggested. Whether we could get to the second trig was another matter. Unless this lot started taking things a bit more seriously, we certainly weren't going to make number two before nightfall. We had our small, one-man bivvies with us and setting them up was no big deal – we just needed a good and possibly sheltered spot.

The farmhouse was further than we thought but we pushed on with an amount of determination. The going wasn't too easy as the moorland was soggy in places and up and down like a roller coaster. By mid-morning we heard a vehicle and then, a few minutes later, an old Land Rover with a trailer came into view. The farmer stopped and dropped off a bale of hay, saw us, and drove over.

"Hi lads, where are you off to then?" he said in a strong Welsh accent.

I showed him the trig point on the map and asked if it would be possible to fill our water canteens up at the farm if he didn't mind.

"Hop on the trailer, I'll take you all to the farm."

We did and one of the lads jumped into the passenger side of the Rover. We all hung on as we hurtled and bounced across the moorland and down to the farm.

There was a large barn next to the house that he kept his vehicle and a tractor in.

"Make yourselves comfortable in the barn out of this wind. It's going to rain again soon, too, but would you mind not smoking in the barn as I have a lot of dry straw bales in there."

We opened the door to the barn. It was massive inside, dry, and out of the wind. There were lots of bales of hay around and the odd farm implement. We chose some comfortable bales to lean against and dropped our packs. One of the lads gathered up our water bottles and disappeared to the farmhouse. We reckoned we could rest here for about an hour, max, and would then have to move on. We took stock of our remaining food supplies and knew we were going to run out during day two. On the last day (day three), we'd have to tighten our belts and be a bit resourceful. The lad who had gone to get the bottles filled was taking a long time and when he came back, he had the farmer with him. They came in and the farmer sat on a bale with us.

"I've been having a chat with the farmer here, Mr Jenkins," he said, nodding at the ruddy faced farmer in his cloth cap. "He is willing to do us all a big favour. I showed him where we are heading, to the various trig points, over the next few days and he says he knows all of them."

We all looked at the farmer. He smiled. "Look lads, if you are willing to give me a hand with getting these bales out to the sheep grazing areas, I can take a couple of you to all these trig points, you can get your information, and rest here for the night. What do you think?"

We stared at him with our mouths open.

"All I stipulate is that you give me a hand with the bales and don't smoke in the barn."

"How long would it take you to visit all five?" I asked.

"Well, we can do three today and the other two tomorrow morning. What do you think?"

We all fell about laughing and whooping.

"I take that as a yes then," he said, grinning. "Mind you, you'll earn it, these bales will take some shifting."

And so, it was agreed.

A little later, his wife came into the barn with a tray full of hot tea.

"I take it you lads will be staying for dinner this evening then?" We all just nodded numbly. "Ok, that's settled then. I'm cooking roast pork. If you want to use the convenience, there's a small outhouse round the back of the barn and the horse trough has running water."

We all murmured our thanks.

When she had gone, we grinned and looked a bit stunned, pleased at the prospect of a hot meal that evening.

We chose our spots to sleep for the night and got ready to help the farmer. It went like clockwork. The farmer's wife came and showed us how to hook up the tractor and the trailer and we started loading up the bales. One of the lads went with Mr Jenkins to the trigs while his wife jumped in the tractor, and we all piled on the trailer and went out to the grazing areas. The wind picked up further and just as we dumped the last of the bales it started to rain heavily. We were back in the barn by mid-afternoon.

About 04:30 p.m., the farmer arrived back in the Land Rover. Pete, who had gone with him, came in with all the info, looking well pleased. Mr Jenkins stuck his head in the barn.

"I'll see you lot around six then. Come eat in the house, we've enough room."

We couldn't believe our luck. All trigs cleared by tomorrow morning! We all swore an oath of absolute secrecy as not only could we get severely done for this, but the farmer would be in trouble too. I called it using your initiative but, somehow, we all knew HM Military back at AAS Chepstow wouldn't.

That night was amazing; good food and even beer to follow. We were back at the house the following morning at five. for a 'full English' (or Welsh as the case may be).

By mid-morning the deed was done, and the remaining trig information was gathered. We stayed a second night, having spent the rest of that day chatting with the farmer and his wife.

On the morning of the third day, we were all dropped off at the fifth and final trig point and shown which way to head off to meet our rendezvous with the sergeant and his truck. We said our thank yous to the farmer and got underway in a slow, steady hike. Along the way we dug a small hole and dumped what remained of our rations. We were all in good spirits and decided to 'muddy up' our clothes and gear to make it look good.

En route to the pickup point, we came across an old quarry near a disused railway line. Not far from this quarry was a small village that had a post office/village shop. We all trooped in and while one of the lads distracted the elderly lady behind the counter, we pinched some sweets and biscuits. The poor woman didn't stand a chance. We made our way for a further couple of hours to the pickup area and sat down by the side of the road, waiting for the truck, and stuffing ourselves with our ill-gotten gains.

The sergeant was surprised and *very* pleased with our progress and result, stating that we did a lot better than the other group who had run out of time and only managed four of the give trigs. I did catch the sergeant looking a bit suspiciously at us from time to time over the next few days, but nothing was ever said and, as far as I know, to this day, we got away with it.

In April of '63 my dad died. I was called to the CO's office on the morning of April 9th and informed. I was upset but more numb than anything else. I was given compassionate leave immediately and went home.

I remember sitting on the train, looking out of the window, and thinking about Dad. He was never very pleased with me for joining up and we hardly ever spoke about the Army when I was home. He was a bit of a mythical figure to me as he never seemed to be around at home in those latter years. By then he was the manager of the Londoner Hotel.

Dad was always a bit of a ladies' man and I'm sure he had another woman somewhere. Mum never seemed to be unhappy, although she was pissed off with his gambling on the horses. But I was worried about Mum now that he was no longer around.

When I arrived home, there were people milling about the place and talking very quietly. Mum gave me a big hug and we clung to each other for a while. I asked where he was and she said he was still in bed, where he had died during the night. For some reason, him and Mum were using the girls' room which was much smaller. Mum said it was okay to go in and see him.

I'd come home in my No.2 dress uniform, and I remember pulling the jacket down and straightening my tie as I stood outside the closed bedroom door. I looked back at Mum, and she just nodded and shooed me in with her hand. I tentatively opened the door, stepped inside, and closed it behind me. Dad was tucked up in bed as though still sleeping. I walked over and looked down at him.

"Christ, Dad, what have you done?" I said softly.

He didn't answer.

I sat down on the bed, leaned forward, and kissed him on his brow. His eyes were closed but I had a strong temptation to open his eyelid and look at his eye. I did but I don't think he was paying attention.

I took his hand from under the sheets and held it in mine, resting on the covers. I thought of our times together: his laughter and tap dancing; his snoring after Sunday lunch; sitting in the rocking chair with the newspaper, open at the racing section, over his face. His Cuban Havana cigars that he smoked now and again. His thing about wearing new ties and us lot saying to him, "What? a new tie?" His Pashana toilet water and Mum saying to him, "Keys, wallet, glasses," as he was leaving for work.

It was all these silly little things that came flooding back in my head. I did wonder, for a moment, if he could hear me or would gently squeeze my hand as I sat there. But no, death is pretty final, I guess, and nothing like that happened.

I kissed him again to say goodbye, stood up, looked at him quietly lying there, oblivious to the world, turned, and silently left the room.

16

Settling back at school was a bit difficult. There were many times my thoughts turned to my dad. I was feeling a bit removed from it all and I knew it must have been difficult for Mum.

Dad was Jewish, although he didn't practice it much. He was probably the black sheep of the family, and his family was quite large, spread across the country and abroad. Dad was seventy when he died.

He was one of the youngest so already quite a few of his family had died. He never kept in close touch with them all, but his death had stirred a few of them. His sister Esther was living in Cheltenham, and she was married to Alf Valentine. I had heard of Auntie Esther and Uncle Alf but knew little of them and Dad was never one to mention his family much.

One day at mail call, I found a letter on my bed when I got back to the block. I didn't recognise the writing, but the postmark was Cheltenham. It was from my Uncle Alf inviting me to dinner one Saturday if I could get permission to leave the school for the day. My CO granted me the day off, so I contacted Uncle Alf and arranged it for the following Saturday. He would pick me up from Cheltenham Station.

I was certainly a bit bemused by all this because I had never met these people before and couldn't think why they would contact me out of the blue like this. I supposed it was that, with Dad's death, they felt it a duty to meet me and express their condolences. I couldn't think of any other reason.

I did ring home and speak to Mum, and all she said was that they were the very wealthy side of Dad's family, and it was nice of them to contact me. Other than that, she had about as much idea as I did as to what this was about.

On the day, I dressed in my civvies for the first time in quite a while – chinos, blue shirt, sweater, and my suede bomber jacket. I remember because these were the only civvies I had...! When I came out of the station in Cheltenham, there was Uncle Alf in a chauffeur driven 'Roller' waiting for me.

On the way to the house, he asked after Mum and the girls and how much I was enjoying life in the forces. I said it was okay but didn't enthuse too much. His house was a grand Georgian residence in the 'posh' part of Cheltenham. A maid opened the door, and I was welcomed in. I met, for the first time, my aunt Esther and my three cousins – Lorry, Iris, and June. They were all very friendly and pleased to see me.

I began to wonder why my dad hadn't kept in contact with these people; they were really nice – and very rich.

Over tea and cakes, it wasn't long before Alf got down to business. His son Lorry was a dentist and I believe one of his daughters was a doctor. He, Alf, ran a small clothing factory making children's clothes. He was getting on and needed someone to learn and take over his business. Neither of his kids were interested. It seemed I was his only hope of keeping it in the family and, as a young lad to teach the business to, a viable apprentice. I was the nearest relative that fitted that requirement. He wanted to buy me out of the Army and set me up in his business, training me to take over from him.

I was dumbstruck. I told him I didn't practise my dad's faith and had been brought up a Christian. He wasn't bothered by that at all. He said he would give me time to think about it but first he wanted to show me around his factory. This was in Cheltenham, and we would be visiting it before lunch.

Alf's factory made children's clothes and the label and brand was a Ladybird – Ladybird children's clothes. Now I don't know whether they owned it outright or were part of a franchise, but I much later came to learn that this brand was well known around the world and was renowned as a good quality product.

He took me on his own to the factory and gave me a guided tour. The place was a hive of industry. The floor manager was a man, but all the machinists were women. Everyone called me 'Sir' and there was some giggling amongst the women. We spent about an hour there, looking at all the stages of the process. After this we went into the office that overlooked the work floor and the list of orders for the clothing was explained to me. Most of the time, I was struck dumb. We then left for home and lunch.

Dinner was served in a large dining room that had one very long dining table. It was like something out of *Downton Abbey*. The food was served by a host of servants in the traditional black with white lace aprons and caps. Once we had been served, the servants stood throughout the meal, to the rear of us. My one embarrassing moment came when I was cutting into a roast potato and it shot off my plate, down the table, to be expertly picked up by my cousin Lorry who gave me a wide grin. The maids to the rear were all smiling at my little 'faux pas'.

I had a good chat with Lorry about the whole issue and he explained that his dad was desperate to be able to pass the business on. I explained that I was nearing the end of an Army apprenticeship and he understood that. I needed time to think about things, and Alf was happy to give me that time.

It was an amazing and life changing offer and I needed time to think on it and to have a chat with Mum.

When I arrived back at Chepstow, I phoned her. She was quite taken aback, and I could tell that she was not too happy about it either. It would mean that I would suddenly be launched into the wealth of the upper class and, to be honest, it frightened the hell out of me. Now that I was in my last year at Chepstow I was not that far away from my final exams and graduating. I knew I wasn't going to win any scholarships, but I had been looking forward to joining my unit and getting onto the ships. The lure of overseas travel with the forces loomed large. I would not get any of that in Cheltenham. Also, I never had the head for the sort of business that would be expected of me.

In the end, I wrote Uncle Alf a letter explaining my decision to remain in the Army. He understood and was very nice about it. Mum breathed a sigh of relief and I got on with my life. To this day I don't regret my decision. It's not that I couldn't handle the society that I would have had to fit in with, it was more that I would be terrified of making a hash of the business. No, I had the world ahead of me in the Services and overseas, not at a factory in Cheltenham.

I still had many months to go before the final exams and the passing out parade and they were going to be very busy. I had joined the Scots Pipe Band as a side drummer, a hang-over from my days in the ATC. It didn't last long, though, as I wasn't comfortable wearing tartan trews and a forage cap!

I also decided to get baptised. Every Saturday morning, we had a 'drill and turnout' practise. This was a competition between A, B, and C companies. It was fiercely competitive, and we had to practise every Saturday morning. The only lads excused this were those that attended Holy Communion. I decided I would do the religious bit and partake of this. When I went to see the chaplain, he informed me that he needed to see my baptism certificate. I phoned home to ask Mum to send it to me when she promptly informed me that I had never been baptised.

Oh, shit, now what? I thought.

I informed the chaplain who told me that wasn't a problem as he had one other person who needed to be baptised and I could join her.

"Her?" I said with a surprised look.

It turned out that the Camp Commandant Lt. Col Keymer's daughter was also up for this. So, I agreed, in the mistaken belief that it would be a small ceremony with perhaps the colonel and his wife, their daughter, and the chaplain. How wrong I was.

Meanwhile I had to undertake five weeks of bible study at the chaplain's house with the colonel's daughter. At least we had lots of teacakes from the chaplain's wife and the commandant's daughter was very nice but a bit wild.

It later transpired that the two of us were to be baptised by the Archbishop of Gloucester in the school chapel. I had no problem with that except for one thing: it was to be in front of the whole school – over one thousand boys – and in full No.2 dress uniform.

On the day, the two of us had to stand out front and lean over the font backwards while we were dribbled with holy water by 'His Grace'!

All this just to get out of early Saturday morning parades...

As it turned out, I got off the parades but had to do cleaning duties in the block. It really wasn't worth all the bloody trouble.

As the days rolled on, studies got harder, and the revision started. Lots of trade training exams, written and practical. We were also doing 'Drill and Turnout' practise so any breaks we had were made up of trips to the NAAFI Club in the evening for a few games of snooker, a beer, and a large plate of sausage, egg, chips, and beans.

One of the lads bought an old Morris Minor and four of us would go into Chepstow at the weekend for a drink. One particular weekend we decided to go a bit further afield to Gloucester. They had a well-known inn there that was good for quality beer and the number of unattached females that frequented the place. We all had a good time but were quite late leaving, hoping that we could sneak back in without too much trouble. However, fate had other ideas.

On the way back, about twenty minutes into a one-hour journey, we broke down. There was no way we could get this thing going. Also, we were all quite pissed. So, we decided to abandon the car and try to thumb a lift back. By 02:00 a.m. I'd sobered up enough to know we were in trouble. There was no traffic on the road, so no one to get a lift from, and we had no means to telephone the guardroom to let them know we had broken down. So, all we could do was walk. Unknown to us, the MPs had been informed that we were 'absent without leave' and one of the lads in our platoon had mentioned that we intended going to Gloucester. So, they came looking for us.

At a little after 03:00 a.m. they found us. Truncheons out, they stopped us and started shouting all manner of abuse at us. They then made us remove our shoes and socks and walk the remainder of the way back to the school, barefoot, in the middle of the road. It was quite uncomfortable and by the time we reached the guardhouse we were knackered, tired, and sore. We were strip searched and put in the cells. Even there we weren't allowed any peace. Every time someone came into the cell block, either NCO or officer, we had to jump up and stand to attention.

The following morning, we were marched under guard to breakfast and then sent in front of the CO. He gave us all seven days in the guardhouse. It was here that I learnt to paint coal white. Daytime duties included cleaning latrines out, plus the cells and the guardroom, sweeping the parade square, peeling sacks of potatoes in the school cookhouse, and any other manual job going. As it turned out, we only did a few days in the nick because they needed us for the 'Drill and Turnout' competition and also because it was our final year of trade training, and we couldn't afford to miss too much.

When I now look back at the punishment received for breaking down in the car and being late back, it seems grossly out of proportion. Especially being made to walk barefoot back to the camp. By today's standards, completely barbaric and we could have probably sued the school for all sorts of reasons.

The final months leading up to the passing out parade were a blur of pre-exams, marching practise, and kit preparation. Practising formations for the final parade and swotting for the exam finals were paramount. While I would like to say that I did buckle down to my trade studies, I have to admit to being somewhat lax in this. I had lost the heart to really continue with anything to do with the school and I was beginning to wish I had stayed at Norton Manor.

It was during the many days of classroom study that I started writing poetry. I did this quietly but got a lot of satisfaction out of writing it. This habit of drifting off and writing poetry was to follow me throughout my army career and beyond. When I read them, some are still very evocative and instantly take me back to the time they were written.

I had read a lot of books throughout my Chepstow three years. Looking back, I never really did enjoy my apprenticeship years as much as I think I was supposed to, mainly because of the bullying. But I absolutely loved the blacksmithing and it still lingers large in my mind from that time. I have no idea why. The smell of hot metal, the heat from the forge, the sweat, and the physical effort. I found all these a wonderful experience and I'm glad that I had the opportunity to do it.

My book reading was mostly fictional adventure stories, and I developed a passion for Westerns, reading books like Zane Grey's *Riders of the Purple Sage*. Frank Gruber and Louis L'Amour also featured heavily. They were extremely descriptive and full of adventure. At this time, the days of the Beachley Ferry were running out. The Severn Bridge was under construction, and it was amazing to watch the massive suspension cables being put into place. It also heralded the death knell of the school, although we weren't aware of it at the time.

My last leave before the finals was the Easter of '64. Because of Dad's death I didn't feel that spending my days with Les and Hayden was fair on Mum, so I tended to stay closer to home. One of my few good mates from Chepstow, Roger Hayward, came to London to stay for a while. However, when we were dispersed to our units, I lost touch with him and many others.

During that spring leave I met a girl in London who had a flat in Earls Court. She was the sister of one of the girls we had met in Chepstow, and I had promised to look her up. That spring was a particularly hot one and I remember one afternoon walking along a side street off the Earls Court Road to visit her. It was after 02:00 p.m. and the air was still and very hot. All of the houses were Victorian terraces along both sides, and most had been converted to bedsit apartments. As I walked along, windows were open, people were sitting on the sills, and music was predominant in the background. I was particularly aware this afternoon as I had a strong feeling I was going to get a bit of 'nookie'! She was definitely up for it and unbeknownst to her, this would be my first time, in earnest. When I arrived at her place, I could see her room window open on the second floor. I called out to her from the steps leading up to the front door.

"Lesley, Lesley, are you about?"

A head poked out. "Hiya, come on up, the door's open."

I pushed the black painted front door and walked into the gloom. As I went up the stairs, the butterflies in my stomach started, as well as a rush of blood to the groin.

By the time I reached her room, I was ready for it. It was a small one bedroom, with a chest of drawers and a small table and chair. The window overlooking the street was wide open, music was drifting in from one of the apartments across the road. It was hot and sultry with not even a slight breeze to stir the air.

I sat on the edge of her bed, and she sat next to me. We discussed that I had to return soon to Chepstow. She mentioned her sister meeting me on a pub crawl there and how it was lucky I met her. At the time we'd had a good laugh and she'd told me about her sister, Lesley, living in London. It was then that I was given her phone number and had promised to look her up. I did, we met for a drink, and arranged to meet again this day.

I thought back to that pub crawl in Chepstow, attempting to have a pint in all of the thirty-six pubs in the town. Needless to say, we never made it. Now here I was, and it didn't take long before we were stripping our clothes off… possibly due to the heat.

One thing led to another, and it wasn't long before we were into the main event. I didn't tell her that this was my first proper sexual encounter that ended in the actual act. It was a great experience, probably enhanced by the hot weather, and we were at it like bunnies… going for broke.

About an hour later I rolled off her with a view to just letting the sweat dry in the sultry air from the open window. What I ended up with was loud cheering, hoots, whistles, and clapping. When I turned around and looked out the window there was a bunch of faces looking out of the window directly across the street from us – waving and laughing! One even held up a camera with a telephoto lens, shouting, "Magic, great show."

I flopped back down.

"Oh no, do you know what just happened?" I said to Lesley.

"I can pretty much guess," she said, rolling off the bed and pulling on a long T-shirt. She turned to the window and waved. I grabbed my jeans and tugged them on. We both stood at the window laughing – there really wasn't much else we could do.

Later on, we strolled out, me taking bows and waving to the folks across the road, found a pavement café and sat outside. Lesley asked me if we could keep in touch and perhaps meet up again on my next leave. I was okay with that but knew it would be pretty doubtful.

However, much later when I was back at Chepstow, she came to stay with her sister for a while and we made up a foursome and had a good day out. That was the last I saw of her. She was a good girl and we enjoyed being together; I'm sure we could have become more of an item if circumstances were different. But I wanted to travel and once my exams were over, I had everything in front of me.

Those final months at AAS were all hands to the wheel. I didn't feel particularly confident about the trade exams. We had the practical first, which consisted of fault-finding on an engine. Our coursework over the final year was taken into account and I was pretty much 'average' on that. I never thought I was going to be their ace student however much I studied.

The swot sessions intensified with the odd visit to the NAAFI Club for food replenishment. 1963–64 was certainly an eventful year and, with the assassination of President Kennedy as well, things were happening on the international front.

Dad's death, my first bonk, leaving Chepstow – it was a bit like being fired from a cannon. Although I'd been with these guys for the past three years, I was aching to get away to my new unit and start my real military career. First, however, we had to get through the exams and that would be followed by the results and then preparing for our passing out parade.

Exam day came in a blur. I had prepped as much as I was able to and went into the first exam with great trepidation. I was never any good at taking exams and my nerves were all over the place. Two hours later, however, it was all over, and I was emotionally drained. I didn't feel confident at all and, for a while, had an awful feeling I would have to do another year as part of 62C. Not a prospect I relished.

The whole day was spent doing the various exams in the different categories. By 04:00 p.m. it was all done. My three years of trade training had come down to this one day. That evening it was up to the NAAFI Club for a good meal and a few pints. It would be a week before we had the results.

That week was spent cleaning and polishing our kit to get ready for the big parade. On the day of the results, I was convinced that I had not passed. We were all called over to the workshop classroom in an air of silence and expectation. Once settled down, we waited.

Nothing was straight forward in the forces. No individual calling to the office to be told how we had done. Instead, the trade training master came in and we all went quiet. He then started reading out our results in the order of the highest grades first. Those that we knew would come top, did. After twenty minutes or so, we came to those who had just managed to scrape through. That was me – by a cat's whisker!

I had just managed to avoid coming back next year. I didn't care that my results were not brilliant, I was through. Later that day they posted the results in our rooms as well as where our postings were to be. Mine was to what was then the RASC – Royal Army Service Corps – to the marine engineers' barracks in Gosport, Hampshire. However, the RASC was in the throes of being amalgamated into a new corps called The Royal Corps of Transport (RCT). I was to join 20 Maritime Regiment, St Georges Barracks, Gosport. It was to be my home, where I would convert to a marine engineer, be taught seamanship, and be assigned to a ship. I couldn't wait. But first we had to get the passing out parade done. Letters were sent to parents, inviting them down for the occasion. Mum was going to come with Di. They booked into an hotel in Chepstow.

Our C Company top cadet was a lad from Cornwall – Mike Opie. For this, he was promoted to Jnr. Sgt Major, complete with pace stick. He deserved it. He'd done well in the exams, never got into any trouble, and his kit and turnout were immaculate. He was a nice lad too and the promotion didn't go to his head.

So, we drilled and drilled and drilled. A few days prior to the passing out parade we had the 'Drill and Turnout' competition with A, B, and C companies competing for the cup. It turned out well and I have to admit that seeing us all together like that in top kit certainly looked good. In the end, A Company won, and we came second. Our final day drew near.

Even though I didn't particularly enjoy my three years at Chepstow, I can remember a sadness hanging over many of us as we started clearing out our rooms, packing our cases, and getting our gear ready for the final parade. Unknown to us, the Army Apprentice School's days were numbered. The military was cutting back and the apprentice scheme was going out of fashion. The scheme was eventually ended in 2004. This was to be a big mistake, but as successive governments came and went, the forces were to undergo severe cutbacks. Several

Middle Eastern conflicts later and, although the need to go back to the apprenticeship scheme in the civilian world is recognised, it would seem, for the moment, too costly for it to be re-introduced to the forces.

The need for recognised trade training in the services continues and all three forces have their own schemes in place. But the Army Apprentice Colleges, of which there were four – Chepstow, Harrogate, Arborfield and Carlisle – were to go. A scheme no longer deemed necessary as the reduction of the Army made these institutions too costly and lacking support. A sad loss indeed.

Meanwhile, Mum and Di had booked a hotel in Chepstow and the evening before the parade, we met in town for dinner. Many other boys and their families did the same. During the day, we had a walk around town and met other lads from our section. Before long, the big moment came. Wooden tiers had been set up to one side of the main parade ground, much like American 'bleachers. We were all dressed and ready well before time.

We stood around, outside C Company block and talked nervously. A moment came to mind of a day we were on parade outside the block being inspected by our platoon sergeant. He came up to a lad called Henderson standing next to me. He was a very gentle boy with a baby face who never had to shave. The sergeant inspected him and asked him, "Why haven't you shaved, Henderson?"

"But I don't need to shave, Sergeant," said an affronted Henderson.

"What's all this stuff on your nose then?" he said, leaning over into his face.

The lad had a fine down of blond hair on his nose. "What stuff, Sergeant?"

Pointing to his own nose, the sergeant said, "Here lad, all down here. I don't want any bloody excuses, get it off."

By this time, we were all falling about laughing.

"And you bloody lot can shut up or I'll have you on extra duties."

Those times were now past, and we were moving on into the real world. We were carrying the Belgian FN 7.62mm rifles for this parade with fixed bayonets. A good, all-round rifle but heavy and not that versatile. They looked good when on parade, though, because of their long barrels.

I was feeling a bit numb that day; it had all come around much quicker than I had expected. I began to realise that this was the closing of a chapter in my life, and I was now moving on. The regular Army, a new unit for me and, with the impending relocation to ship-board life, a whole new world. I was excited, nervous, apprehensive, and sad, all in one brief span of time. But I wasn't sorry to see the back of these guys; I needed to be in the real world now and, hopefully, it was just around the corner.

As it turned out, the parade went well. The various companies were marched through the campus and on to the parade square, accompanied by the different school military bands.

C Company was led by Jnr Sgt Major Mike Opie, and we marched on to the pipes and drums of the Pipe Band, by far the most popular and the most stirring. Each company formed up and we went through our various display routines and marches.

I could see Mum and Di watching from the stands.

We were all inspected by the Commandant, Lt. Col. Keymer and best cadet of the year was presented with the apprentice sword. Eventually, we marched off the square, down a small side street, and were dismissed.

I met up with Mum and Di, and we walked around the camp chatting. That was it for me. I just wanted to get home and put this place into the past where it belonged. My new career in my unit was ahead of me and I was looking forward to that.

I have some nostalgic memories of Chepstow but never really enjoyed my time there, mostly because of a few of the arseholes in the group. I was always seen as the boy that came from the Jnr Leaders Regt who thought he was better than them and wanted the prestige of the Chepstow apprentices. By missing the first six months of basic training with them I never got to form the same kind of bond that I did at Norton Manor. So, I was always seen as the outsider – thanks to the bloody incompetence of the War Office for sending me to the wrong place in the first instance!

I only ever saw one guy from 61C again, and he happened to be one of the bullies that I hated. It was three years later, in Aden. I was on a weekend off at the NAAFI Club in Steamer Point, and there he was. He had completely changed and was very friendly. But I didn't have too much to say to him.

I guess that's how it goes. Time changes and heals. I sometimes wonder who from those Chepstow days is still around, how their careers went, and who has died. I'm over seventy now so we must all be around the same age. Frightening and rather melancholic if I think about it. The AAS is just a piece of history now and I sometimes wonder what the place is used for now.

There were some good and funny times there and I haven't forgotten those. But life aboard the LCTs was a whole new ball game and I was looking forward to the next chapter of my life

PART III
THE LCT YEARS

17

My time at home had been a quiet affair. Things had changed since Dad's death. Mum seemed a lot more serious and quieter, and Jo's friend Mavis – my childhood love from years ago – often came up from her flat below us and dropped in more regularly. She got on well with Mum, who treated her like a daughter. I think Mum was pleased that I was going to Gosport as it was a pretty simple trip on the train, which made it easier for me to get home at weekends if necessary.

I arrived at Gosport in the autumn of 1964 with just my one, green army suitcase. I was in my No2 Dress uniform. I reported to the guardroom that was on one side of the road, across from what was known as St George's Barracks. The duty MP had a list on a clipboard of new arrivals. My name was ticked off and the duty sergeant invited me in to sit down whilst we waited for someone to come and show me where to go. I was quite surprised as it seemed far more relaxed than I had been expecting. I asked how many new arrivals there were and was informed there were around fifteen. They were all coming from various units. Most were coming to do their seamanship training but there were a few engineers like me. Most were ex REME that were converting to the RCT to serve aboard the LCTs. I was now part of 20 Maritime Regiment, RCT.

A little while later, I was taken across to the barracks by one of the duty corporals. St George's Barracks were originally designed for a British Army barracks in India but, as the story goes, the wrong set of drawings were sent out. So, Gosport ended up with the Indian ones and India received ours. Either way, they were pretty impressive; one long block with stairs at intervals, leading up to a veranda that ran the length of the block. There was a basement level, but the rooms located there were for storage and the Quartermasters' office and stores. The rooms on the veranda level were massive, each holding four people. The ceilings in these rooms were very high. I suspected it was to keep the rooms cool in the Indian climate. Here in the UK, they would have been cold had it not been for the massive central heating radiators in each room. The road in front of the barracks was used for parades, and across from this was the mess block and kitchens.

Our trade training classrooms were back across the road and down the side of the guardroom in Weevil Lane. This was another long building but without the veranda. Classrooms were mostly on the lower levels and admin offices were on the upper. It was here that I was to carry out my conversion to marine engines and also study basic seamanship.

The first thing that happened to us 'new guys' was that we were issued with our uniforms. These were what the navy called No.8's: dark blue trousers, lighter blue shirts, white roll-neck sweaters, thick, white woollen socks, and 'sea-boots'. Not a sign of khaki. In fact, the only army item of clothing we retained was the beret.

Winter dress included the wearing of the white sweaters. Great, I was well pleased. We also wore black shoes, no DMS boots at all. These weren't allowed on board ships.

I met the lads I would be training with and most of them were seamen. There were only a few of us engineers.

It was here that I met Andy Mortimer and Malcolm Thomas, and we were to become close mates.

Trade training here was enjoyable and also more diverse. In between the conversion to marine diesels, we included gearboxes for ships, pumps and compressors, refrigeration, and air conditioning. Seamanship was two periods per week, and this included different types of ship and boat hull construction, seamanship aboard LCTs, and even how to tie knots. I settled in well and really enjoyed the start to my military career in the 'real' army. It was a far cry from Chepstow and had none of the bullshit they had there.

Training often entailed going out on one of the boats they had at a jetty nearby, close to the large sailing boat manufacturers, Camper & Nicholsons. This was often a test to see how capable we were on small boats. The two I knew were a small fishing boat and a fast launch. Being winter, you could guarantee the seas were none too smooth.

On one such trip, we were going to Guernsey in the Channel Islands. When the four of us stepped on board the Yarmouth Navigator, the skipper said, "I hope you lot didn't have greasy eggs and bacon for breakfast 'cause you'll more than likely lose them. It's likely to be a tad rough out there."

Oh shit, I thought, *I hope I don't throw up.*

As the boat bobbed about alongside the jetty, I felt fine. Our engineering instructor was chuckling away to the skipper. Once aboard, it was nice and warm below decks but outside it was cold and blowing a bit and we were still in the harbour. I put my overalls on as we had been told to bring them. The chief came up from the engine room hatch and told us that once we had left the harbour, we could take it in turns going down into the engine room. The place was small down there, but large enough to hold the four-cylinder Crossley marine diesel.

A couple of the trainee seamen who had come with us were told to let the lines go and away we went. I sat on deck on a hatch cover and watched as Portsmouth harbour slid past on our left – or 'Port side' as we were told.

There were quite a few Royal Navy ships in, and they looked stunning as we sailed past them. On our right, 'Starboard side', was the submarine base of HMS Daedalus. I could just see the conning towers of a couple of subs and, in this grey light, they looked quite sinister. As soon as we cleared the harbour entrance, the seas picked up. To my untrained eye, the waves looked to be coming from all directions.

The boat was rolling from side to side as well as up and down. A couple of the lads sitting near me were starting to look a little queasy. I felt fine so far and adjusted my position to the roll of the boat. The chief came on deck and asked one of us to go down to the engine room with him. One of the lads immediately made his way down below. I sat there a moment longer and watched the forts that were dotted about the place go past. These were built during the war but were now either derelict or being used by pirate radio stations. I think Radio Caroline was on the one with all the antennae.

I made my way forward and asked if I could have a look in the wheelhouse. They didn't mind so I slid the door open and almost fell inside. There wasn't a lot to see but it was good to get out of the cold wind. The skipper was chatting to our instructor, and I just stood back and watched. There was a small Decca radar unit to one side, but it wasn't switched on. He obviously knew the route by compass bearings alone. I asked him about this, and he did know the bearings but would be turning the radar unit on in a while.

Looking out the front windows I could watch the sea state starting to pick up. Every second or third wave a mass of spray came over the bows and slammed into the wheelhouse. In the middle of one window, directly in front of the helmsman (the skipper) was a circular piece of Perspex that was connected to a small motor. This kept the circular window spinning and clear of water and ensured pretty good vision looking out despite the spray. Behind me was a hatch with stairs that led down below. I turned and went down. There were two bunks on either side, a small folding table, as well as the hatch to the engine room. I sat on one of the bunks and one of the other lads came down and sat on the one opposite me.

"Quite cosy down here," he said.

It was. It smelled a bit of stale air and diesel fumes but, otherwise, not too bad. Just then, the lad who had gone into the engine room came up looking a little pale.

"One of you can go down next. I think I'm gonna feed the fish," he said, and off he went, out on deck.

"I'll go have look below," I said and went down the few steps to the engine room.

You could tell this was a military vessel as everything was neat, tidy, and even looked freshly painted. The chief was standing wiping his hands on a piece of rag. We shook hands and he started explaining various details of the engine room and engine, shouting over the noise. It didn't smell too bad, mostly of hot metal and diesel. I took it all in, fascinated by what I was looking at. This was my first time in a boat's engine room whilst underway.

We all took it in turns going down, but I noticed that only two of us came up feeling ok. Every now and again one of the lads would hang onto the side and heave up over the rail. After watching this a couple of times, I made my way forward, past the wheelhouse, to a winch unit near the bow. Hanging on to one of the side lines, I let the spray hit me. We were ploughing our way forward and off in the distance I could see other boats and ships. It was quite exhilarating, and I was pleased I wasn't feeling sick.

As we approached Guernsey, the wind and seas calmed, and it wasn't long before other boats were near and also heading for the harbour. Once we had manoeuvred our way to a berthing place, the two seamen jumped onto the jetty and tied us up fore and aft. We'd been told all about 'springs' – a way of tying up the rope lines that also enabled you to slip it whilst on the boat's bollard to allow for the tide drop whilst tied up alongside. Guernsey is notorious for having quite an extreme tide drop, so we had to make allowances for it.

We stayed there at St Peter's Port for about one-and-a-half hours. Time to have a mug of tea and some sandwiches in relative calm. The two lads who had been sick were now starving and made short work of lunch. Strong mugs of tea helped. We asked questions about the engines and other mechanical issues then it was time to head back.

We navigated our way out of the port and headed back to Portsmouth. By this time, I was becoming acclimatised to the smells and noise of the boat whilst underway. We all took turns doing engine checks, having been instructed on what to do and where to check. It was just as rough going back but I was getting used to the roll of the boat. The skipper told us that each boat or ship has its own little quirks including how it rolled in heavy seas. They were all different. It does help not to have too large a fried breakfast, but you can still be ill just on cereal. So, eat hearty, I say. However, it doesn't help when you have your instructor hovering nearby as you wobble about the deck, looking a bit green, saying things like, "Oh, I had a double helping of really greasy bacon, dripping in really slimy fat!"

You really would be sick if you listened to that too long, but they wouldn't persist, because on the LCTs everyone gets sick at some time due to the nature of the vessel, especially in heavy seas.

Life on the town in Gosport was pretty boring; there was a pub just outside the back gates of St George's Barracks called The Fox, and this was our main watering hole. Most of the nightlife was on the other side of the harbour in Portsmouth. But we didn't bother going there together yet. There were several other pubs in Gosport, most in the high street, with one in particular noted for its music. The Fox had a landlady who must have been all of eighty-years-old. She was made up like Aunt Sally and we always used to imagine that she put her lipstick on whilst in a force nine gale. So, for me, the pub with the music – The Nelson – was far better. There was little else in Gosport High Street. The other hangout was a Wimpey hamburger bar. The days of Starbucks, Costa, McDonalds, Burger King, and pizza Express were a long way in the future.

One night, whilst drinking in The Nelson with a couple of the lads, a group of 'bible pushers' came in. One of them was an extremely attractive young girl. They singled us out as we were the youngest lads in the place. We started chatting and I paid particular attention to the girl, introduced as Penny.

It was probably a bit of a ploy to attach such an attractive female to the group in the hope of hooking a new recruit. They only drank soft drinks, and it turned out that they were Evangelists from the local church group. I got into conversation with them, Penny in particular. The lads I was with weren't in the least interested and drifted away. I found out that going around pubs, trying to recruit people was called 'fishing'. Well, Penny had me truly hooked. Somehow, I agreed to meet them on Sunday morning, at the local Evangelist church, after morning service. When I caught up with the lads, they thought I was nuts. They agreed Penny was a looker, so we had a bet that I would try to get a date with her. The object was to get her in the sack, so to speak!

Sunday came and, I had to admit, I was really looking forward to seeing her. I found the church, which turned out to be an old hall at the back of the High Street. I waited until I saw people starting to come out and made my way in. The place had that musty smell of an old building. A group of people about my age were stood around to the rear of the place, talking to some mums with their children. As soon as I was noticed, Penny came over.

"Hi, I'm surprised. I didn't expect you to turn up."

I can't remember what I said back, but she took me over to meet the vicar. He was quite young and was pleased to see me. Apparently, he had been told I may be coming. I was invited to join their bible class. This was held in a small room at the back. A couple of the girls left to do the children's Sunday school and the remainder of us sat around in a small circle. Bibles were handed out.

Passages from the New Testament were read out, taking it in turns around the circle. Following this, a discussion was then held amongst the group, discussing how each individual interpreted the section. Tea and biscuits were handed around and after the Sunday school was over, we all moved to the main church pews. Here, one of the group would stand up and talk about how they had 'found God'. I felt a bit like the devil, sitting there, as my main interest was getting into Penny's knickers! Looking across at her I couldn't help but notice how well formed she was, with a truly decent chest size. Trying not to let the bulge in my jeans show, the chat was soon over, and we eventually left the place.

Most of the others went their way, but a few – including Penny – decided to go for a coffee in the Wimpy bar, so I joined them. The chat was mostly about what I did and what the others were doing. Most were students at college, as was Penny. She lived with her mum in Havant. They tried to get me to go on one of their 'fishing' episodes, but I declined, making excuses that I was studying and doing duty at the barracks.

As the months ticked by, I did go to the church hall on Sundays sometimes and, in fact, took part in the Sunday school readings with the little ones, which I quite enjoyed. I was never committed enough to do the fishing thing but enjoyed the bible classes. They preached a lot about how sinful it was to have sexual relations before marriage, and they were all a bit self-righteous. As for Penny… I did get quite close to her, but she was already in a relationship with one of the guys. In the end, it became uncomfortable. What I did find out, however, was that all the girls were sleeping with the lads in the group!

One evening, whilst having tea at the vicar's house, they were all going on about being 'pure of thought and deed'. After a long discussion on this, I'd had enough. I got my jacket, thanked the vicar and his wife, and told him I wouldn't be coming back anymore. I knew I wasn't going to get anywhere with Penny, so I didn't want to hang around. The vicar walked with me outside his house and asked me the real reason I was leaving, so I told him. I told how much I really liked Penny but that it was a bit of a one-way street. As for the others, I told him they were all very hypocritical as they didn't practice what they preached. He felt I was wrong and thought that, because of my feelings on this, perhaps it was better that I left. But he was very pleasant and wished me well for the future.

About eighteen months later, I came across him in the street in Portsmouth. We stopped for a chat, and he said, "You were right, you know. I wish I'd taken you more seriously and listened to you."

He went on to say that they had become quite disruptive and then the relationships between the girls came to light. In the end he had to disband the group and just concentrate on his church and the Sunday school. I felt a bit sorry for him. He didn't know what had happened to Penny, and I never saw any of them again. It was all rather sad really as the basic idea was good. I just don't think any of them were mature enough. I thought of Penny once in a while, but then things moved on and new horizons were on the way.

18

Being in the services and stationed in Gosport was handy in that I was land-based and most of my weekends were free. However, it wasn't long before I was contacted to report to a senior officer who suggested further weapons training based on my shooting ability. I wasn't that keen, but it would break the monotony of barrack life in Gosport, so I started doing this at times they organised. I still kept up my evenings out with the lads, but it also meant I could pop up to London and see Mum now and again. Guardroom duties didn't come around too often.

Meanwhile, my trade exams for conversion to Marine Engineer were going well. Now I was away from Chepstow and all that went on there, the environment was a million times better for me and studying.

The last part of the training was steam and turbine engines, and this was held at Marchwood near Southampton. The Army's maritime unit had an old steam tug called the Trieste, and it was here that steam boilers, turbines, and engine training took place. The Trieste was a marvellous old pre-war tugboat with a massive open crankshaft. This engine was fired from a large Scott boiler. We all had to take it in turns stoking the boiler with coal to get up a good head of steam and then get the engine going. We'd take the Trieste out, around Southampton waters. A real treat as this was a taste of what the old steamship engines must have been like. Every now and again you had to throw a bucket of water over the crankshaft as it ran. Apparently this mixed with the oil and made a milky lubricant that also kept it cool. The smell of hot metal and oil is something you don't forget. The old telegraph system was still in use and, as they rang down, you had to adjust a brass wheel control to either increase or decrease the revolutions of the engine. The scent of hot metal, oil, steam, and coal was very evocative.

Eventually the exams came, and I did well in this one. We were then told which ship we were being sent to. Mine was the LCT (Landing Craft Tank) HMAV Audemer L4061. She also happened to be the flagship of our fleet. Some of the other LCT's in home waters were Andalsnes, Arrowmanches, Abbeyville, and Antwerp. Agheila was in the Middle East and Arezzo was in the Far East. Our ships were still army vessels, and our flag was the Blue Ensign with crossed swords. We also wore these as shoulder flashes on our shirt uniforms. The ships were often tied up at the HM Gunwharf on the Portsmouth side, part of HMS Vernon and adjacent to Portsmouth railway station. Otherwise, they were tied to buoys at the top end of the harbour. The Gunwharf could only hold two ships at a time, so most of the time we were on the buoys. To get to the ship if she was on the buoys you had to go to the Gunwharf to pick up the tender that took you out to the buoys. If the ship was tied up at the Gunwharf, life was a lot easier.

My first sight of Audemer was as I was taking the tender out to the buoys where she was tied up. It was a cold, crisp but clear, January morning and the harbour was choppy. I stood on deck as the tender left the Gunwharf moorings. On the way across, we passed what was called the 'kingstairs' where the navy tied up. There were a couple of destroyers and an aircraft carrier in port at the time, and it was a fantastic sight to see these ships so close as we made our way up the harbour.

As we neared the Audemer, she looked resplendent in the morning sunshine as she swung lazily, chained to the buoy. She was to be my home for the foreseeable future and, in that moment, I felt a thrill I hadn't experienced before. Looking up at her as we neared the boarding stairs alongside her, I also felt a swell of pride.

Her grey hull had the look of a working ship with small lines of rust from scupper ports at the deck level and from the anchor port. Steam drifted lazily up from the generator outflow in the cold morning air, and the slap of waves against her hull echoed with the cry of a gull overhead. I knew my life was once again taking a turn of direction that I had little control over.

As the tender came alongside, I grabbed my kit bag, slung it over my shoulder and made my way up the gently swaying stairs that were hung over the side of the ship. When I stood on the steel deck of the catwalk, an Indian looking lad with the two stripes of a corporal on his white, turtleneck sweater, came out to welcome me aboard and mentioned that he had been expecting me. He introduced himself as Dip Surgreve, one of the ship's engineers and said I was to report to the Chief Engineer once I was settled in. He was then joined by one of the seamen and we were introduced.

"JC here will show where to put your gear and where your bunk is, then I'll take you to the Chief. I'll take you after and show you around."

I thanked him and shook hands, then he disappeared along the catwalk.

I turned and offered JC a hand shake too.

"My name's Johnny Crack but everyone calls me JC," he said, grinning. "Is this your first time aboard?"

I nodded. "Yes, except when we were in training. My name's Dave English."

I looked up at the superstructure as the wind gusted across the deck, snapping at the Ensign flying aft. The harbour water was showing the effects of the wind, white crested waves making it very choppy. In the distance, towards the harbour entrance, I could see the Gosport Ferry in its green and white livery, pushing its way through the waves as it crossed the harbour to the Portsmouth side.

"You'll get used to things. They are a little cramped, but we're quite relaxed here. This is the squadron flagship so we're a bit more spic n' span than the other vessels," JC said. "Come into the mess deck and I'll introduce you to the lads."

We went inside to the crossroads of the corridor. Turning right would take me to the mess deck. To my right was a metal railing around a hatch in the deck that was open. I looked down into it and saw a steel ladder going down and a deck grating below. I could hear the generators running and someone down there whistling. This was the engine room, my domain. Opposite this hatch, to my left, was another hatch with more robust steel steps leading down. This was the accommodation.

"It's pretty quiet at the moment as a lot of the lads are on leave and many of the married lads are still ashore," JC explained.

I nodded. We turned towards the mess deck, and he pushed the door open for me. I stepped over the lintel and into the room. It was not very deep but covered the width of the ship up to the catwalks on each side. In front, against the forward bulkhead, under three portholes, was a sink and drainer unit. The portholes looked out towards the bow of the ship, and you could also see down into the tank deck below. On each side of the room were two long tables with benches along each side. Around the room was cushioned bench seating. It all looked pretty cosy.

A lad sat drinking coffee at one of the tables and reading a newspaper. He looked up and JC introduced us. He was also a corporal engineer and would be one of the guys I would be working with. He stood up and grinned as we shook hands.

"You drew the short straw then," he laughed. "I'm Corporal Lawrence but you can call me Brummy."

I grinned and introduced myself.

"And that fat git over there is Clarky the cook," he said, laughing and pointing over to one of the benches where a large lad in the grubby clothes of standard army catering – a white jacket and blue striped trousers, was sitting reading a paperback.

"Fuck off, you bastard," he said. He stood, came over and shook my hand. "Don't pay any attention to Brummy, he's an arsehole."

"Oh right," I said with a laugh. "Feels like I'm at home already."

We all laughed, and I dropped my kitbag to the deck while JC got me a coffee.

"You're going to find it a bit of a ghost ship for a while," said Brummy, "but there's plenty to do and we're about to start painting the engine room – that's the next job. The Chief will fill you in. The Buffer, that's JC over there, will issue you with overalls and any other items you might need."

I had all the uniform I needed and had come across in the standard Maritime Regt dress: No.8 dark blue trousers and a light blue shirt over which was the off-white roll neck thick wool sweater. We usually wore soft soled black brogue-like shoes, but sea-boots were a standard of wear also. These were large black wellies with long off-white woollen socks that folded down over the tops of the wellies. These were usually reserved for really rough weather, and it was shoes most of the time for the engineers. I had the wellies, but the seamen wore these most of the time. Headwear was always the beret.

I sat down at one of the tables while JC handed me a coffee.

"You can help yourself to tea or coffee any time, and dinner tonight is around six. I have some things to do, so will see you later. Welcome aboard."

I said my thanks and relaxed. I sat back, trying to get my head around things. I could feel that the mood aboard was good. This was such a far cry from Chepstow and being in Gosport barracks. Like it or not, it was to be home for some time.

Brummy popped his head around the mess door and said he'd show me where my bunk was down below and to a locker. I had a choice of about four berths as we weren't at full crew status.

Back at deck level, the 'heads', as they called the toilets, were in the opposite direction from the mess, past the galley, on the same side. There were shower stalls and sinks there also. I have to say, I felt instantly at home on this ship. Being the flagship, she had an extra deck – loosely termed 'officer country'. Up there, they had their own officers' mess and cabins. The middle deck was the wheelhouse, and the skipper's cabin was adjacent to this. The Chief's cabin was on the main deck, next to our 'forward mess' and opposite the hatch down to the engine room. Below deck, our bunks were three tiers, and I chose the middle one of a group central to the space. My clothes locker was next to me, so I didn't have far to grope on a dark night in a force eight gale. I stowed my gear, and JC popped down with a pair of dark blue overalls. "Hope they're not too big. I'm afraid it's one size fits all until I get a new batch in. I'll keep one by for you."

I thanked him and struggled into them. I had to roll the sleeves and the legs back as it was a bit of a sack of potatoes job. I still wasn't much over eight stone and that wasn't about to change anytime soon.

I had my meeting with Warrant Officer 2nd Class, Keith 'Granny' Hopping, the Chief. He was pleased to get another pair of hands. He opened his office door and called out to Dip Surgreve to show me the ropes. He turned back to me, closing the door.

"It's quiet at the moment, so I'm getting the engine room painted. Sorry about that but it's only a touch-up job until we sail. Welcome aboard. Any problems, I'm available most times."

We shook hands and stepped out into the corridor. I would be added to the duty roster but for the first month would share the watch with one of the more experienced lads until I found my feet. He was a good chief and easy to talk to but could be a bit of 'an old woman' hence the nickname 'Granny'. Dip met me by the hatch and grinned seeing me in my overalls and beret.

"You don't need to wear your beret around the ship while we're working. Come on, I'll show you below."

I shoved my beret in one of my pockets and followed him down the metal ladder into the engine room.

We had four V12 Paxman-Riccardo diesels. Two on each side, linked to an epicyclic gearbox. This meant there were two shaft inputs on the engine side of the gearbox (one from each engine) and one shaft coming out the other side of the gearbox that passed through the ship to the props, one on each side. At the bottom of the ladder were the engine controls from which all four engines could be controlled. They consisted of four brass levers set in a small metal housing. The two outboard levers controlled the gearbox connection and were, in fact, clutch levers. The two central levers were slightly taller, and these were the main engine throttles. Pushing them forward controlled the engine revs – slow, medium, maximum. The two outboard levers, if pushed forward, would put the ship into forward drive. Pulling them all the way back, towards you, put the ship into reverse. Above these were two large telegraphs, linked to the bridge telegraphs. An interior needle on them indicated the instruction from the bridge and on each was another handle that you moved to be over the interior needle that informed the bridge that you had complied with the order. There was an engine room to bridge communication system below the telegraphs and a ship's chronometer between them.

To the rear of the engine room ladder and behind the gearboxes was the main switchboard which ran about two metres in each direction. This controlled all the ship's electrics. There were four main breakers, one for each of the generators and all the power supply readouts. To either side, port and starboard were the generator rooms. These were accessed by hatches that had two metal steps leading up to them from the engine room. Each of the generator rooms held two Foden diesel generators. Each room also housed a Worthington-Simpson ballast pump with control valves. These were rugged, reliable pumps that kept the ship trim and pumped sea water in or out of the various ballast tanks that ran the length of the ship on each side below the various store compartments. These generator spaces were 'neat' to say the least and I'd get to know them well. Carrying out an oil change in the tight space with a lot of noisy, hot metal around you was a challenge, carrying it out at 03:00 a.m. in a force 8-10 gale was mind numbing, but we did it...!

The total crew was around thirty-six. There was the skipper, the first lieutenant, the chief, the bosun, and it worked down from there. The majority were seamen and there were generally around six of us engineers. There was a radio operator who also doubled as the ship's clerk. Along the catwalks on each side there were hatches that carried the ship's stores, from food to engineering equipment and what was called Bosuns stores. At the pointy end (bow) were the winch, bow door and ramp housings where both the doors and the ramp could be operated from. These took the form of small rooms, one each side, and consisted of a large winch drum and an operation console for one bow door. The ramp could be operated from either side. They were dirty, noisy, confined spaces but we had to keep them spotless, a daunting task.

It was January 1965, and it was a quiet time for us on the LCTs. This was the best opportunity to get things 'ship shape' on board, hence the painting of the engine room. But I didn't mind; it was good to be a part of the crew and I started to feel that I belonged.

It had been a good January so far, and on Saturday 30th January I was on watch. We'd been out on the buoys for quite a while. The engine room work was going well, and I'd come up on deck for a breather and a roll-up. It was a crisp, clear day with bright blue skies. I stood on the aft deck looking out towards where the navy ships were tied up. All the flags were at half-mast on the ships and the admiralty building and ours as well. Winston Churchill had died on 24th January and today was his state funeral. The lads had it on the TV in the mess. You could have heard a pin drop across the harbour. Nothing was moving, just the flags fluttering in the gusts of wind. As I stood there, I remembered the time I'd been introduced to Winnie at Brighton racecourse and shook the hand of that great man. Dad had been so pleased that day. Now just a memory of places and faces. I remember well that cold, bright day, standing on the aft deck of Audemer, wondering what my future would hold. To this day, whenever similar weather descends, I think back to that moment, looking out across the harbour on Audemer.

Some of the crew were married and lived ashore when we were in our home port. They were known as 'pads' though I had absolutely no idea why. Most lived in the married quarters adjacent to the admin buildings in Gosport, in Weevil Lane. They would come out to the ship between

08:30 a.m. and 09:00 a.m. and leave between 05:30 p.m. and 06:00 p.m. unless they were on duty watch.

It wasn't long before we moved back from the buoys to the Gunwharf where we were tied up alongside. This made it a lot easier for coming and going ashore. If the ship was out on the buoys and we'd been ashore it meant coming into HMS Vernon, past navy security, and then a long walk to the Gunwharf to pick up the military tender out to the buoys. This tender operated hourly. If we missed the last one at midnight, we had to sleep ashore somewhere. There were a few incidents of lads missing the last tender and, on one occasion, a couple of them stole a rowing boat to get out to the ship. As they neared the buoys, they were caught by a naval police launch. Needless to say, they got into deep mire for that, and we were all warned about missing the last tender. No, being alongside at the Gunwharf was good.

HMS Audemer L4061

19

February and we were continuing to spruce things up on the Audemer. Being the flagship of the fleet meant that extra bit of spit and polish which included painting the engine room. This was not the most inspiring of jobs, but it was something we were expected to do. It amounted to covering the four large Paxman twelve-cylinder diesels with old sheets, man-handling large ladders in an already tight space, filling our overall pockets with loads of cotton waste, and humping large pots of paint down the steel engine room ladder.

Because I was one of the smallest engineers on board (if not, in the fleet) it became my job to squirm between the deck plates and the engine mountings to recover any tool (or paint brush) that had fallen into the bilges. This entailed wriggling under the engines, groping around in semi-darkness while balancing between structural beams below the deck plating. There was always an amount of water and oil slopping around in the bilges and although we could pump them out, there remained a significant amount of muck down there. Also, we weren't allowed to pump them out while in port. So, whatever was down there, we had to wade through it to get the dropped item. I was the proverbial 'bilge rat'. Carrying this exercise out while at sea with the engines running flat out, hot metal all around me and the ship rolling in a force seven gale was not to be taken lightly. But if a tool had been dropped down there, you could guarantee the buggers would leave it until I came on watch to get it out.

Because these engine rooms were a mass of pipes, cable trays, and fixed equipment, painting the bulkheads and deckheads was another challenge. Many an hour was spent doing this, but the end result was worth it. The main colour for these areas was white. Engines and gearbox covers were sky blue but, thankfully, they weren't painted very often. Once done, the place looked a treat and with the telegraph, chronometer housing, and controls being brass, once polished, they made the whole engine room sparkle.

Touching up was always being done, quite often whilst at sea. We were due to go to Milford Haven for a refit later in the spring, which would include a major engine overhaul, so the painting was just to keep it looking reasonable in the meantime.

I was starting to get settled into shipboard life. This was to be my home for some time to come and I quickly adapted to it. I'd been a part of military life since I was fifteen. Most of that time had been in barracks and I hadn't enjoyed it much at all. I didn't mind the discipline of military life; it was just that the lads I'd done my apprenticeship with at Chepstow didn't impress me. By the time I arrived at Gosport I was almost nineteen, starting to find my way and adjust to life in the 'real' military.

I turned nineteen in the December of '64 and when I joined Audemer most of the lads were in their twenties, with the exception of the more senior NCOs and some of the officers. This made it so much easier to settle in as part of the crew.

Audemer had spent most of the winter of '64 up in Scotland. We had a base there at Helensburgh and our vessels took it in turns at being stationed there in the winter months. Audemer had cut short her time up there as she was due the refit and also because, as flagship, she had other duties down South. When I joined her, she hadn't long been back, hence the painting. It also meant that she would be around Pompey for some time.

When I had weekends off from duty, I would sometimes make the trip up to see Mum. She was living mostly on her own now. Jo and Di were still there but that was about to change; Jo had met an Australian guy who was a friend of my uncle Hayden. They had both been mercenaries together, fighting in the Belgian Congo, as it was then. When that all went 'tits up' they came home.

John Hoey was typical of his type; ex-military (2 Para), lean, blond, and rugged looking, and Jo was smitten – hook, line, and sinker! He was Jo's dream and so she started the relationship. Mum didn't much like the idea and, in her way, made it abundantly clear to Jo that she wasn't happy about her getting married so soon. Although I believe she was perfectly justified in this belief, Mum's intransigent, Victorian view on these things had a negative effect on Jo who just dug in. And so, Jo and John were married in a registry office in Brixton that March, and it wasn't long before they moved into rented accommodation in Balham, Southwest London. Mum and Jo hadn't fallen out over it, but Mum had made it plain that she didn't agree with what she was doing.

At this time, Di was working as a legal secretary for an Inner Temple solicitor, and it was just her and Mum now in a large, four-bedroomed flat in Stockwell. It wasn't long before Jo and her new Australian husband decided that they would move to Oz. As this was where we had all been brought up, Dinah, who had made many friends from that time and still corresponded with them, decided that she would quite like to go with Jo and I guess that Mum's worries were very much eased by this. So, in the end, that is what happened. Jo and Dinah were to live in Melbourne where both girls had friends and John Hoey was originally from. Di was going to rent her own place. They were to leave in the coming November. I don't think Mum put up any resistance but had just resigned herself to it. She was never one to display or discuss her emotions on things. If she had, I think the outcome may have been different.

Jo's friend and our family friend, Mavis, was still living with her mum, Maud, in the flat beneath us. Her father, Frank Chiles, had died suddenly of cancer and this hit their family quite hard. Mavis spent quite a lot of time up with Mum and Di in the evenings, and I think they both liked having her there. For Mum, it was like having another daughter, especially with the girls disappearing overseas. My eldest sister Delia had married some time before and had been living in Muswell Hill, London. Then later, they had moved to a house in a recently developed area of Bishops Stortford, on the Essex/Hertfordshire border, about an hour's train journey away. I was starting to visit home on odd weekends and had been getting on well with Mavis for some time now. We'd been close since childhood, and it started out like having another sister.

Meanwhile, life on board soon settled down for me and I gradually gained my sea-legs. These ships were flat-bottomed and with an overall length of around seventy metres and a width of twelve metres, which meant she was a bit of a beast in a stormy sea. Because the primary role of these LCTs was to carry tanks and heavy vehicles, the flat bottom enabled us to run the ship up onto a designated beach area, open the bow doors, lower the ramp, and drive vehicles on and off. Once at sea, the ship could be ballasted to suit the cargo and conditions.

Along each side of the hull were ballast tanks that ran almost the length of the vessel. This meant that we could lower or raise her position in the water. Quite often, in a particularly rough sea, we could pump seawater into the ballast tanks on either side which would lower the ship's position in the water and make her more stable and less likely to roll. However, the trade-off for this was that she would be slower and use more fuel. Although all the ships in our fleet were more or less identical, with the exception of Audemer and her additional deck, theoretically, they would all roll the same. However, this was never the case and we had to 'bodily adjust' to each vessel. I was generally pretty good and rarely ever was seasick but that's not to say I was *never* seasick. There were odd occasions when I would be quite ill and, if you have ever been seasick, you'll know that all you want to do is to lie down and die!

Finding my way around the engine room didn't take too long. Everyone was helpful and, although a little nervous of the electrical switchgear, I soon got the hang of it. Controlling the main engines underway required concentration as we had to respond pretty quickly once the commands came down from the wheelhouse. It was quite a while before I was allowed to operate them, so I always ended up with the jobs nobody else liked to do. One of these was checking the prop-shaft bearings, aft, down where the ship's hot water boiler was. The shaft tunnel could only be accessed whilst lying on your stomach and wriggling through to the prop-shaft bearings. Because I was one of the smallest on board, it wasn't difficult to see why I got the job.

Packing the stern glands meant using asbestos string to pack around the gland. This bearing was also fed by a remote Tecalemit grease pump located on the rear bulkhead of the engine room, just behind the telegraph and control station. Oil changes on the generators, whilst underway, was a squeeze as well and if the ship was riding a heavy sea, getting a five-gallon drum of dirty oil up on deck via a small, steel, vertical ladder and out a steel hatch was no mean feat. The dirty oil was normally to be emptied into a large forty-gallon drum on the tank deck. This meant that once I had manhandled the five-gallon drum of dirty oil (open at the top and carried via a rope handle) up on deck, I then had to carry it along the catwalk to the first vertical ladder down into the tank deck and hand pumping it into the forty-gallon drum. If I had to do this in the dead of night, in anything over a force five gale, with heavy seas, it was little wonder that quite often the five-gallon drum of dirty oil ended up being thrown over the side. This, of course, was provided I made sure I was on the side of the ship where the wind wasn't blowing towards me. This was a highly illegal manoeuvre but did happen once in a while underway at sea. I certainly wouldn't do it if tied up alongside or out on the buoys!

Changing the oil on the main Paxmans was a bit more of an issue. The sump drain was under the engine, at one end, below the level of the deck plates. Again, because I was small (and the junior) I could crawl under the engine, undo the large sump nut to start draining the sump, ensuring that a drain tray and drum was in place between the bilge ribs and the bilges. It was not unknown for people to drop the dirty oil straight into the bilges and then pump them out over the side. Again, this was illegal, and you were in serious trouble if you were caught doing this. Hence, it was a case of lifting deck plates and this 'bilge rat' crawling around the bilges. Once in a drum I could then pump the dirty oil through a hose and a hole in the forward deck head out to the tank deck and the forty-gallon drum on the other side.

The work was good, and we would work the normal 07:00 a.m. – 05:00 p.m. Duty watch keeping came around every four to five days, depending on how many engineers there were on board at the time. When at sea however, we worked a four hourly shift. Mine was usually what was called the 'middle watch' which was from midnight until 04:00 a.m. I liked the solitude of this watch and seeing sunrise in the mornings. It also meant I would be one of the first to the galley to get breakfast. There was always plenty of work to do and sometimes we'd muck in with the seamen and help chipping or sorting out winches and deck gear. My responsibility most times was the port winch and housing, in the bow. This was a small winch room under the forecastle, that housed the main winch drum for the bow doors and the ramp. It often meant that I could squirrel myself away in there and carry out general greasing and maintenance on the winch and keeping the place tidy. If things were really slack it was a good place to read a book or have a quiet roll-up.

When I was previously ashore at St. Georges Barracks, I had made friends with a lad who was learning seamanship – Malcolm 'Tom' Thomas. We became good mates and drinking buddies. He was from Tenterden in Kent and had a great sense of humour. He was about six inches taller than me and had the kind of looks that made him favourable with the opposite sex. He also had the 'patter' so whenever we went out there was never a dull moment. Fortunately, he was drafted to the Audemer like me, although he was a 'deckie'. Off watch, we continued the drinking partnership, and it was always on the Portsmouth side.

Going ashore to the NAAFI Club in Portsmouth was the most usual choice. Tom and I had started to become known around the club and made friends with many of the matelots (RN Sailors). It was mostly the navy that used the place and of course, our lot from the LCTs. I very rarely saw an Army lad there and I don't recall ever seeing RAF bods there either. If Tom was working, or any of the other lads were doing other things, I'd quite happily go there for a pint and a meal. If any of the RN lads or girls that we'd got know were there, I'd have a drink and a chat with them.

The other watering hole was the Still & West, a large corner pub that fronted the entrance to the harbour in Old Portsmouth. The pub was over two hundred years old but was a main focal point and meeting place. The upstairs bar overlooked the harbour entrance and the massive glass windows also gave a good view of the 'King Stairs' where the Navy tied up. This way, we could see which naval ships were in and – as we knew a lot of the ship's crews on these various vessels – it was good to know who was likely to be around. We could get Fullers London Pride on tap here, a cracking good pint of ale. There would always be someone you could chat to just by sitting at the bar. A lot of tourists used the place, too, and it was always packed with people at the weekends.

20

It was in the early spring of '65 that we were informed that we would be going into dry dock at Milford Haven, Pembrokeshire. It was time for Audemer to have her hull scraped and painted, the main engines overhauled, and general work carried out around the ship. This was done by the local dockyard workers. The dry-dock stay was usually around six to eight weeks with a skeleton crew kept aboard to maintain watches and keep an eye on things. The married pads hated being away from home too long, so it generally came down to us single guys to put the time in. I was keen to do it, but I knew it wasn't up to me and of course, the old adage, 'never volunteer' always rang true. I needn't have worried, however, as sure enough, I was one of those chosen to make up the engineering side, along with Dip Surgreve. He hailed from Fiji originally. He was a really nice sensible, quiet guy but we got on well...! In total, there would be around eight of us staying on board whilst the remaining twenty-eight or so, would return to Portsmouth once we had arrived, and would be farmed out to other ships in the squadron, take annual leave or work ashore in Gosport. Our sailing date was just after Easter in April.

It wasn't long before we were underway to the Pembrokeshire coast. Most of the crew were on board for the trip. The trip round to

Milford was uneventful but it was good to be at sea and the prospect of spending some time in Milford Haven was something to look forward to. There was a newly opened refinery located near the dry-dock area and as we came around the headland, you could see the town of Milford stretching from the hilltop down to the dock area. It was also a large fishing port and just across from the dry docks were the large sheds where the fish was unloaded from the trawlers and auctioned off – usually on a Thursday morning. In those days, fishing was the mainstay of Milford and probably at its height in business.

As we slowly navigated past the oil tanker jetty, where the crude was off loaded into large storage tanks, we turned in towards the dock area. There were around three docks here and ours was the first on the left as we sailed in. The tide was high and over on the right-hand side was the jetty for the fishing fleet. It was a sunny, clear day and I remember completing my watch as we came in. I came up on deck from the generator room hatch on the starboard side and watched as we slowly approached our dock. The decks were a hive of activity as ropes were made ready whilst the bosun was shouting out his orders. Up on the headland, people were starting to gather as it wasn't often that a military ship came here. Many of the crowd watching were girls and it wasn't long before they were waving, responding to some of the lads as they waved to them. This drew a sharp rebuke from the bosun. The ship was backed into the dry dock very slowly, then engines in neutral and she was slowly pulled in and lined up by the dock workers. Dip came to stand beside me, and we watched the manoeuvre into the flooded dock.

Once we were positioned in line with the dock, the engines were kept ticking over. The pilot had come aboard as we neared the refinery area, and I could see him up on the bridge giving directions. Soon we were slowly gliding into the dock. Dock workers were taking the ropes as our lads threw them to the dockside. Once the ropes were on the winches, the ship was slowly pulled into the position necessary for her to settle onto the cradle as the water was gradually pumped from the dock. The massive dock gates were closed behind us and slowly, the water was being pumped out. Before we had entered the dry dock the ship was turned around 180° so that we were facing the way we came in. The stern ropes, still on the winches, were slowly let out as the vessel dropped with the water level. It was a tricky manoeuvre to ensure we settled correctly on the cradle that was to support us once the dock was dry.

Gradually we were lowered onto the cradle, the ropes were secured and all you could see now was the green/black of the dock walls, dripping in water. Fortunately, our extra top deck was just above the walkway on the dock. A gangway was put in place on both sides of the ship, the generators were put on internal running until we hooked up to the dockyard electrical supply and the main engines shut down. We migrated to the forward mess for a chat by the chief and the bosun on what was to happen next. For me, it was a cup of tea and relax a bit. Six weeks was a long stay in one place, and I was looking forward to a run ashore with the lads. Little did I know what this visit to Milford Haven was about to do to me.

It wasn't long before the chief and the bosun set up a rota of watch systems for those of us that were to remain behind. Once this was done, the chief, bosun and the others of the crew who weren't staying, left with the officers. In charge of us was the bosun's second, Joe Buckley, an experienced, elderly sergeant who was on his last year of service before retiring. He was a seaman by trade. Dip Surgreve was the senior engineer. We'd all been given an in-depth chat on what our duties were and there was nothing that any of us wasn't expecting.

Over the next few days, the time was spent getting things organised. A landline was put in place, and we were told we could receive mail from the dockyard office. A couple of us wandered over there later to introduce ourselves. The receptionist was a young girl of around eighteen called Valerie and, for a while, Val and I were going to be 'an item'.

The rota as to who was going to be doing the cooking was made. Most of the guys couldn't cook so there remained three of us who elected to do this. We would be using the ship's galley, which was well stocked. It was mid-week and Dip agreed to do the first set of meals. Myself and another lad, one of our engineers, would be doing the food shopping in town. But for the first few days, we had existing food supplies we would be using.

The dockyard people made themselves known to us and started setting in place their work cradles down in the dock itself, which was sixty feet below. Their intention was to start scraping, de-rusting, and painting the undercoat of red admar on the hull. This was a lead free, anti-corrosive paint, a sort of brownish red. Joe Buckley nominated a couple of his lads to help him start chipping the hull the following day when the dock workers would start doing their bit. Us engineers were to carry out work on the generators not in use. It also gave us the opportunity to service the Worthington-Simpson ballast pumps and any other odd jobs that required doing. Everything was quite relaxed.

That evening, on our first run ashore, we found a decent pub right outside the dockyard gates – The Railway Tavern. This pub is still in place today and now known as the Railway Hotel. The beer was good, and the locals were very interested to chat and fraternise with the crew of the first military ship they'd had in port for some time. Like all small coastal towns, it wasn't long before word went around. Military ship, single guys… the girls were not far away. One of the guys, Alan, managed to organise a date that night but for the rest of us it was mostly getting the lay of the land, what the beer was like, and getting to know the locals. We all made it back in one piece and sat around the mess deck having a late supper and taking the piss out of Alan and his 'first date'.

I slept well, although it was odd being in the bunks and the ship not rolling or the mains rumbling away. I awoke at 06:00 a.m. to the sound of someone clattering around in the galley. When I stepped out of the accommodation hatch, the smell of eggs and bacon cooking was mouth-watering. Breakfast was always my favourite meal. Brummy was making breakfast for all of us, although I was early. I took my towel and made my way to the heads. The water was good and hot, so I let it wake me as I stood under the shower. I finished, wrapped my towel around me and still in my flip-flops made my way back down the hatch to get dressed. The lads were just starting to rise. It was a working day so that meant No.8's, the working dress. As the weather was warming up, that also meant the light blue, short-sleeve, No.8 shirt and darker blue trousers.

I made my way to the mess deck, having collected my full English breakfast from Brummy in the galley on the way. I made myself a coffee and dropped a couple of slices of bread in the toaster. Over the next hour, guys started to appear with their breakfasts in the mess. Nobody said a great deal and we all just tucked in with brief chat about the previous night's escapades. This was to be the pattern of behaviour most mornings to come.

Brummy, Dip, and I sat around after breakfast and discussed what our plan was for the day. I was delegated to go over the dockyard office each morning and collect any mail as well as pick up a couple of newspapers. Following that, check the power supply and get the first generator, not being run, ready for an oil change.

That morning, as I went across the gangway to the office, I noticed how quiet it was. This was unusual as the dock workers usually started early, around 07:00 a.m. It was 08:30 a.m., and all was eerily quiet. The dockyard was silent and there was hardly anyone around. I wandered into the dockyard office and tapped on the window of the reception area.

"Hi, Val, good morning. I've come for the mail. Bit quiet, isn't it?"

She looked at me shyly and handed over the ship's mail. "That's because they're all on strike," she said, grinning.

"You're kidding me, right?"

"Nope, message was sent out yesterday afternoon."

"Well, we never received anything."

"Oh, sorry, I thought you got the note. I'm sure one was sent over yesterday."

"Oh, okay, well thanks Val, maybe see you later."

I walked out of there a little stunned. I hurried back on board. As I went into the mess, most of the lads were still having breakfast but also, hoping to get some mail.

"Okay lads, I have some news for you all," I said as I was handing out the mail. "The dockyard workers are on strike."

The bosun came in just as I was announcing this.

"What?!" he said.

I repeated it to him.

It was then that I noticed the envelope pinned to the notice board. I pointed it out to the bosun. He took it down, opened and read it.

"Looks to be indefinite, until further notice. I better get on the radio to HQ," and off he went.

The strike didn't make a lot of difference to us engineers, at least, not at this stage. The mains weren't to be overhauled until about two weeks' time. But it did matter to the ship as a whole. The powers that be back in Gosport would have scheduled military exercises and operations after we returned there. These would now have to be postponed or taken over by other vessels in the squadron. Our stay was meant to be six weeks. As it eventually turned out, we were in Milford Haven for eighteen weeks – twelve weeks over our allotted time. We were all okay to stay and our first lieutenant came from Gosport to talk to us about anyone wishing to go back. No one did, so we all stayed. The majority of us were single, so I guess that was the main reason. It was to be a fascinating eighteen weeks.

The Audemer in dry dock - Milford Haven

We continued with our engineering bits and the remaining lads carried out duties both on and under the ship. A lot of dock work was necessary to keep these vessels afloat, safely. They were built in 1945 and were originally intended for the invasion of Japan. However, with the dropping of the atomic bombs on Hiroshima and Nagasaki, there was no need for them. This particular ship, Audemer L4061, was completed on 22nd December 1945, originally for the Royal Navy. It wasn't named but was given the designation L4061. She was then transferred to the Royal Army Service Corps in 1957 where she was given the name Audemer. The fact she was commissioned two days after I was born made her quite special to me.

The lads couldn't carry out much work on the hull, so they concentrated on all the deck equipment, catwalks, winches, stations, hatches, deck plates, and the superstructure. All required chipping, scraping, and coating with the rust resisting paint. So, they had loads to keep them busy. It was decided that we would take the main engine room forward bulkhead off. This was so that the mains could be manoeuvred out to the tank deck, ready for the dockyard engineers to work on them whenever the strike was over. So, there was also plenty to keep us busy. It meant re-scheduling the work and to do what we could. It was good that the warm weather had arrived as it made working and shore runs so much the better.

21

As the days warmed up, our work continued in a more relaxed manner. The noises of a busy dockyard were stilled; just the cry of gulls looking for scraps of fish and flotsam in the bay. The fishing fleet went out on Mondays and returned and off-loaded the catch early on Thursday mornings. That was when the noise was compounded by the cry of gulls and the thumping of fully laden boxes of fish being unloaded on the wharf alongside the fish auction sheds. The large, refrigerated trucks were lined up and the cry of the auctioneers was a continuous background clamour to all of this. A few times, if I wasn't on watch, I would wander over to watch the off-loading and capitalize on being in uniform by picking up a bargain selection of fish to take back to the ship for our dinner. I loved the hustle and bustle of the fishermen and buyers wrangling over the week's catch. The smell of fish was not unpleasant, and I found the whole thing absolutely fascinating to observe.

There was a smokehouse in Milford where freshly landed herring was filleted and smoked to produce kippers. You either love or hate them but it is a particular favourite of mine. The funny thing was that Alan's new girlfriend, who he'd met on our first run ashore, was a twin and both siblings worked in this smokehouse. They were known locally as the Picton Sisters, and Alan was enjoying himself. One fact emerged from this particular relationship, and that was the girls' hands. They both worked in the filleting section of the smoker and one night, when a few of us were in The Railway, Alan came in with one of them. Alan had mentioned that their hands were a bit weird, and he asked her to show us.

She put her hands, palm up, on the table. They looked a bit scratched. If you ran your hand over her palms one way, they were smooth. But when you did it the other way, it was like running your hand over sandpaper. It was awful to feel, although I got the impression it was the twins' party-piece. It didn't bother Alan as long as he was getting his 'nookie' and we had a hoot when he mentioned how uncomfortable it was if she grabbed his 'member' in the wrong direction!

One morning, Alan asked me if I was interested in going on a blind date with him.

"I thought you were okay with the Picton girl," I said.

"I am, but she said she has a friend who'd like to go on a date."

I thought about this and, to be honest, I wasn't in a rush to date. There were some great pubs in Milford, and Dip and I were working our way through them, enjoying the beer. Well, I thought, anything for a laugh... so I decided to do it.

We arranged it for the following Saturday. Both Alan and I were off duty, so it was arranged that we meet the two girls at around seven in the evening. The summer evenings stayed light until quite late and, on that particular day, it had been quite a hot one. We were to meet outside a small supermarket at the top of the high street. Alan and I had gone ashore earlier and had a couple of beers during which we decided that we'd take the girls for a drink and then maybe sneak them back to the ship for a couple of hours. This had happened a few times and the sergeants on board had 'looked the other way' as long as we were discreet about it. Alan had already had his girl on board a few times, but it didn't happen very often. Most of us were more interested in drinking in the pubs.

A little after 07:00 p.m. we decided to make a move and made our way up the high street. I have to say that I was feeling a bit apprehensive but, hell, it was something different and, who knew, she might be really nice. We wandered up the hill towards the top of the high street. As we got nearer, I saw two girls appear out of the doorway of the now closed supermarket on the other side of the road. We crossed over and I noticed that one of the girls was wearing a topcoat.

"Bit warm for her to be wearing that, isn't it, Alan? Is that your Sue?"

"No," he said. "It looks like that's your blind date, Joan. Sue, has the cardie on."

I looked hard and tried to make out what she was like. She had a mane of hair and, even from about two hundred yards away, I could see that she wasn't bad looking. As we got a bit nearer, I noticed that she had her coat buttoned up most of the way. As we approached, I realised why.

This girl had the biggest pair of breasts I had ever seen. And I mean *big*. These mothers were humungous! We nervously greeted each other, while I tried extremely hard to not look anywhere else but her face.

I could see that Alan was struggling with this as well. Introductions were made and when Alan suggested going to one of the more well-known high street pubs, Sue declined. The girls didn't want to go to any of the more popular ones. My date, Joan, said she knew of one in a back street down at the lower end of town. That was okay by us, and it was also nearer the dockyard, so off we went.

She told me later that her bust size was 46" and it was because, as a child, she had been diagnosed with a gland problem. The fact that she was quite a petite girl only emphasised her 'assets'. Anyway, I was game; she was still very attractive to me, and I figured that, if I was lucky, I might get the chance to 'meet n' greet' these two lovely 46 inches. I have to admit, it turned out better than I had expected! Indeed, we ended up going the full nine yards (as it has been known). But, alas, our dalliance didn't become anything more lasting.

The next day we were to meet near the home of the Picton girls. A shortcut to this was along a small, wooded path. Alan and I went, and we met up with the two girls, Joan, and Sue. As we were walking them along this path, a monster of a guy appeared and came towards us menacingly. Both Alan and I let go of the girls' hands and considered our options. None of them were very good. This guy insisted that Joan 'the bust' was his girl. At first, she denied it, but I looked at her and asked, "Is this true?"

She hesitated then nodded. The guy came on, and Alan said something to him. The next minute, Alan was on his back, looking dazed. I started forward, quickly taking off my glasses and shoving them into my jacket pocket. Joan then stepped between us and begged me not to, saying that she would sort it out. Sue, on the other hand, legged it, shouting she was going to get the police. Joan went towards this guy and, in a flash, he backhanded her across her face. She went down, screaming curses at him. Next minute, he grabbed her by her hair as she sat on the ground and, with her feet dragging along the dirt track, he hauled her back the way he had come. I started after him, knowing I was going to get my lights knocked out. Still holding onto her hair, he turned to look at me and said, "Let it go, you don't want to get involved in this."

I didn't and Alan stumbled over to me. "Best let her go mate. He'll kill both of us and you've only known her one night."

I was glad he said that; the guy was a mountain and, as far as I was concerned, he could have her. I felt really bad for her but my survival, in this case, 'was common-sense before valour' so we both stood there, watching her disappear up the path with him.

The police did finally arrive, but the two of them were long gone by then. One of the policemen said to me that I had had a lucky escape.

"You don't want anything to do with Joan. She's been with this guy for years and he is always knocking her about. Best find a less complicated date next time," he said, laughing. I asked him if he was going to do anything about it and he said probably not. Apparently, he was often doing things like this to her but unless she brought charges, they couldn't prove anything.

"We'll get him on something fairly soon, don't worry. Best you don't get involved with this girl."

I took heed of his suggestion and, looking across at Alan as the police left, said, "Any other good ideas, mate?" We both grinned and decided it was time for a Sunday lunch time pint.

My lasting image of Joan was as she was being dragged up the track by her hair. However, there was an epilogue to this event a few weeks later. We had learned that her violent boyfriend was a motorcycle fanatic, and that his pride and joy was a big old Harley. We were tipped off that he was visiting a mate of his in a back street of Milford and that his motorcycle was parked outside the house. Dip took a two-pound bag of sugar under his jacket and three of us decided to make a small diversion on the way to the pub. We found the bike parked alongside the kerb on this quiet backstreet. We watched the road for a while, then Dip nipped across the road, opened the fuel tank cap, and emptied the whole bag into the fuel tank. We then legged it to the pub. We never did hear the outcome of this, but that little bit of revenge really was sweet, if you'll excuse the pun.

Despite what was happening with the dockyard strike, life was pretty good on board. I was occasionally cooking the main meal and learning to play bridge as well as carrying out my everyday engineering duties and work. The weather was getting hotter, and a sort of calm and routine settled over the ship. One day, the local chaplain dropped by and asked to come on board. The duty watch brought him into our mess deck and introduced him to those of us who were there. The object of his visit was to get us to pay a visit to his church on Sunday mornings. After he had left, our bosun threatened us to attend or he would find us all jobs to do aboard, even if we were off watch. So, it was decided that a group of us would go. His church wasn't far from the dockyard gates, so we decided to make the effort the following Sunday.

It was a small Baptist community and on our first Sunday there, I saw Val from the dockyard office. She was pleasantly surprised to see us and after a few prayers, some hymns and a 'view from the pulpit' in which we had to stand up and were welcomed into the community, we met up outside. After some small talk, I walked her up the road. She wouldn't let me walk her to her house, but we got on well and I said I would see her the following day in the dockyard office. I then met up with the others in the pub. This Sunday chapel was something a few of us continued for most of the time we were there. The vicar had meant us well and it was through his say-so that we became better known throughout the town of Milford in a favourable light.

A few days later, when I went over to get the ship's mail, I plucked up enough courage to ask Val to go on a date. She declined at first but, after some persistence, I managed to get her to agree to meet up one evening that week. She had some errands to do for her mum so we wouldn't be meeting up until around eight thirty in the evening. Yet again, little did I know what I was letting myself in for...

David in Milford Haven, on board with the chef's hat on

Work continued on board, with no sign of the dockyard workers returning. We tuned the ship's radio in to BBC Radio 2 and had it playing over the ship's speakers wherever we were working. I remember that *Mr Tambourine Man* by The Byrds was top of the charts that summer and it certainly had a lot of airtime on board. Along with The Beatles, The Supremes, The Stones, Bob Dylan, and Barry McGuires's *Eve of Destruction*. 1965 was a year for some pretty good music. All these groups and tunes were the background to many of those weeks in Milford Haven.

There was, however, a sad moment to these times and one that came back to haunt me a year later whilst on active service in the Middle East.

Our runs ashore were nearly always drinking sessions in the local pubs. It was too good an opportunity to miss; being close to the town centre, good pubs, and interested locals. We all drank quite a bit more than we would have back in Pompey, and the weather here was hot with the longer evenings. It was an unwritten duty that whoever was on watch for the night – one seaman and one engineer most times, although there were occasions when it was just one or the other – made supper for the lads when they returned. It was usually leftovers from the day made into either soup or a stew. The lads looked forward to it and it was a good opportunity to catch up on the evening's adventures.

This particular night, I was on watch. It was a warm evening, and everyone had gone ashore. Around 11:00 p.m., I had a large tureen of soup on the go in the galley and was sitting in the mess writing up the watch notes from my hourly engine room checks. Apart from the radio being on, all was quiet. I heard someone singing in the distance on shore. I turned the radio off and listened again. Sure enough, it sounded like one of the lads was returning. I sat a moment longer then heard them singing near the gangway. I went to the galley to make sure the soup was hot then went out onto the catwalk and looked up. At first, I couldn't see anything, just heard someone singing. Then I saw Dave Ridley near the dockside end of the gangway.

He was on his own, a bit unsteady on his feet, and looked quite happily pissed. I called up to him, "Dave, come on, I've got the soup on mate."

He looked down and said something that sounded like, "Hi..." He hesitatingly made his way onto the gangway and started to stagger across. He got about halfway and stopped.

"Come on mate, stop messing about," I called up to him.

The gangway was on the left, above me. He started swinging on the wire handrail, singing, and laughing. Dave was quite a big lad, not so much in height but thick set. Hanging on to the top wire of the cable handrail, he started to lean over it.

To me, it was as if this all happened in slow-motion.

As Dave leaned over the handrail, the wire started to sag under his weight and the momentum carried him forward. I guess at that point, gravity took over. He tumbled forward and fell head-first into the dry dock, sixty feet below. He tumbled right past me but didn't cry out or say anything.

I heard the thud as he hit the bottom and I just stood there for a moment thinking, "Oh fuck."

After catching my breath, I looked over the handrail and could see him lying face down below. I quickly ran back to the mess deck and grabbed a torch. The fastest way down was to go along the catwalk and climb the ladder into the tank deck. The bow door and ramp were left in the open position, so I ran out to the ramp and jumped down from there onto a wooden trestle and dropped down into the dock. Turning the torch on, I ran to where I could see Dave – about halfway along the side of the ship. I shone the torch on him. He was lying face down and he didn't look good.

"Oh, shit Dave, what the fuck have you done?"

I wasn't expecting an answer. I pushed my hands under him and rolled him over. For some reason, I'd got it in my head to carry out cardiac massage and started pressing down on his chest. I knew he was dead but thought I had to try.

When I saw what was coming from his head, I stopped.

I called out loudly as I knew there was a dockyard night watchman. I kept shouting until I saw torchlight appear at the far end of the dock.

"Down here, I need help!"

I saw him looking for a ladder down.

As I knelt there, I felt numb. All I could think of to do was to say the *Lord's Prayer* over him. My other thought was that I hoped this didn't fuck up our stay in the dockyard. I wasn't ready to go back to Pompey just yet and hoped that this wasn't going to mess with mine and all of us, our time here.

As it turned out, it didn't. I went back up to the ship and cleaned up. The watchman had called the local 'Bill' and an ambulance crew. I sat in the officers' mess and gave a statement to the police when they arrived. I was certainly shaken up but when asked if I wanted to go home on leave, I declined. I didn't want to dwell on this, so getting back to work and duties was the best thing for me.

All of us went to Dave's funeral in Devon but, to be honest, I don't remember too much about it. I do know that his brother couldn't make it; he was in the Green Howards and was on active service in the Middle East. However, something else happened in relation to this which is worth a mention.

A year later saw me on a sister ship, HMAV Agheila, in Aden. This was an active service drafting, and we were kept very busy here. Dave had died in Milford Haven on 20th May 1965, and a strange twist in the tail of this story happened.

We had been pretty busy for a few weeks now, going back and forwards to an island in the Indian Ocean that had terrorist activity on it. On this occasion, we were tied up alongside at HMS Sheba, a shoreside naval station, and were taking on some Special Forces guys who we were to drop off on this troubled Island. It was mid-morning, and I was in the mess having a break from the heat of the engine room. Most of the troops we were taking on were taken down to the tank deck. On occasion, an NCO would be allowed in our forward mess to get some ice water and have a quick break. This time, as I was getting myself a coffee, I heard these guys being led into our mess by one of our NCOs.

"Have a seat, guys, and cool off for a minute," he said. Then to me, "Dave, can you show these lads where the coffee is?"

"Will do," I said, not turning.

He went back out and I turned to talk to them. In that moment, I nearly wet myself. Sitting there, on the bench, was Dave Ridley.

"Bloody hell," I said, just standing there, unable to move. "Your name is Ridley, right?" I said, looking the man in the face.

"How the hell did you know that?" he replied.

"You're Dave Ridley's brother Michael, aren't you?" I said.

He nodded and just looked at me as if he knew what was coming.

Taking a deep breath, I said, "I was there the night Dave died."

He nodded again but didn't say anything. I made the two of them a coffee and showed them where they could fill their canteens up with ice water. Then I sat down opposite Dave's brother and finished my coffee. It was difficult to take my eyes off him, but I didn't want to stare. I asked after his folks, and he said they were okay. I could see he didn't want to talk much.

"Well, I have to get back to work," I said. "Hope it all goes well for you."

He just nodded and said thanks. Nothing else. Just, "We better get back to the lads. Thanks for the coffee."

I nodded and shook hands with him, and he went out the mess door. I stood there for a moment, a little shocked by the encounter. He looked so much like Dave that they could have been twins. Then, for some reason, I looked across at the calendar on the bulkhead... the date was 20th May 1966. One year to the day since Dave had died.

A footnote to this is that Michael died ten years later and both his parents shortly after within a year of each other. There are no surviving members of the Ridley family.

22

The summer was truly warming up in Milford and, with no end to the dock strike in sight, it looked to be a long, hot one. I was looking forward to going out with Val. She wasn't a stunner, but she was pretty, dark haired, and fair of skin; undertones of her strong Irish makeup. She was shy, quiet, and about my height at 5'6". None of the guys were surprised when I told them I had a date with her. They had all seen her from time to time in the dockyard office.

The evening of the date, I met her after she closed and locked up the office. We walked slowly outside the dockyard and up the hill to a quiet pub Dip and I used from time to time, just off the high street. We chatted but it was hard work. I kept the conversation light and talked a bit about life on board an LCT and the work we did. As the evening wore on, she loosened up a little. I could see that this was going to be a hard slog, but I didn't mind, and she was nice to be with. She talked about her Irish heritage and had the soft accent of Southern Ireland. There was quite a large community of Irish in Milford Haven, and I could only assume it was because of the fishing industry and Milford's proximity to Ireland on that Pembrokeshire coastline.

After we had been in the pub for an hour or so, we decided to go for a walk. It was a really warm summer's evening and night was closing in as purples and deep blues stretched across the skyline as the sun quickly set. We continued walking up the hill. There was a bus shelter at the top that had a great view of the harbour, looking West, and the lights of the refinery. Val had said it had a good view, but she had understated it; it was stunning. The shelter was one of those Perspex covered ones, so we were sheltered from any breeze, and the view over the harbour at night was amazing. It was a feast of twinkling lights and the deep purple hues of the setting sun. There was an oil tanker alongside the refinery jetty, which added to the scene. We both sat there taking in this amazing view for a while in silence. The breeze was cool, and I was starting to feel a bit chilly.

"Are you warm enough?" I asked.

No answer.

I sat there for a moment longer and, without looking at her, I asked Val how long she had been working at the dockyard.

Still no answer.

She had on a mustard yellow topcoat and a skirt beneath. I turned and looked at her. She was staring out at the harbour scene.

"You alright, Val?" I asked.

Nothing.

"Val, Val? Are you okay?" I was starting to worry now.

No response.

I sat back for a moment trying to think whether I had said anything that might have upset her. I couldn't think of anything and, in fact, I'd been on my best behaviour all evening. I tried again. "Val?"

Nothing.

I waved my hand in front of her face. She didn't even blink, just sat there staring straight ahead.

"Oh shit, come on, Val. Talk to me." Now I was really starting to panic.

Not a sound.

I sat back again, wracking my brains.

By now it was truly night and the glow of a nearby streetlamp washed across her face. Half-suspecting she was winding me up, I thought of a good test. Her knees were showing from beneath her dress, so I gently put my hand on one and started to slide my hand up her skirt. She still didn't move. I didn't really want to continue but was out of ideas and thought perhaps a bit of shock therapy would bring her round!

It did. Just as my hand reached her thigh, she sat quickly back, blinked, and looked at me. I whipped my hand away and said, "Val, are you okay"?

She looked at me for a moment and then nodded, "Sorry, yes, I'm fine."

"Val, you were in some sort of trance. I tried to talk to you, but you didn't respond. I'm sorry I touched your leg, but I didn't know what to do."

She didn't seem to mind or hadn't noticed. She apologised again and then told me that sometimes she went into trances – as if it was perfectly ordinary.

I didn't know what to say to that.

"Can we go for a walk?" she asked.

We both stood and made our way out of the shelter.

A breeze was picking up and I felt a bit of a chill. I put my arm around her for a moment as we walked along. My mind was racing. Was this some kind of epilepsy? We talked briefly and continued back down towards the town. There was not a soul around and, in fact, it seemed unusually quiet. I moved my arm down her coat sleeve and took her hand. She didn't seem to object so I kept it there, warming her cold hand. We talked a little and I asked her how long she had been experiencing these 'trances'. She said that she'd had them since she was small, but they didn't happen very often. The doctors didn't seem to know what they were and had also told her that she wasn't epileptic.

As we were talking, I was unconsciously moving my fingers across her hand. I paused. It felt like there were a lot so, discreetly, I started to count her fingers. I kept getting six, which made me a little more alert. Without being obvious, I started counting her fingers in earnest. I still kept getting six. That couldn't be right; surely, I'd have noticed when she was back in the office.

"Val, can I ask you something?"

"What?" she said.

"Don't take this the wrong way, and I do apologise, but how many fingers have you got on your hand?"

She was silent for a moment, then in a quiet voice said, "Six on each hand."

I stopped and turned to look at her, lifting her hand at the same time. "Six," I said. "How come?"

She told me she had what is called a supernumerary digit on each hand. Apparently, this was quite unique; having them on one hand was not unheard of but to have one on each was quite rare. She lifted the hand I had been holding and, sure enough, she had two pinkies, both about the same size and looking perfectly normal.

"Wow, that's really cool," I said, trying to appear normal.

We continued walking in silence for a while, but my mind was all over the place. Perhaps it was something in the bloody Milford Haven water! After a time, and thinking to myself that it really didn't change anything and I liked her company, I was considering ways to play it all down. I decided that I wouldn't mention it to the lads because I could just imagine their response; they'd fall about and find it highly amusing then find excuses to go over to the office to see. No, that would embarrass her and put any relationship I had with her in the pan. I put my arm around her and hugged her closer. She put her head on my shoulder as we walked.

Neither of us said anything for a while, and the street was dark and quiet. As we walked, with the closed and darkened shop fronts on our right, I looked for a doorway that was set back. I fancied taking things a little further, more to let her see that I was quite comfortable with what I'd discovered about her but also to have a snog if I could!

We carried on chatting in the quiet, warm air as we drifted down the silent high street. It was like the world was holding its breath. I saw a likely doorway; the recessed front of a hairdressers. I slowed down and she looked at me. I nodded towards the doorway, and we wandered into it, my arm around her, holding her close. Obviously, she didn't mind, and this was the opening I was looking for. I held her against me, her thick black hair smelling fragrant and slightly musty at the same time. Our faces came together. I kissed her gently on her lips as I felt her press against me. Slowly, she opened her lips, and my tongue lightly brushed her teeth. I decided to go for it and pushed my tongue in further as her teeth parted.

I don't know when it was that I detected something wrong. As my tongue found hers, it seemed as if I was finding two tongues. In nanoseconds I decided I was paranoid and continued. We were crushed together but, as my tongue explored, the realisation started to dawn on me; she had two tongues!

Half thinking I must be imagining it, I explored with the tip of my tongue, and felt the split in hers that seemed to go halfway to the back. There were definitely two halves. I carefully pulled back, not wanting to alarm her but feeling stunned.

"Val, your tongue, it feels like there are two halves… look, I'm sorry, I'm getting a little confused now," I said, unsure of what I was feeling.

She was quiet for a moment, then said quietly, "I do, but I've learnt to keep them together when I talk." Her eyes were beginning to tear up.

Looking at her, I said quietly, "Val, for fuck's sake, what else is there that you haven't told me?"

She looked down, "I'm sorry, I should have mentioned it."

Seeing the expression on her face, I felt awful; I'd reacted on impulse and now felt a bit of a chump. After all, it was me that pushed her for a date in the first place.

"I also have webbed feet," she quietly said, looking at me expectantly.

Oh shit, of all the girls in Milford, I'd ended up with someone from the pages of Irish mythology! *Well*, I thought, *if likes attract, this could be one hell of a ride…*

"Blimey Val, you're certainly some catch. I think I've got one in a million," I grinned, trying like mad to play it down just in case she pulled a wand out and started throwing spells around. I gave her a hug and pulled her close, kissing her forehead. I had to resurrect this and fast. I'd been rude and had reacted on impulse, which was not surprising.

"Come on, let's go get a coffee at Dino's," I said.

She was quiet for a while as we walked slowly down the darkened street. Then her arm came around my waist and I relaxed. I had recovered the situation, but I was still reeling inside. Blimey, she had six fingers on each hand, went into trances, had a forked tongue, and webbed feet. Shit, it didn't get much better than that. I was now hoping she didn't have teeth in her 'nether regions' as well! If there was another surprise waiting to reveal itself, there was a good chance this was where it was going to be. I considered whether maybe I should quit while I was ahead.

Life in Milford Haven was settling down again. We got on with our work, and the warm summer days were truly upon us. At a local dance in the next village of Pill, one evening, I met Carol. She was tall with long hair and a strong character. I liked her immediately. We got on really well and, although she couldn't often get to Milford, I was happy to go and see her in Pill.

We would go out for walks or would stay in at her place where she lived with her mum and dad. They were very nice, and I got on well with them. This was a strange relationship and, as much as I wanted to see and do more with her, it wasn't to be. I even went as far as to buy her a 'friendship' gold ring – two hands holding a heart with a tiny ruby in the heart. I also got her a locket with my picture in. I think this was an effort on my part to try to consolidate our friendship in the hope it would lead to more. We both wanted to, but family constraints on her part were keeping it from happening. We knew it wasn't going to work, but neither of us said anything. For me, I was disappointed as I knew that with Carol I could have taken it a lot further into a serious relationship. Her strength of character was very appealing, and she looked good too, but it wasn't to be. I probably should have pushed it further but with other things going on back in Milford I was a bit too relaxed about it.

I also continued to go out with Val, and we formed a sort of clique with her friend Kathy who was dating one of the lads. I think we all knew it was a temporary thing, but it certainly lightened the days up. There were never any repercussions from the sugar in the petrol tank and, in fact, I never saw Joan again.

Meanwhile, Dip and I started using a pub halfway up the high street. The landlady was a bit of a nutter, but the place was small and friendly. One afternoon we were laughing and joking at the bar, and she spilt some beer over my arm. She then proceeded to lick it off. I was quite enjoying this, except that her twelve-year-old daughter happened to wander in. When she saw her mum doing this she was horrified and said she was going to tell her dad and stormed off. He worked away but came home at weekends. The landlady said that she was 'in for it' and, after a brief snogging session at the bar, much to Dip's amusement, she said that we'd better not come in there for a while until things cooled down a bit between her, her husband, and her daughter. That afternoon, Dip and I slept it off in the small local park, under a tree.

In Milford Haven on board with Dip Surgreve

The dockyard workers eventually came back to work and, at last, we could get things sorted. Once again, the ship hummed with activity and noise. One of the last things to mark our stay in Milford was a massive 'punch-up' in the little dockside restaurant called Dino's. We often went there in the evenings and the place was run by a Greek Cypriot.

One Thursday evening the trawlers had come in that day with a good catch. At the same time, a Turkish oil tanker was off-loading at the refinery. Dino's was quite full, and a crowd of us were in there with some of the girls, having drinks and a meal. It wasn't long before all hell broke loose, and glasses and fists were flying between the Turkish sailors and the mostly Irish trawler-men. We all dived under our table, grabbing our drinks as we went. The sides of the tablecloth mostly hid us, so we sat there and finished our pints. Peeping out, we grabbed some more beers from various tables which had been vacated and carried on drinking. It was a fitting end to our time there, as it would not be long before we returned to Pompey.

The work was going well, and the trauma of Dave Ridley's death had passed, although the memory of it hung around a few of us for a while. The general mood amongst all of us had been a little dented. But life goes on. We were all quite young and could absorb much of this type of thing. I had got better at roast dinners and elected to do the cooking most Sundays. Out of respect for the community and the locals we had made friends with, we still did the Sunday morning church thing and then, if I wasn't cooking, it was off to the pub to meet up with the girls. The weather had remained great, and I don't think that any of us were looking forward to returning to Portsmouth.

Our last week there, we were re-floated, and members of the crew started arriving back on board. We then took the ship out on trials around Milford Sound and apart from a few minor tweaks, the main engines were running well. It was good to have her back up and running. The last couple of days were very busy getting things ready to sail. The fuel tanks were filled up and supplies of food and stores loaded.

Saying goodbye to all the people we had befriended was difficult. I felt really sad for Val but knew we couldn't take things any further. Kathy, her friend, was quite distraught but we couldn't do anything. I contacted Carol, too, but she got upset about us going and I couldn't get to see her. She said she would see us sail the following day. I wanted to keep in touch with Val but knew that was a waste of time. So, we had a last run ashore the night before we left. All of us were off duty that night as the returning crew took those duties on. We met up in The Railway with most of our girls and had a good night, if tinged with the sadness of leaving. Carol didn't appear. We had been in Milford for eighteen weeks and I was returning to Portsmouth a slightly different person than when I had first arrived. I think most of us had changed a little.

The following morning, we were up early and the buzz of a fully operational Audemer was great. She hummed with activity. All her paintwork was newly done, and everything was polished and in place. I would be taking the second watch, so I would get to see Milford as we sailed away. The day was bright and clear with crisp, blue skies and a light breeze with a hint of autumn in the air.

The engines were running, the seamen lined the decks, the Ensign was flying stiff in the breeze as the bow and aft lines were cast off. Slow ahead meant we crept out of the dock. Most of the dock workers lined the dockside and I saw Val. She was crying along with some of the other girls, but she was smiling too. I knew I'd never see her again. We cleared the dockyard, and the skipper sounded the ship's siren several times. As we swung out into the bay, we could see loads of people standing on the headland waving. It looked like most of Milford Haven had turned out to see us off. I really hoped that up there somewhere, there was Carol. I stood at the rail and felt a huge lump in my throat. Val had run to the end of the dock jetty, and I moved to the stern to wave to her as the engines increased, the waters churned, and the bows swung to port, and we picked up speed. I waved one last time and went into the mess, made a mug of tea, and sat down with some of the others.

"Shit, Dave, that was hard," Alan said as he came in.

We both looked at each other and shook our heads. Another new chapter was beginning.

23

It didn't take long to get back into the routine of operational life on board. We had a few military exercises where we took troops and tanks to places in Europe but, mostly, we spent time in Portsmouth, either in the Gunwharf at HMS Vernon or out on the buoys.

At this time, the Vietnam war was getting underway and there was a lot of racial unrest in the States. The Beatles were pumping out top singles every week and, along with the Supremes, the 'hippy' generation was in full swing. In the services, this didn't really mean a lot and life seemed to carry on much as usual. When ashore, it was either the NAAFI Club in Portsmouth or some of the more popular pubs around the area. A few times we had some more serious drinking sessions where we ended up at the Still & West in Old Portsmouth. This would be followed by a curry and back to the ship.

On one of our jaunts ashore I met a very dark-skinned Ghanaian girl in a bar along the Southsea front. She turned out to be the daughter of the High Commissioner for Ghana. There was a meeting of Commonwealth ministers in London that particular week and her father had been staying with family in Portsmouth. We got chatting and she mentioned a party her friends were having in the town. I left our lot and went with her to a very smart residence in a side street in Old Portsmouth. It was drinks and canapes and what I thought to be some pretty silly people. I remember the music was good though. We arranged to meet up later in the week. She wanted to see *The Sound of Music*, which hadn't long been out and was currently showing in Portsmouth. This was my first date with a black girl. I was enjoying her company and, to me, she was stunning to look at.

Later that week, we met up for a coffee and then went to the cinema. Because she was so dark, I did get a few looks but, being brought up in a predominately black area like Brixton and Stockwell, it was water off a duck's back for me. However, it didn't help having a bunch of the lads from the ship, sitting nearby us murmuring things such as, "Dave, ask her to smile so you can see her," and hurling popcorn at us. She took it in good heart, but I decided it was a bit much, so we decided not to stay for the whole movie.

We went back to her place as her folks had gone up to London, and it was much more enjoyable. However, it was never to last and was doomed the moment I had mentioned it to the lads on board. I had enjoyed our brief time together and when I got back on board, I thanked the lads for their 'thoughtfulness' in providing popcorn during the film. We all had a laugh, but I wasn't that pleased about it. She eventually left for London, and I never saw her again.

There were always a few heavy drinking sessions, but I never drank so much that I couldn't stand up. We had to get back through the naval checkpoint at HMS Vernon and they would put you in the cell overnight if you were unable to walk. You would be in deep mire back on board ship the next day if this happened.

It was during this period that I became well acquainted with the Still & West at Southsea. This and the NAAFI Club became our main watering holes, and I loved all the places we frequented. Malcolm 'Tom' Thomas was a seaman aboard and I'd known him in Gosport barracks where we had first met. We became close friends and he joined

Audemer just after I had. It was usually the two of us that did the Portsmouth run. As we got to use the NAAFI on a regular basis, we were gradually building up a bunch of friends ashore. Most were Royal Navy lads and although we were the 'hated' Army, we were known as Sea Gypsies as we didn't conform to normal army dress which included haircuts and the fact that with permission from the ship's captain, we could grow beards.

The NAAFI was situated across from 'Vicki' barracks or HMS Victorious. This was the WRNS barracks, and they too frequented the NAAFI. Being mates with Tom had its advantages. He was tall, quite good looking, and with an outgoing personality. This was always going to be a bit of a magnet to the opposite sex, and he used it to full advantage. It never bothered me and, in fact, I was pleased as he knew all the chat up lines and I was more than happy to observe and learn. It didn't always work, though, and sometimes my quiet observing ways brought a better result. So, between the two of us it was quite a workable arrangement.

Whatever Royal Navy ships were in, the first port of call for the naval lads, when ashore, was the NAAFI Club. Our list of mates from the naval ships was growing and, before long, evening and weekend runs ashore became the NAAFI Club.

The ladies that ran the bar were mostly middle-aged women and I got to be known by one lady, named Olive, quite well. She would always put a bar bill on the 'slate' if I was a bit short; something they were not allowed to do.

It wasn't long before Tom and I hooked up with a group of Wrens. They were all DSAs (Dental Surgeons Assistants) and the nights in the club became a hoot. We would always meet up and start off there and then gradually drift off to one of our favourite pub haunts. The Dolphin in Old Portsmouth was one such place. This pub is reputed to be the oldest in Pompey, around three hundred years old. There were four DSAs – Sue, Ingy, Babs, and Sarah. Sue was by far the most stunning and I secretly adored her. Ingy was bubbly and innocent and very English whilst Babs was dusky, somewhat exotic, and mischievous. Sarah was very bright, a bit plain, but with a great sense of humour. Tom and I never disclosed who we liked and when we went out it was as a team, nothing serious, we just loved each other's company.

Sunday lunch times in the NAAFI were some of the best. If a naval ship had recently returned from overseas duties, having been away a long time, its return heralded some good times, especially the large aircraft carriers. Many of its crew would descend, en masse, at the club and you knew you were in for a good time.

One Sunday lunchtime, Ark Royal had returned from a Far East trip the previous Friday and the Club had come alive. It was magic and it wasn't long before the fun started. A couple of local girls, not WRNS, were drinking at a table in the main lounge bar. A few of the navy lads had tried to chat them up but none had been really successful. Tom, me, and the girls were sitting at another table having a laugh but watching these two girls. Now, if you were a local girl and you decided to go in the NAAFI for a drink, you obviously went in there because of the lads. For the past hour, these two had been turning away offers for drinks and chats with several matelots. The latter were now starting to get a bit wary of these two.

The fun started when about a dozen of the navy boys started to play 'shit the penny'. This entailed having two teams of around six per team. They'd stand in two lines and in front of them, about five metres away, was an empty pint glass on the floor. The two front lads from each team would then proceed to drop their uniform trousers to their knees, bend over and place a coin between their bum cheeks. They then had to hobble up to the empty glass, stand over it, drop the coin into the glass, pull their trousers up, run to the back of the line and the next man goes. If you missed the glass, you had to go back and start again. The winner being the team with all their coins in the glass.

It was great fun to watch, and we were all shouting and cheering the teams on.

There was a club doorman who was an elderly chap in a commissionaire's uniform, but he never tried to stop these games. This particular Sunday 'shit the penny' had been going full tilt and when it was over everyone was in high spirits. The two girls sitting at the table were not looking very amused. At this point they decided to go to the ladies' toilet, which was just across the main room in one corner.

I noticed that a group of the lads who had been playing the penny game were pointing at the girls as they both went to the loo. As soon as the door to the ladies' closed, about six of the lads quickly ran over to the toilet door and stood in a line in front of it. They had their uniforms on and their white naval flat hats under their arms and started to sing, in a chorus, some sea shanty song. As they sang, they swayed from side to side. This went on for a minute or two and then, still in single file, they trooped into the ladies' toilet.

There was a stunned silence in the room and then we all started cheering and laughing. After about five minutes, they still hadn't come out. Then the door opened and out marched all of them in a line, totally stripped with just their underpants on, their uniforms neatly folded over their left arms. Well, the place just erupted. Everyone cheered and clapped. It was pure theatre, absolute magic. The two girls still hadn't reappeared and, in the end, one of the bar girls went in to see if they were okay. When they did eventually emerge, we again cheered and clapped. They quickly left the place.

It was a typical Sunday lunchtime drink. The atmosphere was brilliant. The six of us trooped down to the Dolphin for some lunch. A truly great run ashore. These sorts of antics were not uncommon in the Club, especially when a naval ship returned from a long trip overseas. Being nicknamed as 'Sea Gypsies' really did work for us. That and the fact that we were always seen with the girls who were WRNS. So, although they all knew we were military and army, no one minded. However, if an army lad came in whilst in uniform from a regular unit, he would get a lot of black looks and rarely stayed beyond one pint. It really was a navy establishment and who was going to argue, surrounded as they were, by naval barracks?

When I had weekends off from duty, I would sometimes make the trip up to London to see Mum. As stoic as always, she was getting on with life. When I look back, it must have been a difficult time for her. One minute all your family is around you and the next they have uprooted and gone. I'm sure that she was very lonely at times and, apart from Mavis who would pop up from her flat below, from time to time, she must have felt the change coming. Dinah was busy working for Clare & Clare, a legal firm in the city and Jo was consolidating her new matrimonial life in Balham and working for the Toronto Dominion Bank, also in the City, as a teller. This was all soon to change as her and her new husband were making plans to go to Oz to live. Mum wasn't happy about the move, and I don't think Dinah was either. Delia was wrapped up in her life with Ken and pregnant with her first child. Living in Muswell Hill, London, she was soon to move to a new house in Bishop's Stortford, about an hour Northeast of London.

24

It wasn't long before we were heading towards winter. 1965 had been a busy year and I don't think I noticed the seasons changing much. Between work and life aboard, as well as the runs ashore in Pompey, the time flew by. As summer wound down, we were anchored, more often than not, on the buoys at the far end of the harbour. That meant having to get the military ferry out and back. I would quite often stay aboard and either catch up on my letter writing or learn to play Bridge with the duty watch guys. I was useless at it, as I invariably made a wrong call, but none of us took it seriously. It was good to play on long voyages. Being on watch when on the buoys, usually meant carrying out oil changes on the generators or top-end overhauls on some of the pumps. Mostly, it was quite boring, just my hourly checks through the night.

It was November and, on the home front, Jo was leaving for Oz with her new Australian husband and Dinah had decided to go with them. I think she was a bit concerned about Jo going so far and I knew Mum must have had some influence on that. Mum wrote to me and mentioned it in her letter. I felt a bit guilty for not keeping in touch with her more regularly and decided that I would see her more often. I don't remember the actual day the girls left for Oz, but I think I rang home to say my goodbyes. It had been agreed that Mavis would be popping in to see Mum on regular occasions and I felt a lot happier that she wasn't going to always be on her own living in that large four bedroomed flat. With the girls gone, I felt happier that Mavis was around, and I quite enjoyed seeing her as well when I visited.

If duties and runs ashore didn't intervene, I made a point to pop home. Mavis wasn't always there but on the occasions she was, the three of us had a laugh. It also meant that I was getting closer to Mavis and, to be honest, I probably aimed it to be that way. One such weekend, things suddenly took off and, that Friday night, we slept together. It was the start of a close relationship and I think Mum was pleased, although she never mentioned it other than telling me to 'be careful'. I was comfortable about it, and it seemed inevitable that it would happen.

So, on the weekends that I came home, we would go out places around London, see a movie, go to the park, or go for drinks. Quite often we would just spend time in bed. I was trying not to be too obvious about this as my main reason for coming home was to see Mum and to try to bring some normality to life for her.

About this time, I developed an increasing liking for cooking and, coupled with my attempts at it in Milford Haven, Mum showed me how make a proper roast dinner. I would leave on the Sunday evening to go back to the ship, so it was good to have the vessel around and that we weren't doing any long trips away from Pompey. Curries and such were not in vogue yet. At least, not on the scale that they are now. So, I learned about roasting lamb and beef. A good English Sunday roast was the real deal, and it would stand me in good stead in later years. Lamb and beef were popular meats and were nowhere near as expensive as in current times. Chicken was becoming more popular although still quite expensive. Fish was Mum's and my favourite, but it was usually cod, haddock, plaice, or coley.

Being ship's crew meant that you couldn't settle in to a comfortable 'home life'. It wasn't long, therefore, before we were underway again. This usually meant military exercises with various army and navy units. My comfortable time with Mavis was in serious conflict with my work and my shore-side life in Pompey. The two didn't mix at all and I was in a bit of a quandary where Mavis was concerned. Being with her wasn't a problem; we both enjoyed each other and being together. However, although I hadn't quite picked up on it at the time, I think our relationship meant a bit more to Mavis than it did to me.

This became apparent one weekend when I was up in London, and I wanted to pop over and see my Aunt Lil and Aunt Doll. They both lived near each other in Forest Gate and my main reason to see them was to see my cousin Pete whose mum was Aunt Lil. We had been good mates long before I joined up and he was thinking of going to the States with his brother Doug to set up a pipe-lagging business. It never occurred to me to ask Mave if she wanted to come, partly because I was only going to stay there a while and would be back home in a few hours. Pete, myself, Uncle Wal, and Uncle Ern went up the pub and when we got back to Aunt Lil's she invited me to stay for lunch, so I did.

By the time I arrived back in Stockwell it was late afternoon. Mavis went ballistic. I began to realise then that she was taking our relationship a lot more seriously than I was. To be honest, it frightened me, and I knew Mave deserved better than that. I felt terrible and, although we made up before I went back to my ship, I decided that I had better cool things off. I'm sure Mum must have realised my dilemma as she had previously mentioned about me making sure I knew what I was doing. I said I did but in actual fact, I don't think I had at all. I was sort of leading two lives. My infrequent one at home in London and my more time-consuming military one aboard ship and in Portsmouth.

That winter was to be my first trip to Scotland and our excursions to deliver mail and supplies to the Outer Hebrides. The Orkneys and Shetland Isles had issues getting mail in the bad weather. This was normally delivered by local ferries but when the weather conditions became too difficult, as it often did in winter, we were on hand to deliver supplies and mail. Our main reason, however, was to supply the early warning missile bases up in these northernmost of locations. The Cold War was far from over and with the large Russian 'Bears' making incursion flights in UK airspace, the missile bases were quite often, facing alerts.

Our home base in Scotland was Helensburgh, which took us up the Firth of Clyde not that far from the naval submarine base at Faslane. We would take on supplies, provisions, necessary cargo, and mail, and then move up to Faslane to load up more 'military' supplies and equipment.

This was to be my first trip north from Pompey and it came at a good time because of the Mavis issue at home. I was looking forward to this trip and, as expected, it was fascinating. The nearer we got to the Highlands and Islands, the more rugged and riveting became the scenery. On the way up, the weather was getting rougher by the hour. We pulled into Douglas, in the Isle of Man, and once we had rounded the spur of land, the sea calmed, and we could tie up in Douglas harbour.

We had pulled in to seek shelter as storms were making it very difficult and hazardous to continue. The high winds, dark skies, and the stark outline of the castle cast a gloomy spell over the place.

I remember standing on the aft deck as the winds clashed the masts of yachts and boats rigging in the marina, the flag upon the castle battlement snapping like a whip being cracked. In the two days we were sheltering there, everything on board was subdued and melancholy.

It was not uncommon to seek shelter during some of these winter storms as they could be quite fearsome when at sea, especially on a flat-bottomed LCT.

Underway to the Scottish Isles

We continued north a few days later, the sea gradually calmed, and we were all looking forward to seeing Ailsa Craig as we sailed past. We came upon it a little after dawn and it was quite a sight to observe. Sea mist had surrounded part of it and the cries of the gulls seemed to echo across the water. There were literally thousands of them, most nesting in a blur of white and grey, like a blanket of snow across her top. We sailed on, passing Arran on our left and being a lot more sheltered from the North Atlantic weather. It wasn't too long a hop from there up the Firth of Clyde, round Gourock Head, and across the Clyde to Helensburgh. A few of the lads had been here before but it was all new territory to me.

As news spread of a military ship alongside at Helensburgh pier, a number of spectators soon arrived. One of the older lads aboard had been here a few times.

"Here come the Dumbarton Debs," he said, pointing to a group of girls that came wandering down the jetty. From a distance they didn't look too bad but as they got closer, they were certainly on the 'rough side'. They started waving and yelling various things to the seamen tying up the spring lines forward. I was looking down from the wheelhouse as I was still on watch. Everyone ignored them. When I saw some of the lads later in the mess, I asked what the girls were saying.

"Did you see what she was doing with her hands?"

"No, although I saw one of them waving and shouting something," I said.

JC looked at me and laughed, "She said, 'I ken what you mean but I'm too wee!'"

I laughed at his attempt at a Glaswegian accent.

One of the lads said, "That's typical Dumbarton Debs speak. Should be a good run ashore tonight."

Unfortunately (or fortunately), I was on duty watch that first night in and never did see 'the girls' but the pub runs were interesting, if a bit on the rough side. A couple of us found a hotel bar along the main road to Rhu and frequented that when off duty.

The next day we moved up to Rhu and took on fuel there. Then on to Garelochhead to take on equipment for the missile bases. The thing that struck me most about the place was that as we sailed up this 'dead end' I realised that here was where the Royal Navy brought all their decommissioned ships to be broken up. It was, for me, a truly sad place to see; this was where the breakers yard was. There were destroyers, frigates, cruisers and even an aircraft carrier there. It was sad to see these leviathans just sitting there, looking empty and desolate. The grey, windy weather didn't help but I could almost hear the echoes and shouts of crews long past. It was one of the saddest places I had seen to date, and I just stood on our deck watching as we sailed quietly past.

I think there were a few of us that felt the sadness on that bleak day. Was this fate to happen to Audemer one day, I wondered?

Years later I found out another fate awaited her which, in many ways, was worse. When I went into the mess, many of the lads were chatting about the ships. Someone said that the razor blade company, Gillette, had bought some of them to make razor blades! Quite often, a few were 'mothballed' and later sold to foreign navies. To me, these ships were 'alive'; they had characters and each one was different. Maybe a somewhat romanticised view of these vessels but, to this day, I still feel that sadness, especially for my own ships that, for a time, were our homes and kept us safe.

Audemer coming alongside at Helensburgh

Audemer moored at the Helensburgh jetty

25

Those winter weeks in the Northern Isles and waters were all new to me. We beached on Benbecula and waited as the tide receded to the distant horizon. The bow doors were opened, and the ramp lowered. Joe Buckley, the bosun, took a spade in one hand and a bucket in the other and walked down the ramp and on to the flat sands. A short way from the hull, he started digging in the sand. He was after cockles, a lot of them. We suddenly caught on and those of us not on duty were soon doing the same. That evening we had a feast of them, liberally sprinkled with vinegar and black pepper.

The mail and equipment were off-loaded, and we moved on to St. Kildare. This was the furthest of these isles and an experience. We tied up alongside a wooden jetty for the night and, with the exception of the duty watch, were invited ashore to a ceilidh (pronounced 'cailee') – a Highland dance party put on by the local crofter community. The girls weren't exactly stunning, but the music was great. Fast and flowing with accordions supplying the lively, foot tapping rhythms. I'd never been one much for accordion music, but this certainly got me clapping and foot stomping along. I wasn't confident enough to join in the dancing but decided to prop the makeshift bar up with some of the lads and drink the strong local ale. There were other military there, from the early-warning stations, some officers, and NCOs but everyone mixed in. How the locals lived in these bleak, windswept places, I couldn't imagine but they were certainly a tough lot – even the girls we saw.

We visited most of the larger isles, sometimes just to carry out mail runs. Skye was probably the best. There was a medical clinic/hospital there and nearby, set back in the side of a hill, was a nurses' home. Chatting these girls up in the local pub was entertaining. Depending on the weather conditions, we could be alongside these islands for a while.

We always returned to Helensburgh to load up again before doing the island runs. The weather sculptured these places, making them dramatic to the eye and at times, dangerous to navigate. Mostly, we stayed aboard and carried out routine maintenance and when not on duty, played bridge or caught up on letter writing. My bridge playing hadn't significantly improved, and I remained a 'last resort' to partner. By the time it came to leave we were all looking forward to getting back down south to our regular haunts

We were now into '66 and ship-side life in Portsmouth continued. The fashions in civilian life were changing rapidly. London was the swinging place to be and flower power continued to make an appearance. I was no fan of it, although I loved some of the music. The Beatles and The Rolling Stones were getting into full swing and men's hair fashion was long and free flowing. Being in the military showed as we all had short hair, but it didn't deter us; we just stuck to our familiar haunts and Pompey was well used to that. At this time, I became a fan of rock bands like Hendrix, Pink Floyd, The Cream, and John Mayall's Blues Breakers. Their music burst on to the scene, but it was still early days for it to really take off. At the same time, Vietnam was hotting up and the Americans were having race problems.

Despite all this, life aboard Audemer continued, and I was now fully integrated into the crew and quite at home. Military exercises kept us pretty busy, and I managed to get some time ashore, at certain places, to continue practicing and honing my shooting skills on odd weeks here and there. I was getting skilled at it but never wanted to shoot competitively. Troubles in the Middle East were escalating, and the UN and British Military were trying to keep abreast of it all. It never made the media as much as it does these days, but things were brewing in Saudi and the Yemen. Because I was enjoying life aboard ship and, in particular, in Pompey, thoughts of going overseas were all but forgotten.

Meanwhile, military exercises continued. One such week, we had been operating in the Irish Sea and were on our way back to Portsmouth after manoeuvres. It was early March and the weather had turned atrocious. Force eight and nine gales had been blowing around the western coasts and Atlantic for days and the sea conditions, especially for a flat-bottomed Landing Craft, were grim. Nobody said much to anyone during these conditions. We just crawled out of our bunks, carried out our duty watches, tried to eat something and back to the bunk in the hope of snatching a few hours' sleep, if possible.

I was on the four to eight watch as we were approaching Portland Bill in the early hours of the morning. I couldn't eat anything and just managed to drink a hot coffee. I'd gone down to the engine room at 04:00 a.m., we'd had the watch hand-over, and I was trying to keep warm between the main engines, cleaning oil spills and checking temperatures. The waves were enormous, and they were coming at us, bow on. Twenty- and thirty-foot waves that lifted the propellers out of the water at each peak making the engines race as the ship dived down the trough only to face the next one.

I was not prone to sea sickness, but this took the biscuit. I was feeling grim. I went to the port side generator room to do my hourly checks and stuck my head out of the deck hatch at the top of a four-rung ladder to get some fresh air. All was as black as pitch and the wind was blowing fiercely. As I clung on, half out of the hatch, I could see the periodic flashing light of the Portland Bill lighthouse almost directly on our beam. The engines were going flat out and had been for some hours. It was apparently too dangerous to turn in and seek shelter, so we just kept on, towards Portsmouth. I returned to the engine room and continued my watch. Brummy saw my face and shouted in my ear, "You alright mate?"

I looked at him and shrugged, hating to admit that I felt like shit.

"Shouldn't have had that greasy bacon sandwich earlier," he laughed.

"Fuck off, Lawrence," I shouted, clinging to a hot steel railing as we hit another wave.

By 05:30 a.m. I was useless. I'd thrown up hot air and bile and just wanted to curl up on the engine room deck plates and die. In the end, Brum called the chief and mentioned my state. I was relieved from watch duties in the hope that I would be okay for the afternoon one at 04:00 p.m.

I crawled my way up the engine room ladder, timing my climb up to coincide with the excessive rolling of the ship. By the time I got up on deck, I made my way to the port side hatch, ready to throw up again. As I looked up, I could see that we were still in the same place. We hadn't moved one jot. Portland Bill lighthouse was still off the port beam – in the same place I'd last looked two hours previously. I stumbled my way down to our bunks and, as I groped my way along the space between the bunks, I came to my middle one and stared at it in horror. The bunk above, which hadn't been occupied at the time, had been shaken out of its brackets by the constant shuddering and rolling of the ship and the metal bolt that kept it in place had jumped out of its housing and the whole weight of one side had collapsed down onto my pillow. The bolt had gone right through the pillow and hit the wooden slat beneath. If I had been in the bed, it would have quite likely killed me. A seaman coming on watch stood with me looking at it.

"Fuck me Dave, you were bloody lucky," he said as we both stared at the bunks. He helped me get it back in position.

"Well, there is no way I'm getting into that in this fucking weather," I said.

I followed him back up the accommodation ladder and went into the mess, my sea sickness gone or forgotten, and hunger now gnawing at my sore stomach. Daylight emerged as a gloomy, wind-screeching grey, and I made my way to the galley and got the cook to make me a breakfast.

"You alright mate?" he asked. "You're looking a bit grey?"

I nodded and just said I needed some breakfast. He had plenty as many were not eating. The shock had sorted me out, that and a decent breakfast and loads of coffee.

It wasn't until around 10:00 a.m. that the storm eased, and we started to make headway to Portsmouth. We had used up excessive amounts of fuel and had to pull in on the way and take on more. Many of the crew had been sick that trip but the collapsing bunk stayed in my mind for a long while. It was extremely fortunate that I wasn't in mine when it went.

Later that week, once back on the buoys, we wired up all the bolt fittings on the bunks to prevent it happening again. If you could make it on an LCT in bad weather you could probably sail on anything, as I was to find out, many years later, in something that would make this a mere picnic.

26

We continued to do small trips in local waters but most of the time we were tied up to the buoys out in the harbour. I was offered an NCOs course to go on in Aldershot but turned it down. I'd had enough bullshit at Chepstow, and it was still a little fresh in my mind. The skipper was curious why I didn't want it, so I told him. He understood my reasoning.

January and February were always 'grey' months to me. Back from Christmas leave and straight into the routine of work and cold, wet, dismal days. Runs ashore had been fairly quiet and the usual crowd were either still on leave or busy doing other things. Portsmouth had a Mecca Dance Hall. It was not a place I frequented, although quite a few did, mostly matelots. It was rumoured that once the navy ships were away on duty, some of the wives of the married lads would go there to see what they could pick up. I didn't know how accurate that rumour was but one evening a couple of us decided to find out. It was a Friday night, but the place wasn't packed. They sometimes had a band playing but this particular time it was a disc jockey playing records.

The bar was pretty busy at the back of the dance floor and both of us made for it and observed the 'talent' as we stood at the bar drinking. There were quite a few couples dancing and the tables around the dance floor were starting to fill up. Clocking the talent was a great sport but you weren't going to get anywhere just watching. We had both noticed two girls dancing with each other and I nudged my mate. "What do you think?"

He watched for a moment then agreed it was worth a try. We finished our beers and wandered across the floor. Keep in mind that we had spent a good ten minutes debating and plucking up the courage to approach these two. They didn't look like tarts or dressed in a flashy way. They were younger than many of the women there, probably around eighteen years old. We agreed which ones we were going for and sauntered over as a particularly good record for dancing came on.

"Hi," I said. "Would you like to dance?"

The girl I'd chosen looked up scathingly. "Fuck off, arsehole."

I stood there, shocked. I certainly wasn't expecting that. "Oh, nice one," I said, now feeling pretty stupid. I looked at Andy, who shrugged, and we both wandered back to the bar rather sheepishly. We ordered two more beers and sat at the bar deciding whether or not to make this the last one and go back to the NAAFI Club.

As we were sitting there, I noticed three middle-aged women sitting together at one of the tables around the dance floor. One of them kept looking over at us. I nudged Andy and mentioned it. He wasn't too impressed.

"She's about your mum's age, isn't she?"

"You reckon? She's got a nice face and, from where I'm sitting, the rest looks pretty good too."

"Ok mate, she's all yours. I'll just watch as you crash and burn," he said laughing.

I can't remember what music was playing but I wandered over, butterflies taking root and feeling nowhere near as confident as I may have looked. I nodded, smiled, and asked her for a dance. She agreed. Not expecting such a positive response, I must have looked surprised. She was definitely older than I was; I'd have said somewhere in her thirties. She had a great figure and danced well. There was a spell of slow dances and we chatted. She smelled good up close – it wasn't cheap perfume. I noticed she didn't have a wedding band on but that didn't mean anything. I assumed she was married.

We continued dancing. During the third dance, Andy came over with one of the other women that had been with her. The evening wore on and we'd danced most of the time. Andy disappeared with the other woman and, shortly after, we decided to leave as well. She went and got her coat and we both left. She said she didn't live too far away and had her car in the back car park. It was a red MG; I was well impressed.

The initial outcome of this was that once back at her place, I kind of recognised the area. This was definitely 'married quarters' but it was for officers. I didn't remark on it but had a bit of a funny feeling.

It wasn't long before we made our way into her bedroom. I definitely wasn't going to tell her I was in the services, so I avoided the issue completely. However, I had a feeling that she already knew. Much later, I told her I had to leave. We got out of bed, and I started to get dressed. She went out of the room to the bathroom, and it was then that I noticed two picture frames, face down on the dressing table. I picked one up and turned it over. I was shocked – it was Captain M, one of our skippers on the LCTs. I quickly thought of which ship he was on. I was sure it was one of our T's, which was currently up north on the Scotland run. She had taken over from us. That would make sense; his wife could be certain he wouldn't turn up at the door. I heard the toilet flush and quickly put the photo back as I had found it.

Mrs M offered to drop me home, but I insisted on getting a cab and told her it was no trouble. She went back to bed. We kissed goodbye and arranged to meet again. She gave me her phone number. When I got in the cab, I felt sick. Jesus, I really had to be careful here. But I liked her, she was really nice, and I certainly didn't feel sorry for Captain M. I knew I couldn't tell anyone of what I had found out, certainly not Andy. I only hoped that he hadn't met with too much success with the woman he went off with. As it turned out, they went for a drink in a pub and parted ways.

Spring came and, one morning, we were tied up at Gunwharf and I had a day off. I had arranged to meet her early in the morning. The weather was good and sunny when our sergeant engineer Des Stokes came into the forward mess.

"Dave, can I see you for a moment?"

I was ready to go ashore and looked up as he held the mess door open for me.

"You have a visitor, mate, down on the jetty." He lowered his voice. For a moment I went cold and almost felt the need to run to the 'heads'. My career flashed before my eyes as it crashed and burned, and I quickly shoved my hands in my pockets to hide the tremor. "I know her, Dave, and you are going to get into trouble with that one mate."

"For fuck's sake, Des, don't tell anyone will you? It's only a brief fling. I never even told her I was in the military. I don't know how she found out I was here aboard Audemer."

He looked at me and grinned. "I live a few doors away from her. Those flats are for NCOs and officers."

Oh shit, I hadn't a clue that non-coms were living there as well.

"Des, please don't…"

He held his hand up. "Don't worry, none of my business, but I suggest that you get rid of that one, sharpish!"

As softly and quietly as he said it, I recognised an order if ever there was one.

When I went out on deck and looked over the side, there she was, bold as brass, top down, gleaming red MG, headscarf and sunglasses, grinning. I waved and quickly went down the gangway. Word must have spread quickly and soon some of the lads started appearing on deck, grinning, and giving me the thumbs up. She realised I was uncomfortable, and we took off along the jetty. Once we'd cleared HMS Vernon, I asked her why she came to the Gunwharf. She just laughed and said she'd known I was on the LCTs. I had a feeling I'd been played; a pawn in some game she was playing. I wasn't too happy about that but thought I'd see how it went. In the end, I decided it was too risky and we amicably parted ways. I never went to the Mecca Dance Hall again.

There was, however, a possible outcome to this dangerous liaison as it was shortly after this that the overseas draftings came up and *yours truly* was on the list. My short relationship with Mrs M came back to haunt me at a later date too – if it hadn't done so already.

Work continued and, just as I was enjoying the early spring weather, the overseas postings came up on the notice board. This was an annual occurrence but was mostly for other units. I had just come up from the engine room and was sitting in the mess. JC came in grinning.

"Dave, looks like you'll be joining me in Aden with Brum."

I looked nonplussed. "What? You're kidding, right?"

"See for yourself," he said, pointing over his shoulder to the mess door.

I stood up, trying to ignore the sudden gut clenching butterflies in my stomach.

Looking at the notice board, there it was. I was to join the L4002, HMAV Agheila in Aden – three of us from this ship and some others from other ships in the fleet. It amounted to a crew change out there, where Agheila had been for over a year.

The skipper sent for us and individually wished us luck. I was excited and sad at the same time. I explained that I required a new passport and he said that it was being sorted out in London and I could collect it while on leave.

Aden was an 'active service' posting. This meant it was a war zone. The British Forces had been fighting a war there against terrorists from the Yemen and it wasn't going well. I knew we would be aboard ship, though, so didn't see as how it would affect me much.

My departure date was to be 15th April. In the first week of April, I was given leave, during which time I would get my passport sorted. The Army had filled in the necessary forms, and I had signed them aboard ship. These were then sent off and I was to pick the new one up in London on 14th April.

Mum was still in the flat in Stockwell and Mave was there occasionally. She was working in Marks & Spencer in Oxford Street and now had a boyfriend, of sorts, who was a telecoms engineer. Things were good for her and between us; we were still good friends.

Mum never said much about my posting to Aden but may have asked my uncle Doug about the place as he was staying with us for a while. He was the manager of the Dominion cinema in Tottenham Court Road and lived in Brighton, but sometimes – if some premier was on – he would stay with us. Every once in a while, Hayden dropped around too, so she had company. When I rang and told her, she was pleased for me, but I knew that she hated it really.

I'd said my goodbyes back on Audemer and many of the guys were envious. JC and Brummy were joining me, and I was quite pleased about that. But I was sad to leave Audemer.

The day I left her, we were tied up alongside the Gunwharf. I walked around the ship on my own, looking at places that had meant 'home' to me. I felt quite sad about that but hoped I'd be back on her again one day.

As I walked away from her with my kit, I stopped and looked back, remembering Milford Haven, and Val, and Dave Ridley, and the times I'd had aboard her. A lump formed in my throat. She was a very special ship to me; my first and, probably, the best. A ship has a way of doing that to you and leaving a ship you've served on for a while is always hard.

It was arranged that we report to Brize Norton early Friday morning on 15th April. I'd said my goodbyes to Mum and to Hayden, who happened to be there. Leaving the flat in Stockwell and Mum was also quite hard for me. I didn't know it at the time but that would be my last sight of 35 Enfield House as home. While I was in Aden, Mum would move to Bishops Stortford on Thursday 5th May 1966.

At Brize Norton it was a matter of checking in, handing over my case, and waiting around to board. JC and Brummy were there as well as a few faces I recognised from some of our other ships. The aircraft was a VC10 in RAF Service. We were all in 'civvies' which was the norm for these flights. Now this was for real, and I had to admit to a few nerves.

Two things struck me about flying in the VC10. One was that the seats faced to the rear, rather than as normal. I guessed that as it was an RAF aircraft, it was felt to be safer this way. The other thing was the flight attendants. These were RAF staff, but they were great, just as on civil airlines. One girl in particular, I got on well with. She chatted about Aden and told me what she knew of it. Following this particular flight, she was having a twenty-four-hour turnaround and would be staying at the base at Khormaksar. She gave me the name of an hotel in town and a contact number. If I was allowed out, we could meet up.

On arrival, we were all disembarked to a convoy of armed vehicles. They had anti-grenade cages on most of them and each one had an armed escort, sitting in the back with us. This was my first Middle East visit, and it was extremely hot. It was a blanket of very dry heat, which suited me well, but many of the guys were grumbling already.

We were taken to a barracks that was well guarded and laid out in rows. The camp was called Normandy Lines and it was to be home for a few weeks until LCT Agheila was ready as she was undergoing a minor refit.

Being issued with our new uniforms was the next stage. This was the tropical kit for this region, which consisted of khaki shorts as well as long trousers and lightweight shirts with our Maritime Regiment shoulder flashes. None of us liked it at the camp and were keen to get to the ship. Meanwhile it was barrack duties and all the usual army bullshit that entailed.

I don't remember a great deal about my time at Normandy. However, a few things do stick in my mind. One of them was the laundry. This was where the word 'dhobi' really came into play. It was rotated amongst us to collect the dirty uniforms, take them to the laundry area, and collect the clean ones. The laundry itself was a compound within the camp to the rear. It was a wire, fenced in compound as the Arabs that did the laundry were all local and the Army, obviously, wasn't taking any chances.

On my first trip to take the dhobi in, I managed to get a good look at how it works. I also had to collect the clean uniforms and it was when doing this that I saw how they ironed and starched the uniforms. No electric steam irons here. These were heavy irons where the top hinged to one side of the sole plate. Beside the lad doing the ironing was a brazier with glowing, hot coals in it. Using tongs, he would pick up a number of the glowing coals and place them inside the hinged open iron, on the sole plate, then close the top. As the iron was already hot, he could continue ironing almost immediately. The 'steam' was provided by a jug containing a mixture of water and starch. He would take a mouthful of this and then blow it onto the item he was ironing. Once in full flow, this guy was good. The creases in the jacket sleeves, trousers and shorts you could cut your finger on, and they stayed in for most of the day. There were dozens of these guys doing the laundry and ironing and in the darkness of the night it looked like a scene from Dante's *Inferno* with all the braziers full of the hot coals.

From time to time, while living on the base, we were all expected to carry out patrol duties. This entailed being issued with Sterling SMGs and a spare magazine. We were then allocated to either Land Rovers or three-tonners. These had a wire mesh grill over the back which were intended to be anti-grenade cages. We would then sit in the back and patrol the streets. We started off just outside the RAF base at Khormaksar and then made our way to Steamer Point via Maala Strait. Maala Strait had another name that the squaddies knew it by, which was why I was just that little bit nervous. It was known as 'Murder Mile'!

Maala Straight - 'Murder Mile'

Along both sides of the street were tall, multi-storey blocks of flats. These were the married accommodation blocks for the military. All of the married pads lived here. It was along this street that more servicemen, including families, had been killed. It was patrolled 24/7 and all service units had to take a turn at being on patrol.

Aden was my first combat location and the thrill of being here was constant. It was also one of the best duty-free ports in the world. Being at Normandy Lines was not the best but they had a reasonable NAAFI club on the camp and the food was just about edible.

Forces housing blocks along Maala Straight

The heat and dust got to everyone. I got sunburnt playing football on a square of dust in shorts and t-shirt and got into trouble for it. Discipline was tight and before long I was doing extra duties for answering back. This was infantry life and those of us from the LCTs weren't infantry.

There was a firing range at the back, and I did manage to get plenty of practise in. I tried to get to see the stewardess at RAF Khormaksar, but she had gone back to the UK. So, we sweated, cursed, and slept restlessly, waiting to get to the ship.

Eventually, our time came to board Agheila, and we couldn't wait to get away from the Army life that was Normandy Lines.

Agheila was very similar to Audemer back home, only she didn't have the extra deck. Captain Venmore was our skipper, and he didn't have a very good reputation amongst the crews. But we had a good No.1 (he was a First Lieutenant and spent a lot of time amongst the crew).

It was good to get back on board ships again and our main docking location and base was HMS Sheba. This naval base had a secure jetty, and it was here where we would be tied up, for the most part, when we were in Aden. As we walked down the jetty, to the right, about six-hundred metres offshore, was a sewer outlet from the city. If the breeze was blowing our way, the smell literally took our breath away. It was something I never quite got used to, but it became 'the smell of Aden' for me.

Alongside at HMS Sheba

When I was first sent to Aden, ocean-going liners were still stopping there for the duty-free. Quite often, these passenger ships were en route to Oz, many with families aboard that were emigrating there. My sisters, Dinah and Jo had come this route just a few months earlier on their way to Australia. Passengers were allowed ashore to visit the port shops to get their duty-free but had to be escorted by British soldiers. The main two regiments in place at the time were the Argyll & Sutherland Highlanders and the Cameronians. Often, on runs ashore, we met these passengers and enjoyed chatting up the girls although the parents were never very far away.

Getting used to Agheila was not difficult as the majority of LCTs all had the same layout internally. The main difference was the heat in the engine and generator rooms where the average temperature was around 140°f. It was sweltering down there and any metal surface we touched was red hot. We did have air-conditioning units in the mess deck and down in the sleeping accommodation. These required constant maintenance as they were running twenty-four hours continuously.

There was always a lot to do to keep the ship running, so we were constantly busy. Every day there were incident reports of army incursions into the Radfan mountains against Yemeni rebel outposts and quite often the retaliation was in Aden itself. The commander of the

A&S at the time was known as 'Mad Mitch' and he was getting a lot of news coverage back in the UK. On my shopping forays, I purchased a YashicaFlex 2½ x 2½ format camera for what was then fourteen pounds. This would equate to around one hundred and eighty-three pounds in today's money. So, this was quite an outlay for me at the time, but I was into photography, and this was my opportunity to get something a bit more serious. My other purchase was a Seiko Chronograph watch which I still use, on occasion, these days.

There was a NAAFI Club at Steamer Point. When off duty, it was a good place for a beer and a meal in the evenings. At weekends it was the favourite haunt of married service personnel and their families as it fronted onto a guarded and fenced in beach. Once or twice, we'd go there for a swim and some different food and beer. It was during one of these visits, whilst playing handball with a couple of our lads on the beach, that I heard someone calling my name. When I looked up, it was Wes Modlin, one of the guys from my group at Chepstow and 61C. We were sworn enemies when I was there but at this meeting he was as friendly as could be. I wasn't particularly impressed but did say hello and told him what I was doing when he asked. He seemed really pleased to see me, which kind of threw me a bit. That was the one and only time I ever met anyone from 61C. To this day, I never did again.

Also, on that particular day at the beach, while swimming, I lost a gold crucifix necklace that Mavis had given me. I was not best pleased but never did tell her. Meanwhile, I was beginning to settle into Aden and getting used to the heat, the smells, and the ship.

27

Mail was always welcome, and I started to get regular letters from Mum, Di, and Jo. The girls seemed to be settling into life in Oz. Jo was looking forward to moving into her new home with 'Digger' and Di was moving into her small, rented apartment. Both had been having driving lessons and were now able to get around independently. Di had a light blue Volkswagen Beetle and was well pleased with it. They were both still quite homesick but were getting on with life. Jo worked for a bank and Di worked for the Prudential, both in Melbourne.

It was always nice to get mail. Late mornings, if we were in port, was mail-call time. Jo was intent on finding me penfriends from amongst the girls she worked with, and I also received mail from Dip Surgreve, Les Topping, and girls that I knew from home. So, I spent much of my off-duty time, writing. Mum wrote every week; it was always good to hear from her.

One lad we had on board used to write to his girlfriend every day, often to the accompaniment of a Jim Reeves album played on a small turntable we had in the mess. It used to drive us all nuts. Apparently, it inspired his love letter writing and, even to this day, I cannot hear a Jim Reeves song without thinking of that lad writing his letters. Mind you, it must be years since I last heard one. But I loved to write and would tell of incidents from life in Aden and on board which always brought a good response.

Apart from drinking in the NAAFI club, there were a few bars in town. The town itself consisted of lots of little alleyways with the shops selling cameras and watches mostly on the front streets. But up the little side streets you could find hairdressers, haberdasheries, grocers, bakeries, leather wear and hardware stores. All seemed to be doing a thriving business, especially as the married families were living close by. All of these areas were heavily patrolled by whatever regiment was in town.

The first time I went browsing, I was nervous but after a while I soon got used to it. We rarely went ashore alone. Mostly it was in groups of three or four. One of the lads I met on Agheila was Stuart. We became good mates, and it was usually him I went ashore with.

Goats wandered around everywhere, quite often eating cardboard boxes in the gutters but not bothering anyone.

Tom had also joined the Agheila crew, so we teamed up. Many of the local Arabs were friendly and I don't ever remember feeling threatened. Quite often, it was not unusual to see teenage Arab lads walking along holding hands. It was the first time I had openly encountered gay couples, although the word 'gay' was not used in those days. To us, they were 'queers', which now seems an awful thing to say.

There were not many bars in Aden but there was one on the front that we would frequent. Dark rum and coke was the popular drink then and, of course, beer. The beer was Amstel, and this was the first time that I had come across 'stubbies', the small bottles that Amstel was sold in. The bar we used had an upstairs balcony that was open but had wire anti-grenade netting over the exposed sections. This was our favourite spot as it overlooked the main street and the harbour. It was in the shade so a little relief from the 33°C average temperatures. Sitting there watching the world go by was our favourite pastime. Quite often there would be foreign ships in port, and these were often American cargo vessels or Dutch tankers. Some of the crews used this bar as a watering hole and the place was never empty. However, we always got our regular spot upstairs on the balcony.

One visit to this bar turned out to be our last, although we didn't know it at the time. The three of us strolled into the gloomy interior after having wandered around the shops. As we came into the bar downstairs, we noticed there were two distinct groups of drinkers. One group of guys were sitting at the tables and the other group were at the bar, on stools.

We went up to the bar and ordered our drinks. While we were chatting amongst ourselves, the guys at the tables started arguing with those at the bar. They were Americans, all from the same ship, it seemed, a freighter. The comments shouted across the room were starting to get abusive and slowly became more aggressive. Tom said that we should take ourselves off upstairs to the balcony, but the barman said that it was being repainted at the moment and we'd have to stay in this main bar. It wasn't long before one of the guys sitting at a table threw an empty beer bottle at one of the Americans at the bar. Then all hell broke loose.

The bartender quickly told us to come with him and we grabbed our drinks as he took us to a back room with a curtain over the entrance. There was a small round table in there and some chairs. The barman started apologising to us but said we should stay there. We had no intention of going back into the bar. It started to get really out of hand, and we could hear tables and chairs being thrown around, glass breaking, shouts, and screaming. We carried on drinking and thought it was hilarious.

I guess the barman must have called the police, and army patrols outside must have heard the commotion and called the military police too. From what we learned later, knives had come out and some of the guys had been stabbed.

It was a good ten minutes before the MPs arrived and waded in. An MP sergeant stuck his head around the curtain, saw us three sitting there drinking and came in. He checked our ID, and we informed him we were nothing to do with what was happening in the bar, which the barman confirmed. We were told to stay where we were until it was clear to come out. Eventually, amidst the groans, screaming, and distant sounds of sirens, the MP came back in and said it was okay for us to leave. It was a scene of carnage in the main bar room. There were two guys lying on the floor being attended to by medics and several more being handcuffed by the MPs. The bar was completely wrecked. We made our way past the bodies and broken bits of furniture and glass to the front entrance.

As we went out of the main door to go down the steps to the street there was a large crowd of people being held back by MPs and local police, and a press reporter complete with camera. As I stood on the top step, I adjusted my shirt sleeves and dusted my arms down just as the photographer took the picture. We all three did the same, adjusted our uniform berets, and an MP came over and asked us if we wanted a lift back to base. They agreed to drop us off at the gates to HMS Sheba. While he went to get the Land Rover, we stood looking at the crowds of people watching. They were watching the walking wounded and a couple of others being helped out on stretchers to a waiting military ambulance from the military hospital. People were staring at us; there was not a mark on any of us.

The next day, there were our pictures in the local newspaper, brushing ourselves down, grinning. The headline was, *'American sailors in brawl at local bar, many injured'*. We were heroes of the day on board. I only wish I had taken a cutting of that newspaper. The civilian bars were off limits to most military personnel after that for a long time.

High Street near the infamous bar

Life on board Agheila was getting back to the routines I was familiar with on Audemer. Only here it was the heat that slowed things down. As I mentioned previously, quite often, the temperatures in the engine room were around 140°F and anything metal was very hot. We had blowers running but they weren't near effective enough. That meant that wearing overalls was out. It was shorts and t-shirt and not always the t-shirt either.

When we were tied up at HMS Sheba, we had to get to the jetty via a naval guard room. Once past this was the long pier where we tied up at the end. Immediately outside the base was a clear, sandy bit of waste ground where various Arab hawkers would sell things. These traders had been there for many years and must have done a reasonable business as the base was a busy place. There were fruit and veg sellers and a stall selling fresh and roasted nuts. The naval boys didn't move them on as they were quite useful and were a regular feature. Our chef often bought these enormous watermelons from them – these were long, sausage-like in size rather than the round ones you get here in the UK with a light green skin.

One day an Arab appeared with an accordion and a small music machine on wheels, much like the old music accordions that were seen around the streets of London. He'd turn a handle and play different tunes for a few pennies. But the main attraction was a small monkey that would dance and perform tricks and come round with a fez hat to collect money. This type of entertainer was known as a Hully-Gully man. At first, it was amusing to watch but quite often the monkey wouldn't perform to the satisfaction of the Arab. At these times when the monkey was being a bit reticent in his performance, the man would hit him with a stick. It didn't always work but usually did. Quite often, the lads would come back aboard complaining of the way this man was treating the monkey.

Johnny Crack or 'JC' as he was known was one of the seamen aboard. I'd known JC back in the UK and we'd served on Audemer together. He was particularly incensed by the monkey's treatment and took it on as a sort of mission. His intention was to buy the monkey from the Arab.

First, he had to get permission from Captain Venmore, the skipper, to get it aboard as the 'ship's mascot'.

I don't know how JC did it, but he got the necessary approval and him and a couple of the lads went to bargain with the Hully-Gully man. I believe the sum agreed was £5, which was quite a lot in 1966, somewhere around eighty-five pounds at today's value. JC had a whip round the ship's crew, and we all contributed. The monkey became the 37th crew member. After a brief discussion, JC named him Zippy. From then on, life aboard the ship was never the same again. It was a hoot. Zippy loved it. He was well cared for, and JC took him to heart. He quickly became a cult figure in Aden and whenever the officers held parties aboard, everyone wanted to meet him. During one of these 'parties', Captain Venmore had a hold on him while introducing him to the British High Commissioner and his wife whereupon good 'ole Zippy decided to pee, in his excitement at meeting such exalted company, over the High Commissioner's wife.

Following this, it was decided that Zippy needed some clothes. A call went out and one of the married guys informed his wife back home. A couple of weeks later, a knitted uniform, complete with beret, was sent out. It was perfect and he didn't mind wearing it for short stints. Even the beret, held on with a small piece of elastic under his chin didn't seem to be a problem. He quickly became a character of the forward mess. At meal times he would sit on someone's lap and be quite happy to be fed from that person's plate. If you didn't feed him quickly enough, this little hand would sneak up, grab a handful of whatever you were eating (peas were his favourite), and leg it. He could drink a pint of beer by putting his foot on the bottom of the glass to support it and then lift it with his hands. He would polish off the lot then drunkenly stagger around the mess. We were never afraid to let him out on deck when we were at sea, he loved it. He could always be found sitting on someone's shoulder, about the ship.

Zippy in his knitted uniform

It wasn't long before he became known back home in the UK. On Forces Family Favourites, the radio programme, which was broadcast on Sunday lunchtimes back home, requests were often made to Zippy from families. Pictures were requested and sent. He quickly became a normal part of life aboard the ship His favourite pastime was to sit on your shoulder and pick through your hair. I assumed it was what they normally did to each other when looking for fleas, etc. Whatever he found, he would eat. I later found out that it was the salt crystals that collected on our scalps that he was after.

He was now officially ship's crew and would be coming with us when we sailed home. Initially, we thought that he would have to go into quarantine, but he drew the attention of Dr Desmond Morris. A sample of his blood was taken, analysed, and sent to the UK. It transpired that he was a Rhesus Monkey and quite a rare one. He ended up in Whipsnade Zoo and grew to quite a large size. Meanwhile, he was great to have aboard Agheila and JC was his personal care person. If he got sick at all, he was cared for as a human and he always recovered well.

Zippy 'uncloaked'!

28

In this region of the Middle East, the US 6th Fleet was patrolling the waters at this time. They may still be doing this, but it wasn't something you noticed very often.

We were all getting used to the routine of life in this hot and arid country. There was still something mythical about the place and it didn't take a great deal of imagination to see why.

Whenever we were entering the port of Aden, as we rounded the headland from the East, we saw the hills and rocky outcrops. Behind these, laying back into the hillside, were the Arab homes. It was something akin to the tales of Arabian Nights. The wattle and daub buildings stretched back up the hill creating a pale, dreamlike picture. Mosques with their tall minarets gave the scene the quality I'd imagined as a child, all pushed together from the coastline, up into these craggy hills.

I could imagine the little narrow streets between the houses, the alleyways almost closed off as the buildings leaned into each other. The foot-worn steps and oaken doors smoothed to a bronze patina by a thousand years of hands and feet. Walking around the backstreets of the city of Aden, as I had done on a couple of occasions, I could see the cool interiors and, in some places, the ancient glowing bread ovens, the smells of which mingled with the freshly roasted local coffee, nuts and cardamom. Over this, at various times of the day, there hung the cries of the muezzin as prayers were called from the minarets. From the sea, I could see the dhows at anchor with fishing nets strung out on wooden poles along the beaches. It was truly beautiful to behold. All of which added to this very Arabian scene.

When I see the tragedy that is Aden today, the damage that has and is being inflicted by air attacks, I can't help but feel a great sadness at the loss of this piece of living history and the many lives that have been devastated in this meaningless war. This particular peninsular of Arabia is no stranger to war as the various tribes have fought over the centuries. But the damage inflicted by later technologies has been far more than any one person could ever have envisaged.

In 1966 the reality was also not so pretty. The constant fear of terrorist attacks was a sort of guerrilla war that kept us all on our toes. The smells weren't too good either. Near where we tied up at HMS Sheba was the sewerage outlet. This was a little way out in the bay and was constantly bubbling up from under the water, producing a small fountain of effluent. Onshore breezes coming off the hills moved the smell out to sea, at least, I think that was the idea. However, the smells, generally, wafted around the place. We couldn't escape it and on extremely hot days, which were quite often, it invaded everywhere. In the end we sort of became used to it but, to this day, I can still recall the smell; it was a tangible thing, a part of life in Aden.

Perhaps the smell was why we didn't see the Americans in port very often. However, once in a while, they would put in an appearance. They rarely came in and tied up alongside. Most often, their destroyers were anchored off and 'bum-boats' would ferry crews ashore. We all hated it when the Yanks were in as all the prices suddenly shot up and even the NAAFI club at Steamer Point was caught up in this. I'd been ashore a few times in the club when these guys were in town. They were noisy, arrogant, and took the place over. American ships were dry which meant there was no alcohol allowed aboard, so when ashore they tended to overdo it a bit.

I remember overhearing them talking about the currency (which was Dinars). They considered all money (including ours) 'funny-money'. It was quite amusing to hear, if not a little irritating.

One day when the 6th Fleet paid Aden a visit, their flagship, USS New, came into port and tied up behind us at HMS Sheba. It became a natural progression of events that the officers of both ships got together and arranged a party on our ship. It also came to pass that some of their off-duty crew could come aboard ours for a 'darts match'. This was the term for a piss-up, but we did actually have a darts board. That day we set up the ship's speakers so that they were connected to the ship's record player which we located in the tank deck. A bar was constructed out of old crates and a table together with buckets of ice. Crates of beer were taken from the ship's stores and put in the buckets of ice. The dart board was set up at one end and the cooks had made a stack of burgers, sausages, fries, and bread rolls. Bunting was draped along the tank deck sides and by 6pm we were ready to receive our American guests.

At around 07:00 p.m. they started to arrive in their white, summer uniforms. JC was tending bar and once my watch duties were over, I came and gave him a hand. I was useless at darts, so it was the best place for me. The officers were having their 'do' up on the top, open deck with some people from the British High Commission and their wives. Needless to say, Zippy was doing the rounds and entertaining all. The Yanks thought he was a hoot, especially in his knitted uniform. They'd never seen anything like it. Both parties were going down well. Music and alcohol were flowing, and no punch-ups had occurred.

By 10:00 p.m. we were running out of beer and both parties were well underway by this time. I mentioned to JC whether it was possible to get some beer from the NAAFI at Steamer. He said they don't usually allow it to leave the premises.

"What if we tell them that it's for the officers party with the Yanks?" I said.

"They won't believe us."

"They would if we took one of them with us."

"They're not allowed out of the dockyard," he muttered, rubbing his chin.

"What if I asked if I could borrow one of their uniforms and you came with me?" I ventured.

"Worth a try," he said, grinning.

Bearing in mind that we had both had a skinful of beer, it seemed a sensible idea. I'd been chatting to this one particular guy from the US, and he also seemed to think that this was a good idea. We were both about the same size. We went into our mess deck and swapped uniforms. When JC saw me, he fell about.

"Come on then, let's do it," he laughed.

So, off the two of us went. As we left the dockyard, JC told the Naval Security that we had been sent on detail. They didn't argue. We picked up a cab from outside HMS Sheba gates where they used to park and went to the NAAFI Club at Steamer.

The place was heaving when we arrived and I did sort of stick out like a sore thumb, wearing the white US sailor's uniform. As we went in, JC informed security of our mission and they let us in, nodding to me as we went to the bar. I sobered up quite quickly and didn't feel so brave.

"Perhaps this isn't such a good idea JC," I whispered to him as the sweat of fear started to trickle from under my white sailor's hat.

"Nah, don't worry, we'll be okay."

There was a queue at the bar, so we joined the end of it and stood in line. Meanwhile, I noticed that a large group of Aussie soldiers were getting a bit loud, over at one of the tables. Some of our lads were not taking too kindly to what was being said. It wasn't long before the comments between them started getting more abusive and louder. Next minute all hell broke loose; fists, bottles and glasses started flying.

"Oh shit, that's all we need," I said. "Come on JC, let's go."

"No mate, don't worry, it'll die down, just stay here, we'll be okay."

Our turn at the bar came as security was trying to sort out the fight. JC explained to the barman that we required some crates of beer to take back to the ship. He went off to get the bar manager. At this point, someone had probably called the police as the fight was getting out of hand. Before we knew what was happening, the MPs arrived, red caps and batons swinging.

"Oh fuck, now we're in for it. Just stick to the story, JC."

Even he was starting to sweat, and I could see that he was as scared as I was. Shit, that's all I needed.

The MPs managed to get things under control and were rounding up those involved in the fighting. Then they went round all the tables asking to see ID Cards. An MP sergeant came over to those of us waiting at the bar. The sergeant made straight for me.

"Hello mate, what are you doing here?" he said. "I didn't know there were any US ships in."

I explained, in my best American accent, that we were tied up at HMS Sheba and pointed to my ship's name 'New' on my shoulder tab.

"Our officers are having a party with the English officers and the British High Commissioner at Sheba on board the LCT Agheila. They're getting low on booze and sent us to get some crates to take back." The sweat was running down my back in streams. He looked at me and checked JC's ID. Fortunately, he didn't ask me for mine.

"Have you got your beer?" he asked me.

"Not yet," I said. "The manager here said he was thinking about it."

The MP looked over at the manager and said, "Well, are you going to give it to them then?"

The manager nodded and asked me how many crates we wanted.

"Can you manage fifteen?" JC said to him.

"Er, yes, I suppose so," he said, looking at the MP sergeant.

The MP grinned and slapped me on the back. "Got to keep up our Anglo-American relationships," and winked at me. "Sorry you have to see this fighting," he added. "Just some of the lads letting off a bit of steam."

"Sure," I said, "happens with our lot too."

The manager went off to get the beer.

"How are you getting the beer back to the ship then?" the sergeant asked.

"We'll get a cab," I said, hoping that he would be satisfied with that and go away.

"Oh no, no, no, can't be having that." He called the manager back. "I'm moving one of our Land Rovers around the back, stack the crates and we'll pick them up."

I looked across at JC who by this time was pale and terrified.

"You don't have to do that," I said. "We'll be okay."

"Oh no, we have to do our bit for our American cousins," he said, grinning under his peaked cap. He turned and said something to one of his subordinates then turned back. "We'll meet you out back."

One of the bartenders led us behind the bar and out a back door. The beer was being stacked up and JC started asking the manager for the cost. While he was sorting that out, a police Land Rover backed into the small yard. Two MPs and the sergeant jumped out and started loading the crates into the back of the vehicle. By this time, I had sobered up fully and was quietly terrified, hoping that it wouldn't show as the beer was being put aboard.

Very quickly, all was loaded. JC had paid off the NAAFI manager and the MP sergeant came over to us. "Jump in the back lads, we'll take you to the ship."

So, we did.

My knees were trembling as I was either coming off the alcohol or an adrenaline rush. JC was trying not to look at me, but I knew we both felt that we just might have pulled this off. I felt like pumping the air but was still nervous about what was to happen when we arrived at Sheba.

We needn't have worried. The Naval Police waved them straight through and they drove to the jetty where both ships were tied up. The duty watch from our lot stood at the gangway with their mouths open. The MPs jumped out and started unloading the beer. JC went up to them as they stacked the crates on the jetty. "Keep a crate for yourselves," he said. "Thanks for helping us."

We all shook hands and off they went.

"I'm going to get this fucking uniform off before any of our officers see me," I said to no one in particular. The duty watch guys stared at me as I went aboard. "Dave, is that you?"

"No, it fucking ain't," I replied over my shoulder as I hurried through the hatch and went below to change into my No.8's.

I'd never been so happy to be in them again. I could not believe what I had just done and was still trembling. When I came up into the mess, the Yank was still there, chatting to one of the lads with a stubby in his hand but now in his own uniform. "I went back and got another one," he said, "You can keep that one if you like."

I did and would use it again back in the UK.

The lads thought it was a hoot, especially as we had managed to get all the extra beer. I also knew I would have to keep out of the NAAFI for a while just in case someone recognised me. Our officers aboard Agheila never knew what I had done, thank goodness. To be caught impersonating another country's sailor, in a war zone, was a major offence and I think they would have thrown the book at me. I was very lucky, and both JC and I realised the enormity of what we had done. We did laugh about it though, for some time.

29

The work was pretty constant now and quite often we were asked to go to certain locations to take supplies which were mostly ammunition and equipment. One of these places was Perim Island. This island was along the West coast of the Arabian Peninsula, going North. It sits about mid-way between the Arabian and African coasts in the Mandab Straits. On a clear day you could see the Djibouti coastline, part of East Africa.

The island itself has a natural harbour where there was an old, small rock jetty. This place was ideal for Agheila to come alongside to offload supplies and pick up any necessary cargo. There were several beaches where we could go in, open the bow doors, drop the ramp and either off-load or pick up vehicles and heavier equipment. If we were to stay overnight or for a few days, we would anchor off in the bay. It was safer and less of a security risk. At those times, if we were not on duty, we would go snorkelling and swimming, jumping off the back of the ship.

The water was crystal clear and although I was never a strong swimmer, this place was ideal. I had never seen so many tropical fish. The colours were amazing and the coral reefs alive with all manner of tiny, iridescent fish. The largest I saw were parrotfish with large eyes and what looked like lipstick on thick lips. Some of the guys went spear fishing but I just used to like watching these amazing fish. The seabed was white, coral sand. I trod on a sea urchin one time, and it was an extremely, painful experience, laying on my stomach whilst the ship's cook pulled the black spines out of my heel.

In the evenings and night we would fish with lines over the side. If you hung a lamp over the rail it was fascinating to watch all the fish attracted by the light. Predominant were the gar fish of varying sizes. It was always very hot at Perim and while on duty that often meant carrying out maintenance and oil changes for the generators or main engines. The average temperature in the engine room was between 130° – 140°F and every piece of metal you touched was red hot. So going swimming over the side was the obvious choice.

However, not all the visits to Perim were pleasure.

In early July we were told that the island had been harbouring insurgents and the RAF wanted to go in and bomb locations on it. The island is around three and a half miles long by two miles wide. At the time we were there, the only settlements I knew of were small, where Arab shepherds kept their goats and some sheep. Along with their families, these people scratched out an existence based mostly on fishing. Perim had virtually no drinking water so any visit we made often included tankers with fresh water that we would offload.

On the occasion of the RAF strike on Perim, the island had to be evacuated and so our final trip there was to do this. We stayed there two days whilst we took on the refugees, complete with livestock. The sheep, goats, and chickens were loaded into the tank deck, and it wasn't long before we were at full capacity. The trip back to Aden would take a casual one and a half days. We were to drop them off just north of 'Little Aden', on a sandy beach. I've no idea what was to happen to them after that.

However, once fully loaded at Perim, we pulled off the beach and as dusk settled, we began the journey back to Aden. The noise and bleating of goats and sheep was quite odd to get used to but, once underway, they settled down. The Arabs and their families were not allowed in the ship's quarters at all and had to remain on the tank deck.

If they wanted to go to toilet, two sections of our own 'heads' were allocated to them, down aft.

There were lots of children, but they were very quiet and subdued. The women were tall and thin, and all wore colourful Arabic clothes similar to saris with head scarves loosely draped either on their heads or around their shoulders. None of their clothes appeared very clean looking. The men had on these long, dirty white robes but all were quiet and didn't say a lot. Altogether, it was a sorrowful sight. Their only home was on Perim but because of rumours of dissidents being harboured on the island, the RAF were going to bomb it.

During the early evening loading of these people at Perim, I was off duty. I remember this being a good opportunity to take some photographs, especially as this was to be our last visit to Perim. As the loading got underway, people were being directed around the catwalks and down the vertical ladders to the tank deck. Most of the men were with their animals, getting them settled down. Women with their total family possessions in large cloth bundles on their heads were passing these down to their men in the tank deck.

Meanwhile, the children were just following Mum or helping with the livestock. One little girl came along the catwalk and tugged at my arm, "Aqua, aqua," she said pointing at her mouth. When I

looked down, I was stunned. She had a purple flowered head scarf loosely draped over her hair and a dirty, grey dress/robe. Her hair was jet black and straggly, lots of it, and her skin was a rich coffee colour. But her eyes were an almost fluorescent brown. She was absolutely stunning. This was crying out for a photograph. I told her to wait by the side of the hatch into the ship and went to get my camera from the mess and a glass of water. When I came back, she was waiting patiently. She drank the water and just stood there. I made sign language for taking a photograph of her and she grinned. Just along the deck was an air vent and I took her over to it. I picked her up and sat her on the vent. It was difficult to gauge her age, but I guessed that she was around ten years old.

One of the evacuees from Perim Island

That night, as we sailed through the darkness back to Aden, I was on watch. Part of my watch duty was to check the security of the bow doors. I had to make my way along the catwalk to the forward Port side ramp hatch. As I made my way along the catwalk, a hand came out of the darkness to touch my arm. It was a young woman, probably in her twenties, holding out a plastic container and asking me if I would fill it with 'aqua'. In the glow of the navigation lights, I could see that she was absolutely beautiful. I took the plastic container from her and told her to wait where she was. I went back to the mess and filled it up. We were not supposed to talk to these people but, other than the guys on watch, there was no one around. I filled the container and took it back to her. She smiled gratefully.

I sat there a moment, leaning on the tank deck railing, looking out to sea in the darkness. She leaned beside me, against the railing, looking at me and across the water. It was an odd moment and all I could think of was these two people, worlds apart, never to meet again. It was a moment when these two lives touched, and it would stay with me forever. I later wrote a poem about that encounter called 'Of an Arab Girl'.

Fresh the face emerging from the night
Sweet with Jasmine, scented right
Beauty enhanced, a smile given
For moments as these, thoughts had striven
Not merely etchings of a dream
But here to touch and feel this scene
That's captured a velvet night within
Her eyes and settled gently on her skin
And all the while the wind has played
With a strand of hair that's strayed
From sheen of black that holds the moon
And hint of dawn that breaks too soon
Feeling love befits the part
That heats the face and pounds the heart
And drowns the sound that wants to come
From the heart onto the tongue
What distance lies between these lands
That can be bridged with ease by hands
And sets an English mind awhirl
By the touch of an Arabian girl
God to His children has been kind
And left this distance far behind.

30

It was July and life aboard was a continuity of hot engine room and the stinky smell of Aden while in port. Mail was regular now and I was getting weekly reports from Mum and the girls in Oz. Eventually, Hayden got in touch and invited me to stay awhile with him in Muscat where he was working. He was with a quasi-government organisation called Airwork Services and was living on a military airbase just outside Muscat, called Bait-el-Falarge. He had gone to the Omani Embassy to arrange for my visit, and I had applied for two weeks leave. Around the middle of July my visa came through plus a very elaborate document from the Sultanate of Oman giving me access to the military base and permission to fly directly to it from RAF Khormaksar. Approval was given for me to go from the skipper who was well impressed by the Sultan's seal.

I was driven to the RAF base and boarded a Beverley B101 transport plane. These were purely for cargo, but they had a few 'sling' seats on each side. They were not the most comfortable, but it was only a two-hour flight. I was treated by the RAF as a VIP, probably because it was very unusual for a military person to be given special permission to fly into Bait. However, first we were stopping at Bahrain where I would have to wait overnight before going on to Bait. The RAF were dropping in supplies there and the Beverley had to be loaded. I stayed on the RAF base of Muharraq overnight. The following morning, I boarded the onward flight to Bait. It was only an hour's flying time in total, from Muharraq.

Bait was a frontline airbase in the fight against terrorism in that region and was also home to the Trucial Oman Scouts. These were a notoriously tough regiment, equivalent to the SAS. This unit was a mixture of nationalities that spent their time in the desert, fighting the insurgents and were known for their tough, no nonsense, techniques.

We circled the base once before landing then dropped down on to this dusty, desert strip. As we had circled, I noticed the barrenness of the place with what looked like rocky escarpments surrounding the place. As the Beverley taxied to a halt, Hayden was waiting for me at the steps in his Adjutants uniform, as he was seconded to the Scouts. The RAF guys saluted him as he took my bag and we walked to the set of low-level buildings that made up the base. I was given a small room with a single bed and desk in it. The air-conditioning was welcome as this place was hotter than Aden. Hayden introduced me to his personal 'batman' and showed me the shower facilities. I showered and changed, by which time lunch was up. The food was excellent and after this Hayden took me on a tour of the base. The hangers held the fighter aircraft, Jet Provosts, fully rigged for air-to-ground combat.

They also had a De Havilland Otter that was used for spotting. I was told that I would be going up in the Otter the next day, on a patrol and maybe later, go up in a Provost. I was given a green flying suit for the period of my stay. All the buildings were single story structures consisting of accommodation, admin, canteen, and a briefing hut. There were also 'secure lockups' and an interrogation area behind razor wire fences. This was the prisoner compound. Apparently, not many of those that went in there, came out again.

The town of Muscat was about a half hour's drive from the base, along a road that went through a mountain pass and then down into the town of Muscat. The place was a walled, coastal city where, at 06:00

p.m. every evening the place was closed off by two massive gates in the wall. This closure was preceded by the firing of a large 16th Century cannon. Once in the city after 06:00 p.m. you stayed in until 06:00 a.m. the following morning. After dark you had to carry a lantern with you. There was no electricity for streetlights. The place was a thousand years old and walking down the alleyways and dusty streets was how I imagined 'Arabian Nights' would have been like. For me, it was fabulous and the stuff of dreams. Very few of the shops and stores had glass fronts. Most were shuttered with wooden screens, when closed. The bazaar was ancient and sold everything from vegetables and spices to silks, vehicle parts and gold. In one place, I watched this little old man melt a ten Talos bar of gold and make a ring out of it. He used a small pipette in his mouth and a lighted oil lamp wick, to produce an intense flame to melt the gold and form it to make the ring. The gold bars bore the stamp of James & Mayhew, London.

The call to prayer would echo around the city and while prayer time was being called, Hayden knew a small 'open-plan' bar that sold iced beer. We'd sit in the shade watching the dusty streets, relishing the cool and chatting about Aden and home. There were very few motorised vehicles there; the main transport was a donkey and cart.

The majority of the buildings were the white, adobe mud-type with narrow alleyways leading back into the rocky hills. Along the seafront were the fishing dhows, either tied up alongside the jetty or moving in and out of the harbour. This section of the city was a busy fishing port, and you could buy freshly landed barracuda, marlin, swordfish, or shark. The whole place was medieval, and I felt privileged to see it like that. It wouldn't last and prosperity, oil dollars, and modernisation were to follow.

Today, the old town is still there but blended in alongside modern businesses with tall, high-rise buildings. Some sensitivity has been applied and the stonework of those modern buildings is similar in colour, if nothing else, to the existing old town. The wall is still part of Muscat, and the massive, gated archway now has a two-lane highway running through it. Progress stops for very little, and a busy seaport and modern airport contribute to the expansion and continuity of this most ancient of Arab cities.

Back at Bait, I had my first flight in the Otter. It was my chance to gear-up in the green flying suit and as we walked out to the aircraft, I really felt the part. Hayden was working but I had been introduced to the pilot who also doubled as the medical officer. He walked around the aircraft carrying out his pre-flight checks. I had my camera with me and persuaded one of the ground staff to take a picture of me, helmet, and all, stood alongside the aircraft. We climbed aboard, fired up and taxied out to the strip where we received flight clearance. The noise was quite something and as we rolled down the tarmac, I felt the exhilaration of take-off. First, the tail wheel lifts off and as she sped up, the wings bounced, the struts creaked and as he pulled back on the yoke, all the bumps and creaks ceased, and we lifted effortlessly into the air.

Going on flight patrol - Bait al Falaj, Oman

The brown and grey dusty hills slipped away beneath us as we gained height. At nine thousand feet we levelled out and turned south. That's when I came to realise how rugged and mountainous this country was. The view was amazing. We both had headsets on, and it was explained to me what we were looking for. The idea was to sight a 'caravan' or 'train' of camels. There were Bedouin in the area, but these were the 'friendlies'. We flew a grid pattern, well away from the base and Muscat, which was far behind us. After about twenty minutes, I settled into the flight.

It was all a far cry from Aden and Agheila. No stinky ocean breezes here, no 140°C engine room; all of that was a long way away. I felt quite privileged to be here – not many lads would get a chance like this. The pilot was sitting on my right-hand side. I had an identical yoke and set of controls on my side as well. I felt the aircraft bank as we moved on to a westerly heading.

"Have you done any flying"? he asked me.

"Only in the ATC, that was a Chipmunk, out of RAF Northolt."

He looked across at me. "Would you like to take the controls for a bit?" he said over the headset.

I looked at him and grinned. "Sure."

"Keep the rudder as it is, feel the yoke and relax. Here's our heading," he said, pointing to the dials between us just right of centre. "Keep her level for a few more minutes, then head towards those hills over there," he added as he pointed out of the Perspex window to his right. He took a large Nikon camera and started looking with it out of the side window. He didn't take any pictures.

I gave it around six minutes then slowly turned the yoke towards the right. I was a bit nervous at first, but the aircraft slowly dipped the right wing and we turned. I let it go until I had the hills coming round towards the forward screen. He nudged the throttle, which was above us in a stirrup form, central in the upper console, increasing the speed. I looked at the level indicator with the horizon and moved the yoke to get the wings level. She responded well. After a couple of minutes, he pointed. "Over there, see that smudge of dust on the ground? Looks like a camp or a train of camels."

I looked hard for a minute then saw what he had been pointing at. It was vaguely bluish.

"Looks like smoke to me," I said. He agreed. He took back control and we headed towards it. A few minutes later we were lower and nearer, and it was easier to see. There was a camp with two large tents and a group of camels tethered nearby. It was difficult to make out how many people there were at this distance. He asked me to take the controls again and to stay on the current heading. He wrote something down on a knee pad and then got the Nikon going as we neared them.

"Are they Bedou then?" I asked.

"No, I doubt it. Bedou nearly always have a flat-bed truck nearby and lots of goats. I can see none of that down there."

He took back control and eased the aircraft in a long, angled turn, gaining altitude as he did so. He then came around for another pass and then headed north-east. After a while, I could see the hazy blue of the ocean.

"I'll show you 'Starkers', the little beach cove where we go swimming. I'm sure Hayden will take you there sometime."

We dropped lower once we had cleared some hills and the coastline came into view. He followed it for a while then drew my attention to a horseshoe shaped bay.

"That's Starkers, about a half-hour drive from the base.

"What was that place with the tents and camels, back there, that we were looking at?" I asked him.

"Could be a rebel camp. I've taken some pics so that intel can get a closer look at it. The smaller tent behind the larger one could be the stores. The boys will have a briefing on it when we get back and we will keep an eye on it for the next few says."

That evening I discussed it with Hayden over dinner. He didn't say too much about it except to say that they may have to do something to confirm it and then they'll take it out if it's still there. Apparently, these guys had a habit of disappearing pretty quickly. The food was good and, later that evening, we sat outside under the stars, having beers and telling stories. Some of the other guys joined us and we had a good evening. The next day we would pay a visit to 'Starkers'.

The little cove was indeed, secluded and the gentle lapping of the warm water on the sandy shoreline was inviting. The trip had taken a good half-hour in the Land Rover Defender, and I quickly realised just how rocky and barren this place was. It was the nearest thing I'd seen to what I imagined a lunar landscape would look like. However, no matter how devoid of life and barren this place was, you couldn't afford to be complacent. Hayden and a couple of the guys that came with us were armed. We parked up close to the beach and took the cool box down to a sandy area. I had my swimming trunks on as did the other lads – no one was going in 'Starkers' even though that's how the place got its name.

It was a nice break and, after an hour swimming around the cove and observing the marine life in the crystal-clear water, we were stretched out enjoying a smoke and some beers. For me, it was a much-needed respite from the heat and stink of Aden. It was also unusual to see my Uncle Hayden like this. This was his territory and where he belonged. I began to understand something of the man and why he could never settle down in the UK. There was too much 'military' in him and all that that entailed. He'd had several marriages and relationships that were never straight forward. He was like a fish out of water back home. Here, and in places like this, he was in his element. He was a man's man and was respected and feared by most of the people he worked with.

My uncle Hayden on 'Starkers' beach, Oman

My flight in the Jet Provost T55 was an experience to remember. It was a two-seater jet where the pilot and navigator/gunner, sat side by side. We hurtled down the runway and were quickly airborne. Once again, the dusty, rocky landscape stretched before us and once we'd reached our cruising altitude, the air was sharp and clear. We circled around and turned South-West towards the coordinates where we'd recently seen the encampment in the Otter. This aircraft was fast, and the sense of speed was exhilarating. After flying along valleys and mountainous escarpments, the pilot picked up something. He pointed forward, to the left. "Can you see that dust rising in a line over by the base of that pointy ridge?"

I looked hard but couldn't see a thing. "No," I said, "I can't make it out."

He banked slightly and reduced speed and altitude, came around and pointed again.

I looked hard and then saw it. "I see it, a line of smoke or dust."

"That's it," he said. "I'll have to radio that in. Let's go for a closer look, you ok?"

"Fine, I said, let's do it."

We carried out a long, angled turn, dropping lower as we came around. He then followed the escarpment that ended in a flat, sandy, valley floor. At the lower altitude everything was much clearer but whizzed by that much faster. As he lined up along the rocky walls you could feel the aircraft being buffeted by updrafts. In front of us was the dust cloud and then appeared a line of camels with packs loaded on the back of them. You could just make the tribesmen out, with some walking and some riding. Most seemed to be armed with what looked like rifles. As we shot past them, a couple waved their rifles at us, then we were climbing up into the azure sky.

Over the radio, the pilot said we would be heading back shortly and report the sightings. We levelled off at around twenty thousand feet and seemed quiet and smooth again.

"Would you like to take her for a moment?" he asked.

"Love to," I said.

"Keep it on this heading for five minutes," he said pointing to the compass, "and then ease to starboard fifteen degrees. Maintain altitude."

I took the stick, and my hands were clammy. It felt extremely powerful. Nothing like the Otter. "Take her down to fifteen thousand feet," he said as he proceeded to show me how to gently ease the stick forward, watching the altimeter. This gauge also showed the horizon, so gave a good indication of whether you were flying true. It didn't take long to master. I loved it; my childhood dreams were partly realised, and I felt comfortable and confident. My moment of flying her stretched to a little under an hour and I was ecstatic.

We circled the base and then landed, taxiing to the pan in front of one of the large hangers. I didn't want it to end. As we climbed down the short ladder and I stood on terra firma, my legs were shaky, and I felt exhausted. I had been quite tensed up but the feeling after the adrenalin rush soon passed. I took off my helmet as we walked over to the briefing room. Hayden was sitting inside having a mug of tea. "You okay mate? Enjoy it?"

I just nodded. "Shit, that was magic."

The pilot looked at Hayden and said, "The boy did good."

I turned and thanked him.

"No problem, you're a natural. You handled that as good as any I've trained."

I grinned and sat down with a freshly brewed mug of tea. I was knackered.

The rest of my days there went by in a whirl. Good food, good company, lots of drink and, pleasant evenings under desert skies. It was a break to remember. Seeing Hayden like that gave me a greater understanding of the man and I felt privileged to have been with him, like that, in his preferred environment. By the time I came to leave, I felt quite sad, but I knew I'd be seeing him again back home.

My flight back via Bahrain was in a Beverley. These old pack horses were rickety things. They had a large cargo hold and troops could sit in the tail-boom. This was a narrow space with two rows of seats each side. I had a surprise when I arrived at the staging area at RAF Muharraq. A large number of 2 Para were going on to Salalah, so it looked like it was going to be pretty crowded in the Beverley. I got a sandwich and a coke and sat amongst these guys. There was to be a wait whilst their gear and heavy equipment was loaded on to the Beverley. These lads were in full gear and looked ready for anything. I got talking to one of them as I waited to board again. They were 'on operation' and were off to do something in Oman. I explained what unit I was with (I was in jeans and t-shirt) but he'd never heard of LCT's and the Maritime Regiment. As we sat chatting their sergeant major came in. All went quiet as he entered. He was a tall man with a stern face and a patch over one eye. He looked fierce. He told them to get their gear and start boarding. They did this immediately and it was clear to see that this character was 'in charge'.

By the time we were seated in the tail-boom of the Beverley, the temperature inside was starting to rise. We buckled up and the aircraft taxied out to the end of the runway for take-off. As we sat there with no air conditioning working until the aircraft was airborne, it started to get hot. These guys were in full combat gear, I was lightly dressed.

After ten minutes of nothing happening, the engines suddenly shut down. An RAF engineer came along and said they'd had a generator failure and we may have to get off the aircraft for a while. After an hour of sitting in a bloody metal tube, out in the blazing sun of a desert airstrip, they decided to let us off the aircraft. We went back to the building we'd originally waited in. These lads had all their packs to carry as well. We sat down, drank loads of bottled water and waited. The Sgt Major was pacing up and down, chatting now and again, with some of his men. I started chatting to the lad sitting next to me, a corporal. He told me they were 2 Para.

"I know someone who was in 2 Para," I said, thinking of John Hoey. "My sister's husband. He was an Aussie lad, name of John Hoey." One of his mates had overheard me and looked a little stunned. I looked over at him. "You know John Hoey"? I asked.

Both Para lads looked at each other and laughed. "Hey, Sgt Major, Sir", one of them called out. It all went quiet. The guy with the patch turned and looked across at us, sitting there.

"This bloke just asked us if we knew John Hoey," he said grinning. The sergeant major looked stunned.

"Hoey!" he shouted. "That bloody waster!" He marched over to where I was sitting and glared down at me with his one malevolent eye. "You know John Hoey?" he asked. "What's he to you"?

I could feel the heat on my cheeks and face, I must have been glowing.

"Oh, I er, met him in a bar in Aden and he said he had been in 2 Para," I stammered. With that kind of reaction there was no way I was going to tell him he was my bloody brother-in-law. I just hoped that the other two lads I was sitting next to, either hadn't heard me or didn't say anything. No one said anything then the lad next to me looked across and winked. I just sat there with the sweat suddenly running down my back.

"He was a bloody waster and a blight on the regiment. He got thrown out." He glared down at me for a moment longer. "What unit are you with?"

Oh fuck, I thought, *now what?*

"Maritime Regiment, RCT, I'm a marine engineer on the LCTs, stationed in Aden, Sir."

"Humph," he said, glaring at me a moment longer, then turned and stormed off, mumbling about Hoey being a bloody little arsehole.

It was at this point that an RAF sergeant came in and said we could board. I was never so glad to get back into the hot, stuffy tail-boom of the Beverley. Shortly after, we took off for Salalah.

"You don't want to mention Hoey anywhere near 2 Para," the lad sitting next to me said. "He's persona-non-grata in our lot."

We touched down in Salalah, a desert airstrip that looked in the middle of nowhere. I could see mountains some distance away and a coastline on the other side. The airstrip at this time was just a few huts and dusty roads in and out. Now, of course, it is an international airport with quite a thriving city around it.

I sat in a lounge area whilst 2 Para deplaned. When I got back on board there were only a few others, that like me, were going on to Aden. I was actually looking forward to getting back to my ship. I never did find out what John Hoey had done but, as it turned out in the end with my sister Jo, he was better off forgotten.

31

Things were hotting up in Aden. It didn't look like we would be staying there, and it was becoming obvious that a British withdrawal was on the cards. Meanwhile, life aboard was good. We were kept quite busy and Zippy had become the darling of the air waves even if he was a bloody handful on board. Our next trip was to Assab, in Ethiopia. We were taking a group of Army Officers on a three-week hunting/shooting trip, as you do! Not so sure they'd be allowed to get away with that, these days. We were dropping them off in Assab and they would make their way overland, towards Addis. We were to wait in Assab a week then move on to Djibouti. Assab was part of Ethiopia in 1966 and was one of its major seaports. Currently, it now belongs to Eritrea, but Ethiopia is trying to get it back. Looking at current pictures of Assab it doesn't look much different now to what it was in 1966.

We tied up there around midday on a Saturday. The dockside was dusty and deserted, except for a small convoy of military vehicles that were picking up the officers for their expedition. Once all the gear was off-loaded, things quietened down. Our skipper, Capt. Venmore, was going with them for the first week and we were to pick him up in Djibouti. The No.1 was left in charge of the ship. There didn't seem much to go ashore for here but one of the lads had been speaking to a dock worker who said there were plenty of bars along the main street, outside the dockyard. That was all he needed to say.

Alongside in Djibouti

Later in the afternoon, once the duty watches had been arranged, a group of us, around 8, decided to explore the town. JC was with us, and he had decided (unwisely, as it turned out) to bring Zippy along with us, tucked in his shirt front. We had a lead for him, but he soon snuggled down inside JC's shirt. All you could see was the top of his head. In part, this was because of the heat. At that time of the day, it was probably the hottest. As we came outside the dockyard gates, the high street was in front of us. It reminded me of something out of a Clint Eastwood western. Boarded sidewalks and a dirt road. Some of the bars even had batwing doors.

We wandered up the left side of the street, trying to decide which bar we liked the look of most. Word had obviously spread, and these tall, very dark-skinned Ethiopian and Somalian girls were standing around outside the bars, calling us to go in. It wasn't long before we found one we liked the look of, if only to get out of the burning, afternoon sun, so we headed in.

Inside it was cool and dim. A little way inside the batwing doors was a large circular table in the middle of the floor. We all piled into the chairs around it and ordered beers. They came, quickly brought by a handful of the girls. The icy cold beers, most of which were Amstel, were welcome. With the beers on the table, more girls appeared and decided to space themselves between us, around the table. There was plenty of groping going on by the girls much to every one's amusement. The favourite thing was to rub the front of your trousers.

"You like to fuck me?" was the most common question.

"Me very cheap, you handsome man."

None of us were very bothered at this stage; we had only just sat down in the place. Before long, the beer was flowing well, and we were starting to relax. Zippy hadn't put in an appearance at this time, he was fast asleep, clinging to JC, inside his shirt.

We'd been in the place for about an hour when I noticed that the girl that had been sitting on Stu's lap opposite me had disappeared. He was still sitting at the table but not joining in with the chatting and joking. I could see that his face was looking a little strained and then I saw him suddenly sit a little straighter in his chair. No one else had noticed as they were all laughing and chatting to the other girls. I quietly pushed my chair back, enough so that I could see under the table without being too obvious about it. All was explained. The girl that had been on his lap was now sitting on the floor between his legs. She had his 'ole todger' out and was going to town, giving him a blow job. Well, I sat up and looked across at him and couldn't stop laughing. He was trying so hard to look nonchalant, hoping no one would notice. Jesus, what a place this was! Apart from that, we all stayed there and carried on drinking for quite some time. Eventually, having paid up and too much moaning and groaning for us to stay, it was decided to move on to another bar.

We crossed the dirt road of the main street, to the now cooler side where the bars were in shade. We chose one where we could get something to eat as well as drink. We found this place that was quite small but served food. We pushed a couple of tables together and ordered up some grub that consisted of chilli beans and flat breads to dunk in it. Just behind our table was a long bar with a mirror behind it. By this time, it was early evening and Zippy had smelt the food and was getting hungry. JC was giving him some flat bread with some of the chilli sauce on it. Meanwhile, as seemed to be common practice in all these bars, the girls sat amongst us. They all thought Zippy was cute once they'd got over their initial surprise at seeing him. We were also a novelty as UK military rarely came to this place.

We were getting a bit louder as the evening wore on and one of the lads decided to have a nipple measuring contest amongst the girls. We managed to coax the girls to get their tits out on the table and we would measure their nipples against a large coin, about the size of a 50p piece. I have no idea why this seemed to be so funny, but I guess when you're pissed it made for good entertainment.

Zippy was still sitting in JC's shirt with just his head sticking out. The girls didn't seem particularly bothered by him and in fact were quite amused. When Zippy saw all these tits out on the table and us lads touching them on the pretence of measuring, he must have got a bit jealous. He climbed out of JC's shirt, sat on the table for a minute, then made a beeline for one of these girls' tits. He grabbed it, put the nipple in his mouth and bit down hard. All hell broke loose. The girl screamed and frightened Zippy, who took off like a banshee. He jumped onto the long bar and then saw himself in the mirror behind it. He also screamed and then tried to attack his reflection. We had all jumped up by this time and JC leapt behind the bar counter to grab Zippy. The girls meanwhile had run out of the bar and up the road screaming. We knew we had to grab Zippy and get out of there and back to the ship as quick as we could. By luck, JC managed to get a hold of Zippy and stuff him inside his shirt. We paid up the bar owner plus extra for any damage. He was not happy and said he was going to call the police. We left and made our way back to the ship, laughing most of the way.

Needless to say, Zippy didn't come ashore with us in Assab again. Most of the remaining days there, we were busy working on board. A police jeep did arrive the next day and spoke to the duty officer, but nothing happened, to my knowledge. On the evening of the day before we were due to sail for Djibouti, I went ashore with Stu. He was meeting the girl he'd met the first day ashore. The intention being to have a few beers and say goodbye. We met her outside the dock gates, and she had another girl with her. This other girl tagged on to me. They wanted to show us where they lived. It was on a hillside, behind the town in these tents and corrugated shacks. Stu was keen to get his 'nookie' before we sailed, and I had to admit I was tempted but way too frightened of catching something. We made our way partially up the hillside and were taken to these little shacks. Stu disappeared inside one and I went into one, just a little way back from his, with this young girl. Inside, it was very clean and tidy. I had made it quite clear that I was not interested in having any nookie with her, so she introduced me to her little corner where she stayed with her mother. There were magazine cuttings of Elvis and Cliff Richards stuck to a cardboard shelf. It was then that I realised how young this girl was. She must have only been around fourteen, although she maintained that she was older. I didn't want Stu to leave without me, so we sat outside her shack, looking down the hill. Stu's shack was not far in front of where we sat. Being on the hillside, you could see down to the dockyard, and I could see Agheila, twinkling in the night with the ship's lights on. I talked about the UK and what life was like back home. When I looked at her, she was quietly crying, and I felt bloody awful.

I lightened things up talking about Zippy, who was by now quite a celebrity. I took out a handful of US dollars, the currency we were using, and gave them to her. Eventually, Stu appeared from the tent, and I called out to him. He came up the hill with the girl he had been with, and they sat down with us. They got us some cold beers from a bucket of ice, and we sat looking out at the night and the harbour, chatting. We left to go back aboard, and I felt a little saddened by the whole episode. These people were eking out an existence but had little hope for the future. Some years later, the war between Eritrea, Ethiopia and Somalia started and these lands are still in the various throes of this, to this day. The next day we left Assab for Djibouti which was further down the coast.

Djibouti was a different ball game altogether. As we entered the harbour, there were several large cargo ships at the dock, either being off-loaded or taking on cargo. On the way down the coastline, it was obvious how dry and dusty this place was. Every now and again there would be clumps of palms, small adobe dwellings or the ubiquitous 'Kelongs' where fishermen had set bamboo poles in the shallow waters and strung nets around them.

As we entered the port of Djibouti you could see the town spread out beyond the port. There were two- and three-story buildings enabling you to see that the town stretched back quite a way. I was finishing my watch as we entered and there were various dignitaries waiting dockside, to come aboard. We tied up behind an Ethiopian naval vessel that looked very much like an ex Royal Naval minesweeper and probably was. Relations between Britain and Ethiopia at this time, were very good, so you didn't feel threatened in any way. We all had to wear uniforms and for a change, it looked quite strange seeing our lot looking like soldiers for once.

By midday we were all 'tied up' and keeping out of the very hot sun. The dignitaries had been and gone and the dock work had all but finished. Silence seemed to have settled over the place. We were sitting in the mess, after lunch, discussing going ashore. Zippy was on 'lockdown' and was confined to ship but he didn't seem to mind as we all laughed and joked about his nipple biting exercise. By 02:00 p.m. there was a group of about six of us that had decided to explore the town. We'd been told that somewhere, not that far from Djibouti, was a French Foreign Legion outpost and if we were to come across any legionnaires from there, not to get involved. The skipper had returned to the ship and therefore, we were all a bit more 'disciplined' in our dress and behaviour.

We made our way ashore, feeling a bit conspicuous in our khaki uniforms, complete with lanyard braid and berets. The town was wide and dusty and silent. Notwithstanding that it was probably the hottest part of the day, we wanted to do a bit of shopping. These were not the normal shops that you'd expect to see. These stores had open fronts where you just wandered in, no doors, no windows, pretty much the same as I had seen in Muscat. Only, at this time they were all shuttered and closed. I guess they didn't open until the later and cooler part of the day. Although a bit disappointed, we chatted and laughed as we wandered down the dusty main street. There was the odd mangy looking dog eying us up warily and scrawny cats lying in the shadows, but nary a soul stirred and not a bar in sight. We followed the main street as it curved away to the left.

"Surely there must be a bar open somewhere, especially as they must know a military ship is in port," JC said in an unbelieving manner.

Someone mumbled, "Yeah, has to be one around here somewhere."

We carried on meandering, getting thirstier by the minute. After a while, we came to a long stretch of street that seemed to go on forever. Not a cat, dog, vehicle, or person could be seen. We were still in good spirits and laughing when JC held up his hand,

"Hey, shush, listen a minute," he said, looking ahead, down the street. We all stopped and listened. At first, I didn't hear anything, then I heard what sounded like people singing. We all slowly walked on, no one saying anything, all listening intently. Sure enough, people were singing. We stopped as it seemed to get louder. As we listened, I began to recognise the tune.

"Hey lads, that sounds like the Horst Wessel," I said, amazed I'd remembered it.

"The what?" JC asked.

"The Horst Wessel, a Nazi marching song. I think it was taken up by the Wafen SS during the war as their anthem." I still couldn't believe it. We listened further. No one said anything and we slowly carried on walking. By this time, it was quite loud and then JC pointed to a place across the road. Amongst the dusty, shuttered store fronts was a small, open-fronted, café/bar. Staying on the opposite side of the road, we wandered forward to get a better look. Sitting at the back, inside the café were 6 guys in legionnaires uniforms, sitting around a table, a large pitcher of ale in front of them, raising glasses and singing. We looked for a moment, then JC grinned.

"Couldn't be better, lads, come on, we'll show them how we can sing, let's get some beer."

We crossed the road, the emptiness of the street enhancing the singing as it drifted in the still air. As we approached the café, the singing quietened down then stopped altogether. They just sat there watching us. We walked into the shade of the café and made towards an empty table in the opposite corner from the legionnaires. A scruffy Somali was stood behind the bar, watching. We pulled the chairs out and they scraped loudly on the wooden floor. The barman looked frightened and continued to watch. JC waved across at him, pointed to all of us now sitting around the table and said, "Beer, kemosabe." The barman disappeared behind a bead curtain whilst the legionnaires continued to watch. One of them said quietly to one of the others, "Wer dieses loss dann sind?"

JC looked at me with raised eyebrows.

"I think he said, 'Who are this lot then?' but my German isn't that good," I said.

Stu suggested we started singing our own songs, but we all needed the beer first. So, we sat there, both tables eyeing each other up, getting the measure. These guys looked tough and there was no way we'd come out tops if it came to a scrap. I noticed that several had tattoos on their upper arms, and one had one on his neck – a swastika. From what I could see, a couple had the double lightening symbols of the SS on their arms. I looked at JC. "They all look like German SS soldiers – ex, I hope."

We all looked at each other. Just then the Somali barman came back with 6 frosted pint glasses and a pitcher of lager and set it down in the middle of the table. Stu asked how much in dollars and the guy held up five fingers. Stu dropped a ten dollar note on the tray and asked for another pitcher. He went to get it as JC poured. By the time he'd come back we'd almost finished the first one. He set the pitcher down and some small dishes of pistachios and olives.

As we settled down into drinking and quietly chatting, the Germans started singing the Horst Wessel, this time a little quieter.

"Come on lads, our turn," JC said.

He started with, "Pack up your troubles in your old kit bag…" and we picked it up slowly then got into the swing of it and turned the volume up. The Germans responded and they started to sing louder too. By this time, the Somali had taken himself off until the legionnaires shouted for more beer. Then, in a show of camaraderie, one legionnaire pointed across to us and said to the Somali, "Beir fur das Englanders." We nodded across to them, raised our glasses and carried on singing.

From out of nowhere, a session had started, and it wasn't long before the two tables were pushed together, and the beer was flowing freely. These guys were tough buggers, but the barriers came down and we were soon swapping stories. I can't recall how long this went on for, but it was well after dark. I do remember exchanging cap badges and belts with one of them. I guess we staggered back to the ship but how they let us on board, I've no idea. The following morning, with a thick head I was hauled up before the skipper and with him was a Commander from the Legion. It turned out I had also swapped shirts with this guy and in the pocket of mine was my ID card and I had his. Needless to say, the consequences of this could have been quite severe for both of us. I think leniency was given and I got off with being confined to ship for the remainder of the week. The rest of the lads fared similar fates, but the skipper was pretty good about it.

As it turned out, I only had to spend three days aboard. In between my duty watch I managed to get ashore and visit the town, picking up a few souvenirs. I don't know what happened to the legionnaire, but I think the skipper requested to the commander that he be dealt with lightly. We hung around Djibouti until all the officers returned from their hunting escapades and we sailed back to Aden. I think it was during this rather hectic time that a funny incident happened. Now I may be wrong, and it may have been back in UK waters that this happened but for some reason, I have a strong feeling that it was during this trip.

The day we left Djibouti I was on watch. We had not long left port and were heading out into open sea. I went around the ship to check that all my areas of responsibility were secured and one of these checks included the steering pedestal in the wheelhouse. The system was hydraulic, so I went to check the couple of connectors that were located at the base of this pedestal. The seaman on watch was, at that particular moment, on his own. He was watching his compass heading and just standing there giving odd turns at the wheel to make minor adjustments.

"Hello Dave, everything ok?" he asked

"Yeah fine," I said. "Not too rough out there today. Should make reasonable time."

I looked down and at the bottom of the pedestal and there was this really nice looking, lacquered wooden box with a closed, hinged lid.

"What's that then?" I said, pointing at the object in question.

He looked down with a slightly puzzled expression.

"Dunno mate. It was there when I came on watch and I didn't ask," he said.

I looked around the bridge and could see the bosun out on the wing-bridge. There was no way I was going to ask him, so I bent down to pick it up. It was too heavy, so I thought better to just leave it. However, it had a hinged lid, so I thought I'd open it and see what it was. I got down on my knees and gently lifted the lid. Inside was this gray/white powder. A lot of it. The seaman looked down and was as puzzled as I was.

"What the fuck is that?" he asked.

"Haven't got a clue mate," I replied, frowning. I gently put my finger in it. It was loose and powdery. I put my finger lightly on my tongue, then dipped it in the powder and tasted it. Very bland and didn't taste of anything.

"What do reckon then?" He still looked puzzled.

"No idea, can't taste anything. You have a try," I said.

He licked his finger, leaned down, and gave it a good old rooting around. Tasting it, he looked puzzled.

"Thought maybe it was some dope, waiting to be chucked," he laughed.

I closed the lid back on the box and stood. "The officer of the watch should know, he probably put it there. I leave you to it, then," I said, and left.

At lunch time, in the mess, I mentioned it, and nobody had a clue what it was. Quite a few had done what we had done and tasted it. Later that day, all was revealed. A member of the RCT who had served for many years on the T's, Duffy, had died – I assume of natural causes. However, his dying wish was that he wanted his ashes to be scattered at sea. Quite a few of the lads turned a peculiar shade of green when we were informed. But Duffy wasn't finished with us yet. There was to be a small 'on board' ceremony in which the ashes were to be dumped over the side. The bosun went to great lengths to make sure we had the right wind direction and the ship adjusted accordingly. The engines were temporarily slowed and those of us not on watch were allowed on deck to observe the 'ceremony'. When the moment came, the skipper gave a few words during which we found out his name (Duffy) and his wishes. He picked up the box, held it at armslength and opened the lid. Just as he started to tip it into the sea, the wind shifted dramatically and as he tipped the box over the side a strong gust of wind blew the lot back over the ship and everyone standing in the way. Fortunately, I was sitting in the mess, watching from one of the portholes with some of the others. It went bloody everywhere and there was a lot of it. Some of the guys were coughing and spluttering and rubbing their eyes. We were all laughing like loonies in the mess; Duffy certainly had the last laugh...!

Duffy was scattered throughout the ship and quite a few of us now knew him a little more intimately.

32

Following our return to Aden we were fuelled up and at the request of the British High Commissioner for Aden, we sailed for the Kuria Muria islands. This was a disputed area, regarding the sovereignty of these islands. The Yemen were claiming them as belonging to them but in actual fact, they were in Omani territorial waters. Word had filtered down to us that the locals were causing trouble to passing ships and so we were requested to pay them a visit. We didn't know the full story, but something else was going on as well. We were instructed to stop along the Omani coast and pick up some of their National Guard, to accompany us.

The trip to the pickup point was interesting for me. We hugged the coastline, and it was fascinating to see the distant dunes and villages of these ancient, desert towns and dwellings. It was like something out of Arabian Nights. I should think that nothing had changed in these places for centuries. The only transport you could see was donkey and cart. Now and again, a small oasis of palms made a green splash against the sandy background. We eventually pulled into an old wooden jetty where we were to pick up the Omanis. It was to be an overnight stay. The jetty was a small wooden affair and thanks to our flat-bottomed design, we could tie-up at the end of it. We'd pumped the tanks out, so we were sitting quite high in the water. This part of the Arabian Sea was not known for bad seas and dodgy weather, so it was all pretty smooth. I managed to get ashore to stretch my legs here and it was interesting to see the small village huts and the oasis date palms.

Other than a few stray dogs and scruffy kids, there wasn't a great deal to see. But I was interested to get a feel for these places and as a scented evening breeze came off the desert, it enhanced the quiet atmosphere of the place. A couple of us wandered around the area then sat against a date palm and watched the sun set. There was a light breeze and together with the almost pastel colours around the area, we watched as they were slowly turning to purple/blue when the sun slipped below the dunes. Sitting there, quietly smoking a rollup, we chatted of home. This was a magic moment for me and good for the soul that allowed you to disconnect from just about everything else except that moment in time and space where you felt like you almost didn't exist and become one with the surrounding area. That simple act of sitting there in the warmth of the setting sun and the light scented breeze, watching the sun set, remains with me to this day. It is a place to return to amidst the chaos of everyday life and I often used to think of it when at work in a particularly boring meeting.

We took the Omani guards on board the following morning and these guys were impressive. We had been instructed not to say too much to them and to just be courteous. They were allocated a section of our 'heads' (toilets) to use but they would remain on deck for the duration of the trip. They certainly looked the part in their white, long robes, headdress, and weapons. Some wore crossed bandoliers of cal.303 cartridges and the dagger they all wore in their belts. The dagger was known as a 'Khanjar' and was in a sheath of beaten silver and gold. These were extremely ornate with handles of horn or ebony. These guys all looked like weathered old men. All had beards with very lined, nut-brown faces. They all sat in a group up on the forecastle head on an ornate, Persian type rug and drank Arabic coffee from flasks. Their rifles were mostly Lee Enfield 303s but there were a couple of much older ones that almost verged on the musket.

We left that morning and reached the larger of the three islands just after midday. As we approached, there was a large hill in the distance with a flagpole atop. We'd all spotted the Yemeni flag that was flying. As soon as they saw us, this flag was taken down and a Union Jack hoisted. It was quite amusing, but the Omanis were not impressed. Once we were alongside a small, wooden jetty and secured, a group of our lads were issued with weapons and under the bosun and first officer, made their way ashore accompanied by the Omani guards. We carried out normal maintenance and then sat about on deck, having a smoke and a mug of tea. The silence of this place was eerie. No curious locals came to see the ship and in fact, apart from our own lads, we saw no one.

Omani Guard

By late afternoon, they all returned to the ship. No one else, other than the Omanis, were with them. As soon as they were all aboard, we prepared to leave. We sailed back up the coast and dropped the Omanis off. By this time, word was filtering amongst the crew about what had happened. Apparently, they came across the main village and met with the village chief. The Omanis took him to one side, out of sight and interrogated him. They had all noticed the lack of women and children in the place. Eventually, with the headman in tow, he took them to an escarpment. At the bottom of this was a deep ravine into which had been thrown the bodies of dead people. The lads said that from the smell and the quantity of bodies, it had been in use for some time. Later, we heard that the Omani Airforce had been in and fire-bombed the ravine. The Union flag was to remain flying until the Omanis officially took the islands over the following year.

Back home, things were going through some difficult times. Mum had a part time job, cleaning in a local school and Britain was going through what Mum described as a 'credit squeeze'. These days, we call it a recession. Prices of food and commodities were on the increase, and we had just beaten Germany in the World Cup. A cheery statement on the football pitch, for all.

Meanwhile, things in Aden were hotting up. The attacks on British soldiers were increasing and the number of ships bound for Oz and stopping at Aden had diminished significantly. The Gordon Highlanders took over from the Argyll & Sutherlands and 'mad Mitch' went back to the UK. The Gordons came with a bit of a reputation and within a few weeks, the number of attacks lessened. Life aboard was hot and sweaty but stable. We were pretty much in a world of our own. We still had to do our share of patrol duties ashore, in the backs of Land Rovers or three-tonners.

One morning, a couple of civilians came aboard for a discussion with the skipper. It turned out that an Italian oil tanker, the Mare Nostrum, had gone aground on reefs just off the island of Hallaniya which was part of the same Kuria Muria group we had previously visited following the Djibouti trip. These islands were around forty kilometres off the Omani coast, in the Arabian Sea. After a few days, the skipper had us all assemble in the tank deck. He explained that it was not clear how this tanker had managed to go aground as it was a bit off the normal shipping lanes. The crew had been rescued by an RFA (Royal Fleet Auxiliary) ship on 20th September. However, reports had come back that she was in danger of being raided by local pirates that were well armed. Because Agheila was flat bottomed, we could get alongside her, above the reefs she was on, and take off any valuable cargo that had remained on her. Apparently, she had been empty of oil when she struck the reefs, so there was no breach or local contamination.

Late that afternoon, we sailed. We were getting to know these waters well. Zippy was now fully integrated into the ship's crew and most of the time we didn't even know he was there. Early the following morning we were in sight of our destination. As I came out of the engine room onto the deck, I saw the massive bulk of the Mare Nostrum, slightly canted over to one side with quite a bit of her hull showing. All engines stopped as we waited some five hundred metres off her port side. The tide was high, and it gave us plenty of scope to come alongside. There was a lot of activity on deck as the bosun and deckhands readied the ropes that would be used to secure us to this massive ship. It dwarfed Agheila. Orders were shouted and slowly, metre by metre, we gradually closed on her. The port side of her had nets running down her hull where the crew had previously evacuated. This part of the coastline was rugged. Shore-side, you could see the mountains rising away from the coastline. This was a partial cove and with the mists lifting off the sea, the orders shouted out, echoed off the cliffs and the massive hull of the tanker.

Several of the lads clambered up the netting to get the ropes secured. Once this was done, the engines were idled and the ship was slowly pulled in by the ropes, using the winches. Buffers were slung out along our starboard side as we came up against the tanker's hull. Once the skipper was happy, everything was shut down. We were in place. Our bridge was just below the level of the tanker's main deck and a wheeled gangway was hauled in position and a temporary boarding point was now set up. The tide was still coming in, so lads were stood by the ropes constantly to keep watch. The silence, combining with the size of this massive ship was eerie. The cries of the gulls echoed around the bay and the only other noise was that of our generators.

We were asked to assemble in the forward mess and the first lieutenant came in to discuss how the boarding parties were to work and what we were expected to do. The officers and senior crew members were to take the officers' quarters and senior crew accommodation, wheelhouse, bridge, and main crew areas. The rest of us were organised into afterdeck details and would join the crew accommodation areas. I was detailed with Brummy and a couple of other lads. We were told to take the lower decks, aft. The object was to collect any personal or valuable items that may have been left behind and bring them back to Agheila. As the sun rose steadily, the day began to heat up. It was going to be a hot one. Standing on the canted deck of the tanker felt odd but once we had made our way to the cabins, we soon got used to it.

Wandering through the ship's lower crew decks was spooky. It was obvious that the crew had left in a hurry. Some of the cabins had been broken into so it was assumed that some of the looters had made it this far. After a couple of hours of this, Brummy and I were getting bored. Nothing much had been found by us but some of the officers had managed to locate the ship's chapel. Some damage had occurred, but they did salvage some valuable pieces. Groups of the lads had been set up on both ships and equipment and items were passed across to Agheila.

By early afternoon, Brum and I were hot and tired. We'd been going through the catering section of the ship and the galley. It was in a bit of a mess with dried peas scattered across the deck flooring making it a bit perilous. Not finding much, we wandered down aft to the very rear of the ship. There was a tarpaulin covered rear deck section and it provided some respite from the sun. We were knackered, it had been a tiring morning. We sat on a large, wooden hold cover and rolled a couple of smokes. The others were still going through all the other areas, but we were well out of the way, and no one could see us.

"Dave, you know, I had an uncle who served on an Italian ship for a while and he reckoned they liked their wine and lager," said Brum as he puffed on his roll-up.

I sat back on the hatch cover and thought about this. "Do you think this ship has a liquor store, then?" I asked Brum.

"I don't see why not – these ships are at sea for weeks on end," he said.

We both laid back on the hatch, thinking about this. "Well, we've looked in all the places we were asked to check and found nothing that looked like a wine store or, in fact, any alcohol at all!" I said.

"Well," Brum said, "if you were loading this ship, where would be the most likely place?"

"I should think it would be near the food storage, wouldn't it?" I asked.

"Yeah, but we've just looked around the galley and local food storage spaces," he said, looking a bit puzzled.

We both sat there awhile, leaning back on the hatch cover on the deck and in the shade, feeling nice and cool and rested. As I leaned back with my hands behind my head, I looked up. In the deck head immediately above me there was a block and tackle with a rope tied up to a metal strut. I sat up and looked down, wondering what the block and tackle lifted. In the middle of the hatch, we were sitting on was a large, metal eye bolt. Brum saw what I was looking at.

"What do you think is in this hold then?" he asked, "I mean, it's just adjacent to the galley where we've been looking, isn't it?"

I thought about this a moment. "It's big, Brum, do you think we can lift it?"

"Worth a try, no one's been down this end yet."

We both looked back down the ship. There was no one in sight. Most were storing gear on our ship and probably having lunch and a rest. It was the hottest part of the day.

We stood and flicked our butts over the side. "Come on," he said, "let's give it a try."

We untied the length of rope that was on the strut and Brum threaded it through the tackle block. I pulled the loose end and threaded this through the eye bolt in the hatch cover, back up through the tackle swivel, leaving a long piece of rope loose. We both got on the end of the rope and heaved. It was solid and nothing budged. We both took a breath,

"Come on, let's really go for it," he said.

We took deep breaths and pulled. Both of us were straining when we felt something shift. We looked down. The hatch had moved. Tightening our grips on the rope, we looked at each other, grinned and hauled our butts off. With a soft groan, the cover moved. We took up the slack further and pulled again. The hatch suddenly came free, revealing a large 4 x 4 ft deep black hole from which erupted the most pungent aroma. Alcohol. Hanging onto the rope, we both looked at each other. "Bingo!" we said together, grinning.

Brum tied off the rope to the ship's railing, leaving the hatch cover suspended in the air, gently swinging. We both looked down into the hold. It was pitch black, we couldn't see anything, but we could certainly smell it.

We both stood a moment, looking around the deck. No one had seen us or were nearby.

"Come on mate," said Brum with almost tears in his eye. "Let's investigate."

Down one side of the steel hatch rim was an iron ladder, descending vertically into the darkness. Very slowly I swung my legs over the side and started down the ladder, hand over hand. I had no idea what I was descending into or how long the ladder went down but I knew this was a big ship. As I was a good part of the way down, Brum started to come too, above me. Eventually, I touched bottom. It was cold down here and pitch black. I moved back a bit from the ladder to let Brum down. The smell was overwhelming, it was alcohol, lots of it from the strength of the smell.

Brum made it down and we both stood there a moment, our eyes slowly becoming adjusted to the dark.

"Blimey, Dave, the smell, it's unbelievably good!" he laughed.

He pulled out his Zippo lighter and flicked it on. The sight was staggering. We were in the booze store. There was rack after rack of wine, hundreds of bottles. There were dozens of cases of Champagne, arranged in columns across the floor. In another area of the hold crates of Drehers beer was stacked ten high across two bulkheads of the hold. Brum pulled a crate down and opened it, took a couple of bottles, and passed one to me. We opened them on the side of one of the metal racks. It was cold, premium lager beer. Wonderful stuff. We polished those off and got a couple more. I said to Brum, "You know what, I think this calls for some champagne. Let's have a champagne moment."

We finished the beer then I opened a case of Moet Chandon, pulled out a bottle, and handed it to Brummy. He worked the cork out and it shot out and hit one of the bulkheads. The champagne bubbled forth. By now, our eyes had adjusted nicely to the darkness and with the light from the opened hatch, we could see quite well. We sat down in a corner, away from the light from the hatch and passed the bottle between us.

"This is worth being sent all this way from Blighty, just for this moment," he said, grinning.

"Shit," I said, "this is magic, wait till the others find out!" We both laughed.

Halfway through the second bottle of champers we decided it was worth singing.

I think we must have been down there for a good hour before we were missed. One of the lads must have heard us and we saw this shadow of a head appear, up above, in the light of the hatch.

"Brum, Dave, is that you guys? Jesus is that booze I can smell?" he said. It was one of the seamen. We heard him calling out, so we went quiet and listened, trying not to laugh.

Next minute, we heard the gruff voice of the bosun. "Lawrence, English, is that you two down there?" he shouted.

"Yes Bose," Brummy said. "We've found the Holy Grail."

"Don't move, either of you, wait there," he called down and we heard him leave. We both looked at each other and burst out laughing,

"I ain't going anywhere, are you Dave?" Brummy said.

"No mate, think I'll sit here for a bit. Fancy a beer?"

"Why not?" he said.

A few minutes later another shadow appeared at the top of the hatch. "I'm coming down," a voice said. It was the skipper.

"Oh Christ," whispered Brum.

We both struggled to our feet, bottles in hand. When Venmore reached the bottom and turned, he still couldn't quite see us.

"Afternoon, Sir," Brummy said. "Your sight should clear in a mo."

Up above, more shadows appeared at the hatch. Venmore called out, "Wait up there and tell the No.1 I want him down here." He turned around as his eyes adjusted and he looked around. "Good God, you two, what have you stumbled upon?"

"The booze locker, Sir," I said.

"I think you bloody well have."

Brummy handed the skipper the now half-full second bottle of Moet. "Have a toast, Sir, to all those poor Italian lads of the Mare Nostrum."

The skipper took the bottle and had a mouthful. "Blimey, that's good," he laughed.

Just then a voice called down, "I'm here, Sir."

"Ok No.1, come on down, tell the others to wait up there."

A few minutes later we were joined by the first lieutenant. Once he had gotten over the shock of what was presented before him, we all sat down on the cool floor, taking in the implication of what we had here. Opening a third bottle of Moet, it was discussed how the spoils would be passed out among the crew. There was more than enough to keep us all going for the remainder of our stay in Aden, and in all likelihood, the trip back home to the UK. Also discussed was the long, slow process of hauling all this lot up, out of the hold and across to our ship.

Once the bosun understood what we had come across he quickly set about organising a means to get it out. With the help of some of the lads, he rigged up a hoist with a large tray on the end. This was lowered into the darkness where we were waiting and so began the long haul to get this store emptied. Brummy and I initially helped in between slugs of beer. The skipper and No.1 were also swigging the champagne. After a while, the skipper said we could leave and head back to the ship, sending the bosun down. Crawling up the ladder was a feat in itself and emerging into the late afternoon sun, was blinding. The lads, who had by now formed a chain and were passing the crates of beer, wine, and champagne back to the ship, stopped what they were doing and cheered and clapped as we took bows and rather wobbly, made our way over the side netting and back on board Agheila. It was a day to remember and as Brum and I settled into the mess for an early evening meal, the atmosphere aboard was good. Amazing what a few crates of alcohol can do, especially when it is free and unexpected, and in such large quantities.

33

Aden was starting to look like a transit camp, more than it ever had. Patrols had been stepped up, but this didn't seem to deter the odd sniping and grenade attack. About midway between Steamer Point and Khormaksar was a military ammunition store. I think it was at Maala. Tensions in the region had been 'ramping up' as the British withdrawal came nearer. We were looking forward to the trip home. Because of the Mare Nostrum affair, the ship was well stocked with beer and wine. It had been an interesting time. We had to leave a group of lads behind to look after the tanker until the tugs came to move her off and claim salvage because these islands were still under the British flag at this time. When we went back to pick them up, a couple of weeks later, we heard tales of how a group of 'pirates' had tried to board her again. This time our lads were waiting for them and after a brief gunfight, they cut their losses and departed. They never tried again. The guys were glad to get back aboard Agheila.

The whole business of how the Mare Nostrum ended up on the reefs of Hallaniya Island was a bit of a mystery but foul play was not ruled out. It was pretty obvious something dodgy had gone on there, especially being so far off the main shipping route. We never did find out, at least, us lot 'below decks' didn't, but we enjoyed the fall-out.

In preparation for our trip back to the UK, we had to go to the ammo store at Maala to take on stores and supplies. We normally held duty guard watches on the ship every day that we were tied up alongside, either at Steamer Point (HMS Sheba) or at any location. This duty watch entailed being armed and usually consisted of two of us patrolling the ship, one at each end. There had been several attacks in Aden during these closing stages, that had become more daring. One of these was a mortar and grenade attack on the High Commission, but it failed. However, it meant that we were all on heightened alert. On the day that we tied up at the ammo dump, Brummy and I happened to be on duty through the night. The only difference was that we had to change out of our overalls and wear our khaki uniforms. We were both issued with SLR rifles.

The jetty we were tied up alongside was a concrete landing stage. The whole place was behind a razor-wire compound. Also within it were the fuel tanks. There were at least two of these large, circular tanks that reminded me of the gas storage tanks at the Oval, in London. It was from these fuel tanks that we took on our fuel, when required. This particular night, nothing untoward was happening. Both of us would wander up and down the catwalks, one on either side of the ship. By midnight, all had quietened down on board. The generators were running but that was the only sound. Every now and again, Brummy and I would meet up, have a chat and a smoke before resuming our shipboard patrol.

The SLRs were on slings so both of us had them over our shoulders. At 01:00 a.m. we both met up on the bridge. From up here you got a good, overall view of the ship and the area we were tied up at. There were a couple of sodium lights atop lampposts on the jetty, spaced apart, but this was the only light apart from our shipboard lights. Our starboard side was against the jetty and our port side faced the open water. About a half mile from us, across the water, was an island. There were the odd lights from passing dhows but little else was stirring. It was going to be a long night. Brum decided it was time for tea.

"You hang in here; I'll go and make us a cuppa. Be back in a moment."

With that, he went below to the mess deck. It felt suddenly quieter. On the extreme wing bridges, were large searchlights, one each side. I wandered over to the port side wing and stood looking out over the water towards the island. After a few moments, I thought I heard something. At first, it sounded like a fish had jumped in the water – a small splashing sound. I wasn't particularly worried as it was not uncommon for fish to jump, catching insects attracted by the lights. I relaxed, leaning against the wooden handrail. There was hardly any moon, just a glow from behind clouds. It was then that I heard a different kind of noise. It was hardly there but it seemed different from the other noises, like the gentle lapping of the water against the hull. Or the odd engine sound from a distant dhow as it passed on the other side of the island. I listened hard, trying to isolate the sound. It sounded like someone breathing, but from up where I was standing, it was quite faint.

It was while I was listening intently that Brum arrived back with two steaming mugs of tea.

"All quiet then mate?" he asked, handing me my mug of tea.

I took it and said nothing for a moment. I took a sip of tea. "Tell me," I said, "can you hear anything odd?"

He looked at me quizzically. "What's up, mate? Are you hearing things?" he laughed.

"No, but listen, out there." I pointed out and down to the darkness and the water.

He stood quietly, frowning slightly, but listening. "Sounds like heavy breathing. You don't think one of the lads is playing with himself next to an open porthole, do you?" He burst out laughing.

"No, you bloody idiot, it's not that far aft. Sounds a bit further up this way," I said, rolling my eyes.

"I was joking, you dick."

"So, you can't hear anything then?" I asked him.

He listened a moment longer. Then, all of a sudden, a much louder breath came, almost like a whoosh and a splash of water.

"Shit!" he said. "What the fuck was that?"

We both listened. It was quiet for a moment then the breathing sound came again.

"Shit," he said quietly, "do you think there's someone in the water?"

"Like who? A frogman?" I whispered. "What the fuck would he be doing swimming about at this time of night?"

He looked at me, astonished at my naivety. "How about planting mines on the side of the ship?"

I stared at him. "What, you mean…?" then fell silent.

We both stood looking down into the water. The sound was still there. I put my mouth to his ear, "I have a plan," I said, quietly putting my mug of tea on the deck. "Why don't I put the searchlight on the area?"

He thought about this for a moment. "Tell you what… I'll go down to the catwalk and aim my rifle roughly in the area of the sound and, on my nod, you turn the searchlight on, down into that area," he said, pointing.

"Hadn't you better call the DO first?" I said.

"It may be too late by then. Time he gets out of his pit and on deck it'll be all over."

I thought about this. The duty officer wouldn't be in bed, but he was probably asleep on the bench in the officer's mess. This was not unusual.

"Ok, I suppose so," I said, still feeling a bit nervous. "What are you going to do if you see someone in the water?"

"Shoot the bastard," he said, pulling the slide quietly back on his SLR and putting a round in the breech.

"Jesus, Brum, don't miss him or we could all be in the shit."

"Listen, I heard a rumour that you're pretty good with a rifle – I don't mind if you do it."

I looked away, hoping he didn't see me go red. "No mate, it's just rumours. Besides, you're the NCO here, not me."

He looked at me a moment longer. "Okay," he said and started to walk to the ladder down. "Don't forget the light on my nod."

I gave him the thumbs-up, turned back to the lamp and moved it into position. I could reach the breaker for the lamp without moving away. I picked up my tea, took a swig and waited.

It was scary. If it was a frogman planting some kind of magnetic mine against the hull, it wouldn't take much to sink Agheila. Fortunately, it was pretty shallow here. But the fallout would be bad. I certainly didn't want the trip out here to end like this. All these things went through my head as I waited for Brum to get in position.

A few minutes later I saw him slowly moving along the catwalk, his rifle ready. As he moved towards the port rail, I could hear the noise of what sounded like heavy breathing coming from the position not far below where I was standing. Brum carefully raised his rifle and, leaning awkwardly over the side, got into position. He looked up at me and nodded. I hit the breaker that turned the searchlight on. The light came on, full power, with a hum. I grabbed the handles and aimed it down as far as I could, to the area of water at the side of the ship. It was tight and was at maximum depression. Brum hesitated a moment, then with the rifle on single shot fired a round. In quick succession, he did a 'double tap', firing two more rounds. In the silence of the night, the sound was deafening.

There seemed to be a few minutes when nothing happened at all. Then all hell broke loose in the area. Sirens went off, armed units started turning up at the jetty, and then Venmore appeared on the bridge in his PJs. He came over to me and I explained what had transpired. Next minute, Brum was joined by the duty officer, both armed and pointing their rifles over the side. Venmore disappeared below and as I probed with the searchlight, we all saw this long, black object, floating in the water near where we had heard the sound. It flapped about a bit and then was still.

It was a large porpoise, quite dead.

Later, it took some explaining to the skipper and the commander of the base where we were, what led up to it and our opinions. For some reason, they didn't quite see it our way. We should have called the officer of the watch before we decided to take action. Our defence was that we didn't think there was enough time. By the time the 'interrogation' was over, everyone was up, and the base was lit up like a Christmas tree.

Brum was fined for the cost of the three rounds of ammunition he expended. As if the bloody army couldn't afford that...! However, we did get some praise from the base commander for being alert. The lads on board thought it was a hoot and took the piss for the next couple of weeks. Never did find out what happened to the poor bloody porpoise. Apparently, it's not uncommon for these creatures to rub themselves against the ship's sides, sort of like an underwater scratching post.

34

One of our last pieces of work entailed a trip up the East coast and round to Bahrain to assist in the decommissioning of one of our LCTs that was being sold to the Bahrain Navy. When we arrived there, we tied up to a buoy, about 600 metres from the LCT and three of us engineers and a handful of seamen from Agheila were taken out to her in a small launch. Our job was to check out the engine and generator rooms whilst the deckhands would lay out the ropes, deck equipment and carry out a general tidy-up. After tidying up the engine room and carrying out last minute checks, I remember walking through the forward mess and thinking of all the stories and crew that must have passed through her during her life as an Army ship. I think the silence of her was unexpected and I couldn't help feeling melancholic. Another engineer and I were the last ones aboard her and as we climbed down a rope ladder to the waiting launch, I felt particularly sad. I knew she was saying goodbye in a kind of way, and I certainly felt that moment. In fact, it never left me, as I still feel it to this day. As we pulled away from her, I had to swallow hard. I didn't want to leave her like this. Ships will do that to you.

Once back in Aden, we were busy getting things ready for the trip back home. We took on cargo and before long, had quite a load in the tank deck. The military situation in Aden was deteriorating quite rapidly. All the married personnel who had been living in the high-rise blocks along Maala Strait had sent all the wives and families home. The blocks were then evacuated. Word had filtered down that the 'sappers' (Royal Engineers) were laying explosives in all the blocks and were going to destroy them as we withdrew from Aden. A sort of, 'last man out, turns the lights off', scenario. I'm not sure if they actually did carry that out but I like to think that that is what happened.

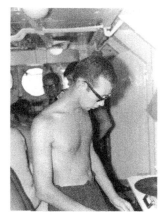

In the Forward Mess on board

We finally sailed from Aden in early November '66 and fortunately, I wasn't on engine room duty, so I had the opportunity to watch as we left HMS Sheba for the last time. I doubted that I would ever be back there again but as I was only twenty at the time, it could have been a possibility. The rocks and mountains that form the backdrop to the city of Aden are around 900 feet high and to see these dusty, adobe type dwelling with their square, box-like construction with minarets scattered amongst them, cramped together, and crowded up the hillsides, is quite a sight. It was early morning when we left, and the watery sun made quite a visual impact as it reflected off these ancient dwellings. I stood on deck as we sailed away, turning right, and heading up the Red Sea towards Port Said and the Suez Canal.

Seeing land on both sides is interesting. It was an experience of sight and smells. Although it was quite wide between coasts, you could see the distant hills and dunes. We stayed closer to the Saudi Arabian coast but the scents and views of, at first, Eritrea, then Sudan and then Egypt, all wafted across to the ship. It was fascinating and passing the enormous ocean-going dhows, was quite a thing to see. These craft were serious sea vessels, and it was not difficult to see how the tales of Arabian Nights could easily be imagined. The scent of spices was always hinted at on the offshore winds. This seaway was busier than I had expected, and it wasn't difficult to imagine a sea-going traffic jam as we neared the entrance to the Suez Canal.

We had to wait to take on a pilot before we embarked on travelling the Suez waterways. This pilot would remain with us all the way to what is known as the Great Lake, about halfway up. From there, another pilot would take over and see us through the rest of the way. I was fascinated and in between engine watches, I spent a lot of time on deck, observing the sights as we passed along. We were tiny compared to some of the ships going through. As we entered the canal, we had a massive cargo ship ahead of us and nothing behind for quite some distance. The shoreline on both sides rapidly closed in and you felt as if you were on a road. The sights have probably changed quite significantly in 50 years, but I doubt by much. Date palms and small villages were spread out along the way. Sometimes, an old ruin or mosque could be seen but mostly it was small fishing villages with young children running along the banks, waving, and shouting. Our ship, Agheila, was the last military vessel to pass through the canal before it was, yet again, shut down. This time, I think it was the Israelis that may have had something to do with that. There were wrecks of ships that required careful navigation past, hence the pilot. Halfway through the canal, we came to what is known as the Great Lake. Here we stopped and dropped anchor for the night. The pilot that had seen us this far, left the ship and in the morning, another came aboard. He would see us through the rest of the way to Port Said. That night, I sat on deck and had a smoke. The desert air was clear and all the twinkling lights of other ships, also at anchor, made for quite a sight. There was certainly an atmosphere about the place.

We left at dawn the following morning, having taken on the pilot for the final section. It was slow progress and in places, reminded me many years later, of some of the Fen waterways of Cambridgeshire and Norfolk. We passed through another lake by Ismailia then the final run to Port Said. Here, we dropped anchor again whilst the pilot left, and clearance was obtained for us to continue. It was a case of turning left after leaving Port Said and the long haul across the Mediterranean to Malta which was to be our next stop. As this was quite a way to go, we took on fuel at Port Said from a fuel jetty. There was no shore leave although the skipper and some of the senior crew were allowed ashore. I managed to get a post card off to Mum from here. Once we'd fuelled, we moved to a buoy to await departure. It was here that the so called, 'bum-boats' came alongside selling just about everything. The skipper allowed a 'hully-gully' man on board who sold schmutter trinkets, dates and nuts and did 'magic' with card tricks and the proverbial pea under three eggcups. The lads were in hoots over this, betting like loonies. You could even get an Arab girl on board for a 'quick one' but that was definitely not allowed...! These boats sold everything.

The trip across the Med was quite a long stint. It was also quite rough seas. It is about one thousand nautical miles from Port Said to the Maltese harbour of Valetta. I think it took us about four days to cross this stretch. I do remember it being quite rough as we turned to enter the harbour at Valetta. It was November and we all noticed the change in the weather. It was sunny and clear, but quite cool compared to Aden. We tied up alongside a wharf about halfway into the harbour entrance, right-hand side as you enter. Across the way, on the other side of the harbour, there was a fortress which in ancient times would have guarded the entrance to the island's capital.

This part of Valetta was a walled city and from the wharf side where we were tied up, were steps leading up to the town centre. We were all glad to be here and stationary. It had been a bit of a rough crossing and it had been tiring. There was work to do however, maintenance schedules and fuelling up for the next stage of the trip to Gibraltar. We had stores and fresh water to take on, but it was also a chance to get some shore leave. We would be here for about two weeks.

Most of the first week we were busy, but it was good to be alongside and not rolling about. Once the work was done, we were given our duties. In between our duty watch work, we were given shore leave. Some of the lads had been ashore already and reports were coming back about a place just outside the port area where we were tied up, called 'The Gut'. I'd heard tales from my brother-in-law Ken, of this place, as he had been stationed here on minesweepers during the war, and I was looking forward to visiting it. It was of course, the red-light area of Valetta. The main thoroughfare was Strait Street which consisted of narrow alleyways and cobbled, twisting roads full of bars. There were a few shops there but mostly it was these little tavernas.

My first run ashore was with a mate of mine, Stu. JC and some of the others had been already and found their favourite bars. It was early afternoon when Stu and I went ashore. It was hot and dusty and much as we had been told, narrow, cobbled streets and mostly full of bars. At this time of day, all was very quiet as they had *siesta* here, which meant that not a lot was open. Most of the bars were open but these were pretty much empty although they would still serve you. One thing we had noticed were that these places were mostly staffed and run by women. Because there were so many to choose from, we hardly came across any of our crew. Wandering around sightseeing was thirsty work so in the end, we found a little, quiet bar, not far from the harbour and went in for a drink. It had plastic, bead curtains over the entrance and it took a moment for your eyes to adjust to the dark interior. It consisted of a bar counter that ran almost the length of the room, facing the entrance. There were a few bar stools lined up and an elderly woman and a younger one behind the bar. Both were sitting reading local newspapers when we entered. We were in uniform and luckily, were the only military ship in port. We were warmly greeted and ordered a couple of beers. They knew we were English, so I guessed another of our lads had been here already.

The beer was good, cold, and reasonably priced. Both women spoke good English and, before long, we were chatting about the UK. After a while, another, younger girl joined them and they made it clear that if we wanted any of the three, they were available. Well, I'd made it this far without one and we were almost home. A few more weeks was not going to hurt. So, we both declined the offers. They didn't seem to be bothered by this and in fact, I got the impression they were a bit relieved. Instead, they offered us a meal each, to go with the beer, so we stayed for that. There was a jukebox in one corner of the bar and Stu put some music on to play. It was pleasant there. The beer and the food were good, and the women were good fun and chatty. We'd tried other bars earlier but both of us found this one the most relaxing. The day went quickly and by early evening we decided it was time to get back aboard. They were sorry to see us go but we promised to be back. We did too. Every run ashore we went back to this bar. Some of the other lads dropped in from time to time, had a couple of beers and left. We both remained and asked them about places to see. They told us about this cave you could go down that had some religious significance and the horse-drawn carriages, called 'Garrys' by the Brits. So off we went. I took my camera, determined to get some photos.

Walking through the centre of Valetta you began to realise how much influence the Catholic church had. There were churches everywhere, the largest being a big cathedral. I stopped outside one particular ornate church and took some pictures. Almost immediately, these two clerics came running out shouting and waving their arms.

"No pictures, no pictures," they shouted angrily.

They wanted me to open the back of my camera to expose the film. We both told them to take a hike, army style. Later on, as we were walking past shops towards the main cathedral, an enormous stretch limo with darkened windows pulled up just near the cathedral entrance. An extremely large, fat priest in a black cassock with an odd, shaped hat was helped from the back of the car. As he stepped out, women, who had been walking by, immediately ran over and got to their knees in the street in front of him. He stood there, holding out his left hand. On one of his fingers was an enormous ruby ring. They grabbed his hand and kissed the ring. Children also ran over to him and did the same. It was sickening to watch. This place was quite a poor nation, yet the Catholic church was very wealthy. Not untypical of many very catholic countries.

One of the sights to see was a coastal section of road where all the houses along it were painted a different colour. In the afternoon light it was quite something to see. We visited the cave where you had to go down this long staircase that took you deep into the bowels of the rock. There was some religious story behind this cave, but I don't remember what it was. Later that day, the two of us took a 'Gary' around the town centre of Valetta. Eventually, we migrated back to the bar. As we entered, the women were all looking excited about something. It turns out, they had heard that an American warship was due in the next day. How they knew, I've no idea but they had a favour to ask us. As we were both regular customers and they trusted us, would we mind tending bar for them for a few hours that following evening, whilst they 'entertained' the Americans. It was an opportunity not to be missed. They told us how much to charge the Yanks and that we could drink for free. The 'mother' would be around but mostly, upstairs. We agreed.

The next evening, we arrived around 5pm and were shown where things were and what to do. Sure enough, the Yanks came, and they kept the place busy. Both Stu and I loved it. We charged them extra to what we were told to charge, and they didn't argue. Some of our own lads had heard what we were doing and popped in for a beer. It was great fun and we both enjoyed working behind the bar, serving the lads (ours got their beer cheaper, of course). We did this for two days running but then had duty aboard ship so that ended our run. But we had both enjoyed it and the girls were pleased with our easy-going style, as barmen. They'd made a good profit too.

My last run ashore was with a group of the lads. Some of them had found a bar with a gay pianist in that was a hoot so we all descended on this particular bar. We sat around the piano and got this elderly gay to play all the songs we asked. He was very good and funny too. Weeks later, when I was back home, I mentioned this place to Ken, my brother-in-law. He said he knew the bar and the pianist and was surprised to hear that he was still alive and playing there.

Our next stop was Gibraltar but on leaving the relative calm of the protected Valetta harbour walls, we were soon hit by the choppy seas of the Med. Apparently, several tides and currents meet here, and the initial ride was rough. Fortunately, we were fully fuelled up and had heavy cargo on the tank deck, so we were quite stable in the water. Some of the lads were quite green around the gills but once we were past Sicily and coursing round the top of North Africa, it eased off. Next stop was Gib, a final refuel, take on stores, then the run for home. It took us almost a week to make Gibraltar. We would be spending a few days here before making the final run.

We arrived in Gibraltar on 28th November and this time I was pretty busy. The generators needed servicing, work which couldn't be done easily whilst underway. So, I only managed to get one run ashore. This time it was the usual group of about six of us that went. It was decided that Gib was too tame, so it was suggested that we go across the border into Spain, to the border town of La Linea. Some had obviously heard that this was the place to go, especially, to see an 'exhibition'. Once we crossed the border checkpoint we came onto the main street of the place. Again, it was like a scene from an old western. It was a hot, dusty, scruffy place with bars and a few stores.

With a couple of the lads asking directions in various bars, it wasn't long before we found this dusty backstreet with what looked like adobe shacks. We were directed to one by the taxi driver that took us. We were met by two women who showed us into one of these adobe dwellings and into the cool interior of a sparsely furnished room. We sat on a mixture of chairs in the room, were offered beer and asked what we would like to see. The older of the women, who looked like the boss or 'madam' of the place, took us into a curtained side room. I noticed that two of the lads remained outside chatting to other girls that had arrived on the scene. In this little room was a rickety old bed, a small wooden table, and some chairs. On the table was a small shot glass and some candles. In our naivety, none of us knew what to expect. We handed over the money that she asked for and she laid herself down on the bed. She lifted her skirt and took off her knickers. Bringing her knees up and opening them wide she proceeded to insert the shot glass into her vagina with the open end of the glass in first. When it was right inside, we were then invited to look through the bottom of the now inserted glass. I suppose if you were a medical student, it would be an extreme teaching session...! In all its glory and detail, there was the cervix and the entrance to the uterus for all and sundry to see. She gyrated her hips and all the 'bits' moved. Most of us grabbed our beer bottles and took a heavy pull on them.

Removing the glass, she then started inserting candles into the same orifice. Each was about three inches long. She inserted about four of these then asked one of the lads to stand in front of her to catch the candles as she then shot each one out individually. We all fell about as these things shot out of her like a bullet.

Her final 'trick' was to put about a dozen quite large coins in a stack inside herself, stand up, and then drop each one individually into the shot glass. By this time, we were all laughing and marvelling at the control she had. The final part was when she asked who now wanted to have sex with her. There were vigorous shakes of heads all round. As we went into the main room, she pulled aside a curtain and there was one of the lads in 'full flight' with his trousers around his ankles, giving one of the girls a good rooting from behind. We all clapped and cheered. He didn't bat an eyelid, just carried on and told us to leg it.

By the time we got outside I think we had all had enough. There was a small stable across the way. The older woman went inside and came out leading a donkey that had seen better days. There appeared to be various straps across it and as the woman started taking her clothes off, we all looked at each other and decided that we had had enough. She'd already been remunerated for her 'entertainment services' so we called out to the lad still inside that we were going and walked out of the place. Once all together again, we picked up a taxi and made our way back to Gib. We soon found a bar where we slaked our thirst from some well-deserved beer and gave a toast to the poor donkey. By this time all we wanted to do was get back aboard. There had been something unsettling about our visit to La Linea and I think we were all glad to leave and get underway for the last leg of the journey home.

35

The weather changed quickly but the winds and seas were in the right direction. We'd left Gibraltar on 1st December, so our arrival home was estimated to be the 6th or 7th. It would have been earlier but crossing the Bay of Biscay was notorious for its rough seas and of course, we weren't disappointed. Out warmer clothes came out and for once, I was pleased to be down in the engine room. Time off duty was mostly spent sleeping or playing bridge in the mess.

As we rounded France and entered the Channel you could feel the mood change aboard. People started chatting again and the atmosphere that you always get on long stints at sea with no sight of land, changed. Spirits were high and we were longing for the sight of Portsmouth harbour. First, we had to clear customs and just outside the harbour, a customs crew from a launch, boarded us. The other issue was Zippy, and we were all concerned about how long he would have to go into quarantine. However, our fears were put to rest when a day away from home, word came back from no less than Dr Desmond Morris that Zippy was a rhesus monkey and had a blood type that was the same as humans. A blood sample had been taken in Gibraltar, analysed, and confirmed. It also turned out that Zippy was a rare form of Macaque and on the endangered list. No quarantine was necessary for him

Customs cleared us, after a team went through the ship checking for contraband, allowing us to enter harbour. It was good to see Pompey again and as we turned into the Gunwharf, I realized how scruffy looking our ship had become compared to the other LCTs tied alongside. Agheila had served us well and shutting down the engines brought a lump to my throat. Even the hum of the generators seemed muted. We all met in the Mess and the skipper came down to thank us all. Many of the wives of those married had come to the quayside to see us tied up and these lads were given their shore leave. The rest of us packed our gear and prepared to leave the ship. Agheila was going to be taken over by another crew and was off to dry dock for a paint job and general overhaul. However, leave would wait until we had completed our work aboard. Many of us had outstanding leave and I was due three weeks. This would take me to the end of December, and I was looking forward to the time at home. It was 7th December and, as the married lads left the ship, I remember sitting in the mess with a few of the lads, wondering how it had all happened so quickly. They were all talking about what they were going to be doing at Christmas and I felt a little knot of excitement about going home. I would leave Agheila the next day for my three weeks leave.

For some reason, I had decided not to ring home but turn up as a surprise for Mum. In my kit, I had packed the US Naval uniform on top of my other bits, in my case. I thought, as a joke, I would put it on whilst on the train, on the final leg home. On my return from leave I was to join HMAV Andalsnes for a spell before re-joining Audemer. Back on the train, I changed into the US uniform that I had got from the lad when I went to get the beer at the NAAFI club, back in Aden. The only trouble was, it was their summer uniform, and it was winter here. Still, the day was bright and sunny so I didn't mind too much, hoping nobody would notice.

I arrived at Bishop's Stortford station and took a cab to Mum's house at Beldams Lane. The cab dropped me off a little down the road, so I walked along the pavement until I spotted the house.

It all looked very quiet, and I didn't even see anyone else along the road. As it was a Thursday, I assumed most people were working. It was just after 01:00 p.m. when I strode up the drive with my case and knocked on the door. There was no answer and looking through the windows it was pretty obvious no one was home. I could only guess that Mum was at Dee's, so I put the case around the back of the house, went down the street to the telephone box and called a cab. He dropped me off at Dee's and I knocked the door. There was no answer... I couldn't believe it. I'd come all this way, and no one was in. My little joke with the US sailor's uniform had fallen flat. I'd slung a small kit bag over my shoulder in which were some gifts for Mum, Dee, and Ken as well as a bottle of vodka. I decided to sit on the front step and drink the vodka. My intention had been to tell them I had joined the US Navy. Bloody daft now I look back at it. So, I sat back and enjoyed the vodka until Dee's neighbour, Sue, came out and saw me. She guessed who I was and invited me in to warm up. By this time, I was starting to get cold as well as nearing the limit of my alcohol intake. All I really wanted was to sleep. I stayed with Sue who plied me with cups of black coffee until I was eventually, rescued. When Ken came round to collect me, I was pretty much out of it and remember very little of what happened after that. The best laid plans, etc.

I loved Mum's little house. It was cosy and she had put a lot of effort in to make it home. After the months aboard ship, it was good to get into a proper bed and back to some home-cooking. The leave was a blur of events, but it was mostly, just good to be with Mum as well as Dee and Ken. Little Debbie was a joy, and I could see how close Mum was to her. I think it was this that had kept Mum going, through the lonely days. Mum didn't drive so when she went to town shopping, it meant either getting the bus which came only once an hour, or walking. Knowing Mum, she spent it walking, most times. She missed not having people around her and the spaciousness of the London flat. She also missed her neighbours. This was country life and Mum had been a city person most of hers. One evening, sitting in front of the fire, she told me that she had been so depressed at one point, that she had wanted to end it all. Thank God she never went through with it, but I was starting to get the picture. Now, as I write this, I feel that I had somehow failed her. I really should have given her more of my time and been a lot more thoughtful. I was too wrapped up in my own life and friends, mates and of course, the ship. But I guess that's life and we just have to get on with it. The bond between a mother and son is nearly always very strong but at twenty-one I guess I was too full of the adventures of life and missed the little parts that would have meant so much to Mum in those days.

Christmas was over and all too soon, it was time to go back to Portsmouth and my new ship posting. I was sent to Andalsnes L4097, as a temporary measure as they were short of crew, but I was told it would only be until she was ready to go North on a Scotland run. Because the internal layouts of the LCTs are pretty much all the same, it didn't take long to get settled in. However, it did mean lots of painting of the bloody engine room and Mess once more. Life in Portsmouth settled back again and very little had changed in the NAAFI club and the Still & West.

36

As I have said, the layouts of all these ships were pretty much standard. What was different was how the ship was looked after. Some were certainly better than others. The '97 needed a lot of paint jobs, and it wasn't long before we were at it again. The military was quiet at this time and not a lot was happening. We were spending most of the time in the Gunwharf at HMS Vernon which was good for runs ashore. There was a sort of post-Christmas lull in the talent at the NAAFI Club. Mum had started working at the Herts & Essex Hospital and this opened up the nurse scene a little later in the year. Meanwhile, I was having fun with a Wren DSA, Babs. She was a coloured girl with a great sense of humour, and we had some good laughs.

Dip had met and got on well with my family and that winter of '67, we went for a long weekend to Brighton. I had relatives that lived in Hove, so Dip and I managed to get a B&B nearby. My two Uncles, Doug, and Ern both lived in the same street as each other but because their wives had had a falling out some twelve years previously, they never spoke to each other. Bloody ridiculous but Dip and I decided to meet them in a nearby pub. Well, we had a skinful and a really good laugh. That Friday night we sort of staggered our way back to the

B&B. Also staying at this place were a group of nuns. To save money, Dip and I were sleeping in a double bed, pushed up against a window. In the middle of the night, I woke up wanting to take a leak. I was still feeling the effects of the alcohol and knew the WC was down the hall a way. Because I was sleeping on the inside, under the window, I would have to crawl over Dip to get out of the bed. I didn't want to wake him, so I decided to pee out of the window.

I sat up in just my underpants and opened the window fully. It was a sash window, so I had room to easily get to the sill and sit on it whilst having a pee into the back garden. We were on the first floor and directly beneath our window was the slanting, glass roof of a lean-to greenhouse, attached to the rear wall. From the guttering that ran the length of the glass roof, ran a short downpipe into a metal dustbin which was being used to catch the run-off water or, as I intended, my pee...

As I sat on the sill I must have briefly nodded off and slipped. The next thing I knew I was sliding down the sloping, glass roof of the greenhouse, came off this and hit the tin lid of the empty, metal dustbin and knocked the dustbin over. The noise was enough to set a dog barking across the way somewhere. Otherwise, all was dark, silent, and very cold, as I sat there, now fully awake, thinking, *Oh shit.*

Somewhat dazed, I sat there a moment and took stock. I was fine, only a lightly grazed leg. The only thing damaged was a bent dustbin lid and my dignity. I gingerly stood, took a pee on a flower bed, and then realised how cold it was. The garden was quite small, with about a two square metre patch of grass that was showing the frost beginning to settle and I was getting mortally cold. For a while, I jumped up and down to keep warm and then started running around in a circle on the patch of grass. If I didn't die of exposure in the meantime, I suppose I could wait until morning and then knock on the door, explaining that I had been sleep-walking and had gone out for a run. However, I guess rigor mortis would have set in by then, especially as it was only just after 02:00 a.m.

Looking back up at the open window, I worked out a route whereby I may be able to climb back in. Putting the lid back on the dustbin I could just maybe get back up onto the greenhouse roof. I righted the dustbin and as quietly as I could, put the lid back on it and gingerly, managed to get on the top of it. By this time, I was frozen and was shaking. I looked up at the sloping, glass roof and could just get my nose to the lowest part. Gripping the glass edge of the roof I started to haul myself up. When I managed to get the edge to waist height, I swung my legs sideways and managed to roll onto the sloping roof. It was a good job I was a lightweight. Halfway up the roof was a leaded ridge that separated the panes of glass. I managed to grip this and gradually get a purchase on it with my now frozen toes. Very slowly I got to my hands and knees and carefully made my way to the top of where it was joined to the brickwork of the house. The open window was quite a way above my head. So, very gently, with my hands on the brickwork, I stood up. The sill was still a way above my head but stretching out with my hands, I just managed to get a grip on the rough stonework of the ledge. Taking a deep breath, I started to haul myself up. Fortunately, although I wasn't particularly strong, I was quite agile and bit by bit, I hauled myself up so that I could swing a leg over the sill. The stone was rough, and I knew I'd grazed my leg and it was now starting to bleed. With a final heave, I fell back into the room, narrowly missing Dip's sleeping form. As I was bleeding, I decided to sleep on the floor so as not to make a mess of the sheets. Grabbing a blanket, I rolled up on the carpet and covered the blanket over me. I breathed a massive sigh of relief and once the shaking had settled down, I slept.

As daylight dawned, I woke up to see Dip looking at me over the side of the bed. "What the fuck are you doing down there?" he said.

I explained what had happened and he fell about, thought it was a hoot. "It's not that bloody funny," I said. "I was freezing and if anyone had seen me, running around the garden at 02:00 a.m. in me underpants, I'd have been locked up!"

I had a nasty graze on my thigh, so it was just as well I'd slept on the floor. Once dressed, we went down to breakfast, and I was so glad that no one had seen me in the garden at that time.

There were four nuns sitting at a table having their breakfast as we pulled out a couple of chairs at an adjacent table. I looked across at the nuns and said, "Good morning sisters."

One of the sisters looked at me, saying, "Good morning, Mr English, I trust you slept well last night?" She looked at the other three nuns who grinned and looked down at their plates.

I swallowed hard. "Oh yes, fine thank you."

"Did you not find it a bit chilly?" she said.

I looked at Dip, who looked at me and grinned. I could feel the colour rising to my face. She had obviously seen me last night.

"Er, well, it was a bit, yes." I smiled hesitatingly at her, now feeling very hot under the collar. Just then, the lady came to take our breakfast order. A little later as they got up to leave their table, she came across, put her hand on my arm, smiled and said, "You might want to think about wearing pyjamas during these cold months," smiled and followed the other nuns out.

In May '67 I was sent on an engineering upgrade course. This meant moving ashore to the Gosport barracks. The upgrade was to a Marine Engineer Tech.II and I was currently a Tech.III engineer which also meant that if I passed the course my pay would increase. The course was spread between Gosport and Marchwood. The Wilson government was not doing too well at this time, and we were still in the throes of a biting recession. The military was probably a better place to be during this spell although I didn't really appreciate that at the time.

The course went well, and I actually enjoyed it. One of the highlights was a trip out on a fast patrol boat. We had one of these in the fleet, but I'd never been on it before. It was crewed by civilians and its sole purpose was for training. The engines were Vosper Thornicroft turbines, and this boat could shift. They were used in Hong Kong for patrol duties alongside police and customs vessels out in those waters. Should I be so lucky as to get a posting to Hong Kong, these were the craft I would be serving on.

The day of the trip was good. It was sunny, blue skies with a bit of a wind. There were three of us engineers from the course and we'd left from the wharf at Gosport to sail across to Cowes on the Isle of Wight and back. The objective was to give us a taste of these craft, observe the performance and work in the engine room. Once out of the harbour, the skipper opened the throttles, and the craft took off. It was amazing but even the slightest wave was a bit like hitting a rock. Out on deck, you really had to hold on whilst, in the engine room, you had to use ear protectors. The high-powered whine of the engines was head numbing, even with the ear protectors on. In the wheelhouse, the skipper sat on a high stool with the throttles, like those of an aircraft. The wheel itself, was a large, thin spoked, stainless steel one that looked almost too large. The entrance to the engine room was to the rear of the helmsman's position. Steps led down to a small galley area, a couple of bunks on each side and then the hatch to the engine room. It was fascinating and the thought of being posted to serve on one was exciting.

A couple of hours at Cowes and then we turned for Portsmouth and back to base. During this run back we were going to be given the opportunity to steer the craft. Each of us took a turn at it and I was the last. We were about a ½ hr away from the harbour entrance when I was allowed to sit in the helmsman's chair and take control. It was great. I was shown the course to steer and what side of the buoys to be. Everyone settled down and the skipper went below with the others for some tea and a chat. The power at your fingertips was immense and although we were not at full throttle, we were moving well. A landmark to aim for was a large block of flats in the far distance, at Eastleigh. The minutes ticked by, and the guys were still below, chatting. After a few minutes I gently nudged the throttles forward a little. There was only a slight change in noise, but the launch picked up speed. I tried to keep the buildings lined up and was doing well. I gently nudged the throttles forward a bit more. It was brilliant. The spray was hitting the forward screens, but the visibility was good. In the distance, I noticed a large naval ship leaving the harbour. She was still within the harbour but was slowly making her way out. It was one of the new frigates, looking sleek and big from where we were. As I looked, I noticed we were coming up on her a bit faster than I had expected. I moved the throttles back to the position they were originally in and called out to the skipper. They either didn't hear me or were too busy gossiping. I shouted a bit louder. We were now approaching the harbour entrance. I'd gone the correct side of the first buoy but looming in front of me was the pointy end of this now, massive looking frigate. The skipper must have heard my louder shout and wandered rather aimlessly, into the wheelhouse, mug of tea in hand.

"What's up?" he said, then he looked out the front screens. "Oh shit." He pushed me off the chair, grabbed the wheel, and started to move us over across the front of the bows of the frigate.

A large siren boomed across the harbour as the frigate warned us of our approach. Sailors were now lining the bow, waving their arms about. I grimaced and seriously felt like waving back but thought I'd better not.

We narrowly avoided the bows of the frigate and managed to squeeze down the side of her, between the hull and the marker buoys. Our course instructor came into the wheelhouse and looked at both me and the skipper. The skipper was good about it though, saying, "We arrived here a bit sooner than I expected."

Meanwhile, the admiralty sent a not too pleasant message to the craft. My legs felt like rubber and my hands were trembling. I never did tell them that I had opened the throttles up but then, they never told me which side of the harbour I was supposed to be on when entering, at least, if they did, I couldn't remember. Fortunately, it didn't affect my course results and I passed the upgrading course, well.

Following the course, I was sent back to my old ship, Audemer L4061. I was a happy boy to be back aboard her. I had kept in touch with my old mates Les Topping, Tom Thomas and of course, Dip. He was now a corporal engineer on Audemer, and our friendship was firm. Andy Mortimer was also aboard her and it was good to be back together again.

37

We were on the right side of the year, and we had summer ahead of us. The weather was improving and as usual it was time to get stuck into more painting. This time it was our own forward mess that needed doing. This was to be a joint venture between us engineers and the seamen. Six of us carried out the work done in shifts of two during our watch time. The lad working with me was an engineer called Harry Marsden from the Isle of Man. He had been an engineer for a couple of years and most of that was on Audemer, I believe. Harry used to like his bed. On his days off duty, he would spend the majority of his time sleeping, tumbling out of his pit sometime around 04:30 p.m. to 05:00 p.m., in time for dinner and a night out. He had a very calming presence about him, was quietly spoken and game for anything. I hadn't spent much time with him ashore as it had been, up until then, Tom that I had mostly gone ashore with. But Tom had hooked up with a Wren called Steve, whose full name was Stephanie, but we all knew her as Steve. She wasn't a part of our little clique of DSA Wrens that we usually went around with. He'd met her, I think, at Marchwood and they had struck up a close relationship. She was a Londoner from Charlton and was quite a strong character. Their relationship was getting serious, and they were making wedding plans for some time early in the following year of '68.

So it was that Harry and I spent a few runs ashore. Once Harry had a few drinks 'on board' he was a total nutter. Following a particular heavy drinking session one evening, Harry and I staggered through HMS Vernon and turned right for our walk round to the Gunwharf. Harry decided to do this on his hands and knees. I just wandered along beside him, laughing my head off. Once at the gangway of our ship, the duty officer refused to let him aboard unless he entered the ship normally. This was Harry, he had his own agenda.

One Saturday we had both gone for a lunchtime pint in the NAAFI club. Sitting around with some of the lads off the RN ships, we heard about a naval officers wedding that had taken place that morning. The reception was being held in the Naval Officers Club that afternoon. I didn't even know where the Naval Officers Club was, but Harry did. He suggested that we gate-crash the reception. He said that he had been in there before and got away with it. There are usually so many people at these do's that nobody knows all of them and who was with who. Also, as they nearly always put an amount behind the bar, drinks are free as well as the food. In my slightly inebriated state, it seemed like a good idea. As it turned out, we happened to be quite reasonably dressed, perhaps what you would call, 'smart informal' and I also carried my ubiquitous umbrella. It was a full-length job with a lacquered wooden handle. I was hoping this would add to the air of the dapper 'Man about town' – foolish boy...!

The club was quite near Vernon, and I was feeling a bit self-conscious and nervous to carry this out. Harry assured me it was fine, so we tentatively made our way up the steps of the club. Once inside, it felt better. There were plenty of people standing around chatting, some in uniform, others in civvies. Harry immediately went up to one of the club staff and asked where the groom was, pretending to momentarily have forgotten his name. The staff member told him and Harry just grinned and said, of course. Then I saw a board with the names on of the couple. Once armed with this information, the rest was easy. We were either old friends of the groom or the bride. Harry knew where the bar was, so we went through. There were not too many there. Many couples and friends were still arriving, so we didn't feel out of place. Once we'd ordered our drinks the rest was easy. We stood at the bar, chatting and drinking, speaking in our best quality English and laughing. After about an hour of free booze, I asked Harry where the toilets were.

"I'll come as well, he said, follow me."

We went down a short corridor and there it was. Once inside, we both wandered over to this long urinal trough, unzipped and proceeded to pee. We were stood in the middle of this long run of trough and well into my pee I heard the door open behind me and someone come over to stand on my left. I didn't look up as they unzipped.

"English, Marsden, do you mind telling me what you are both doing in here?"

I suddenly looked to my left. To my horror, our No.1, or first lieutenant, was stood next to me.

"Er, having a pee, Sir?" I said, timidly.

"Do either of you know the bride and groom?"

Harry zipped up and said, "We just thought we would see what it was like here, Sir."

"Well, get back to the ship now and I will discuss this with you later."

We left. Of all the luck, we happened to run into one of our own officers, from our own ship. I was a bit concerned about what would happen, but Harry didn't appear to be bothered at all. As it turned out, we weren't dealt with too harshly, fined a couple of days pay. The lads thought it was a hoot. For a while after, whenever we went ashore, the duty officer would call out, "Don't let me catch either of you in the Naval Officers Club."

Our workload picked up and it was time for exercises in various waters around the coast and Ireland. My mate, Les Topping married his long-time girlfriend, Roma and I was to be best man. For some reason, I didn't do it but cannot remember why. Les and I went back a long way, to my Chepstow days and he knew all my family. Goodness knows what happened there.

I finally got around to writing to Mum and telling her I had passed my engineering course and she was well pleased, more with just getting a letter from me than anything else. It wasn't until these much later years that reading through her letters to me, I realised just how lonely she was. Now, in my seventies, I read through her letters to me during '67 and realise how much she missed us all. There she was, in a little two bedroomed semi, in a small rural town, on her own. Having come from a large, four bedroomed flat in central London, to this, must have been a shock. From a large place with lots of family and friends, to solitude. I had never given it a thought and it was pretty obvious that Delia hadn't either. Fortunately, Delia had Debbie who was just over a year old. She was Mum's saviour as she would take Debbie out in the pram and walk for miles with her.

Delia's friends and Ken (my brother-in-law) had helped to get Mum's house to her liking, with new kitchen cupboards, fixtures in the two bedrooms and new paint. There was a middle-aged couple with a young daughter next door to her and an elderly couple, Mr & Mrs Perkins, living on the other side. She also had a garden of reasonable size and loved planting and pottering in it. There was a bus stop outside the house, but these were infrequent so if she went into town shopping, she would often walk there and back.

She had tried a couple of different jobs but none to her liking, so she didn't stay in them long. In the end, she managed to get the job of Home Warden at the Herts & Essex Hospital, a seven-minute walk away. She really enjoyed it, and the nurses loved her. The combination of those nurses and Debbie were Mum's saving grace. Many years later, I talked to her about those times, and she told me that at one point, she had contemplated suicide. I felt (and still do), awful for not getting my head around those issues she was having. But in my haste to live and enjoy my life, I hadn't given it a thought. She missed her kids, Di, Jo, and me. Also, all her friends were back in London. It had been a very difficult time for Mum, and I didn't help much by not keeping in touch more regularly. When I did manage to make it home for the odd weekend, I started to meet the nurse friends Mum had made. One of these was Carol, a West Indian girl from Trinidad. She was a midwife at the H&E. We started to date when I was home, but nothing too serious.

Back in Pompey life was good. I tried very hard to keep out of trouble, but it was always hovering in the background. One night, a group of us had gone into Pompey for our Friday night out and this time decided to go to different pubs rather than our normal haunts. Needless to say, we'd all got pretty well slaughtered, and I was not feeling brilliant so decided to get a taxi back to Vernon. Opposite the Guildhall was a taxi rank. As I walked towards it, I could see several taxis on the rank. I walked to the front car and got in the front passenger seat. There was no driver. I sat waiting for a minute or so, but nobody came. I noticed the two-way radio on the front dash, so picked it up, pressed a button on the side and asked where the driver was. A voice came back asking me who I was. I said it didn't matter who I was but where was the bloody driver. I kept asking for a minute or so then all of a sudden, the passenger door was flung open, and a pair of hands grabbed me out of the vehicle and pushed me up against a wall.

"What the fuck do you think you're doing?" an aggressive voice said. He was holding me up against the wall and my toes were just about touching the pavement. As I took stock of who was holding me and looked towards the vehicle I had been sitting in, I realised it was a bloody police car. Because it was in a line of taxis, I hadn't bothered to take in the larger picture.

"I thought you were a bloody taxi," I managed to squeak out, nodding to the line of taxis behind the police vehicle.

He let go of me and, as I slumped against the wall, he shoved me away with a warning of worse to come if I didn't get on my way. I think I sobered up pretty quickly and decided to walk back to the ship.

38

Summer drifted into Autumn and shipboard life kept us all busy. Due to the age of all these vessels, there was always a continuous rota of work to be done to keep them running. Even the paintwork looked good, inside, and out. It was at about this time that we sailed for Bangor, County Down, as part of a goodwill trip for the people of this part of Northern Ireland. The ship was to be opened up to the public which was one of the main reasons we had been painting for a good many weeks previously. The few days that we were to be there coincided with a NATO exercise that was being held at that time that included the Irish Sea and some foreign ships would also be in the port.

The weather had been good and the trip across, unusually for the Irish Sea, had been smooth. As usual, I had been on the night watch with Brum. We were ahead of schedule so had reduced engine speed so that we approached the harbour early morning. The sea was smooth with a light swell and at 03:30 a.m., as dawn was breaking, we'd slowed right down. We were to take on the pilot and the Queen's Harbour Master at 05:00 a.m. As we drifted nearer the coast, we put the engines into idle and drifted on the swell. After a while Brummy said to me,

"Dave, if you pop up and get our breakfast going, I'll organise the handover to the next watch."

At this time of the morning the chef hadn't yet got up to start breakfast, so I made my way up the engine room ladder and into the galley. I washed up and popped out on deck to see where we were and what was happening.

It was a beautiful morning; the mist was rising off the water, and I could vaguely make out the harbour and the town of Bangor in the distance. I could also hear the engines of the pilot's launch not far away. I put a large fry pan on the galley stove, put some oil in it and turned the hotplates on. I opened the galley door to the outside deck a little to get some fresh air and then looked for some eggs to cook. I took four eggs and put them on the stove whilst I got some rashers of bacon. It was at this point that the pilot's launch must have come towards the Port side – the same side as the galley but a bit further aft. As the launch came alongside it must have bumped the side of the ship quite hard. Momentarily, the ship lurched to Starboard which was not particularly helpful.

The deck of the galley consisted of black and white ceramic tiles and as I adjusted my stance to stay upright, the four eggs I'd placed on the stove, rolled along the top. In a sort of slow-motion I saw them rolling towards the edge and was too far away to catch them. All four went hurtling off the top to land on the tiles with a resounding 'splat'.

Just at that moment, in typical bad timing, Brum appeared in the doorway from the corridor. "Fuck me, English, I can't even trust you to make breakfast."

I looked at the mess and grinned. "Oh, for crying out loud," I said. "Brum, push the galley door open mate, will you, and I'll scoop this mess over the side."

Brum went over and pushed the galley door wide. Looking up from where I was standing in the galley, I could see that all was clear.

"Stand back," I said to Brum who stood to one side and was laughing like a loon.

I bent down and scooped up a handful of raw egg and bits of shell and in one movement (the egg was in danger of running through my fingers) threw the lot towards the open doorway and over the side of the ship. At least, that was the intention. But in the second act of pure bad timing, the Queen's Harbour Master picked this moment to walk past the galley door. The trajectory of my aim was up, to clear the deck rail and launch this gooey mess over the side. Which, as luck would have it, coincided with the poor man's face. The complete mess hit him squarely on his right cheek, ear, and nose, which was unfortunate as he had on this superb uniform with peaked cap, gold braid and epaulettes, a ceremonial dress uniform.

He stood there, frozen to the spot. I stood up and put my hand over my mouth in horror. Brum, standing to one side observing all this, just absolutely fell about. I quickly snapped out of my shock, went forward, and took a hold of the man's arm and pulled him into the galley. He hadn't said a word and just stood there as if in a trance.

"Oh God, I'm ever so sorry, I didn't mean to get you, I'm so sorry."

I put my hand under his chin and with my other hand, started to scoop off the bits of yolk and gooey stuff from his nose and cheek. Brummy was still in hysterics, doubled over, laughing like a drain. I looked daggers at him and then emptied the mess onto the stove and got a tea towel, took his hat off and started to wipe it down. Then his uniform front and sleeve. I gave him his hat back which he placed on his head. I dampened another tea towel and finished off his uniform and then wiped his shoes. He still hadn't said a word.

"There, that's better," I said, patting his arm. "You'll be fine, hardly notices."

He turned away from me, looked quite disdainfully at Brummy who was still in a heap in the corner, shoulders shaking and wiping his eyes, walked back out on deck, and disappeared.

"You fucking dick," I said to Brum. "You could have helped."

I pulled him up, we looked at each other and then we both started laughing. In fact, at this point, we both fell about.

"That could only have happened to you, mate, great approach, loved it," he said, blowing his nose.

After we finally calmed down, I went and got a mop and cleaned the remaining mess up.

"You better go mention it to the officer of the watch, I'll make the breakfast," he said.

I thought about it but decided to make myself a coffee first. I went into our mess, made a coffee, and looked out the porthole to see if I could see anyone on deck, but there was just a couple of our lads chatting on the catwalk.

What I didn't know was that a press reporter from the local newspaper had come aboard with the pilot and harbour master. I eventually plucked up the courage to go find the officer of the watch who was in the wheelhouse and tell him. He already knew as did everyone else, so I went back down and had breakfast with Brum.

Everybody thought it was hilarious and the skipper was very good about it, and I didn't get done. But I wasn't to get off too lightly. The following day in the local press, the headlines were as you might have expected: 'Eggs thrown at Queen's Harbour Master', followed by quite an amusing account and a picture of Audemer at the quayside. Although this celebration of 'Open Day' at Bangor was not quite what the skipper had in mind, I think he quite liked the publicity we got. We stayed a few days in Bangor and had a couple of good runs ashore. By this time, my little escapade was a topic of conversation in a few pubs and bars. The Irish loved it.

We left Bangor in the early morning hours and were making our way back to Portsmouth. The weather was unseasonably devoid of storms and the Irish Sea, notorious for bad weather, was pretty good on this run. There had been a large NATO exercise over the past week in these waters so there were still foreign naval vessels in the area. By the time I came off watch, it was just after 04:30 a.m. It was starting to get light, but visibility was poor. As the sun started to come up, a heavy mist was all around us. It was quite eerie. Brum and I made some coffee following our early breakfast and went out on deck for a smoke. We wandered aft and I sat on a winch drum, facing the stern of the ship. A mug of coffee in one hand and a smoke in the other, Brum and I were chatting.

"Can't see a bloody thing," I said.

We both agreed, it was pretty much a blinder. I turned and looked up at the mast. The radar was doing its normal sweep and as we sailed along, the wash at the stern was minimal. Through the blanket of mist, it was as if all sound was deadened. We relaxed in silence for a while, lost in our own thoughts. Then I thought I heard something.

"What's that sound, Brum?" I asked him, frowning. We both listened.

"Can't hear anything," he said.

Then I heard it again. "Sounds like a low boom," I said. "Seems to be coming from behind us." I strained to hear, both of us looking into the wall of white mist, astern. Then we both heard it again and at the same time; it sounded like voices. Brummy shrugged and we both carried on, sipping our coffee.

It must have been about a minute later; I was still looking astern when I definitely heard a siren going and people shouting. Then, out of the mist, several hundred yards behind us, I saw a dark patch in the mist. I put my mug down and went to the stern rail, straining to see. All of a sudden, through the mist, I saw the bow and bow wave of a large ship.

"Oh fuck, Brum," I yelled. He ran over and we both stared in horror. As the mist was parted I started to look up. It was the bow of an enormous aircraft carrier, heading straight for us. "Shit," he said and ran for the ladder to the bridge and wheelhouse. As the mist parted further, I could see all these sailors standing on the edge of the flight deck, shouting down at us. That must have been the voices I'd heard. The carrier was trying to turn to Starboard to avoid hitting us and for a large ship like a carrier, this is not something that happens in an instant. I felt like a rabbit caught in headlights. This ship towered over us, it was like looking up at a multi-storied building, hurtling towards us. Now the sirens were going continuously and suddenly our engines increased in volume as we went into emergency full-ahead and started to swing away to Port at full throttle. It was horrendous and a moment of sheer terror.

Fortunately, our evasive manoeuvre was just in the nick of time, a few seconds later and the carrier would have carved into us. As we turned away at full speed and the carrier slowly disappeared back into the mist, I saw it flying the Dutch flag. My legs were like rubber as I made my way back into the mess. Brummy came in a few minutes later, looking quite pale.

"When I went into the wheelhouse, those silly buggers were stood around chatting and drinking tea and not bloody one of them had been looking at the radar. No one was on the wing bridge, on lookout, I was fucking furious."

He sat down on a bench. Fortunately, no one else was in the mess or had seen what had happened,

"That was the scariest thing I have ever seen, I said, someone will drop a bollock for that. I bet the radio waves will be a bit hot for a while."

"Fancy a tot?" Brum said. "I've got a small bottle of the stuff below."

"Certainly do," I said. "Several bloody tots."

To this day, I don't know if anyone on either ship got reprimanded for that. But a large element of blame must be with the Dutch aircraft carrier. They should have seen our much smaller vessel long before and taken evasive action. Those large ships take a long while to turn or to stop, even if in emergency full-astern.

I was glad to get back to Portsmouth. We were due to go up to Scotland that November and from the weather forecasts we'd heard, it was going to be rough. But we knew the place well and I was looking forward to it.

39

As predicted, the trip up to Scotland was not the smoothest. Having said that, I didn't mind it at all. My sea-legs were fine, and I didn't feel sick. However, plenty of others did and so the days of sailing up that West coast were quiet. There was hardly anyone about the ship as they were either on watch or in their bunks. There were only a few of us around when off watch and we sat in the mess and played bridge. The winter skies always seem more dramatic at sea and for me, the early morning sunrise never disappointed. Once again, Ailsa Craig was stunning, shrouded in mist with the cries of nesting gulls echoing across the water. The swish of the waves against the hull as we moved in near silence through the sea had a calming effect that evoked thoughts of other times. Distance from the hubbub of life in the cities stood out for me during those times and I thought of words to write about. I had started writing when I was back at Chepstow and in odd moments, had carried it on. Whether a poem or just a piece of prose, it would find its way onto any scrap of paper I happened to have handy. In the early morning quiet, as we sailed on, it was easy to think of words and many times I'd jot them down on the back of an envelope or the back of a watch sheet and rewrite them in a notebook later. Very few knew I did this, and I guess I was too embarrassed to mention it. Besides, it was private to me, and I preferred to keep it that way.

We tied up at Helensburgh on a grey, miserable day. Once cargo was off-loaded, we moved further along the coast to Rhu, for refuelling, passing the sad sight of empty ships, abandoned to the breakers yard. The weather didn't help, seeming to emphasise the loneliness of these naval vessels as we passed them. Once fuelled up, we made our way to Stromness via the Hebrides. This was a long trip and most of us had never been to the Orkneys. Fortunately, we hugged the coast through the Sea of Hebrides and then what they call, the March. The scenery was stunning, what we could see of it, as visibility wasn't brilliant. Going around the top, West coast of Scotland, we were soon out from the cover of the islands and the Atlantic was upon us. The weather started to turn. We all knew it was going to be a race to the Pentland Firth before the weather really broke and then on into the more sheltered Scapa Flow. The sunsets and sunrises amongst these waterways were, at times, spectacular but came at a cost. We were getting battered and LCTs were not the best vessels in stormy or turbulent seas. Once we had rounded Flotta, the seas eased a little, but the wind screamed through the ship's cables and mast-head wires. Usually, during these sorts of conditions, people hardly spoke to one another but on this occasion, we were all in awe of the scenery. The final run in to the port of Stromness was good and once tied up alongside the jetty, everyone seemed to sigh in relief.

The weather out at sea was getting worse and a series of bad storms were brewing. We all knew we would be here for a while. Watches were organised and we all settled into a routine. There were not too many pubs in Stromness in those days, but the beer was good, much of it being brewed locally at the Orkney Brewery. The main place to visit was Kirkwall, a good three-quarters of an hours ride in a cab from Stromness. This was along a coastal road via Finstown and was the quickest (and probably the only) route. Despite this, we decided to visit the place. The tourist season was well over, so the 'local talent' was abundant. I remember going into a local newsagent for some postcards to send home and noticed some wide-angled prints of the German Naval fleet at anchor in Scapa Flow before they were all scuttled and sunk in June of 1919, something I'd heard about but had never seen photos of.

We found a bar and settled into some serious drinking. It was here that we learnt of a local dance that was to be held that night. My duty watch aboard Audemer was at 04:00 a.m. so I had plenty of time to enjoy the evening, as long as I left myself enough time to get back to Stromness. We met some girls at the dance and knew we were on to a good thing. As the evening wore on, so too did the storm. Fortunately, we were pretty sheltered in Kirkwall. The girl I was with could drink better than I could, so we were all pretty tanked up by the time we came to thinking about making our way back to the ship at Stromness. We all made our way towards a taxi rank which happened to be devoid of taxis. One of the lads found a local taxi number in a phone box and arranged one for the trip back. We all started making arrangements with the girls to meet up at the weekend. There was a dance being held in Kirkwall, so dates were fixed. Whilst waiting for the taxi, we all found various nooks and crannies to stand in with our dates. Mine took my hand and pulled me into a side alley where there was a bit of a grassy section by a wall. I desperately needed to pee, so I told her to hang on a minute. She must have taken me literally because as I unzipped and started to pee, she came beside me and took hold of it and started aiming it at the wall. I finished and zipped up as she came in front of me, hitched up her skirt, pulled her knickers aside, squatted and started to pee, grabbing my hand as she started to do so. At this point I'd decided to leave her to it and went back to the others just as it started to rain.

The taxi eventually came, and we had to pay him in advance. Once in the cab we started laughing at the merits of the Kirkwall girls. Heading along the coast road we could feel the stormy weather hitting the cab. Waves started to crash over the sea wall, on our right and together with the driving rain, we were taking a battering. By the time we got to Finstown we couldn't go any further. The road was flooded, and the storm was getting worse by the minute. It was now past midnight and the cabby told us to drop in at the local police station as they may have news on getting further to Stromness. He dropped us outside the police station, gave us some of our money back and disappeared back into the murk towards Kirkwall. We made a dash for the door of the police station, which actually, was like a large old house, fell inside and pushed it shut behind us. We went up to what passed as the front desk but couldn't see anyone there. The place seemed empty, but warm. The temperature outside had been dropping all evening and I guessed that by now, it was around 2°C and dropping still. We called out and eventually, this old boy in a police uniform, came to the desk. We explained who we were and where we were trying to get to.

"No chance tonight, lads, the road through to Stromness is flooded and no one is getting through." He knew of the LCT being in port and also knew that there was no other place we could go, other than this police station.

"You better come round into our back room, there'll be no other visitors on a night like this."

We all three, wandered back behind the reception counter and into another room. As we traipsed in, there was another policeman, making some tea.

"You boys look like you could do with a cuppa," one of them said and we all nodded. We explained about being on duty and one said he'd make a landline call to the ship and explain the situation. Whenever we stay for any long period in a place, it's quite customary for a 'shoreline' to be set up. Fortunately, as the ship had been stormbound in Stromness, this had indeed happened. These Finstown police would contact the Stromness police and explain the situation. It looked like we would be spending the night here.

It was a large front room that was almost like a normal room in a house. The main feature was a large, open fireplace with a fire roaring away in it. One of the policemen pulled some easy chairs into a semi-circle around the fire and we all collapsed into them. The lighting was very dim in the room, and it reminded me of what I imagined a Victorian parlour room must have looked like. As mugs of tea were being poured and handed around, the wind really picked up and was pounding the front of the building and the window.

"Would ya all like a we dram in your tea," one of the bobbies said and we all eagerly nodded. He pulled out a bottle of Talisker from the bottom drawer of an old filing cabinet and topped all our mugs up with it. We all grinned at each other; this was much better than being on board. I settled back in the chair, cradling the mug of tea and felt quite cosy. I thought of Audemer getting a pounding at the jetty and was glad I was here.

After some small talk, I remarked on how little this police station looked like one.

"Unchanged for many years," he said, packing a pipe with his thumb and getting out a box of Swan Vestas.

"Been this way from before the first world war, and then some," he murmured.

I mentioned the postcard I'd seen in Kirkwall showing the whole German fleet at anchor in Scapa.

"Can tell you a story 'bout that time. Weren't printed and not a lot of people know," he said. I perked up, all ears, as did the other two lads. For a while, he just sat there, saying nothing, looking into the flames of the fire. Nobody spoke. The wind howled and screamed outside.

"You lot heard of Lord Kitchener?" We all nodded.

"He was the Minister of War during that time and a bit of a forceful character." He sucked on his pipe and the aroma of pipe tobacco, and the coal fire seemed to me, to settle over the place.

"He came here during the Spring of 1916 and in fact, came to this very house. It was a constabulary, even then but was a good meeting place for him and his officers."

He went quiet again and I took a sip of me tea.

"There was a plot afoot, only it was top secret. Officially, he was to visit Russia on some kind of goodwill tour. Me Da told me it was a load of bollocks. Why, in the middle of a world war, would he want to go on a goodwill tour?" He went quiet and the silence hung around us. We were all staring into the flames, lost in our own thoughts.

"No, it was something else. Me Da knew some quite high-ranking people at the time and one of them was a close friend. Da used to get him contraband whiskey and things."

The wind continued to screech. Every few minutes, I could hear the waves crashing against the sea wall in a thunderous roar. The old boy got up and threw some more lumps of coal from the scuttle, into the fire.

"During one visit he got a bit drunk, this high-ranking officer and started going on about Kitchener. Da said you could tell he didn't like him. Da fed him more whiskey and this bloke said there was a plot afoot. He reckoned that Kitchener was going to negotiate a deal with the German and Russian high commands. An agreement between Britain, Germany and the Russkies."

He sat back for a moment, sucking on his pipe and staring into the fire. I looked across at the lads, one was dozing and the other looked across at me and raised his eyebrows. I slightly shook my head and shrugged. We waited.

"Nobody was to know about this, it was highly classified but many of the senior echelons knew about it, and a few were extremely nervous about the whole thing. Apparently, a secret committee was formed, and it was agreed to try to sabotage this agreement. Knowing Kitchener, they knew there was no way they could talk to him about it. Somehow, he had to be stopped. Assassination seemed the only means. He was closely guarded, so it seemed the only way to go about this was a bomb of some sort."

As I sat there, listening to this, I felt a shiver up my spine. Everyone has heard of Lord Kitchener, his was the face on the old World War I poster proclaiming, 'Your country needs you'. But the more I thought about it, the more I realised it was plausible. A good part of our aristocracy was related to the German royal families as well as the Russians and the Czars.

"On 5th June 1916, Kitchener set sail from Scapa on a British light cruiser, HMS Hampshire, with a full complement of six hundred and sixty-seven men. The story goes that she hit a mine just off Marwick Head. There were forty-two survivors. Trouble with that story is that we had laid these mines ourselves and all British commanders at that time, had plots of where all these were located."

By this time his pipe had gone out, but I don't think he had noticed.

"What happened to the officer that told your dad about this plot?" I asked.

"Ah, well there's the thing. The group of officers that apparently were the ones that allegedly, had a hand in this, were all aboard the battleship HMS Vanguard. Rather mysteriously, she blew up in Scapa Flow the following year, with a loss of eight hundred and forty-three men. As far as anyone knows, that group died with them."

When I looked across at the lads, both were sound asleep. For me, I couldn't have been more awake. I sat there for a while, listening to the wind outside and watching the flames in the fire. What was it that disturbed me about this story? Why wasn't this more publicly known? A high-level conspiracy which to me, could have changed the course of history. It appears to have gone unrecorded and even worse, unnoticed, and conveniently lost in the dusty naval archives of time. The loss of so many lives, forgotten in the icy waters of Scapa Flow. Watching the flames in the fire, I thought of those lost men. A strong gust of wind hit the front of the house, rattling the windows, and howling away into the night. I shivered momentarily and settled further back into the chair.

"Thank you for letting us spend the night here," I said.

"No worries. If the roads are passable in the morning, we'll get you a lift back to your ship."

He made me another mug of tea and poured some more whiskey in it. We chatted on a bit longer, about more mundane things and then, thanks to the 'wee dram', I managed to get some sleep.

The following morning, the storm had passed, and the wind had died down. True to his word, we were given a lift back to the ship. The skipper was good about our absence, and we set sail later that morning for Benbecula and then back to Helensburgh. I never did mention what

I had been told on that stormy night in an old police station in Finstown. But it ranked high in my memory of things to think about at odd moments, and I knew that I had to write it down someday. The other two lads barely remembered it at all, and we never spoke of it again.

40

Back in Pompey, for the first time, I had to spend Christmas on board ship. Audemer was short of crew. People had been posted to other ships as there must have been a general shortage in the squadron. It didn't happen very often, so I didn't mind. Andy had bought an old Ford Anglia and we had been running around in that. We decided to travel home in it, after Christmas duties. Andy came and stayed with Mum and me at Beldams Lane for a few days and my brother-in-law, Ken, sorted out a flywheel problem on Andy's Anglia. However, Ken reckoned there were too many other issues with it and recommended getting rid of it. Andy sold it in late January '68.

It was in the January of '68 that Mum heard that Jo's marriage to John 'Digger' Hoey was over. Apparently, it had been over for some months, but the girls didn't want to worry Mum about it. Jo moved in with Dinah and now they were sorting out some of the legal issues. They were hoping to return to the UK in early '69. It was all of a bit of a shock as Jo had been painting a 'rosy' picture of her life in Oz, for some time. I think Mum had an inkling something was up and I'm sure she was quietly relieved and looking forward to having the girls home again.

Meanwhile, things had been happening with Tom. Our drinking

days as a 'team' with the Wren DSAs was coming to a close. Malcolm 'Tom' Thomas had met his match in Steve (Stephanie), a Wren whom he'd met the previous summer, and the two were dating seriously. Come September of '67 they had decided to get married, and I was to be best man. This time, I would be in attendance. The wedding was held the following February, in a Registry Office in Greenwich. The night before, we held the stag do with some of his old mates from where he lived. It was a pub-crawl from around 6pm. Drinking and driving didn't seem to bother anyone too much in those times and as we made our way around the pubs, the driving deteriorated. The last thing I remember was driving the car the wrong way around a roundabout. We eventually all ended up at his mum's place in Kent, crashed out on the floor

The following morning, we woke up a little late and then had to 'hot-foot' it up to Greenwich in time for the wedding. We arrived at the Registry Office in an awful state. Tom looked like death but with all our help we managed to get him and ourselves dressed for the occasion. I wore a light-coloured, three-piece suit and a turquoise 'kipper' tie and desert boots. We filed into the Registry Office and slumped into the chairs waiting for Steve and her parents. It was whilst waiting that I decided to play a joke with the ring. Tom had given it to me earlier and I had it in one of the little pockets in the waistcoat I was wearing. When the time came to hand it over, I pretended that I couldn't find it. Tom just grinned but Steve went puce and just as the sparks were about to fly, I produced it. The reception was held in a large pub in Charlton, where Steve's parents lived. Both Tom and I were running on alcohol fumes from the previous night, and I doubt that either of us knew what was really happening. I remember very little of it. After he left for his honeymoon, I went back to Portsmouth and Audemer. I remember sitting on the train thinking that this was the breaking of an old alliance. We'd been best mates for quite a while, had some great times back in Portsmouth with Sue, Ingy and the Wrens and this unique friendship with these girls was now at an end. I felt sad about that. Of course, I remained friends with the girls, and we would still meet up from time to time. But those magical days had finally come to an end.

I'd been in the services now for 4 years, excluding my AAS (Army Apprentice School) time at Chepstow. My rank was 'Driver' which in the RCT was the equivalent of a Private. I was due promotion purely by the fact of time. It would mean more pay which at that time was around fifteen pounds per week (two hundred and twenty-three pounds in today's money). The next rank was Lance Corporal (L/Cpl) but to attain this, I would have to go on an upgrading course at Aldershot. That meant about four weeks of bullshit. I had little say in it and was told it would mean my promotion once I had completed the NCO course. Bearing in mind that I had been on the LCTs now for four years, where discipline is pretty slack compared to infantry and non-shipboard units – which was most of the British Army, this was going to be difficult. We were quite unique in this instance.

As far as uniforms go, I had my No.2 dress, which was my best kit. My working uniform was dark blue No.8 trousers, light blue No.8 shirt, brogue shoes (no army boots), white roll-neck sweater, white sea-socks, and sea boots (wellies) for inclement weather. They were also lenient on haircuts on board, which meant about once every eight to ten weeks, I'd have a 'trim'. So going on this course was going to be a bit fraught. However, I thought, *okay, they will realize where I work and will, in all likelihood, make a bit of an allowance.* How wrong I was.

I was soon the topic of conversation. The rest of the lads were from different units around the country, and they all had the correct army uniforms. The 'working dress' was called fatigues. Ours was the blue No.8 naval kit whilst everyone else had the proper khaki army kit.

The following morning after breakfast, we all had to parade at 07:00 a.m. on a cold, damp, overcast parade square. A senior NCO formed us into 4 ranks, brought us to attention, then stood us at ease to await our introduction to the Regimental Sgt.Major. About five minutes later the senior NCO marched to the edge of the square where he was met by the Sgt.Major. They talked for about two minutes and as they then both marched over, towards us all, I had a bad feeling. I then wished I'd made an effort back in Pompey, to get the correct kit and had a haircut before I came here. Big mistake!

We were brought to attention, dressed into straight lines (dressing off), and waited. We were then told to 'open order', putting about two paces between each of the four ranks, while the sergeant major would walk down the lines, inspecting us. The accompanying NCO had a notepad with him. No time was wasted in getting to me. He came over and in a gruff voice, asked me where my uniform was. As he looked at me, I answered that this was my uniform and that they were all that I had. Changing colour to a sort of mauve/red complexion, he informed me that I was in the British Army, not the bloody namby, pamby navy. I explained that I was aware of that but that I was ship's crew, and this was my working dress. He didn't seem to hear this and just stared at me. Because it was cold, I'd put on my white, roll-neck sweater which made my hair look longer than it was. The only piece of army kit that I did have on was my beret. I was asked when I'd last had my hair cut to which I replied that it was about six weeks ago. He then made me stand aside from the rest of the squad. While they were marched away to do drill I was left standing there. After about 10 minutes I was approached by the Sgt. Major who decided to march me around the square on my own for a further five minutes. Following this, he came over to me and shouted at me that he was sending me to the barbers on camp and then I would be issued with regular army kit. After informing me that I was a disgrace to the Army, he sent me off to the barbers.

What followed for the next few days was tirade after tirade of profanity at my so called, bad habits. When we were marching as a squad, I would be singled out. When the others of the squad went to tea-break, I was told to continue marching or left standing at attention. My hair was to be cut weekly but I knew I was not going to make the second week. After a week of this, I'd had enough. I had decided that I would rather remain a bloody private for the remainder of my career, than take all this bullshit. On the Friday night I packed what little gear I had, left the camp, and caught a train back to Portsmouth. A welcome sight was the '61 gently rocking alongside the Gunwharf jetty. The lads on board thought that it was hilarious, but the skipper didn't quite see it that way. I was put 'on orders' and on the following Monday had to appear before the CO in the Gosport Barracks.

I was concerned but not really bothered that much. I'd had a chance to think it over at the weekend and decided that as much as I loved military life, my days of square bashing were over. I wanted to continue with my life as a marine engineer but if I had to buy myself out, I would. Apparently, at the time, it would have cost me two hundred pounds. This is approximately two thousand five hundred pounds in today's money. Maybe not so much an amount now but back then, well, I had no savings, and my salary was paltry. The CO decided that I had the makings of a good engineer and my skippers report from the ship was good. So, he gave me another chance. He did say, however, that I would still have to do the next NCO's course shortly. I would be better prepared the next time.

However, at home, things weren't going too well for me either. I must have voiced my concerns about staying in the Army and in a letter, had probably told Mum that I needed two hundred pounds to buy myself out. She knew I never had that amount and so, unbeknown to me, had been asking around the family for a loan. The first I knew about this was when she told me in a letter. I wasn't too happy about this. Next, I got an abusive letter from my sister Dee who, amongst other things, told me I was despicable and that she'd always known that I would amount to nothing. I didn't respond to this and decided to just shut up shop regarding home and decided not to write to anyone. Eventually, Mum managed to get a letter out of me and was pleased to hear that I was ok.

Once the heat was off me, regarding my failure to do the NCO's course, I think some communication between units had gone on and I was sent back on another NCO course, this time in Crookham, Hampshire. I'd learned my lesson and managed to get the correct kit issued to me at our Gosport barracks.

This time there were two of us going on the course, the other lad named George W. Both of us were on Audemer and we got on well. George was a seaman. Once we'd both arrived, we were shown to our accommodation. These consisted of black, wooden 'spiders' with 8 to a room. Being with George in the 'spiders' meant that we got to know each other a bit more than we would have on board ship. His bed was next to mine and one evening when we were cleaning our kit, he mentioned that he was 'in love' with a girl called Geraldine, back home in Melton Mowbray, where he lived. He'd seen me writing poems on board ship and wondered if I would write a poem for his girlfriend, from him, as he was hoping to ask her to get engaged. It didn't take me long and later that evening I gave him the poem entitled, 'Geraldine'.

> I often wonder while at sea
> What words to say to you
> To express the way you mean to me
> So here are just a few
>
> Without a doubt I know of none
> That make my heart so light
> To turn a day so lack of fun
> To sparkle clear and bright
>
> I have heard tales of golden ships
> Seen lands, some far, some near
> But treasures bound upon your lips
> And speak the words I hold so dear
>
> I've watched seagulls on the wing above
> Beheld topaz in the skies
> Greater still this thing our love
> A deeper blue your eyes
>
> Time nor darkness can erase
> No sunsets can compare
> The simple beauty of your face
> The velvet shimmer of your hair
>
> From busy port to shipping lane
> From oceans to a stream
> Time will idle till I see again
> My own, beloved Geraldine.

George was really pleased with this, but he wanted to say that he wrote it himself and if I minded. I told him I didn't mind as long as he paid me for the 'rights' which in this instance was two shillings and six pence (half-a-crown), equivalent to about two pounds and twenty pence today. He paid. I later heard that he did, indeed, get engaged to her, so maybe it worked. As a footnote to this, I have since made contact with him via Facebook and he is still married to Geraldine. Not bad after fifty plus years. Well done, George.

The course this time was good, and I marched and drilled my way through it with flying colours. When I got back to Portsmouth, it wasn't long before I was promoted to Lance Corporal. The only downside to this was a temporary posting from Audemer to Agheila, as they were short an engineer. But I knew her well from our time in Aden and it was nice to be on her for a while. Of course, as with all these ships, that meant a lot more painting and cleaning of the engine room. I was getting quite good at it now.

41

In June, we were back up to Scotland again, this time on exercise. It was whilst up in the Outer Hebrides that I developed a really bad tooth ache. It was so debilitating that they decided to fly me by helicopter to the Infirmary at Belfast in Northern Ireland where I had it dealt with. Over the years, I'd had a lot of trouble with my teeth. Because my body makeup leans towards alkalinity, I tend to get plaque easily, so this really does demand twice daily cleaning. I was only doing it once a day and in those days hygienists at the dentists were rare. I was to suffer many times over the years from tooth issues, but I was conscious of this and tried, as best as possible, to keep these to a minimum. These days, things are considerably different. The trade-off being it costs a lot more.

I stayed on the military airbase, courtesy of the RAF, for a few days until Agheila arrived at Belfast and I re-joined her. One of the things about Belfast was the beer. Guinness was the premium drink, but 'Porta' was the cheaper basic stuff. There was a large pub, not far from the dockyard gates, where in the ground floor bar there was sawdust sprinkled on the scuffed, wooden floor and the Guinness on this level was the basic Porta, considered 1 'X'. It was a cheap drink if you were a bit short of cash and all they had to eat here was bags of crisps, pork scratchings and nuts. Most people here were in their dockyard work clothes and it was pretty busy. On the next level up, they had worn carpets on the floor, a jukebox and the Porta here was better quality, considered 2 'X'. You could get a meat pie and chips or a pasty. You were not allowed up there in your dockyard clothes but jeans, open necked shirt and a jacket were acceptable. On the top level the place was carpeted with plush carpets, comfortable easy chairs, nice lighting, and a small stage for a band. The food here was fish and chip, steaks, and sausage & mash. The Guinness was the premium draught, considered triple 'X', but it was a lot dearer. So, it depended on how flush you were feeling which determined which level you visited. Also, for the top floor, you had to wear trousers, not jeans and a shirt, tie, and jacket. Uniforms were acceptable. But to be honest, the best place to drink was the Seaman's Mission. You could get a good meal there and a game of pool and the prices were good.

When we arrived back at Portsmouth, I was transferred back to Audemer. I was well pleased, and it certainly felt like 'coming home'. Summer leave time came and as Andy and I were on the same ship and both of us lived in the East of England, we decided to spend some leave together. His folks were from Norfolk, just outside Bury, so we decided to book a boat for a week on the Broads. It was good fun and very relaxing. We pootled from riverside pub to riverside pub. As both of us could cook, we decided to give it a go. One lunchtime we'd stopped at a riverside pub that was near a supermarket. We bought some fresh meat and veg and went back to the boat. I prepared the veg whilst Andy got the meat ready. I put the potatoes in a pot with some water and put them on a low heat. We then decided to go for a pint and return to finish cooking the dinner.

Whilst in the pub we got chatting to some locals and time went by. I'd completely forgot about the spuds I'd left on the heat. When we came out of the pub, there was a group of people stood on the towpath, looking over the edge. We could see this smoke billowing up and wandered over to see what it was all about. We went behind the crowd and peered over the edge. There were several boats tied up alongside and one of them had smoke coming from the interior.

"I wonder whose boat that is," I said as we both looked over.
"What colour is our boat?" Andy said.
"Blue, a light blue," I murmured.
"Shit!" We both yelled in unison and tore along the side path and jumped aboard the boat. I hurtled down the short steps into the galley. There was smoke everywhere, but I managed to grab the pot with the spuds in, off the stove and run it under the tap in the sink. Once the steam and smoke had disappeared, there was a charred mess in the bottom of the pan.

To save embarrassment and clear the smoke out of the boat, we decided to leave. We untied, got the engine going and slowly made our way up the river. The boat cleared of smoke, and I spent the next hour cleaning up the pot. We had lunch without the potatoes. In the end we decided to stick to pub lunches and evening meals. When we had signed out the launch, we also took a dingy with sails and towed this behind us. Andy was into small boat sailing and once we'd found a nice quiet spot, he got the dingy out and we did a bit of sailing. He was good at it. His prowess with a sailing boat had an implication a few years later which, at the time, neither of us could have foreseen.

Summer wore on and we were kept pretty busy. Runs ashore were mostly confined to the NAAFI club and the Still & West. One particular weekend I was sitting around the mess deck writing a letter home to Mum. Andy was on duty watch and we'd been chatting. As we were tied up alongside the Gunwharf I decided I would go ashore, post the letter then pop up the Club for a beer. There wasn't much going on although the place was pretty busy. I didn't see any of the Wrens I knew but was feeling pretty relaxed. I sat at the bar and chatted with Olive, the middle-aged bar lady who knew me quite well. She asked if I was on duty this weekend and when I told her I wasn't, she told me I should have gone home to see me Mum. Olive knew me and our clique of friends and realised none of them were around that particular weekend. I told her that I was going to have an early night after I'd popped up to the Still & West. She just shook her head and laughed, making me promise her I would go for a weekend home soon.

It was a warm evening and as I wandered around to Old

Portsmouth, heading towards the S&W, I thought that actually, an early night wouldn't be a bad thing. On the periods we were at sea I had taken to reading paperbacks a lot more and was currently reading a good one. I hadn't done a lot of reading since my early Chepstow days where I found it a means of escape. Here, it helped pass the sometimes-long hours whilst under way. On evenings like this, it was an alternative to spending my meagre amount of spare money and drinking on my own. It had been raining earlier and now the streetlights reflected off the uneven pavement in puddles. As I neared the S&W, I went over to the railings at the harbour wall and looked across at the harbour, towards HMS Dolphin. It was always a comfortable sight with the lights twinkling and reflecting off the choppy, harbour water. I lit up and stood there a moment, enjoying the evening. One beer and then I'd wander back to the ship. I opened the door of the pub and made my way upstairs to the usual bar I drank in. It was moderately busy. I went over to the bar and pulled out a stool, ordering my beer as I did so. Sitting on the stool, I noticed this Asian girl, sat at the bar a little further along. She appeared to be upset and a little drunk. I knew the barman and nodding towards the girl, asked him what the matter was with her. He knew her and said he was a little concerned. She had apparently been in there a while, and he had tried to talk to her but without much luck. It was mostly couples in the bar this time and no one was paying her much attention. After a few minutes the barman came over to me and asked me, as a favour, would I mind taking her home.

 I got off the stool and went over to her. Looking at her I could see that she was quite petite, dressed nicely, and probably somewhere in her late twenties. I asked her if there was anything I could do. She looked up and I could see that she had been crying. The barman came over and I looked enquiringly at him. He said her husband used to work behind the bar there as a part-time barman but was working for the P&O cruise ships and recently, had gone back to sea. He then spoke to the girl and told her that I was a friend and that he felt it would be better if I took her home. She looked up again at me, touched my arm and said that would be nice.

"I'll just finish my beer and then we can go," I said.

"Can I have another drink?" she asked. I looked at the barman and he shook his head.

"I don't think that's a very good idea," I said. "Just let me finish this and we'll go."

She just sat there looking a bit miserable.

I asked her how far away she lived, and she told me. It was about a ten-minute taxi drive, north of where we were, in the Portsea area. I finished my beer, nodded at the barman and stood up.

"Thank you for doing that," he said. I nodded at him.

"Come on then, let's go," I said, zipping up my jacket.

She got off the stool a little unsteadily and I realised she was quite small, around five feet tall.

I walked with her down the stairs and out into the open. "Sorry," I said. "I don't know your name."

"Pema," she said. We walked on along the wet pavement, towards the busier area of town.

"Where are you from?" I asked

"I'm from the Philippines originally but I've lived here a few years now. What's your name?" she asked, looking up at me.

I told her my first name and mentioned that I was in the services, currently stationed in Portsmouth. She was very pretty, and it did cross my mind to work on maybe taking this a bit further. But I knew it would complicate things and besides, if I was being truthful, I really couldn't be bothered. I just wanted to get her home and be on my way.

"Let's get a cab and I'll get you home," I said, looking up the street. There were usually plenty around on a Saturday night.

"Let's go somewhere for a drink," she said, looking at The Dolphin as we walked towards it.

"No, that's not a good idea, I think you've had enough," I told her, thinking *no way*. I knew a lot of people that would likely be in there tonight and that was our 'watering hole' with Sue, Ingy, and the girls. It wouldn't do my street cred any good at all.

"Can we just walk then, for a while?" she asked quietly. *Well*, I thought, *to be honest that's not a bad idea and she'll sober up more quickly*. I didn't want her falling asleep in the taxi as I needed to get her home.

"How long have you been married?" I asked her.

"Quite a long time – a good few years," she said

"Do you have any children?" I asked as we walked, dodging puddles. It was starting to lightly drizzle again.

After a few moments, she said, "Five."

I pulled up short, shocked. "Five? Blimey Pema…" I stood looking at her for a moment.

"Yes," she said and started telling me their names. The youngest being a baby of about eleven months.

"So, who's looking after them tonight?" I asked as we started walking again, still trying to get over the shock of this little Asian woman being the mother of five kids.

"My eldest, she's twelve."

I was stunned. *Fucking hell, what on earth is the matter with these people…?* I couldn't believe she'd leave them at home in the care of a twelve-year-old, especially with a baby of eleven months.

"Come on, let's get that cab and get you home." I felt really bad for the twelve-year-old looking after her siblings, one of whom was a baby.

After a few minutes I managed to flag a cab down and we got in. She told him the address and we sat back. She started telling me about her husband whose sole function, it seemed, was to come home from sea, get her pregnant, then go back to sea again. I'm not sure how much of this I actually believed but it was nothing to do with me, so I wasn't that bothered.

She stopped the cab at the beginning of the street, and I paid him off. I guess she didn't want the neighbours to see her, I think. About halfway down the street we came to her place. These were all Victorian terraces and reminded me of my grandma's old place in London.

I saw her to the door and told that I had better go. She asked me to come in for a moment and I wasn't sure that I should. She saw the hesitation in me and said that it would be okay, so I did. The hallway was as I had expected, with stairs going up on the right and a side passage that went through to the back kitchen on the left. I could see a light on at the far end where the kitchen was and also, I could hear a TV on somewhere upstairs.

I followed Pema through to the kitchen where a rather angry looking young girl asked her mum where she had been and who the hell I was. Pema ignored her questions and gave her a hug, asking her how the baby was. All apparently were asleep. She then introduced me as David, a friend who had given her a lift home. The girl looked rather frostily at me, and I just said, 'Hi.'

Her mum told her to go on up to bed as she was going to make me a coffee. The girl gave me a disgruntled look and disappeared out of the kitchen. Pema looked at me. "I won't be a moment," she said, nodding in the direction her daughter had gone. She went out after her, closing the kitchen door behind her. I looked around, saw the electric kettle, filled it at the sink and switched it on to boil. I leant back against the worktop and looked around. The place was tidy and clean and, as silly as it seemed, I felt pleased to think that it wasn't in a mess.

A few minutes later it had gone quiet in the house and Pema came back into the kitchen. She'd removed her jacket and had put pumps on. She came in and closed the kitchen door. It was nearing 10:00 p.m. and I was thinking I had better be getting back to the ship soon. She got a couple of mugs out of a cupboard and started putting some instant coffee in the cups.

"Would you like some toast?" she asked.

I nodded. "Sure, that would be nice."

She took some bread out of a cupboard, took four slices out and put them in a toaster. Watching her do this simple task I realised that she had sobered up pretty quick. In fact, the moment she saw her eldest daughter she had seemed pretty normal. The kettle boiled so I took it over to the mugs and started filling them. Next minute, a pair of arms came around me from behind and she laid her head on my back.

"You're very kind," she said. "You're the first person that has done something like this for a long time."

"Done what? All I did was bring you home from the pub, I was going to have an early night anyway."

"You helped me without anything in return. You know what I mean."

I went quiet for a moment, then the toast popped up and broke the silence. She went over to it, taking the toast out and putting the slices on two plates. She started buttering the pieces and as she did so, I could see where this was possibly leading.

"Look, it's getting late, I had better get going."

She just looked at me and handed me a plate with the toast on.

"I'll have this and the coffee and then I had better get back," I said.

She came over and stood in front of me, just watching as I took a bite out of a slice of the toast.

"Please stay with me tonight," she said, putting her arms around me. I put the plate I was holding back on the worktop and put my hands on her waist. We kissed. A slight one at first that then became something a lot stronger. I was genuinely surprised and began to think fast of some of the possible scenarios where this could lead, not least of which was staying the night.

We finished the toast and coffee, not saying anything, just looking at each other, turned all the lights off in the kitchen and made our way upstairs. I started to feel the excitement at the thought of what was to come but a part of me was still questioning whether I should be doing this. She took me into a front room where there was a double bed with a cot to the far side with a baby fast asleep in it. She then left me there while she went off, I assume to check on the other children. I was still sitting on the bed when she came back in. She came over to stand in front of me and reached down to undo the belt on my jeans. We sort of undressed each other and then tumbled into bed.

Halfway through the night the baby started to cry, and Pema got up, took a bottle of milk off the dresser, and passed it to me to hold while she got the baby. I had managed to get some sleep before the crying woke me. I glanced at the luminous hands on my watch, it was just after 03:00 a.m. She lifted the baby out of the cot and brought it into bed with us. I handed her the bottle and she started feeding the baby. She looked at me and grinned, "Sorry about this but if I don't feed him, he'll just cry all night."

"No problem," I said, wondering how long it would take. Looking at her, I wondered if this was a taste of things to come, a sort of peek into the future. Her hair cascaded over her shoulders and the baby snuggled into her arm, looking content now that it was being fed. There was no way I was going to be able to get back to sleep now and I was wondering that perhaps this wasn't such a good idea after all. It was too early to leave, and I didn't want to offend her. After a few minutes the baby drifted off and Pema put the bottle down. She let the baby lie between us for a moment, but it started grizzling again. I knew then I had to think of a way to get up and leave but couldn't think of a suitable excuse. I lay back and we both drifted off.

I woke up at around 05:00 a.m. And got up and dressed. It disturbed Pema and I explained that I was on duty that day and had to get back. I crept downstairs and put the kettle on for a coffee. She came down a few moments later and started making some toast and Marmite. We leant against the worktop, drinking coffee, and eating the toast. I explained I couldn't see her that night because of being on duty, so we arranged to meet up on Tuesday evening. I had to get my head around all of this and whilst feeling somewhat guilty at staying the night I knew I'd probably do it again. So started an interesting period of 'life with Pema'.

I didn't regret it for a moment and, of course, it meant I was enjoying the sex side of it. Taking it a bit more seriously was not on the agenda, although I could see that it would lead that way if I let it. But she was married and was playing around. Doing that and having five children didn't exactly sit well with my conscience. The husband's behaviour, leaving her with so many children, was a bit out of line but that was no excuse.

Still, we got on well together and she was interesting to be with. Her kids seemed to accept me with barely a fuss which made me think this may have happened before. The more I thought about it and had a chat with Andy about her, the more clearly I could see through the pink mist that had descended. I started to back off a little but over the next couple of months we still had a few good nights out that usually culminated in a late night back at her place. I had also noticed that she was known in a couple of the pubs in Southsea by the local regulars. On my days off we had some days out with the kids, having picnics and going to the fair, all of which was kind of fun, and the weather was good that summer. It would have been easy to keep that up and I did have a chuckle to myself, thinking of turning up at Mum's with Pema and five children. As August drew to a close, I was thinking about spending a few of my free weekends at home. Pema would have been happy to drift along but I knew this was not a good plan, so I started to pull away from her. With an upcoming trip to Scotland nearing, I pulled the plug on Pema. I never saw her again.

One weekend, I went home to Mum's. She had now been working at the Herts & Essex hospital for some time and was happy in her job. The nurses loved her and as most were from overseas, they saw her as a sort of surrogate mother. That particular weekend there was a dance at the nurses' home and Mum thought it would be good if I went, especially as she had been telling a few of them about me. Most of them were West Indian and all were studying for their SRN nursing qualification, as it was then. She told me of several in particular that she was close to, and one called Carol, who used to pop round to Mum's when she was off duty, mostly to keep each other company. Mum got on well with all of them and they were keen to meet me.

So, like a lamb to the slaughter, I went along to the dance. I was quite overwhelmed; it was a bit like a kid being let loose in a sweet shop. I made for the bar and hung around there, listening to the music. It wasn't long before someone came over and asked me if I was Mrs English's son. That was Carol. We got chatting and I guess I made all the right noises because we both enjoyed the evening and the dancing. I met up with her the next day and we went out for a Sunday lunchtime drink and a bite to eat. Carol and I enjoyed each other's company but the weekend was too short and I was soon back aboard ship.

42

There were NATO exercises in Europe, and we were assigned the task of taking tanks and troops over, dropping them off at the docks at Antwerp, in Belgium. It took us two days there, off load, stay overnight, returning the next day to Marchwood to pick up the next load. This meant making lots of trips weekly, for the period of the exercise. Apart from the duty watch, we had an evening's run ashore in Antwerp. On our second trip there, word had got around the bars in town, of our visits. As the evening twilight settled over the dockside area of the port, where we were tied up, a long stretch-limo turned up at the jetty and adjacent to the gangway. We were invited to town and would be picked up later and taken back to the ship. The only catch was that we spend at least an hour or two in one of their bars. The bar in question was called 'Danni's Bar' in the Leguit district of Antwerp.

The bar was one of a street of bars, but it was by far, the best. The 'girls' in it were some of the most stunning, curvaceous, and pretty exotic that I'd seen and wore outrageous clothes. But of course, they were males in reality. Most had undergone sex changes and all the necessary hormone treatment. The result of which was some of the biggest 'chests' I have ever seen, in one place. The beer and food were excellent, and their sense of humour was brilliant. You weren't pressed to stay but we all were having such a good time there, it wasn't worth the effort of going elsewhere. The music was good, too. There was nothing smutty or uncomfortable in this place. In fact, I would go as far as to say it had an air of sophistication about it. So, we used it every week we went to Antwerp. The place was run by this very big 'lady' called Danni' most likely named after the famous celebrity transvestite, Danny La Rue.

On one such trip to Danni's, we had a young seaman who had recently joined the ship and it was to be his first run ashore to Danni's Bar. 'Chalky' was about nineteen and quite innocent. The girls in Danni's all knew us well by this time and were always pleased to see us. Because I was one of the smallest of our lot I was treated as a bit of a mascot in Danni's. Whenever we first arrived there, Big Danni, who was the governor of the place, would come around from behind the bar, come up to me, grab my head and bury it between her two massive breasts and wiggle them about my ears. At first, I was horrified and embarrassed, but it became her regular intro, and she always brought me my first beer.

We had warned the girls that we were bringing Chalky in, the previous week so they were ready for him. On the way there in the limo, we had rehearsed what we were going to tell him. One of the lads explained that all the girls were specially chosen for their beauty and friendliness which was why this bar was so special. As we all piled into the bar, Danni was on her best behaviour and just winked at me. At first, we all sat at a couple of tables whilst the girls took our orders. Chalky was truly shocked and quite stunned by their looks. Danni had craftily chosen the best of them all to flirt with Chalky. She was a stunning, young blonde, quite petite and very sexy.

We were all chatting, telling jokes and laughing as this cute little blonde started taking an interest in Chalky. He could not believe his luck. She brought a chair over and sat next to him. A couple of other girls had joined us but were not attached to anyone in particular. Chalky was getting on so well with this girl that he must have thought he'd hit the jackpot. We were all pretending not to notice as we laughed, smoked, and drank. After a while, they both moved to another table and were sat together, totally wrapped up in each other. Danni looked over at us from behind the bar and gave us the 'thumbs up'. Chalky started getting a little amorous after a while and they were gently kissing each other. Then we saw her say something to him and his hand disappeared beneath the table. We found out later that he had put his hand up her skirt and was rubbing her thigh. Gradually, he moved his hand higher in attempt to rub her panties at her 'private bits'. What we saw from where we were was at first a frown and then a look of sheer horror as his hand found her 'ole todger'. He suddenly sat up straight and pushed back his chair. He looked across at us and we were all looking at him, giving him the thumbs up.

JC shouted across, "Go for it Chalky!" and we all clapped and hooted.

He jumped up, almost in tears, "You bastards!" he shouted at us and ran out of the place.

We were in hysterics by then and thought it had gone better than expected. Danni came over and said one of us had better go find him and calm him down, she was genuinely concerned. We all thought that it was a hoot, and the blonde girl came over and joined us saying we were wicked bastards.

It was a great watering hole and nothing 'seedy' about it. By about 11:00 p.m. some of the girls' facial 'stubble' had started to show but by then, most were past caring. At that late time of the evening, it was not uncommon to go to the gents and see them stood at the urinal, hiking their skirt up and taking a leak. During the course of the evening, they would take food orders from us, for pizzas and burgers and go out and get them. They made it so that you really didn't want to go anywhere else.

One of the lads we had with us was a corporal seaman called Rick East. He was a married dad and well liked. He was tall, blond, and good looking and we had met his wife when we had gone out on occasions, in Pompey. She was, as you would expect for him, a really nice-looking woman. He'd been married a couple of years by the time we had started the Antwerp runs. Whenever we'd gone to Danni's he would often sit with one particular 'girl'. We were all a bit shocked when he would sit close with her and now and again, kiss her. The outcome of the 'liaison' was that during our trips there he had decided to leave his wife and go and live with this girl. Once the skipper got wind of what was happening with him, he was posted off our ship to one that was doing the Hebrides runs. We never saw him again. He may have taken up with this girl because she too, disappeared from Danni's. It was a shame for many reasons as he was a good seaman and well liked aboard. It also took the shine off going to Danni's and, in the end, we stopped going and most of us stayed on board. Chalky eventually forgave us.

The NATO exercises went on for a few months and the regular 'to-ing and fro-ing' to Antwerp became a bit like a clock ticking. There was always work to do on board and regular maintenance continued, whether we were at sea or not. One particular trip back from Antwerp meant that we were at sea during the night, having left the Antwerp dock area quite late. As usual, I was on the night watch and had been in the generator room carrying out an oil change. The main reason we were late leaving was due to the weather. There had been some storms with plenty of high winds. Once we were out of the network of canals, we soon picked up the rougher waters of the Channel. It was difficult carrying out the oil change but not unmanageable. By about 03:00 a.m. I had completed it and the dirty oil was in the usual five-gallon drum with the rope handles. However, getting these down ladders into the main engine room and over to the drain point would be a feat as the ship was rolling quite significantly. It would be far easier to haul it up the short ladder of the generator room to the catwalk above and providing no one saw me, heave it over the side.

This exercise of dumping waste oil at sea was normally quite taboo, especially in the English Channel but it was not uncommon practice. The powers that be, aboard ship, tended to 'look the other way' so on this particular night, this was the option I chose. I gingerly hauled the five-gallon drum of dirty, black oil, up the ladder, timing my effort between the rolling of the ship. This meant hauling the rope handled drum in one hand whilst grabbing the rungs of the metal ladder with the other. As the ship rolled to Port (I was in the Port side generator room) I grabbed the next rung of the ladder and hauled, waited for the next roll to Port, and carried out the same manoeuvre. Within a few minutes I was head and shoulders out of the hatch. It was blowing quite hard but every now and again the wind would drop to nothing. I grabbed a stanchion and hauled myself and the oil drum up the rest of the way and managed to get the drum of oil onto the deck of the catwalk without spilling any.

The night was pitch black and the sea had a bit of a 'head' on it which meant that the storm winds had whipped the waves up some which was why we were rolling. It was quite a heavy swell. Off in the far distance I could see the navigation lights of a tanker, otherwise all was clear. No one was about the decks at this time of the night and only the watch on duty with lookouts would be about, up on the bridge and in the wheelhouse. Climbing fully out of the hatch, I noticed that the wind had dropped to a whisper. So, taking hold of the rope handle of the drum, I moved up against the ships rail (a wire cable). Timing the roll of the ship, I waited for it to roll to Port. As the ship leaned towards the sea, I used the momentum of the roll to tip the drum of thick, black oil, outboard as far as I could, over the side. Now up to that point, the wind had eased right off and had been like that for several minutes, easily long enough for me to empty the oil drum. The nautical powers that be had other ideas and I was about to learn a lesson for carrying out this highly illegal exercise. As the tipping of the drum reached the point of no return, a massive gust of wind came around my side of the ship and took the oil with it. I could probably, honestly say that not one drop touched the stormy waters below me. Nope. It all came back along the side of the ship, carried up and away by the wind. Not a drop touched me, it all went towards the aft of the ship.

Oh fuck, I was thinking. With luck, the wind had carried the majority of it away to the rear of the vessel. It was just too dark to see as the only lights we had on were our navigation lights which were high up on the ship's masts.

I took the now empty drum back down into the generator room and climbed back up on deck to see if I could see the extent of the damage. Working my way aft, I tried to see the hull, over the side, but it was too dark. Going past the galley, the ship rolled to starboard, and I put my hand out to steady myself, against the superstructure side. As I touched the side, my darkest fears were realized, it was oil. A lot of oil. Slowly, I looked up and in between brief shots of moonlight, I could see the darker coating of oil stretching up the side of Audemer's upper structure in what looked like patches. I knew then that I was in the mire. Considering damage limitations, I thought I had better come clean to the bosun who happened to be on the night watch. I knew he was up on the bridge.

I made my way aft and up the rear ladders to the bridge deck. I came up onto the rear deck and saw the bulk of the bosun standing like a statue in the darkness, facing me. The wind was howling up here as I made my way unsteadily towards him. He had his uniform on and in the glow from the navigation lights I could see his face was expressionless as he watched me approach him. This particular bosun (Mr Taggart) was well known and feared amongst most crews. He was as hard as nails, a tough Glaswegian with a known temper, not someone you'd take lightly. I knew he would eat me alive when I told him what I had done. As I came up to him, my worst fears were realised. His face was mottled with oil and rage. It was on his uniform too and I quickly grabbed a piece of cotton waste I always kept in the back pocket of my overalls. As I held it out, he grabbed it and started wiping his face. In a rare, sadistic moment, I nearly started to laugh. He still hadn't said anything, and I could feel myself starting to grin. I coughed to cover it, but his steely gaze never left me. Handing back the cotton waste, he said, "See me at first light," then turned away back to the wheelhouse.

"I'm sorry, Sir," I shouted to his back, into the wind. He probably never heard me.

At first light, the mess was more apparent. It was all over the side of the rear section of hull and up the rear superstructure. The skipper was not going to have Audemer enter Portsmouth harbour covered in oil. The bosun came on deck looking cleaned up and told me I was to be lowered over the side on a 'landing stage' with a broom and a bucket of soapy water and scrub the oil off. One of the senior seamen, Barry Sealey, would keep a watchful eye and take charge of me. I was required first, however, to scrub the superstructure sides, along the galley area and up to the bridge.

Once the novelty of seeing me carrying out this task was past, the lads stopped gawking and making suitable comments. By mid-morning I had completed the upper ship sections and was to get on the landing stage and be lowered over the side. The skipper had fractionally reduced the ships speed, but the sea was still rough although not too bad. Barry instructed me how best to work from the stage, but I had been up since midnight and by this time was getting pretty tired. I climbed aboard the stage and was handed down the bucket and broom. This was all rather precarious as the stage was swinging side to side and every now and again, banging against the ships side. I had a lot of observers making an assortment of comments, but I was trying not to grin too much as the bosun was watching me from the side of the bridge, together with the first mate, a first lieutenant, officer of the watch. So started my hull washing, with the sea just a few feet below me, rushing past. Every once in a while, I was moved further along, towards the stern.

A couple of hours later I'd been forgotten and just carried on washing the side down. Periodically, I would stop for a smoke and at one time, Barry handed me down a mug of tea and a fresh bucket of water with the detergent in it. Before long we were approaching Pompey harbour, the lads had formed up on the deck above and the ensign was unfurled. It is common practice and naval regulations that military vessels are 'piped' into the harbour. This is carried out by naval ratings from the Queen's harbourmasters lookout station at HMS St Vincent, on the Gosport side. As we were entering the harbour a Royal Naval frigate was coming past to leave the harbour. Unfortunately for our lot, they had forgotten that I was hanging over the Port side with my broom and bucket of suds, on the landing stage. Apparently, the frigates duty watch had spotted me and radioed it into the harbour master, who quickly sent a message to Audemer to, "Get that bloody man back on board."

It was naval gossip for a week or two ashore and was even mentioned to me by a couple of the Wrens in the NAAFI club. Yet another mark against me in the skipper's log!

The runs to Antwerp continued for some weeks and Danni's Bar continued to serve us poor lost souls of the sea. It was a great watering hole and the sense of humour these 'girls' had was brilliant. I believe Danni's continued to function for many years and was known by many a passing mariner. It closed for good in the 90's.

'Smoko', a break in the work on deck - HM Gunwharf

Loading up the tank deck in home waters

43

One of the things about being on the LCTs at this time was that in many instances, we followed Royal Navy rules and regulations. This affected terminology, dress and of course, some perks. For instance, you could grow a beard without too much hassle and your hair could be a bit longer than the Army norm. However, the main one being that we were issued with the daily ration of rum. This was called 'Tots Up' and was usually around 11am every day. At this time, we would usually congregate in the Mess having heard the announcement over the ship's PA system. The bosun would ladle out the 'tot' from a wooden barrel with a special wooden scoop of the correct measurement. As our names were called out, we went forward to receive our ration of rum. This rum was also known as 'Pussers Rum'. This stuff certainly put hairs on your chest as it was quite strong. It was standard procedure to wait until all of us had been issued with our tot then the skipper or the No.1 came in and whilst all seated, we would toast Her Majesty the Queen. This tradition of toasting HM whilst sitting down, came from around Nelson's days. The mess decks on the warships of the time were very tight and cramped, with little head room. So, it was far more convenient to toast the King whilst sitting down. This was the only occasion that such a toast could happen sitting down. The issuing of rum tots was ended in 1970, the last issue of 'tots up' was on 31st July. I was in Singapore at that time, at the Royal Naval Base, Sembawang and was fortunate enough to have my 'last tot'. You can, of course, still buy the rum.

As it was getting towards the rundown to Christmas, it was good to stock up on spirits and cigarettes. Each Antwerp trip meant we could bring in duty-free, so I was stocking up and had orders from Mum and Ken, back home. Quite often, I would 'bottle' my issue of rum in an old HP Sauce bottle and take it back for Ken, my brother-in-law. Some of the lads didn't take their tot so if you were lucky, you could collect theirs.

As I mentioned earlier, when I was in Aden on Agheila, I had, amongst others, been writing to a friend of my sister Jo, in Oz, called Sue Wright. We had got on well by letter and I had been sent a picture of her, a pretty, natural blonde. She also had an older sister called Sandra. I had never written to her but had briefly heard about her from Sue. It turned out that Sandra had had an affair with some Oz guy that hadn't gone well. So, she had decided to return to the UK.

Well, I guess Sandra had been briefed by my sisters in Oz about us lot back here and had promised to pop in on Mum, et al. I can't remember the exact meeting of the two of us, but I guess it was late in '68. Sandy had bought herself a 'Lotus' Cortina once she was back in the UK and it was in this that she came over to Mum's. The car had the Cortina shape with a Lotus tuned engine and at the time, was quite highly rated. It was cream with a green stripe along the sides and around the rear trunk area. I had come home for the weekend when Sandra came over.

Needless to say, I was impressed by the car and when Sandra got out, I was impressed even more. She was quite tall, dark hair and dressed in jeans and a sweatshirt. I had to admit to a 'tingling in the loins' although I'm not sure whether it was Sandra or the car. Whatever one, it was the kiss of death from that moment on. I was hooked. I guess the combination of both, the car and Sandy, was too much for my oversexed, immature senses and I was smitten. From that first meeting we met as often as possible. It was unfortunate for the nurse I had met some months earlier, Carol. We had been getting on well and I had been sharing her bed in the nurses' home at the hospital for most of the weekends from late summer and through early Autumn. Up to that point, we were doing very well.

Of course, my mistake was not to mention Sandy; I guess I was enjoying having my cake and eating it too. When I wasn't seeing Sandy, I was with Carol. One weekend in October, Mum had asked me to pop around to my sister Delia's to give her some vegetables that a neighbour had grown. As I was with Carol that weekend, we decided to pop around together. Carol, at that time, was working as a midwife at the H&E and had attended Dee in the birth of her second child, Sarah. We arrived at my sister's house and knocked. Dee answered the door and just stood there, staring at us.

"Hi Dee," I said. "Mum asked me to drop these vegetables in that she promised you. This is Carol."

Fully expecting to be invited in, I started to walk forwards. Dee stood to one side of her door. However, she had other ideas. She suddenly blocked the way and said, "You can come in, but she's not."

I was stunned. I just stood there staring at her. Carol got embarrassed and tugged my hand to go.

"What did you say?" I snapped at Delia.

"I said you can come in but I'm not having her in my house," she replied, still blocking the way. It was as if we were both going to force our way in.

"Well, fuck you," I said. "Come on Carol, let's go."

I chucked the carrier with the veg into her hallway, turned around and, taking Carol's hand, walked away.

This was my first real encounter with prejudice and for it to come from my own family was stunning. I was furious. Carol tried to make light of it, but I knew she was upset. When I mentioned it to Mum, she was livid. Later that day she went around to Delia's to talk to her. I never knew what Mum said to her, but nothing was ever mentioned again. I avoided Delia for a long time after that.

Meanwhile, Sandy and I were getting on well. Gradually, she was meeting some of the others of our family. Her own family in Oz came back later in the year and set up house above shops in Station Road, Edgware and it was there that I met them. Our relationship was leaping ahead so fast that I really didn't feel in control anymore. Back aboard ship we were very busy, mostly trips around coastal waters. It was sometime that autumn that we had a trip to Guernsey during which the postings came up. I hadn't bothered to look at the notice board outside the entrance to the Mess, so it was to my surprise and consternation that one of the lads told me that I was a lucky bugger.

"How come?" I said, wiping my oily hands on some cotton waste before making myself some tea.

"Have you not seen the postings?" he said.

"No, where are they?" I asked

"Have a look on the notice board."

With trepidation, I rose slowly from the bench and went out the mess door. I saw the list and started looking down it for my name and there it was.

L/Cpl English to join HMAV Arakan, 18 Maritime Regt, Far East Land Forces, Singapore, 19th May 1969.

I remember the icy feeling I felt, standing there, until one of the lads came up behind me, patted me on the back and said, "You lucky bastard, I'll swap you if you want".

"Why? Your name isn't even on the bloody list," I said.

"Exactly, Singers and Hong Kong are the plum postings, you lucky git," he told me, wandering past and out on deck.

My first thought was not about the 'mysterious East' and the excitement of foreign places. It was almost one of panic because I would be away from Carol, Sandy, and the Wrens in Pompey and, although it sounded complicated, I had been managing it well. I leaned against the rail around the engine room and fumbled in my overalls for 'the makings'. I took out a half empty pack of Golden Virginia, a Rizla green and started to roll one. I put it to my lips just as the cook came out of the galley.

"What you looking so glum for?" he grinned.

I nodded towards postings list on the notice board.

He turned and looked at it, seeing my name and the posting. "Come on, tea up," he said, pushing the mess door open for me to follow him.

I went back inside and flopped down on one of the benches. He got his lighter out, lit my roll-up, and lit his own, sitting at one of the tables opposite me.

"I'll swap, Dave, you jammy git, how'd you get that? All I end up with is another LCT or bloody Catterick," he moaned. "Just think, mate, all those lovely oriental ladies, exotic food, good weather... brilliant. What officer's wife you been shagging?" he laughed (a reference to my previous exploits).

I grinned and the other lads in the mess laughed.

"Yeah, well I guess they couldn't send an ugly bugger like you out there... damage the regiments reputation and eat all the sodding rations...!" I laughed.

"Sod off, you skinny git. Blimey, right cushy posting, two years of heaven," he said, taking a swig from his mug of tea.

I shook my head and went out on deck with my tea, watching the gulls wheeling over the harbour as we bobbed at the mooring ropes in the harbour at St. Peter's Port. I had to think about this. Everyone was saying how good a posting it was, and deep down I was thrilled at the prospect, but it did pose certain issues on the home front and for my current love life.

Two years was a long time. I knew I couldn't keep the girls hanging around that long. I wasn't too concerned about Carol, but I was starting to like Sandy and was getting to feel comfortable with her. Blimey, two years... Mum would be saddened by my leaving again but at least she'd have the girls, who were coming home from Oz.

As the days wore on, the more I thought about it, the more I was beginning to come round to the idea. However, I was concerned about my ongoing relationship with Sandy. She was about five years older than me, and I doubted she would hang around for the two years I would be abroad. I was slowly coming up with an idea, but it was one that would require some serious thought. Sandy and I were already sleeping together on the rare occasions we managed to be alone. Family on both sides were beginning to see us as an item. I had a lot to think about and I knew that as soon as I mentioned it to Mum, it would be all over the family. I decided to tell them during my Christmas leave once I had got my head around it and discussed things with Sandy. At least that gave me time to think things through.

Christmas came and went, and I can remember very little of it. The news of my upcoming posting was not taken that well, at least, by Mum and Sandy. I wanted to ignore it completely but that was not possible. Sandy was the most pissed off, and some serious discussions regarding our relationship were required. We had quickly moved beyond being just friends and I knew that if I wanted to keep this relationship going, I needed to come up with something quite quickly. But was I ready to tie the knot and get married? It had certainly crossed my mind and then there were the Wrens in Portsmouth whose company I enjoyed and there was of course, Carol in Stortford. But from where I was standing, the thought of losing Sandy was a no brainer. Putting her 'on hold' whilst I went off to Southeast Asia for two years was the only other option and, to be honest, that wouldn't have been fair on Sandy. So, I knew I would have to give her up.

My head pointed me to a single man's life in Singapore, my genitals and heart pointed me to marrying her. Oh shit...! It was a dilemma I had to face. Back on board the '61, I didn't really want to discuss it with anyone, so I thought about it and all the consequences. Sitting on an aft end hatch cover to the boiler and shaft compartment, having a smoke, I came to a decision. I would discuss it with the skipper. I mentioned to him that we'd planned a wedding some time ago and I wondered if my 'wife' could come to Singapore. He made enquiries and the result was 'yes', she could be with me out there. She would have to follow once I had been out there at least a couple of months providing the political situation had settled down. There were some ongoing issues with the Chinese Communists at that time. I was okay with that; it suited the purpose well. So, the die was cast.

On my next visit with Sandy, I asked her about us getting married and her coming to Singapore. She would let me know. About a week later I was home for the weekend and called her from a public telephone box near Mum's house. We never had a landline at home and cell phones were still in the realm of science fiction. This was probably just as well as I can't imagine the mess I'd have gotten myself in financially and with my love life. I was concerned when I called her that this was going to be a negative conversation. It wasn't and I could tell from her voice that she was as excited about it as I was. In fact, I was pretty ecstatic. I ran back to the house and told Mum. I was jubilant. I guess I was expecting her to say something like, 'let's wait and see' or to put me off until I returned from the Far East.

When I told Mum, she looked at me for a moment then said that if this was what I wanted then she was happy for me. I felt kind of deflated; I could tell that she wasn't too pleased about it. She liked Sandy but she knew me too well and must have been wondering about the other girls she had heard me mention and, of course, Carol.

Meanwhile, Di and Jo were returning to the UK and were due to dock in Southampton, aboard the Australis on Tuesday 15th April. Mum had wanted me to be with her at the dock, but I don't recall being there. However, my cousin Pam and my aunt Doll would be with Mum. A 'welcome home' party had been arranged at my sister Delia's house in Stortford for the weekend of 19th April. I probably did make that, although I can't recall it. Things were still quite 'stiff' between Delia and me.

Sandy and I saw each other more regularly and I remember going with her to see a local vicar near her home, in Brent, to discuss a church wedding and 'the bans'. The odd thing about all of this is that I have little recollection of organising anything. I must have spoken to Tom Thomas about it as he was to be my best man. I had been his at his wedding, as previously mentioned. Yet again, I cannot remember any stag do for mine, yet I remember his well. The only thing I do remember is the actual day of the wedding and then only a small part of it. It was to be on 10th May. My sisters were home by then and, yet I cannot recall them even being at the wedding.

I do remember standing in front of the alter with Tom stood beside me and feeling concerned I was doing the right thing. Sandy was late arriving and, after standing there for a good fifteen minutes, I was seriously thinking of pulling the plug.

I mentioned this to Tom, who told me not to worry and give it a few more minutes. I also remember the vicar getting agitated as he had another wedding the same day. As I stood there, I turned around to look at the people on my side of the church and remember my aunts Alice and Martha and my mum with a large pink hat on. I don't recall seeing the girls there but remember there being quite a number of people, including Tom's wife Stephanie. When I mention this to my sisters, they have absolutely no recollection of it at all either. However, I do seem to remember my brother-in-law Ken, taking a 16mm movie of it as we came out of the church onto the road.[1]

There must have been a reception somewhere but all that I can remember is Sandy's younger brother poking his finger at my chest saying that if I ever hurt Sandy or messed her about in any way, he would come looking for me and 'sort me out'. I said in response, "Yeah, you and whose fucking army?" He started getting quite agitated, but Sandy saw this and came over, grabbed my arm, and pulled me away. I think that was the last time I ever spoke to him. Sandy wasn't too impressed with him either.

We stayed that first night at the Foxley Hotel in Bishop's Stortford and then at my sister Delia's house the following night. It was that night at Delia's, after we had gone to bed, we were laughing and having a bit of fun when my sister banged on the bedroom wall to tell us to be quiet. That was so bloody typical of Delia. And there remains the sum total of my memory regarding my wedding to Sandy.

Prior to getting married, I was due a couple of weeks 'embarkation leave'. These were my last days aboard Audemer, and I would miss her. She had been very special to me and a part of me would always remain with her. I'd spent almost five years on her. After I left the services, she continued in service to the RCT 20 Maritime Regt and was eventually sold to a private company. She worked the inland rivers of the Cameroons between 1980 and 1985. She was eventually scuttled off the Cameroons at Latitude 3°25' North and Longitude 9° 13' East on 22nd March 1985.

I shall never forget her.

NOTES

Chapter 2

1. This scheme was the result of an agreement between the British and Australian governments. It started in 1945 and ended in 1972. It was an attempt to populate the Australian territories, and between 1950 and 1960 around one million people took this on. By 1969 these figures were down to around eighty thousand per year. The condition was that you had to stay there for at least two years. Like my parents, many were disillusioned and, in fact, around twenty-five percent of all immigrants returned to the UK. It was to cost around £120 for the return passage.

Chapter 43

1. There is a twist to this tale that was unexpected. Recently, my niece Debbie, from Canada, whose mum is my sister Delia, visited her for a week to see how she is. Dee is now in her eighties and is suffering a bit from dementia but still living in the same house in Stortford. While visiting with her, Debs asked me how the book was going. As I mentioned about Sandy, she said, "Oh, that's funny, Fred (her husband) and I were looking at that movie just recently." I was stunned. She said that he was stood outside the church as we came out and took the movie of all of us. How was that for a coincidence?

PART IV
THE FAR EAST

44

Arriving in the Far East was an understated culture shock. Singapore, to be precise, was the epitome of the far eastern adventure, especially in 1969. I was twenty-three years old, had been brought up on stories of my uncle's travels and exploits, and had a good imagining of what to expect. But, like many things in life, you are never prepared for it when it actually happens.

I arrived in Singapore on 19th May 1969 at RAF Changi. There were quite a few of us, all going to different destinations. As we descended the stairs of the VC10, the heat and smells assaulted my senses. Unlike in Aden, where it was the sewerage that permeated everything, here it was vegetation. It was not unpleasant, and one could even say it was exotic. There were three-tonne trucks lined up to transport us and our kit, so once we had cleared the customs area, we were directed onto these.

I managed to get a seat near the tailgate, and drank in the atmosphere, a mixture of the vegetation, the heady scent of frangipani, and the smells of garlic and spices. On the drive to the barracks my head was awash with the sights of Chinese shop fronts, palm trees and exotic bushes, and the clamour of the black and yellow Morris Oxford taxis. The closer we got to the barracks, the busier the streets became.

Gloucester barracks was just off Ayah Rajah Road, which wasn't that far from downtown Singapore. I recall seeing people cooking on large steel woks by the side of the road and the smells that assaulted me were heavenly. There and then, I decided I was going to like this place.

Singapore is situated at the southern tip of Malaysia. It's a separate island, joined via a causeway, to Johore Baru. There are lots of smaller islands around Singapore and several of these had British Army bases and facilities on them. Singapore is predominantly Chinese in population with a large Malay and Indian mix. Certain areas were, and I believe still are, areas where there are mainly Indians, Tamil, and Hindu. Lower Serangoon Road was known as 'Little India'. Many Malays lived in kelongs and these houses on stilts were in the more rural parts of Singapore.

Today, Singapore is an ultra-modern city with monorail and major highways criss-crossing the island, and the kelongs have all but disappeared. Obviously, the city has spread out but in '69 it was less so. The Chinese had a specific area – Chinatown – which was in the downtown area of Singapore nearer to the waterfront. Chinese nationalities were in the majority and probably still are today. They are the lifeblood of the nation and are dominant in business and trading.

The main business area was Collyer Quay and Raffles Quay. It was also here that the main ferries to and from the ships anchored in the Straits would come. This area was always a hive of activity with moneychangers, hawkers, and the hustle and bustle of activity where all nationalities mixed and congregated. Lee Kwan Yew was the prime minister and he had introduced strict rules and regulations that hadn't been seen in Singapore since the war. He was well respected locally and on the international scene.

Meanwhile, in Malaysia, the Malays were having a crack-down on the Chinese. The Chinese, being good at business and money-making, tended to dominate the trading and business scene. The Malays had a much more laid-back approach to life in general. I can only assume this applied to business as well. This must have been somewhat frustrating for the Chinese as they had quite a lot of control over commerce. The Malays eventually retaliated in the aftermath of the Malay General

Election. It was reported that as many as 600 had been killed in riots, the majority of these being Chinese. These racial riots led to a state of emergency being imposed together with the suspension of parliament. Eventually, this led to a change in government policy that favoured the Malays. These events led to disturbances in Singapore and my arrival, just over a week later, was no coincidence. The British government, at the request of the Singapore government, had decided to bolster the services contingent in the event of something similar happening in Singapore. Many major British banks and commercial businesses were located in Singapore. It was, and still is, the financial hub of the Far East and any similar riots would have a serious effect on many economies, including ours.

As it turned out, there were a few minor skirmishes in the Chinatown area, but these were dealt with quickly and harshly by British military units. During my first couple of weeks there we had curfews, so I never saw much of the 'real' Singapore. A few of us were allocated to undertake patrols in the Chinatown area during this time but it wasn't long before it all settled down, the curfew lifted, and life returned to normal.

It was during my third week there that I joined my ship – L4128 'Arezzo'. So many different environments happening all at the same time was certainly something of a culture shock. But from the moment I had touched down in Singapore, I loved it. The hustle and bustle of street life combined with the smells of spices, chilli, and garlic cooking, gave it all the air of the Orient that I had been expecting.

Once aboard Arezzo it didn't take long to settle down. The internals of the LCT were mostly the same on all the ships, so once I'd got a locker and bunk it was easy enough to feel 'at home'. It was good to catch up with old mates too; my close friend Andy was also an engineer with me on the ship. The chief was Keith 'Granny' Hopping and he wasn't too bad. He'd been my chief on the Ts back home and we knew each other. The guys were surprised that I had married, and it wasn't long before I started getting advice from some of the married lads aboard about best places to live ashore.

Andy and I teamed up and, once ashore, started exploring downtown and the quieter suburbs of Singapore. I wasn't in a rush to find a place but there were areas of the island where lots of Brit expats lived. I didn't fancy living in an area where there were too many and, as Andy had pointed out, we would be away at sea a lot of the time and Sandy would need to feel comfortable knowing there were other UK families in the area. I knew I had to find a suitable location that had nice houses, local shops, and a market that Sandy would be comfortable using.

Meanwhile, as with all these ships, there was always a lot of housework to do, and Arezzo was no exception. Fortunately, painting the engine room wasn't high on the list. This was a busy working ship and there were frequent trips around the coast of Malaysia, moving cargo for exercises and the like. It was during my first month aboard that Granny sent for me and asked if I wanted to go on a Tech 1 Marine Engineering upgrade course back in Gosport. I was a bit nonplussed by this. Having not long arrived in Singapore, and getting settled into life in the Far East, the last thing I wanted was to go back home again. I turned the course offer down and I got the impression he wasn't too happy about this.

It later occurred to me that perhaps there were other forces at play here. Despite all the later things that happened as a direct result of me being in Singapore, I have never regretted that decision to remain. However, it set in motion a chain of events that made me later realise that it was more than likely 'engineered' to get me to leave. Who or what was doing that remains a mystery to this day but my refusal to take the offer changed my life significantly. I just didn't know that at the time… or what was coming.

Around mid-June I went with Andy to a quiet suburb called Serangoon Gardens. I'd heard that quite a few Brits had apartments and houses there but not so many that it became too much. It was about fifteen miles north from downtown Singapore and pretty central to the island. There was a small shopping precinct that surrounded a car parking area where, at least twice a week, a market replete with local produce was set up. In the evenings, this became a night market with food and drink stalls.

In the window of a laundry store in this precinct there were a number of adverts displayed showing houses to rent in the area. One of them looked particularly good and was not that far away on a street called Blandford Drive. Just across from the precinct was Chartwell Drive, which led to the top of a hill. Off this, to the right-hand side, were a number of drives with detached houses on either side. Blandford Drive was one before the last one, at the top of Chartwell. The house that we were interested in was about half-way down on the left. It was number thirty-one. I rang the number on the advert and the landlord arranged to meet us there.

The turning into Blandford was just across from a church of St. Francis Xavier. The whole road was quiet and suburban, and both Andy and I liked it immediately. The landlord, an elderly Indian man, met us at the gate and showed us around. It was a two-bedroomed house, very compact, clean and had some basic furnishings. The rent was good, and I would be receiving a good allowance for this in my salary. I thought Sandy would like it. The immediate neighbours on either side were Chinese, opposite was a Sikh family, and next to them a Brit family. I think they were the only other Brits in the road. I saw some children playing in their front garden and they were all quite small.

The house had a sloping, short drive up to the front door which was painted light blue with a small window in the centre and, like most of the houses in Singapore, had a lockable metal grill that slid to one side. The door opened onto the front room with the first and main bedroom on the right. Down this right-hand side, the wall continued to a WC and then on to the second bedroom. Opposite this was the kitchen, and at the end of the short corridor was the bathroom with bath and a shower over it. The front room was a decent size for a small family with a polished tile floor, a two-seater couch and two sofa chairs, and a coffee table. Against a back wall was a small dining table with four chairs. It was comfortable and, with a decent sound system set up, would make for a good place to live. Just outside the wire railings of the front garden was a tall Acacia tree on the pavement. It shaded the front garden nicely. The agreement was made, and I paid a month's rent in advance. The landlord said he would prepare the place for me to move in the following week.

The road was definitely what I would call a 'leafy suburb'. Standing in the front garden, both Andy and I acknowledged that we had plenty of room for a couple of motorcycles. These were high on our agenda. We walked out the front gate and I suggested to Andy that we go meet our Brit neighbour. He agreed. We wandered across to the house diagonally across from thirty-one. As I walked up to the gate, one of the children ran indoors and, a few minutes later, a tall blonde woman came out. Both Andy and I looked at each other and raised our eyebrows. She opened the garden gate and invited us in. I introduced myself, and Andy and explained that we would be moving in across the road. We shook hands and she introduced herself as Bronwen Evans. Her husband Evan was in the RAF stationed at the RAF Seletar airbase. She introduced her four children and said she had a full-time job looking after them. They were all pretty well behaved. She had a strong Welsh accent and said that she was from Holyhead in Anglesey.

We were invited to stay for a coffee. I explained that we were working on the LCTs and that my new wife of a few weeks was joining me shortly. She seemed really pleased to think that a fellow Brit was moving in, and I could see that we would become good friends. Andy, who was quite shy, got on with her as well. I was pleased to think that Sandy would have someone she could meet with as company and, hopefully, as a friend.

So far, my Far East experience had been great. For me, it felt more comfortable here than being at home in the UK. The weather was far more to my liking, the food was superb and cheap, and the night life was great. The high humidity didn't faze me at all, and it became, for me, the chance of a new life completely. I felt I fitted into the conditions and lifestyle immediately and I hoped that Sandy would too.

45

Sandy finally arrived and settled in quite well, although I think she found the humidity quite uncomfortable. We bought various pieces of furniture, and it wasn't long before the place was set up as we liked it. I brought a Sanyo 'Otto' hi-fi system and soon the Moody Blues, Jose Feliciano, Deep Purple, and The Carpenters were filling the place with sound. Bron and Sandy got along well, and her kids were a delight. Her husband Evan and I became close friends, and we enjoyed the evenings sitting around outside with good music, iced beer, and good conversation.

Work onboard ship continued but my heart wasn't really in it. Whilst I loved the Ts themselves, the Army bullshit out here, whilst aboard, seemed worse than back home. Still, it was good work, and the skipper was always fair about time off. I started to write home to Mum a lot more and she was pleased that things were going well. Dinah had got a job at Hambro's Bank in the City and loved it. She was a PA to one of the directors and all thoughts of returning to Oz had fizzled away. My Uncle Bert was taken to St George's Hospital in Tooting where, after a short illness, he died later that year.

I needed transport and as soon as a driver's course became available, I managed to get on it, along with a couple of other lads from Arezzo. I enjoyed the course. The main vehicle we were taught on was the Bedford three-tonne truck. As well as classroom work, the course also involved convoy driving. This included driving through jungle highways in Malaysia for quite a few hours. I didn't find it an issue at all. We were taught to 'double clutch' which meant getting the engine revs up when you changed gear, which helped with smoother transmission gear changing.

We drove Land Rovers on the course and also a few of the remaining Austin Champs. These little 'babies' had Rolls Royce B40 engines, and I had worked on these at Chepstow during my apprenticeship. They were really smooth and a pleasure to drive. I never saw them again, after this. One part of the course was to drive the Bedford up a muddy embankment, get to the top then drive down the other side. For this exercise, we were told to keep it in low gear and not to touch the clutch. All made sense and I was good to go. In front of me, in his Bedford, was one of the chefs from our ship, Paddy Clarke. I couldn't go until he had got down the other side of this muddy hill. I sat in the cab with my engine running watching Clarksy make his way slowly up the muddy embankment in front of me. A couple of times he slid back and slithered from side to side. I noticed that if you stayed in the tyre tracks from previous vehicles, you were probably ok. Eventually he made it to the top. His truck stopped and sat there a moment. After about five minutes waiting, he still hadn't moved. My instructor was starting to get agitated. Then the driver cab door opened and Clarksy jumped down; he'd had enough. The instructor with him took the wheel and the truck disappeared down the hill. Now it was my turn.

I put it into first gear, let the clutch out, and she started up the muddy embankment. The cab was swaying about but she kept in the tracks. I very slowly increased the accelerator pedal and could feel it bite. All I could see was sky but, bit by bit, she made it up. As the truck levelled out at the top, I slowly took her to the edge of the way down and stopped. I could see why Clarke chickened out. The drop down looked almost vertical, enhanced, I'm sure, by the height of the cab.

The object was to put it into first gear, feet off the clutch and accelerator and let gravity and the weight of the vehicle take over. With my heart thumping in my chest, I put her into gear and let her go, holding loosely onto the steering wheel. If I held it too tight it would pull my arms out of their sockets. As the truck tilted forwards, I could feel the sweat start to trickle down my back. It just seemed to keep going over, so much so that you felt that it was going to tilt all the way until it rolled over. But then all of a sudden, she started to slide forwards. All I had to do then was keep it in the tracks.

Once we'd reached level ground, I pulled into the parking area and turned the engine off. My legs were like jelly but I had done it. All I needed now was a beer, badly. The final road test was a drive around town in downtown Singapore. It was rush-hour but I felt invulnerable in the three-tonner. Also, I was high up. The roads were chaotic but most of the traffic kept out of the way. I mean, who was going to mess with a three-tonne army truck with 'L' plates on it...! I loved it. By the time I returned to the barracks and parked up, I felt I could go around again. Needless to say, I passed easily. All I needed was that licence.

I bought my first car that year. It was a light blue and cream Ford Consul. Bench seating and column change, four-door with a six-cylinder engine. She growled like a tank, but I loved her. Sandy drove it too. It was a fun car and allowed us to see a bit more of the island. Meanwhile I started to struggle a bit with married life. I felt constantly under pressure in that I always had to remember that I was now a married man! Going out with the lads after work was now not always an option. I missed that, and there were so many things we would do to have a laugh whilst on shore runs that had changed. The upside was Sandy; she was good fun and nice to be around, and I now had different responsibilities.

It was around this time that I met Bron's Indian neighbour. I'd seen her from time to time in Bron's house and also in her front garden, watering plants or playing with her nieces on the garden swing. I'd been introduced to her and felt an immediate bond. Her name was Anita, and she was from a Sikh family.

My life suddenly became full. Work was very busy and, of course, there were duties aboard. Andy and I worked together a lot and there were always things needing fixing and maintaining, even when in Port.

I'd heard from Tom Thomas, and he was due out as well, having finished work in Bahrain. I explained to him about Serangoon Gardens, and he said he would look there for accommodation also. Steve would be coming with him, as well. I was getting used to living and working in this environment and it was great. There were lots of moans from others about the humidity, but it never bothered me. Sandy, however, was struggling a bit with the conditions but we had aircon at home, so it wasn't too bad in the house.

Sandy took on children for some of the service families in the area and, along with Bron, ran a child-minding service. It kept her occupied and she enjoyed the busy days. At weekends we started looking around the island, driving to the beaches and meeting new people. At night, the evening street life was good, and we'd eat at roadside stalls and once in a while, go for a 'steamboat' on Orchard Road. This was a dish where the food was prepared and cooked in front of you, at the table. There was a bar in the Serangoon precinct called 'The Captain's Cabin' which became our favourite watering hole, and they did an extremely good chilli prawns there.

We decided to get a dog. We'd heard that one of Bron's friends had a dog that had just had puppies, so we took one of them. He was a mixed breed and was small like a Jack Russell. We called him Worthington and he fitted in really well. The kids all loved him, although he was a bit of a gutter snipe and would chase frogs and rats along the monsoon drains. I was still struggling a bit with being married but was trying hard to get it right and do the right thing. It was difficult, however, and I began to realise that I had possibly made a huge mistake. Sandy wanted a 'normal' home life and didn't respond well to the complexities of living in the Far East. Bron was helpful and a good friend to Sandy, but she was a 'wild-card' and had a different set of agendas.

Bron's husband Evan was a corporal in the RAF, and we had struck up a good rapport. It worked well for both of us, and evenings became a regular round at either our place or theirs and we all sat around, listening to music, chatting, and enjoying 'sundowners'. Bron was great fun and always straight to the point with a great sense of humour. At weekends, Andy would come over and we'd talk bikes, and he was keen on getting one. Meanwhile, news from home was that one of our LCTs, Abbeville L4041, collided with a French trawler in the Channel in fog. There wasn't a lot of damage to the LCT, but the trawler didn't make it. Apparently, one seaman died and eight were rescued.

One of the things that was readily available in Singapore was Ganja. This was marijuana and was cheap and easy to obtain. One of Bron's friends had some and, one evening, over at my place we decided to indulge. It was a magical night and what sticks in my mind most was playing the Moody Blues album whilst high on the stuff. Sandy had some too and was really funny with it. However, the following morning she was pretty ill with a bad head and felt sick. Both of us decided that perhaps it wasn't for us.

I'd learnt to make curries from various people and started to get really into them, making them often, at home. Sandy was more of a roast dinner person, but we alternated, and home life started to settle down. We had our arguments and, to be honest, it was probably my fault most of the time.

Work on the T's continued and we started doing trips up to places like Penang and various places along the Malaysian coast. It was good to see these and now that the 'troubles' had quietened down, a few of our trips were more 'goodwill' tours.

Borneo was one trip that I really enjoyed. In 1969 it was still very rural. Most of Borneo belonged to Indonesia, and part was also Malaysian. The place we went to at that time was Brunei, which was a separate nation although part of Borneo. We went to the port of Bandar Sen Begawan, which was the main port but up a river. It was a fascinating place but in those days was a bit of a 'one-horse' town. This was one of the last trips on the Arezzo. She was a good ship but starting to show her age, as they all were. She was destined for Bahrain where she was to be sold to the government. Because I was now a 'married pad' I didn't have to sail her there, so I was to be transferred to L4164 'Arakan'. Quit a few of us were moved over to the Arakan, including Andy, which was good.

Another reason I was pleased to remain in Singers was that I was getting close to Anita. It had happened by accident really; Sandy and Bron had gone downtown for the day, and I happened to get home before lunchtime. Sandy had left a message for me to pop over to Bron's to pick some stuff up that Evan had left for me. Anita, who lived next door, had Bron's key. When I went over, she came around and let me in.

It was the first time I'd been alone with her, and we sat and chatted. It was clear to both of us that there was something special between us. There was an awkward moment when neither of us spoke. We just sat there, looking at one another. I touched her hand and held it for a moment, it felt like an electric shock went through me. The next thing, we were kissing. This became a little more intense, so we stopped for a moment, looking guilty but really happy. I needed her over in my own place as it was far too risky here. We were from totally different worlds and the protocols of her way of life were seriously different from mine. We both knew of the risks we were taking even being alone in the same house together. She said she would help me carry the books and items across the road to my house.

The street was quiet and still. The midday sun was strong as it blazed down amongst the suburban sprawl and not a leaf moved on the tall Acacia tree by my house. A bee buzzed amongst the flowers and a dragonfly hovered a moment then darted away, a green blaze of iridescence. I didn't want to look too furtive so made a joke about the heat and stillness of the day. She looked across at me but said nothing. I put the books down momentarily, got my keys, and opened the pale blue front door. Even the colours seemed to be extreme; it was as if the world was holding its breath.

I stood aside and let her pass me into the cool, shaded interior. Her perfume was musky and exotic, and I held my breath for a moment, stunned at what we were doing. I closed the door gently, put the books on the coffee table, and we stood looking at each other. We both knew what was going to happen next. I moved towards her and held her. The muskiness of her scent was almost overwhelming. She took the clasp from her hair and her raven tresses fell around her shoulders. We both knew that she couldn't stay long. We made love and lay together in total bliss for a while, both knowing this was a major turning point in our lives. I wanted her more than anything, and I knew at that moment that my relationship with Sandy was over. It frightened me some as I knew that Anita was 'forbidden fruit' and that the months to follow would be challenging for all three of us, to say the least.

46

Life aboard the LCTs in the Far East was quite different from Aden and back in the UK. On the Arakan it was a bit more relaxed and, quite often, 'show the flag' trips were more of a thing. That, of course, meant a lot of cleaning and painting. Each engineer had a compartment responsibility. Mine was the forward bow door winch rooms. These were small rooms, as far forward as you can go, under the upper deck section. It was here where the bow doors and ramp were operated from. The ramp operated from a large steel cable, wrapped around a winch drum which had to be well maintained and greased. There was one of these rooms on each side of the bows. There were operating controls in both but the main one used to operate the doors and ramp was the port winch room. These rooms were all steel and very confined. In the tropics, this is a bit like working in an oven and although, on most occasions, you are only wearing shorts, it was best, in here, to wear full overalls as the metal parts were often too hot to touch.

On one occasion, we were being visited by one of the 'top brass' to the ship. Our orders for the week prior to this were to get everything gleaming and all compartments clean. It so happened that on Arakan we had a staff sergeant engineer who didn't particularly like me. I have absolutely no idea why this was, although I do remember saying to one of the watch engineers, whilst we were at sea one day, that this particular staff sergeant never carried out full watch duties properly; whenever we took over from his watch, there was always something that hadn't been done. He may have been standing at the top of the hatch when I said this as it was customary at times to leave this hatch clipped open to let the heat out and my voice was often raised when chatting in the engine room. But who knows...? Anyway, because of this forthcoming visit, I was sent forward to get my bow door winch compartment spik n' span. It was extremely doubtful that the visiting brass would be soiling himself to visit the winch space but, hey-ho, that's the customary bullshit that you had to comply with from time to time.

The winch room had steel plate flooring that was not easy to keep clean. Mostly because the drum and cables had to be kept adequately oiled and greased and it was not difficult to get the deck plates beneath the winch drum a bit messy. The heat in the compartment was enough to sometimes partly liquefy the grease, causing it to drip on the plates beneath. However, saying that, I took a large bundle of cotton waste with me and, getting on my hands and knees, proceeded to wipe all the floor areas of the compartment, including beneath the immediate part below the winch drum, even though this part was never walked on. After a couple of hours of this, I had completed cleaning the floor and stowing any tool and spare winch parts, wiped the bulkhead sides down, greased the winch cables and the compartment watertight door. I was pleased with myself. There was a port hole on the right-hand side that overlooked the tank-deck so that when operating the bow doors and lowering the ramp, you could view how things were going. I'd fully opened the port and wedged the compartment door open to allow fresh air in and get maximum light into the compartment.

. . .

Once I had reported back that my section was completed, the staff sergeant decided to inspect it. I followed him up the catwalk to the compartment, and I could tell by his purposeful strides with his clipboard gripped tightly in his hands that he was determined to find fault. I followed him in as he looked at the deck and bulkheads. He then got on his hands and knees in front of the steel cable winch and put his hands as far as he could, under the drum. When he pulled his arm back, he had a greasy hand.

"What do you think this is, English?" he asked.

"Looks like a greasy hand to me, Staff," I said, thinking, *plonker*.

"Right, exactly, I thought you said that this compartment was ready?"

I looked at him for a moment, framing a suitable response. "Well Staff, I thought it looked pretty clean to me".

"Are you taking the piss, English? When I said clean, I meant spotless. This place is filthy," he said, wiping his grimy hand on some cotton waste.

I just looked at him.

"Get this place done again. I want to see a totally clean hand when I come back. And close that bloody porthole, this place looks the pits."

I looked at him for a moment then said, "Yes, Staff."

After he'd stormed out, I stood there watching him disappear along the catwalk, took out the makings and rolled a cigarette. *Arsehole*, I thought.

I stood a few moments outside, looking out at the harbour area, enjoying the smoke. Flicking the butt over the side I went back in and closed the port. Taking a large handful of cotton waste, I was back on my hands and knees wiping under the winch drum as far as I could reach. I then went and found a broom handle and collected a second bucket of hot water with degreasant and suds in it. I wrapped a clean rag around the end of the broom handle and then proceeded to continue cleaning under the cable drum. With the bucket of suds and degreasant, I washed the compartment floor for the second time. It was getting near lunch time when I felt I had completed everything. Looking out the compartment door, I saw him striding along the catwalk, clipboard in hand and that determined look still on his face. Oh dear...!

"Have you cleaned everything?" he asked aggressively.

"Yes Staff," I said.

He looked around a moment then, as before, went down on his hands and knees and put his hand as far as he could reach under the drum. He moved his arm about a bit then stood up.

"What the fuck is that then?" he said, nodding at his dirty hand then looking at me.

By this time, I'd had enough of his bullshit. "This ship has been in service since 1945. These deck plates are steel with oil, grease, and rust on them. This is a fully functional, tidy, bow door compartment and this is a working ship. With all respect, Staff, the visiting dignitary is not going to get on his hands and knees and stick his hand under the cable drum," I breathed a sigh and stared at him.

"You will clean this compartment again and I shall inspect it in one hour. If it is not spotless, I will put you 'on orders'. Is that clear, English?"

"You can stick your bloody orders. I am not cleaning this fucking compartment anymore Staff Sergeant. I hope I have made that clear to you."

He stared at me open mouthed. "You are on a charge, English. Are you refusing to carry out my orders?" he said, going quite red in the face.

"Yes, I bloody well am."

He turned around. "We'll see about this," he said and stormed off, clipboard in hand.

Oh fuck, I thought, *now I'm in for it. Bollocks, I'm going for a cuppa, and made my way to the mess-deck.*

When I arrived in the mess, one of the lads said, "You alright,

Dave? You look a little flushed."

I lit up a smoke and, as I was making myself some tea, I explained what had just happened.

"Oh, shit mate, they'll throw the book at you."

"I couldn't give a fuck anymore," I said. That arsehole has been having a go at me for weeks. This should bring it all to a head and maybe clear the air. "Life's too short to be having issues with the likes of him," I said as I sat down with my mug of tea. I leaned back against the bench seating, enjoying the air-conditioned mess.

Sure enough, an hour later I was told to clean up and appear before the No.1's cabin. I got out of my overalls and put my No.8's on with my beret. I went up to 'Officer Country' and stood outside the No.1's cabin. I was marched in, beret under arm, saluted, and stood at attention.

The staff sergeant was stood to one side. My 'offence' was read out by the staff sergeant, and I noticed that the charge was for swearing at an NCO and refusing to carry out an order.

"What have you to say for yourself. L/Cpl English?" the No.1 said.

I explained all the cleaning I had done and then mentioned what I had said to the staff sergeant about the ship's age and working capability.

"I see," said the No.1. "However, swearing at a senior NCO is not something I will tolerate on my ship. I would like you to apologise to the staff sergeant."

I stood there quietly for a moment, saying nothing. I could hear the noises of the crew about the ship and the gentle swaying motion of the ship as she nudged the jetty now and again.

"Corporal English, I'm waiting," said the No.1.

"My apologies, Staff Sergeant, it won't happen again," I said contritely.

We all stood there for a moment, then the No.1 looked across to the staff sergeant,

"Thank you, Staff, that will be all."

He turned back to his desk and started shuffling some papers. I came to attention as the staff sergeant left the cabin and waited to be dismissed. The sliding door slid shut behind the staff and all was quiet for a moment.

"Cpl English, David, you should know better than to do that. He was only carrying out his orders."

I looked at him as he leaned on his desk.

"I understand that Sir, but that compartment is as good, if not better, than you will see on any ship in the squadron. I felt he was being over the top and excessive. I could not have got it any better than I had, short of painting it, Sir."

"That's no excuse for insubordination and, because of that, I'm going to fine you a week's pay."

We stood for a moment looking at each other. I put my beret on and saluted him, "Thank you, Sir."

He saluted back. "You're a good engineer, English, I don't want to see you in my cabin again, dismissed."

I turned and marched out. I was lucky, it could have been a lot worse. Perhaps now, the arsehole would back off.

I guess, looking back at that incident, it had begun to dawn on me that my time in HM Forces was coming to an end. I'd had enough. I loved the LCTs and life aboard them. The camaraderie was something you never experience in civvy street. I'd served my country well, by choice. They'd used my special skills when it suited them and, although I was not the best soldier or engineer they had, I was consistent, loyal, punctual, and reliable. I loved the discipline it gave me, but the pay was shite and I felt I had given them my all. However, I would not suffer idiots and there were certainly a few of those around. I realised then that I would try and see my time out and walk away.

47

Settling into Singapore life was easy. Every day was filled with either work or my social life. It was crammed with everything I could throw into it. I was, by now, well accustomed to the tastes of the East. Chilli and garlic were the basis, but the heady scents of the local food permeated everything. The exotic aromas didn't stop at food, either. The fragrance of the blossoms was stunning. Frangipani was heady but the more subtle scents from roses, other flowers, and the general smells of wet vegetation after a downpour, were always there. You never noticed them, they just existed alongside you. Once you moved away, at sea, you were reminded of their absence.

Christmas '69 came and went. It had been a few rounds of parties, meeting people, and dancing in clubs and hotels until the early hours of the morning. Then stopping at roadside stalls to have 'murtabak' or drink the incredibly sweet tea, served in glass tumblers, the ubiquitous *chai*. Tom and Steve settled into life in Serangoon Gardens and Steve had Felicia, her first born. Tom joined me on Arakan, although he was deck side, a seaman. He was good at his job and hard working. I think he too found married life a bit of a struggle. For me, I was fortunate that at the time neither Sandy nor I wanted children; I think it would have been disastrous.

In early 1970 we started going further afield with the ship. One such trip was going to be a special one for us; we were to visit Thailand. It was mostly a goodwill trip, but it was also to help cement our relations with the Thais. We were to carry a couple of dignitaries with us and would be visiting some remote areas. The Vietnam war had been going for many years and by this time, it was not going well for the Americans. For Britain to maintain good relationships with far eastern nations, this was a critical point.

Initially, this trip took us up the east coast of Malaysia. We'd normally sail the west coast and had already made several trips to Penang. Going ashore in these places was a must. The beer and food were excellent, and people were very friendly. The fear that used to hang over you in Aden was non-existent here. It made going ashore that much nicer and it was always good to look forward to. What struck me most about Malaysia was that the people were more friendly and approachable. In Singapore everything was much neater and tidier and there was a 'crispness' to life there that seemed to keep everyone busy and 'on a mission'. Perhaps it was because of this that it could be a little less friendly. Malaysia was very relaxed, and people were a lot more relaxed in their dress and pace of life. Quite often you would see people sitting around the coffee houses and food places. These were open-fronted buildings without glass which made it very easy to just drift in from the street to get out of the sun and into the cool interiors. You could sit at a table and eat chilli and noodles or chicken and rice. A little side dish of the green chilli pickle or soya and red chilli and I would be in heaven. The architecture too, was less modern and many times you could see the influence of the past Dutch colonists in many of the older towns.

The east coast was more rural. As we sailed along the coastline, the places we passed were quiet, sleepy little villages, many with the fishing kampongs that made up much of the local lifestyle here. On this particular trip, we were to have a treat. As we approached the coastal town of Mersing there were several groups of islands. We sailed through these, some between us and the Malay coast, others, further out. The largest one of these, on our port side was named Pulau

Tiomen. On the east side of this island was a natural, horseshoe shaped bay. Because the LCTs were flat bottomed, we could get very close in to shore. In this instance, we could beach her, which we did. We gently eased forwards until we were within ramp dropping distance and dropped anchor.

In the engine room it was noisy, and we were all expectant as the ship slowly inched forwards, leaving me to wonder what the scenery from up on deck, was like. The telegraphs rang down to neutral. We were drifting in. The engines were idling as we heard the anchor being dropped. Then 'slow astern' rang down followed by 'stop'. You could feel the ship pull at the anchor, then remain steady. A minute or so later, the 'all stop' was rung on the telegraphs and we shut the engines down. The silence was good. We kept two generators running and once all was secured, I went up on deck from one of the generator room hatches. The sight that greeted me was stunning.

We were facing 'bow on' to the beach. As I emerged from the starboard generator room hatch, the view took my breath away. White, coral sands with an almost iridescent green, backdrop of the jungle set a little back from the beach. Behind that, these tall cliffs arose, and these stretched along both sides of the arms of the bay, surrounding us and the beach. I walked along the catwalk to the bow ladder and climbed up to the foc'sle. The silence, the gentle breeze and the view was a combined experience, something I'd read about in books but never experienced before. There were some local people on the beach, mostly children, just standing and looking or waving. Sat a little way back from the beach, just inside the treeline of the forest in front of us, I could see some huts. Andy came up alongside me, "Well, blimey, that's some sight. I never thought I'd see anything quite like that", he said, as stunned as I was.

Slowly, the bow doors were opened, and I watched from the port compartment, waiting for the bosun to give the signal to drop the ramp. He waved his hands in the 'thumbs up' and I started lowering the ramp. As it went down, I leaned out of the port to watch. Some of the lads were lined up on the tank-deck below, ready to go down the ramp and check that all was secure. I shut the winch drum down and made my way back along the catwalk. I climbed down the nearest ladder to the tank deck. I walked up to the ramp and on it to the beach. The water was crystal clear and lapped gently at the sides of the steel ramp. A few of us were stood there, looking around when a local man in a sarong came over to us. Shading his eyes, he looked past us to the interior of the tank deck. He grinned and nodded to us, "Salamat, welcome to Tiomen". He was wizened and his skin, a nut brown was very wrinkled. We all echoed the 'Salamat' greeting, and he stood chatting to one of the lads. I turned around and went back aboard as I was still on duty and made my way back up to the forward mess.

Later that day, Andy and I changed into shorts and T-shirt and went for a walk along the beach. I wasn't on duty until 08:00 p.m., so I had a little time to explore. The place was idyllic. It reminded me of the old Hollywood musical *South Pacific* with Mitzi Gaynor and Rosanno Brazzi. The beach scene, where the lads all sang, 'There is nothing like a dame,' came to mind. I mentioned this to Andy, but he hadn't seen the film. I'd been brought up on these films and, having three elder sisters, I'd seen most of the big Hollywood musicals and *South Pacific* was one of the best. This place certainly fit the bill, perfectly.

We wandered towards the treeline and the village huts. People watched us curiously and scruffy young urchins giggled and laughed. Set back a little further in the trees, I could hear running water and realised that the cliff face was quite close by. At a section to the left, water cascaded down the rocky wall into a small pool. I saw a woman filling a jug from the run-off at the rock face. Here was fresh water, a necessary factor if you lived here. The exotic sounds of bird calls complemented the place, and the varieties of butterfly were stunning. Iridescent blues and greens fluttered past in a dazzling display and their wings were the size of a child's hand. It was amazing. Many of the trees were coconut palms and there was a smell wafting among them from the village of roasting meat, chilli, and garlic.

Those of the lads that were not on watch were on the beach. A few played footy with some of the local kids while others, like us, were sitting and taking this all in and having a smoke. Many were swimming in the shallows or just sunbathing on the coral sand. The place was amazing and had certainly left an impression on me. Later, in the evening, I sat with Andy and Tom on the aft deck, having a beer and a smoke and watching the sun set. It was a stunning place, very basic but beautiful. I believe it is now a tourist resort and doubt very much if it is anything at all like it was back in 1970, but it would be worth a visit just to find out.

The next day we sailed for Songkhla, Thailand. Sailing up the east coast was a treat. The South China Sea was relatively calm, but this was around May/June and the hurricane season didn't start until around September. On the way up this coast, it took us about two days to reach Thai waters. As we got nearer Songkhla we started to see Thai navy ships. We sailed past a few of these, and I happened to mention it to one of the lads. The ships looked familiar except for the Thai flag they were flying. Apparently, most of the ships we saw were ex Royal Navy boats. Nothing really big, but a few minesweepers and frigates. We pulled into a Thai naval base but there was no shore leave. This was a diplomatic visit, so we all had to stay aboard and carry out our normal shipboard duties.

A few days later we sailed further up the coast to a place called Sattahip and beached on a long stretch of sand. There was a small town here and our 'beaching' caused quite a local stir. This was not a tourist part of Thailand, so the locals were fascinated to see a military ship with the British flag flying. We were to stay here for a couple of days. We had all been briefed and told that we were only allowed ashore in uniform, not to get drunk, and to stay together in groups of at least two or three. We were told that many of these people had not seen Caucasians before, that apples were a rare delicacy here and that it was ok to offer them these. It all seemed a bit of nonsense to me but, sure enough, when we walked off the ramp, we were besieged by kids and young adults. They certainly hadn't seen apples before and some of the lads had great fun handing them around.

A group of us decided to explore a little further and went up the beach to the town. It was not much of one, with just a few coffee shops and stores along each side of the main street. There were no bars, but you could get beer at the little coffee shops. I liked the place as it was not somewhere tourists were ever likely to visit. The majority of lads soon got bored and headed back to the beach and the ship. Andy and I were enjoying the place so after a couple of beers, we carried on up the main street, chatting and looking at the various stores.

As we were walking, we heard a voice behind us saying, "Erm, excuse me, are you Americans?" We turned around to see a rather well dressed, elderly Thai man. He spoke in near-perfect English and said again, "Are you American or English?"

I grinned. "We're English, mate," and pointed to the Blue Ensign insignia on my shoulder tab. "We're off the military vessel on your beach."

His concerned face broke into a large smile. "Oh, thank goodness. I thought that was the case, but I wanted to be sure. My name is Colonel Sussapon and I live here. I am a doctor and I studied at Kings College Hospital, in London."

We were both a bit surprised. It was quite unexpected in such a remote location to come across such a person. We introduced ourselves and shook hands with the colonel. I explained that I was from London and Andy tried to explain where Norfolk was.

"Would you both do me the honour of coming back to my house? It is quite nearby," he said, pointing up the street, in the direction we had been heading.

We looked at each other. We were both thinking the same thing – is it safe? We were two unarmed soldiers in a remote foreign town, in uniform. I looked at the colonel and then around me. I couldn't see any of our crew about and did feel a little vulnerable. He must have seen our hesitation.

"Please, I can assure you, it is quite safe, and it would be a great honour for me to have you both visit my home and family."

I looked at Andy again and then at my watch. It was just after 02:00 p.m. and starting to get hot. I shrugged, what the hell. "Yes, we'd love to, that's very kind of you."

Andy nodded and the colonel beamed. "Let me show you, please to follow me," he said and strode off in front of us.

I looked at Andy and grinned, "This could be interesting."

We walked a way up the dusty street and then crossed over to the shadier side. When he turned up a narrow side street both Andy and I looked at each other. If this guy was going to set us up, we would find out soon enough. We'd all heard stories during the confrontation, of similar things happening and who was to say that the Thais didn't hold similar grudges against UK military personnel. After all, that was the reason we had been told to stay in groups. I looked around for avenues of escape and mentally picked a couple of alleyways leading off that didn't look like dead-ends.

However, it turned out our fears were unfounded; at the end of this narrow street the place opened up into a cleared area to one side of which sat this rather large, sprawling house. It was more along the lines of a Spanish hacienda with a large portico where masses of purple Bougainvillaea framed the entrance.

The colonel stood to one side of the large wooden door and invited us into the cool interior. As soon as we had crossed the threshold we were met by a little Thai lady and three very attractive young Thai girls, all in their late teens or early twenties. The colonel introduced us to his wife and three daughters. The girls all giggled and smiled with an amount of nervousness.

"They have been preparing some lunch and I would like you to join us, I hope you don't mind," he said, rubbing his hands together. "Would you like a cold drink? We have beer and whiskey"

We looked each other and said that beer would be good. He spoke quickly in Thai to the girls, somewhat aggressively, I thought. The girls didn't seem bothered at all, they smiled at us both and disappeared. We were shown through another door and led into a large living/dining room. Two sets of French windows led out onto a wooden veranda that seemed to run the length of the rear of the house. The room was tastefully furnished with a large hardwood credenza to one rear wall. The dining table was massive, a long hardwood table, a deep, rich mahogany in colour. Both Andy and I were impressed with the place that looked like an old bungalow from the outside. There were potted plants everywhere of which some were very large palms. It gave the place the look of a Victorian conservatory/parlour room.

We were invited to sit down, and it was then that I realised the smells that were wafting through. The ubiquitous chilli and garlic made both of us feel hungry. One of the girls brought a tray in with ice cold bottles of beer on and they were handed out. Iced glasses were put on the table and I poured mine into one. Then a very old man and woman came in and these were introduced as grandparents. They joined us at the table. I noticed on the wall was a framed picture of the Thai King and Queen as well as a large, framed picture of our Queen Elizabeth. A few minutes later a large assortment of steaming dishes were brought in, and the smell was stunning. These were placed around the table, filling it with an abundance of Asian food that assaulted the senses. I looked across at Andy and raised my eyebrows. Neither of us were expecting this. I grinned at him and just shrugged my shoulders. It did cross my mind that perhaps this guy was the local dignitary and that I should have told him that I would inform our officers. But things happened too fast and here we both were, sitting at a table with a feast of food, being treated as very special and loving every minute.

The colonel sat at the head of the table and just as I was about to take a large mouthful of the icy cold beer he suddenly stood up and raising his glass, looking at the portrait of Queen Elizabeth, said, "The Queen." I looked at Andy, who looked at me and grinned, and we both said, "The Queen."

As we sat down, I noticed that all the women had risen as well. It was apparent that the colonel was keen for us to try a particular dish. In the centre of the table was a large soup tureen of what I thought was some kind of hot stew. 'Mrs Colonel' picked up a large ladle, dunked it in the 'stew', and brought out a ladle full of little crabs. It turned out that these were rice paddy crabs and were some kind of local delicacy. She placed them in a bowl and passed it to me then did the same for Andy. She placed a bowl full in front of the colonel and he proceeded to show us how to eat them.

"This is very special delicacy in this region," he said, picking one up with his fingers.

"You eat it like this," and he proceeded to pull the upper shell of the little crab off and suck what was underneath.

"They are very sweet, try it."

I looked at my bowl then looked at Andy. He just blinked,

"Fuck it," I said quietly, then fished one of the crabs out, flicked off the shell, and did as the colonel had. I didn't even look down at it, just ate it like an oyster. It was a bit gritty, but I did it. Andy looked at me and did the same. I quickly took a sip of the soup it was in. That was much better. We both grabbed our beer and the colonel held up his hand and stood up.

"I have something a lot better," he said and mentioned something to one of the girls. She left the table then came back with a bottle and three shot glasses. The dreaded Thai whiskey! Neither of us was keen to partake of this stuff; it was pure rotgut, but we didn't want to offend him, so it was a case of taking the 'medicine'. The girls were giggling and tucking into the meal. Two ceiling fans disturbed the air at each end of the table, but it was quite cool in the place. The colonel poured three shots of the whiskey and handed them across the table. Pushing his chair back, he stood, and we followed suit. He raised his glass to HM, "The Queen," he said, and we followed suit. "The Queen," we both muttered and downed the shot in one. But that wasn't the end of it. He refilled the glasses. I don't know what Andy was feeling at the time, but the fiery liquid was like paint stripper. I could feel it burning my throat all the way down and my eyes teared up. Sitting down I took a long swig of the beer. Balm for my damaged throat. His wife said something to him and smiled across at us. "Eat, eat," she said, and I started tucking into the rice and sambals that went with it. He asked us about the trip we were doing but was mostly interested in hearing about where we came from in the UK and telling us about his experiences at Kings College Hospital. We had to 'toast to the Queen' twice more and both of us explained that we couldn't have anymore as we were on duty later that evening. We tucked into the food and the girls tried to converse in English.

All in all, it was a really nice experience, and we were certainly doing our bit at showing goodwill on this trip. We finally left a few hours later. This entailed lots of bowing heads and shaking hands. I think I was too pissed to ask for contact addresses from the girls and

Andy too shy. I regret not getting the address, but Colonel Sussapon's name I never forgot. It was a good run ashore and I couldn't help thinking that perhaps we should have passed the Colonel's invitation on to the officers. I mentioned this to Andy on the way back and he laughed. "Too bad, we enjoyed it," he said, and we got a fit of the giggles all the way back to the ship, every now and again saying, "The Queen!"

48

The trip back from Thailand was uneventful and it was good to be back in Singapore. All was well at the house, and I think Sandy had enjoyed her time with Bron and Evan and me not being there. The car had been playing up and after someone gave us a shunt in the back, we both agreed it was time to get rid of it. But I still required transport to get to work so it was inevitable that I would get a motorbike.

Andy had brought a bike from a Chinese motorcycle dealer in Singapore. This downtown shop was excellent and was to be a regular haunt for both Andy and me. The name of the place was Ban Hock Hin, and the man himself was brilliant. Originally, he was a motorcycle racer, and we became good friends and when Andy bought his bike, he gave him a good deal. It was a Honda 250 racing bike with drop handlebars and a red tank in very good condition. Andy used to come around on it and even Sandy was taking an interest in bikes. Andy took her on the back several times. I'd had a ride on it but wasn't impressed with drop-bars, but it was certainly a powerful bike. Ban Hock Hin knew I was after a bike, but I couldn't find one that I was particularly attracted to.

Much of the work on the Ts was local, mostly getting things ready to dismantle certain bases as the Brits were hoping to pull out at the end of '71. My time in the services would finish in '73 as would Andy's but neither of us wanted to be in the forces back in the UK; I'd heard that things were getting a bit messy in Northern Ireland and that the Ts back in the UK were doing lots of NI runs. I had a gut feeling that that was where I was heading. After Singers, the prospect of NI was depressing. Both Andy and I felt we had to do something to leave the services and stay in Singapore.

On the home front, Sandy and I had a long discussion, and it was agreed that we would separate so I started the process of getting a divorce through the services. This would take a while so I couldn't leave just yet, but Andy could. However, before he processed the leaving bit, he'd need a job. The hunt was quietly on. No one knew of our intentions.

One morning, I went with Andy to BHH so he could pick up a part for his bike. Andy got what he needed and had to get back to the ship as he was on duty. I said I would hang around BHH as I wasn't on duty until later in the day and liked browsing around the bikes that were on sale. The boss came from the workshop out the back and saw me. He knew that I was looking for a particular bike but so far nothing had turned up. We chatted and I mentioned that I was still interested in a bike. He stood there thoughtfully for a moment, rubbing his chin. I could see that he wanted to tell me something but wasn't sure. After a few minutes he said to come back on Saturday morning. He thought he had something I may be interested in.

. . .

Things between Sandy and me were amicable but we both felt that the relationship was over. I had noticed and heard from Sandy that Anita's brother-in-law, who ran the house where she lived across the road from us, had been making advances on Sandy. At first, I thought it was a joke but then I realised that Sandy was encouraging it because she knew I was too close to Anita.

On the occasions we could meet up, Anita and I would meet in a place near where we lived that we had nicknamed 'the desert place'. It was a large plot of undeveloped land a few streets to the rear of Blandford Drive. Part of it was still wooded and the grass was very long. When we met there, we could lay down in the grass and would never be seen. It was here that we would sometimes meet, and it felt a bit like being at home on a summer's day in the countryside. I knew these encounters were wrong but the danger of it, as well as being with Anita herself, was a big attraction. It really was living on a knife edge because if we were ever caught, the resulting issues would be horrendous. I have to say that testosterone levels were overriding all common sense. The silly thing was, I knew this but just couldn't help myself. It was madness. Her brother-in-law had an inkling something was going on and his attentions to Sandy were probably the result of this. Being aware of these things, I knew that we both had to be especially careful.

I went downtown to the BHH motorbike shop on a Saturday morning. I wandered around the collection of motorbikes that were for sale, out front. Nothing caught my eye. As was customary with these Singapore shops, everything spilled out onto the pavement. It all looked a bit haphazard, but it was all there. Bits of part-dismantled motorbikes, new parts, and accessories seemed to be scattered around. A couple of bikes were being maintained within the gloomy interior of the shop which had no glass front or door. It was a large, open area within the building with a large, drop-down shutter that closed it off at night. There was a constant smell of motor oil, hot metal, and exhaust fumes. I loved the chaos of it all. After a while BHH himself came over. He was quite a small man and a little rotund, with a bald head.

"Ah, Mitta Ingrish," he said in his distinctive accent, "good to see you. Come with me…" He walked to the side of the shop where it was a bit quieter. "Are you still interested in a street bike?" he enquired.

I told him I was as long as it was affordable.

"I may have something for you. About a year ago, an American living in Singapore ordered a particular bike from me. He paid a reasonable deposit to me but, unfortunately for him, he ended up in trouble with the authorities and was deported back to the USA. I think it was something to do with drugs, he said, shrugging his shoulders. The motorcycle I had ordered for him, came but he was not in a position to take it. He asked me to keep it a few weeks for him but not long after this conversation he was deported. I moved the motorcycle to my warehouse near Katong and covered it up. At least once a week I go over to the warehouse and during my visit, I start the engine of it to keep it in good condition. My man over there put the battery on charge overnight to keep it in good order."

I could see where this was heading and was concerned that the American would likely want it shipped out to him.

"That was almost a year ago and as he still owed me payment. I have been trying to contact him but without success. He won't be coming back to Singapore. So, I have this bike which I believe is exactly what you are looking for. I will do a deal with you on the price, so don't worry. But first, are you interested? If so, I shall take you to see it," he said.

I said that I was and was totally intrigued by this bike. We would discuss the price once I had seen it.

I jumped into a pickup truck he had with some old bikes in the back, and we drove across town. The place was a small industrial estate with a number of warehouses scattered about the area. We drove between a few and came to quite a large one with a Malay lad stood outside. The large corrugated, sliding doors were fully open and he drove just inside, in the cool shade. I jumped out as a couple more lads came across and started unloading bikes from the back of the pickup. The place was like a small aircraft hangar with some bikes parked up and a few crates with new bikes on, still unopened, stacked to one side. BHH dealt in new motorcycles to order, and I guessed these crates were orders of bikes from Japan. I looked around for the bike in question but couldn't see anything that I would be remotely interested in. After talking to his workers for a few minutes, he came over to where I was standing.

"Right, let's take a look at the bike," he said, grinning. He'd seen me looking around. We walked past some large packing crates and over to a bike that was covered in an old, grubby sheet. I stood looking for a moment while he went over and slowly pulled the sheet off. I was stunned. There it stood, the most stunning bike I had seen. It was black and chrome and it was big. I didn't say anything at first, just walked over to it and looked.

"Sorry it's a bit dusty," he said, blowing dust off the black tank, "it's been here a while." He bent down and turned a small lever on the side of the engine then took a key out of his pocket and gave it to me. The bike was on its centre stand, just silently waiting. I took the key and blew the dust off the black leather seat. It was a Honda CB450 DOHC, the largest bike that Honda produced at that time and known as the 'black bomber'. With a horsepower of 45bhp it was all that I could wish for, and more. The handlebars had been raked to give it a street bike appearance and it had crash bars to the side and rear. The rear one serving as a back rest for a pillion passenger. I loved it. As I sat across it, it felt just right. I put the key in the ignition and turned. The speedo gear lights came on together with the ignition light. I pushed it off the centre stand and felt the well-balanced weight. I checked the foot gear pedal to see that it was in neutral and turned the key. I didn't expect it to burst into life at the first turn, but it did. A light flick of the throttle grip and she roared to life. I was stunned – again. It was beautiful. The engine 'rustled' on tick-over and never stuttered once. It purred like a dream.

When I looked up at the man, he was grinning. "So, what do you think?" he asked.

I just looked at him and shook my head. "You knew I'd be totally smitten with this, didn't you?" I said laughing. I was totally sold. The quickest judgement I'd ever made on a vehicle.

"How much?" I held my breath.

"Well, the majority has already been paid by the American and I can't ask the same again, so it's yours for six-hundred Singapore dollars."

Blimey, that was a steal for this bike.

"Done," I said, and we shook hands on the deal. That amounted to around eighty-five pounds in UK money at that time, which by today's standards was around eight hundred and fifty pounds. I just about had this in savings. We agreed that I would pay him half now and the remainder over a couple of months. I was now the proud owner of my first, decent motorbike. I asked if it was okay to drive it away now, which it was, so off I went. I think I was in a dream all the way back home to Blandford drive. In those days you didn't have to wear a helmet, so it was more comfortable to ride. However, I knew Mum would have kittens, so I decided to get one for any longer drives Andy and I went on. There was absolutely no comparison to riding a bike and driving a car. Singapore had the right weather conditions for bikes, and, at that time, the big superbikes were beginning to appear. Although my 450 was not a superbike, it was well on its way.

Meanwhile, the Army counselling service was assisting and pushing through in the divorce and both of us had agreed that it would be a 'divorce by mutual consent'. So, there were no nasty times or moments between us. In fact, quite often, when Andy was over, all three of us used to have a laugh and either one of us would take Sandy out on the bikes. I guess the pressure was off for both of us once we knew where we were going. Also, Sandy was pleased that her sister Sue was coming out with my sister Jo for three weeks.

The time flew by and, in between exercises with Arakan, things were going well. Arakan was due a refit and service, so we had to be located in Singapore for a while. Most of the lads were sent to other LCTs temporarily but both Andy and I were kept on Arakan. The dockyard where the refit was to take place was at HMS Terror, the Royal Naval base at Sembawang. The main engines and gearboxes were to be overhauled by local dockyard engineers and the few of us kept aboard had to stand duty watches, even in the naval base. None of us minded and the village of Sembawang, outside the base, was an okay place to eat and get a good drink. It consisted of just one street where all the bars and eating places were along one side of the road.

When foreign navies were in port, they usually tied up at HMS Terror, mostly as a break for the crews and to utilize the dockyard facilities. When these ships were in, the village really came alive. The Americans were especially appreciative of the place, and it was great fun. Mind you, Sembawang had a hard-core red-light area which meant that the place was awash with girls, after dark. Most of us got to know the village well and we would eat and drink in a couple of the bars that had become our favourites. Chilli prawns and chicken rice were our favourite dishes complete with side dishes of pickled green chillies that I came to love and still do to this day.

The Honda was a joy to ride. Every day I would ride the twenty-minute journey from Blandford Drive to Sembawang. One morning, coming into the dockyard to start my day of duty watch-keeping, I parked up next to the ship as always. There were a few parking slots near Arakan's gangway. Andy's bike was there as usual as he lived on board most of the time. There were a few seamen that also lived aboard but most lived ashore. I pulled the bike up onto the centre stand and walked up the gangway. In the mess, Andy was sitting at one of the tables writing up the generator logs from last night's duty. Although we were on the dockyard supply, we still had to carry out maintenance and oil changes on the generators. We'd been in the dockyard now for just over a week but there was little movement on board. I could see 'Granny' out on the catwalk chatting to the bosun.

"Granny wants us to help the deckies paint this mess," Andy said.

"Oh, bloody hell, we do more painting than engineering," I groaned. Andy just shrugged. I could hear someone chatting below in the engine room and I knew we were the only two engineers aboard apart from Granny.

"Who's down below then?" I said to Andy, nodding towards the engine room hatch.

"Not sure, must be one of the dockyard engineers," Andy replied.

I listened further. "Sounds like a Yorkshireman," I said.

I went down to the accommodation to get my overalls out of my locker and put them on. As I came back up the ladder, I thought I would pop down and see this 'Brit' working in the engine room. I didn't know that the dockyard had Brits working for them. I made my way down the engine room ladder and noticed that the forward bulkhead had been removed and the deck plates were up, between the mains, so I guessed they were doing some extensive work on the engines themselves.

"Hello?" I called out. It was quiet a moment then I heard the Brit call out.

"What's up mate?" he replied. I couldn't see him, but I heard his boots on the starboard deck plates. "Hello there," he said as I moved off the ladder to stand by the telegraph controls.

I was shocked; he wasn't a Brit at all but a Chinese guy, in his overalls, holding a wrench, with a grin on his broad face.

"Blimey, where'd you get an accent like that?" I said, laughing.

He laughed back. "I been working ships here since I was a young lad. I worked on the Navy ships and the Brits gave me an apprenticeship. Been working with them all my life."

He looked to be well into his fifties.

"Have you been to the UK?" I asked him.

"No, never had the money to do that, maybe one day, when I retire."

I laughed and shook his hand. He explained that he was carrying out a mains overhaul on the engines. I went back up to the mess and told Andy that the Brit below was as Chinese as they come. He had been here, working on Royal Naval ships all his life and had never set foot in the UK.

Years later I was to come across a similar situation in Rangoon, Burma, where a local shopkeeper in the vicinity of the Shwadagong Pagoda was selling Buddhist incense and monks fans. He had the broadest Geordie accent and when I approached him on it, he stated that when the Brits were stationed in Rangoon, he worked for them for over thirty years. Standing chatting to me in his sarong and flip-flops, he was very discreet about what he was saying because it was considered taboo and undercover police were everywhere. He too had never been to the UK, but he wanted a picture taken standing outside his shop so that when I returned to the UK, he would know that at least a picture of him had made it here. Britain had left its mark.

Over the time in the dockyard, I'd made a few friends with some of the local dockies. There was a Malay food wagon where you could get a good *Nasi Lamat* or chilli rice for lunch. I was one of the only Brits getting his lunch there and I used to chat with the workers. One lunchtime, one of them said, "Are you the lad that comes in on that large motorbike?"

"Yes, probably, but there is another lad on a bike with a red tank." This was Andy.

"No," he said, "the one with the black tank."

"Yes, that's mine, why?" I asked, frowning at him.

"Looks like Sabu on an elephant," he grinned. "That's a big bike for such a small lad."

I laughed and, as I walked back to the ship, I realised that he was right; it was a big bike for someone my size. At that time, I weighed in at around one hundred and twelve pounds (eight stone) so I understood what I must look like. Those were good days at Sembawang shipyard, and I always liked the atmosphere of dockyards.

49

August came and with it my sister Jo and Sandy's sister Sue. They were to stay for three weeks, during which time I would be showing Jo around the island, the bars, hotels, food, and my network of friends. By this time, I was well entrenched in Singapore society which included Dennis D'Cotta and his mates. Dennis was from a wealthy Eurasian family, and we became close friends. His father was the supreme high court justice of Singapore and that gave us access to places like the Singapore Yacht Club and other various normally off-limits places. I had a few mates on board Arakan but other than Andy and Tom, saw little of them once off the ship.

Jo started to meet the guys, who included Dennis, as well as some of the shipboard lads. Andy and Tom got on well with Jo and Sue. During a small party I held at home, Sue met Colin, a lad off the ship. They got on so well it soon became 'a thing' for them. I believe they eventually went on to get married.

Meanwhile, Jo was getting into the motorbike thing and one afternoon I took her on a long ride around the island. Arakan was out of the shipyard, but we were tied up at HMS Terror for some time. I showed her the ship and the one street wonder that was then Sembawang. She loved it, especially being on the bike. Once she got into the routine of the bars and clubs, it was like she was making up for lost time after the quiet, leafy suburbs of Bishops Stortford.

She met Dennis and we partied into the early hours. I introduced her to Sonny Rajah, a sort of wealthy playboy who drove a Lotus Europa and later went into GP motor racing in Singapore and Malaysia in F2. The Lotus Europa was bright, canary yellow and shooting around Serangoon Gardens in this was great fun.

One particular evening I decided to take Jo to Sembawang to experience the night life. There was an American ship staying at the Naval Base, so the village was awash with Yanks. Jo was in seventh heaven. One of the bars had a stage with live music playing. Jo did her bit and, before we knew it, was up on stage singing. The Yanks loved it and it turned into a really crazy night but great fun. She made loads of friends and addresses were swapped amidst promises to visit each other's hometowns etc. At one of the downtown hotels, she met a couple of guys from the oil rigs and one lad and her formed quite a close relationship for a while. After that, I let her entertain herself a lot of the time.

She met Bron and Evan as well as Anita. Jo adored Evan and they did go on to meet up in the UK when Evan went back. Things between him and Bron were not going well but they stayed together until they went back to the UK. They left towards the end of Jo and Sue's visit, and it was very sad to see them leave. I was very close with them both and Evan had been a good mate. It was also sad to see Jo go back. We'd had a great time and I'd taken leave while she was in Singers, so we'd had lots of time together. We had many a tête-à-tête about life, love, and Sandy and me. It helped me a lot as I realised that I had great support from all my family, even though I didn't feel I deserved it.

My breakup with Sandy was ninety percent my fault. She was a good girl but way ahead of me. I was too immature, I think, in those days to handle her and our relationship. But sometimes, things happen like that, and I just wasn't ready at that time to take her on as I should have.

Not long after Jo went back, Sandy followed – around mid-September. I remember taking her, in the evening, to Changi airport.

We were both upset because we knew we'd never see each other again. I remember hugging her and telling her that I really did still love her, but just not enough to make it work. We parted friends, two sad people who would have been better to stay as good friends and never marry each other. Watching her back as she walked through passport control remains a vivid memory to this day. I never did see her again.

I now had to find another place to live. Keeping the house on Blandford Drive going was bad news. It was too close to Anita and also her brother-in-law was not a good person. One day, before Sandy left, out of the blue, I was asked to pop over to Anita's house on some pretext. Like an idiot, I went. Her brother-in-law was waiting for me. As soon as I crossed the threshold, he blocked the front door and confronted me. Anita was nowhere in sight, but her younger brother Anil was there. He and I had become close friends but in the presence of the brother-in-law, he was a different person. I guess he was scared of the guy. Anyway, the short of it was that he, the brother-in-law, knew of mine and Anita's relationship. He said that if I didn't stop seeing her immediately, she was going to be sent to India and I would 'have an accident'. He also said that he had had sex with Sandy and that she had welcomed it. I knew all this was probably rubbish but I did realise that I was in danger.

Over a good part of 1970, I had been trying to consolidate my relationship with Anita. She had two nieces who lived with her – Meera and Sita. They also had a baby brother. Quite often, the brother-in-law and his wife (Anita's elder sister) would go away to Kuala Lumpur for a week or so and leave Anita and the three children behind. As this happened quite a lot, I got to know Meera and Sita very well. I learned to love them, and they returned that love. It was amazing. I used to help Anita make lunch sometimes, in their house, and the girls would show me how to make chapatti and sambals. It was a great relationship. Anita also had a younger sister called Sarika who lived on the other side of Singapore with Anita's elder brother who happened to be the Captain of Police in Malaysia. Sarika had had a troubled past. I never did get to find out what had happened but at some point, when she was in her teens, something happened to her, and she tried to kill herself by drinking weedkiller. Fortunately, she was found and hospitalised. Years later, she still suffered from stomach issues intermittently. She and Anita became very close, but I can't help thinking that whatever happened to Sarika had something to do with the brother-in-law. The brother that Sarika lived with was a decent man with a wife and two children and Sarika got on well with him.

One of my friends was called Alan, a Eurasian lad that lived with his mother. I had joined a 'dojo' in Singapore to learn the martial art of Kung Fu and it was here that I met Alan. We became good friends and I often spent time with him over at his mum's place where we would practice our 'katas' in the garden. He had installed a Mukki Warra, a wooden pole fixed in the ground with a coir matting pad fitted near the top of the pole which was about five feet tall. It was this that you punched repeatedly to harden up the knuckles of your hands. We also did breathing exercises and balance as well as having meditation periods. Alan's father had died some years previously when Alan was quite young. He had an Alsatian guard dog that adored Alan and, after a few barks, got to know me quite well.

Like many Asian countries, Singapore was steeped in folklore, legends, and the 'magic' of priests, some of which was a kind of voodoo. Most locals knew of it, but it was rarely discussed. I had never encountered anything like it before and, on the odd occasion we discussed it, was fascinated by the stories. The voodoo side of it was nasty stuff but was accessible to anyone that was foolish enough to dabble in that sort of thing. These people would visit a *bomo* and pay (usually in money, fruits, or food) for a spell for them to use, usually on someone. This was really dangerous stuff and I had heard tales of when the spell had been used on a person but, later, the person who had set the spell had something nasty or unfortunate happen to them. It was not uncommon (apparently) for these spells to backfire with sometimes devastating results. It was more prevalent among the Malays and Indians.

One night, Alan, myself and two other mates were having a drink in the Captain's Cabin in Serangoon Gardens where I lived. I was still living in Blandford Drive at this time. We'd been downtown and had come here for a bite to eat and a few drinks before going on to my place for beer, a smoke, and some music. It was getting near to midnight when we walked up Chartwell towards Blandford Drive at the top. It was a hot, sultry night with barely a whisper of a breeze. We got to the top of Blandford Drive and the four of us were wandering down it, in the middle of the road, chatting. There was no one about at this time of night and the only light was from the occasional street-lamps that were located at intervals down the road. Blandford sloped down with the top end (Chartwell) being the highest, leading down to a crossroad, Corfe Place. My house was about half-way down Blandford on the left side. We were within spitting distance, Alan slightly in front, when I noticed he had come to a sudden stop, frozen still. As I walked towards him, he waved me back.

"Stop, don't come any closer," he whispered urgently.

"Alan, what's up?" I laughed.

"Shush, stay there, don't come past me." He said, turning his head around to look at me.

We all stopped, wondering what was up. I turned to Richard, one of the lads. He shrugged.

"It's Pontianak," Alan said in a harsh whisper. He stepped back, looking frightened. "Can you smell it? Frangipani, right across the road," he whispered.

I walked up to him, and he put his arm out to stop me going past him. I still couldn't smell anything but, standing alongside Alan, I leaned forward and, sure enough, there was the pungent, sweet smell of frangipani. It was like a barrier across the road. The odd thing was, there was not a frangipani tree in sight. None in any of the front gardens on either side of us, ahead or behind.

"Who the fuck is Pontianak, Alan?" I asked him quietly.

The two lads behind me just stood there, not moving, looking frightened.

"Pontianak is the devil," he forcefully whispered. "Usually in the shape of a beautiful woman. She will entice you to her and then kill you for your soul."

We all stood there for a moment, saying nothing. I could see my front gate, about five metres ahead on the left. "Alan, this is daft, the street is empty, quiet, and no one is in sight," I said. I pointed to my house. "It's just there, for Christ's sake, come on."

"No way, we're not crossing the frangipani barrier, it's too dangerous," said Alan. "Is there a back way to your place?" he asked.

"Well, you'd have to back up and round to the next drive and come over the backyard wall," I said.

None of us moved. I looked ahead but all was still and quiet. I was about to say something to Alan when I heard the distinctive sound of high heels on the road ahead. I turned to look behind me only to see the other two lads making their way back up the road as quickly and quietly as possible. Alan, looking terrified, started moving past me, following the other two.

"Come on, now, quickly," he said in a harsh whisper. He then ran quickly to catch up with the others. I stood there and looked back down the road and the distance to my house. Just then, the sound of the heels stopped, and all was quiet again. I looked behind me but there was no sign of the lads; they'd legged it. I thought for a moment longer. Shit, I had to unlock my house to get in, which meant going the front way in anyway. *Oh, fuck it*, I thought. I couldn't see anything, the road was empty, and there was no sound.

I cautiously moved forwards, into and through the scent barrier which, curiously, was only a few feet thick. It truly was a barrier of frangipani scent. No sooner was I past the barrier, then the sound of high heels started. As I looked down the road, there at the bottom on the right, coming out of the shadows and into the glow from a streetlamp, sure enough, was a woman with a light-coloured top, a short red skirt, and high heels, slowly walking up the road towards me. She was very attractive with long, dark hair, possibly Caucasian. I knew that if I continued to walk as I was, she would be almost abreast of me by the time I reached my gate. It was at that point that I knew that I should have listened to Alan. I still couldn't believe this was for real but knew

I couldn't take the chance. I suddenly felt a great fear and goose bumps started up my arms and at the back of my neck.

I have no idea why such a thing should happen but there it was, right in front of me, and suddenly I knew I had to run for my life. So, I did, but not in the other direction. I made a supreme dash to my front gate. Usain Bolt had nothing on me. I hurled myself at the gate, slid the catch across and ran up to my front door, getting my keys out at the same time. Whether it was the adrenaline I didn't know but my hand was shaking badly as I tried to slide the key home. I fumbled with it, all the time hearing the sound of the heels get nearer. Suddenly the key slotted into the lock, I turned it and flung the door open. Then I threw myself in and pushed the front door shut with my back.

I turned and set the deadbolt. I heard the high heels outside on the road and then all went quiet. I stood there with my back against the front door, holding my breath, my heart thumping in my chest, listening intently to the night sounds outside.

Nothing.

The silence was intense. As my breathing started to normalise, I heard a scrabbling at the back of the house. For a horrifying moment, I thought 'she' was trying to get in at the back but then suddenly I remembered the lads. I ran through to the kitchen and to the back door. Richard was just dropping down the wall into the backyard. I unlocked the door just as Alan dropped down, followed by the other lads.

"You're alive," Alan said, astonished. "Did you see her?"

I looked at them all and had never felt so pleased to see them. "Yes, I saw her. I think we all need some stiff drinks," I said, ushering them in then locking the back door.

I closed the blinds on all the windows after looking out the front of the house. All was dark and still and that was another thing that registered with me. All the streetlights in the immediate vicinity were out. It seemed near total darkness, and they certainly were not out when I ran for the front gate. There was no way these guys were going to leave the house in the dark, so it was going to be a long night.

This was one of the facets of living in the Far East. The legends and stories of supernatural happenings are far more prevalent in these lands, and you discount them at your peril. However, what I did realise was that I needed to get out of that house now that Sandy was gone.

Anita had gone up to KL for a few weeks at the time of this incident so I couldn't discuss it with her. Bron had gone back to the UK, so I was the only Caucasian that I knew of living on Blandford at that time. For me, the legend of Pontianak was real but what evoked it or allowed me to see it at that time, I hadn't a clue. It also happened to be the capital city of the Indonesian island of Kalimantan, which I visited many months later.

By mid-October, Andy and I found a place on the other side of Serangoon Gardens. It was Richard who had mentioned it to me as he lived on the opposite corner from this house. So it was that I moved into 28 St Heliers Avenue. This was to be home for a while, and it would be good for both Andy and me. Before we left Blandford, I had a cat called William, a ginger tom, and Andy had taken on Bron's black cat Sooty, who she had given to him before she went back to the UK. So, we moved into St Heliers with two cats. My dog, Worthington, I had given away to a neighbour.

I spent a short time on HMAV Antwerp and then moved back aboard Arakan. There were rumours that we were going to Karachi, in Pakistan with the ship but it all fell through, thank goodness and we stayed in Singapore. Now that Sandy was back home, her parents had pressured her to get me to pay her more money as an allowance. Fortunately, Jo had an incriminating letter from her whilst she was still in Singapore that mentioned her boyfriend and that she would be getting her old job back once she was home in the UK. Army legal aid helped me, and, in the end, I managed to get a good settlement.

50

Another milestone was being reached as fate moved me along the road and opened vistas.

The challenging events of these Singapore days were starting to settle down. Thoughts of the UK and home were distant in my mind at these times. I never missed the UK and on the occasions I did think about it, the scene in my mind was of grey, wet days and cold. I did feel a bit guilty about Mum and not keeping in touch as often as I should have but it really was a case of living for the 'now' and I was a great one for complicating my life, I never had time to think of things back home.

The Honda at St Helliers Avenue

The bike was going well, and Andy had swapped his Honda for a BSA Gold Star that chugged along like an old Harley. We went everywhere on them. Life aboard ship and the military was gradually becoming secondary, and it seemed I was just going through the motions.

I loved Arakan and shipboard life, but it was the bullshit and the odd one or two people that were spoiling it for me. As far as I was concerned, the military phase of my life was fading into the background, and I knew it was getting near time to move on. When the time came, I would take it and leave. The British Government was winding down a lot of overseas bases and Singapore was at the top of the list. Nearly all the work we undertook on the Ts at this time was about closing various bases and transporting trucks, vehicles and various military hardware to Malaysia, Thailand, and Borneo so that they could be sold on. But wherever we were, either UK or the Far East, my work aboard the ship was pretty much the same: maintaining, running, and keeping the mechanics of the ship going and as always, painting the engine room and various compartments.

Meanwhile, my life ashore was running full tilt. Bron was writing from the UK now and again and she hated it there. She had separated from Evan and wanted to come back to Singapore. I owed her some money that I had borrowed whilst she was here, and I needed to send it back to her so that she could get her fare back here.

I could write many chapters on Bron. She was certainly a character. When she was in Singapore, she had taken up with a modelling agency and had done many shoots with them. On one occasion, she contacted me and asked me if I was interested in doing an advert for Carlsberg Lager. I was intrigued and went along with it. We met up in a hotel bar downtown and I was to be an 'extra', sitting at the bar, chatting to one of the models and drinking a Carlsberg Lager. It was good fun and took most of the morning to film. Goodness knows where it was to be shown but I never did see it appear anywhere. However, I got well paid for it and it paid for the outstanding amount on my Honda 450.

I also knew that Bron was 'turning tricks'; being tall, blonde, vivacious, and attractive, she was very much in demand. We went out a lot together, to clubs and hotels, just as friends. Then she met and became infatuated with the leader of a local band called Renaissance that played in one of the major hotels on Orchard Road. I think it was the Hyatt. They had a nightclub there and many an evening was spent with her and the band. The music was great and Bron's relationship with Jeffery Jellah became quite serious. However, she was still a military wife and although Evan's relationship with her had been nothing other than platonic for some time they were still husband and wife. Word soon got around what Bron was up to and I think Evan had had enough. He requested to go back to the RAF base in Anglesey, Wales. She had no choice and was really cut-up about it. So, with her kids in tow, she went back. It was sad to see them both go but I knew that it would be a temporary measure for Bron and that she would be back.

I did, inadvertently, have a few 'times' with her, especially as we got on so well and I used to cover for her on many occasions. Sex with Bron was certainly an experience, and it was with her on those rare occasions that I learnt quite a lot. It never affected our other relationships but, for me, it was a necessary part of knowing Bron. That may seem as if it would carry our friendship to another level but that's how it was with her, and we both felt the same. She had a great sense of humour, and we often laughed our way through those times. Clandestine liaisons in tucked away hotels were not uncommon. Being Anita's neighbour at that time meant that Anita knew a lot about what Bron was up to but just how much, I was never quite sure. It didn't affect my relationship with Anita, but you couldn't know Bron and not be affected by her. She was a very charismatic person and, in those times, a man-eater.

Many years later, long after I was married to my second wife, I came across Bron. She was living with her kids in North London and from what I could gather was a groupie following some rock band while, at the same time, childminding. It was not a good idea to reconnect our previous relationship, so I made a conscious effort to back away. But our friendship was forever and has stayed that way.

Life at 28 St Heliers Avenue was good. I couldn't always get to see Anita because of the risks. Her immediate family, being aware of our relationship, often made sure she was away in KL. It didn't stop us from meeting when she was in Singapore, it just made us more determined and a lot more cautious and craftier in how we went about it. Fortunately, her family kept to their own circle of friends and didn't go out a lot. But we didn't get to see each other as often as we would have liked.

One afternoon, I was sitting at home, cleaning the Honda. We had a small porch area for a car immediately to the right of the front door and it was where we both kept our bikes. I was vigorously cleaning the chrome on mine and getting on well with it when I heard someone knocking on the front gate to the drive. I looked up and there on the other side of the gate was this Indian girl, dressed quite smartly in Western clothes, clutching a red folder.

I stood up, wiping my hands on a cloth and went to the front gate. "Hello, can I help you?" I asked.

She smiled and started asking me about the house and my living there. At first, I went along with her and listened.

"May I come in?" she said. "I'd like to ask you about what fire precautions you have in place here." She was looking up at the house.

"What are you selling?" I asked, getting a little irritated.

"Fire extinguishers," she grinned. "Perfect for the home."

I looked a bit stunned. "Why on earth would I require a fire extinguisher here?" I said, laughing.

She started laughing as well and I could tell she was a little uncomfortable.

"Look," I said, "come in and have a cool drink and you can show me your catalogue. But I have to be honest, I don't think I'll require one." With that, I opened the gate, and we walked up the short drive to the house.

"Nice bike," she said. It was gleaming from where I'd been cleaning it.

We went into the cool interior and I took her through to the kitchen. She was giving the place a good scrutinising as we wandered through. I produced a bottle of Coke from the fridge and two glasses, pouring hers for her.

She asked who else lived with me and I told her that Andy also lived here. In the front room she opened her folder on the dining table, and we sat down whilst she proceeded to show me the various types of home extinguishers.

At this point, I should admit that my interest in fire extinguishers was non-existent. But the girl herself was quite something else. I admitted to her that there was no way I was going to purchase a fire extinguisher. It wasn't my house, and I was just renting it. She nodded and just grinned, asking me if I was from the UK. I explained that I was and mentioned being from London. She said her mum lived in Manchester, but she had decided to stay here in Singapore with her grandma.

"Can I have a look around the house?" she said.

"Sure, but why?" I asked inquisitively.

"I've never seen two guys living together on their own, I usually deal with family homes. Do you do your own cooking, and do you have an Amah?" she enquired.

I thought all this was a bit much and, to be honest, nosey but I let it slide.

"Come on, we'll start with the kitchen," I said, standing up and leading the way. She took her jacket off and hung it on the back of a chair. As she wandered around the kitchen, I noticed that she had a good figure and was quite petite. Her hair was cut short in a sort of pageboy cut and looked good on her.

When she'd finished opening a few cupboards she asked if she could see upstairs. I shrugged and said sure, that was okay. As we went up the stairs, I was asking myself, *Is this girl for real?* She was certainly pretty forward, especially for an Asian girl. I pushed open my bedroom door which was on the front corner of the house. William was asleep on the bed cover. The fact that the bed was made seemed to surprise her. I explained that I liked a tidy place. She sat down on the bed and started stroking William. I sat next to them both and just watched her. William soon made it known that he didn't like his afternoon nap being disturbed and jumped off the bed. We both just sat there, looking at each other.

"You're very attractive," I said, taking her hand and looking at her. She didn't pull back or resist.

"Thank you," she said.

I thought, *This can't be happening.* It was all quite surreal. It didn't take long to get from that to taking our clothes off and getting under the bed covers. I thanked the stars that Andy was on duty that night on board ship.

I remember laying beside her, a little after midnight, looking down at her. She had a beautiful moonstone and gold edged necklace that was nestled against the sheen of her coffee-coloured skin, sitting in the hollow of her neck. In the darkness, the moonlight fell across the bed and picked up the soft, white, opalescence of the stone at her throat. It seemed to radiate the light and glowed. It was like something out of a fantasy movie. I was pretty much taken by this and mentioned it to her as I lay there, propped up on my elbow, looking down at her. She touched it gently and said that it belonged to her grandmother. I touched it and felt encased in her scent and the magic of the moment. It was a stunning feeling and something I had never experienced before. We chatted and laughed in between our lovemaking. I hadn't felt like that in a long time. I didn't want the night to end.

Just before dawn, we both dressed, and I said I would take her where she asked on the Honda, but she didn't want to go on it. It was decided that we would walk down to the Circle (Serangoon Gardens) where she picked up a taxi. We did arrange to meet again but I wasn't sure it would happen. When we spoke in the night, she'd mentioned that she wanted to go to the UK and I did seriously wonder if she saw me as the ticket to do so, although I didn't see anything wrong in that. At the time, I wouldn't have minded taking her on. She was very attractive, well-educated, and would look good on anyone's arm. But as I was in the process of going through a divorce and I was trying to manage Anita, it was all a bit too much too soon. It was a shame because she was a lovely person. The folks back home would have had kittens.

There was an amusing side to this as the lad, Richard Lim, who lived on the opposite corner had seen the girl go into my place. He was well intrigued and even claimed he'd seen me partially clothed in my bedroom with her. I laughingly called him a bloody pervert but for weeks after I was ribbed for days about the fire extinguisher girl who'd come to 'put my fire out'.

She did come by once more but after that I never saw her again.

Social life started to pick up and it was at about this time that I became good friends with Dennis D'Cotta. There was a group of us that became really good mates and so we decided to form the 'Exclusive Club'. This included Thomas Goh, Richard Lim, Henry Lye, and Dennis D'Cotta. There was also Alan, but he was too serious to belong to anything daft like that; Andy was made an honorary member. All the lads were local boys from good families. Thomas was studying accountancy and Dennis was going to officer training school for the Singapore Army. His father was, at the time, the supreme high court justice. All the families were middle to upper class, which was important in Singapore society. Apart from Andy, I had few mates from Arakan who I associated with when ashore. I didn't need to; I had a really good social life now that was definitely on the up.

Weekends were our best time, and this usually meant house parties on a regular basis. Henry played a pretty mean guitar, so after we had done a few of the big hotel bars and clubs it was off to Changi Beach with Henry picking up his guitar and a few crates of beer along the way. Picking up food from roadside stalls meant we had quite a few long nights drinking, singing, and eating. It was good fun. Dennis' father was a member of the Singapore Yacht Club so we would all get passes as 'family members', providing we wore a shirt and tie. It was here that I first came across a Black Velvet cocktail of Guinness and Champagne. Apparently, these were his dad's favourite and soon we were all into them. In didn't take many of those before you knew you had had a drink! Soon, our routine became a light tea at the Yacht Club plus a couple of Black Velvets to kick the night off with and then on to the clubs and/or the beach. Life was good and Andy made it with us too on many an occasion.

Because we loved the bikes so much, Andy and I would quite often ride long journeys on them on a Saturday. We'd leave home early, around 08:00 a.m., head for the Singapore/Jahore Baru causeway crossing into Malaysia and make our way up the main jungle highway towards Kuala Lumpur. We never went as far as Kuala Lumpur but usually found a nice sleepy town about halfway where we had lunch before making our way back. These highways were more or less straight and we could go for many miles without turning the handlebars once. We had to watch out for potholes but, generally, they were pretty good roads. I'd had further crash-bars fitted to the bike plus a new backrest. I could tighten the front damper a bit and lean back, feet up on the lower bars, set the throttle grip, and let the bike just go. It was great. Helmets were not compulsory at that time, so if we were driving around Singapore or in main towns, we never wore them. We did on the highway though.

The biggest problems on these highways were the timber lorries. They had massive trailers attached to them and would hurtle along, oblivious to something as small as a motorcycle. These roads were also used by the rubber tappers. On each side of the road, for mile after mile, were the famous rubber plantations. The rubber tappers would venture forth about 04:00 a.m., either walking or riding push-bikes along these highways. By the time we started out, they were usually pretty clear except for kids chasing us as we rode through the various kampongs along the way.

One good stopping point was Kota Tinggi where there was a natural waterfall with clear, fresh water, running down from the high hills that made up much of this region. We would wear our trunks underneath our jeans and jump in the large pool that the waterfall emptied into. We could stand under the waterfall and enjoy the cool water after a long, sweaty run.

Like me, Andy was looking to leave the service and he was keen to get the process going as quickly as possible. He was therefore looking out for work as a marine engineer locally, although he was looking at the private yacht side of things as well. Like me, Andy knew that if we stayed in until our full time was up – about ten months away – we would end up back in the UK doing the Northern Ireland runs. The 'troubles' over there were hotting up. Andy was still a private whilst I was a lance corporal (L/c). Towards the end of 1970 he submitted his application to get out. I never heard that there was any opposition to his application but knew that the wheels of admin turned slowly in HM Forces. The British pull-out of Singapore and the Far East was destined towards the end of 1971; therefore, I knew that I would have to do something similar.

51

Things were getting difficult with Anita at this time. We would have to arrange meets when an opportunity arose, and these were usually at the 'desert place'. It was important that I kept away from Blandford Drive and now that Bron was gone there was no reason for me to be seen there.

One afternoon, I met up with Anita at the usual desert place and she asked me if I would drop a book over to her sister Sarika. She had been to Anita's place and had left her diary there. She didn't want anyone seeing it, so Anita arranged with her that I bring it over to where she was staying. She lived with her brother and sister-in-law on the other side of the island. He happened to be the Captain of police in the Malay town of Johore Baru, so I certainly didn't need him catching me delivering this. I explained as much to Anita, but she assured me it was fine as her sister-in-law was away in Kuala Lumpur and, during the day, Sarika was on her own. I agreed to do it and took the diary from Anita.

Sarika was living near Seletar, and I knew my way there. It was a hot, still afternoon and the estate where she was living was not dissimilar to those in Serangoon. I drove the bike around until I found her street. As quietly as possible, I passed by her house just to confirm that all looked quiet and had no surprises waiting for me then parked down the end of the road. As I walked back to the house, Sarika had seen me pass by and had been looking out for me. She let me in a small side door. At this point I should have just handed over the diary and left. But we were very fond of each other, and I hadn't seen her in quite a while. So, like an idiot, I sat with her in her room, and we chatted about things. Before I realised it, I had been there for well over an hour. Next minute, we both heard a car door slam and the house door opening. Her brother had come home early.

Oh man, I was now well in deep shite unless I could get out of there without being seen. Sarika quietly told me to hang on a minute while she went out to see him. I waited in her room trying to think of a way I could get out. Her bedroom window had a metal grill over it, so that was out of the question. A few minutes later, she came back in and told me that the best way was to go out of the rear kitchen door into the backyard and over the small wall to the wasteland behind the house. She also said it was too risky staying in her bedroom. She told me that there was a small cupboard in the toilet that had a fine wire mesh over the door and, although you could see out, it was too dark to see in. She said it was best to stay in there until her brother was settled and she could give me the all clear to make my way through the kitchen and over the rear wall.

As she said, I waited until she gave me the signal then I stealthily made my way along a corridor and into the WC room. Sure enough, just inside the door, on the left, was the under-stair cupboard with the mesh door. I crouched down and got in, pulling the door shut as I did.

I didn't have long to wait. A few minutes later, the toilet door opened and, just as I was about to come out of my cramped position, her brother walked in with a newspaper. He then proceeded to drop his trousers and go to the loo. Prolonging the agony, he opened the newspaper and started reading it. Oh Christ, my heart was pounding, and I felt sure he'd hear me. I decided to go into 'meditation mode' and slowed my breathing and heart rate, like we'd been taught in the Dojo. It seemed like he was in there for hours, but I guess it was only about ten minutes. By this time, I was getting a bit cramped. Eventually, he completed his business and went out. A few minutes later Sarika came in and gave me the all clear.

Once out of the toilet, I stretched and emphasised my need to leg it. She told me he was sitting outside, to the left of the backyard, reading the paper. My exit would be through the rear kitchen door and across about two metres of the backyard to the rear wall. I nodded and peeped around the kitchen door. There he was, sitting in a rattan chair, facing me, reading the paper. I'd have to pick my move as for the briefest of moments, I would be totally exposed to him as I crossed the yard to the wall should he look up. It was all about timing, so I watched him for a moment. He put the paper down, opened up another page and held it up in front of him to read. It was now or never. I kissed Sarika, took a deep breath and, as silently as possible, ran for the wall. As soon as I was inches from it, I leapt for the top and swung my legs up and over in one movement.

The trouble was that in mid-flight I realised the house was built on a slope at the rear and the drop on the other side of the wall was at least twice the height of the wall. It was fortunate that the ground was mostly grass and weeds. Down I plummeted, hit the ground like a parachutist, rolled, and came to my feet. I then ran like a lunatic to the right and a distant clump of bushes. A few minutes later, I was back at the bike, shaking and panting, but safe.

Once on the bike, I let it roll down the road a way and then started it. I did a circle round the streets and came back past the house. I could see Sarika's brother on the other side of the railings, still sitting there, reading the paper. Sarika waved from a window, grinning. I couldn't believe that I had got away with it. Absolute madness!

I didn't see Anita for some weeks after that as she went up to Kuala Lumpur. Things at St Heliers Avenue were going well. Andy and I were getting along fine, and Bron was pushing to come back to Singapore and stay with us. Our two cats, William and Sooty, got on well. Sooty was pretty idle most of the time but William was the hunter. It was not uncommon to find the odd, dead mouse around the place, gifts for both of us. William had a routine. He would hang around the house most nights, usually sleeping on the end of my bed.

One night, I heard a cacophony outside the house. It must have been around 01:00 a.m. and I noticed that William suddenly sat up, alert. He looked towards the window, then at me, then back to the window. The noise was a number of cats crying below outside the front of the house. He looked at me again then jumped off the bed and went downstairs. There was a cat-flap in the kitchen door, so he could come and go that way. I got up and went over to the window. These were never closed, and the windows had jalousies over them, which on a still night, I always kept open. Looking out, I saw about five cats, all sitting around the pavement, looking up at my bedroom window. They were calling to William. I saw him come out and go over to them. A couple of them touched noses with him and then, as a group or 'gang' went off, up the road. It was amazing to see. He never came back until about three or four days later. Afterwards, this behaviour happened about once a month and was a regular part of life. He would return, usually about five or 06:00 a.m., looking bedraggled and absolutely stinking. He would spend the next twenty-four hours cleaning himself. I wouldn't let him in my room until he had done this.

My social life was good and balanced between life aboard the Ts, going on the bikes a lot and clubbing with the lads. One weekend, Dennis was throwing a party at his house. His parents had gone away for a week and Dennis took the opportunity to have a house party. It was a Friday night and both Andy and I had the weekend off from shipboard duties. We drove over to Dennis' house on the bikes. The place was massive and had a swimming pool and large, enclosed gardens. There were already many people there, including Richard, Henry, and Thomas. The 'Exclusive Club' was out in force. There were loads of other friends of his there, many I never knew. We wandered around, drinking, eating, chatting, and listening to music. Around midnight Andy decided to go back home but I had decided to hang around a little longer.

I'd moved to the hall area and was mostly observing the people and listening to the music, drinking a beer, and leaning against the doorframe of the kitchen. Over to the right of the hall, stairs went up to the next level. I could hear that there were people up there. Richard came over and we started chatting. I heard a commotion at the top of the stairs and looking up, saw a girl with masses of dark hair and a fairly short skirt, standing at the top landing, looking upset, saying something to someone I couldn't see. She started making her way downstairs and I could see that she was crying. Richard said something, laughed, and wandered off. I watched her come down and she went past me into the kitchen. There was no one else in there and she stood by the worktop with her back to me. I finished my beer and decided I would go in and see if she was okay. No one else had come down the stairs, I noticed, so I went over to her.

"Are you okay, is there anything I can do?" I said, leaning against the worktop with my back. She just looked at me with a sideways glance and shook her head. I gave her a tissue and she wiped her eyes and blew her nose.

"Do you have a car?" she said, looking at me.

"No, I have a motorbike. Why? Do you want a lift ?" I said, grinning.

She didn't say anything for a moment, so I asked her where she lived.

"Downtown, off the Serangoon Road. Can we go now?" she said and started out of the kitchen, towards the front door.

Okay, I thought, *well sure Dave, that'll be great*. Surmising she had a bit of an attitude, I realized I'd have to be a bit cautious here. She wasn't very tall, around five feet, which probably accounted, in part, towards her attitude. She was nicely dressed and looked of mixed heritage, possibly part Chinese.

It was a warm night, so I didn't think she'd have a problem on the back of the bike.

"What's your name?" I asked her.

"Carmen," she said, "What's yours?"

I told her as I took her to the bike. She stood there looking at it for a moment.

"That's a nice bike," she said.

I sat across it and moved it off the centre stand. I put the key in and pushed the starter. The bike rustled into life. I kicked out the two passenger footrests, steadied the bike, and asked her to climb aboard. She hesitated for a moment, looking at me, so I held out my hand. I showed her where to put her right foot and swing her other leg, over the saddle to the footrest on the other side. She grabbed my hand and swung over. The additional weight was not a problem on the Honda; she could handle it easily.

I turned the lights on, revved the throttle a bit, and moved off. She put her arms around my waist and tucked herself against my back. It felt good to have her there and, every now and again, her perfume assailed my senses. It was about 01:00 a.m. and there wasn't a lot of traffic on the roads. It was about twenty minutes to downtown Serangoon Road and not having a helmet for her was not a problem. I'd offered her mine, but she had refused so I was ok with that. After about ten minutes I came to a set of lights at a crossroad and asked, "Are you okay?" half turning my head.

"Yes, fine," she said, pausing a moment, "thank you," and gripped my waist a little tighter. I took it easy along the dark, quiet roads, enjoying the warm breeze as we rode. There was very little chance of having night rides like this back in the UK.

As we came nearer the centre of town, the traffic started to get a little busier and there were still a lot of people about. We came past what is known as 'Little India' and she tapped me on the shoulder and pointed in front, to the left. I slowed down until I saw the street sign saying Rowell Road.

"Here?" I asked.

"Yes, about half-way down on the left," she said, quietly.

"What number?" I asked her.

"Thirty-three, with the green door," she said, indicating.

I slowly rode down the road, avoiding the deep monsoon drain that ran alongside these roads.

The upper floors of these terraced buildings came over the pavement, so the entrances were in shadow. I saw the number thirty-three on the wall, pulled over, and stopped. I turned the engine off and she climbed off the bike. I sat there on the bike, and we looked at each other.

"Thank you," she said, touching my arm for a moment.

"Can I see you again?" I asked, my heart beating furiously.

"Just a moment," she said, turning around, and disappeared into the dark interior of the open front door. It was then that I noticed that in front of the open main door were these two bat-winged doors just like in the old western movies. Further down a couple of doors, I noticed a woman leaning up against the wall, smoking a cigarette, watching me curiously. A moment later, Carmen came out and passed me her telephone number on a piece of paper.

"Call me tomorrow after one," she said.

I nodded and tucked the note in my pocket. I started the bike up and we looked at each other for a moment, not saying anything. I nodded again, slipped the bike into gear, and turned around in the street. She stood outside her place in the shadows and watched me pull away. That meeting with Carmen was fated. Little then did I realise what a significant part she was to play in my life.

I met up with Carmen again, a few days later and we drove out to Changi Beach. I got to know her better but never approached her in a sexual way. Yes, blimey, I was attracted to her, but I didn't want to frighten her off or spoil what could be a good relationship.

One afternoon, I went to her place in Rowell Road to pick her up to go to the beach. I parked up and knocked on the bat-wing doors. A small, Chinese woman in her mid to late forties came to the door and glared at me. She asked me what I wanted in a barely recognisable English. I nodded and said that I had come to see Carmen. She looked at my bike and then at me and stood to one side, inviting me in. The interior of the house was very cool and a welcome relief from the heat outside. She must be Carmen's mum, I thought. She was quite round and about five feet in height. She looked fierce and obviously didn't speak much English. She pointed to a green, plastic covered sofa and gestured for me to sit down. She walked off to the back of the room where, on the left side of the rear wall, a beaded curtain hung. Above this entrance was a framed picture of Christ holding a bleeding heart with rays of light coming from it. Well, that was a surprise, they were Catholics. I could hear voices the other side of the bead curtain. A moment later, two little kids came running in wearing just their pants. One was a little girl of around five and the other a little boy of around three. They stopped and stared at me, started giggling, and ran back the way they'd came. I looked around the room. The sofa where I was sitting was to the right of the entrance and over in the right-hand corner of the room, leaning against the wall, was a massive base – of the musical instrument variety.

The curtains parted and a woman in her twenties came in. She came over to me and shyly asked if I wanted a drink. I said water, to be polite, and she said that Carmen would not be long. I assumed that she was the Amah. She had a sarong on and flip-flops. I noticed that she had a slight hare lip and a small speech impediment, but her face was so kind and friendly that you didn't really notice anything else. She brought me a glass of water and stood there a moment, smiling at me.

"Hello and thank you," I said, grinning, "My name is David."

"I'm Ah-Leng," she said.

I nodded. "That's nice."

"I'm one of Carmen's sisters," she said.

Just then, I heard someone coming down some stairs. I heard Carmen's mother speaking in Cantonese then Carmen replying in the same language. A moment later, Carmen came out and said, "Hi." Ah-Leng grinned, and Carmen said something to her, which made them both laugh.

I stood up, feeling a bit awkward. "Are we ready then?" I asked. Carmen nodded.

"Come on, Mum doesn't like me going on the bike."

"Ah," I said, "just a moment."

I walked over to the bead curtain and looked through. The mother was sitting in a small room area at an old treadle Singer sewing machine. She looked up at me, no expression on her face.

"I'll take care of her, I promise," I said.

She just looked at me. "Humph," she said and wagged her finger at me and turned back to her sewing machine. I fully understood my commitment. When we got outside, I handed Carmen a spare helmet I'd got for her.

"My mother trusts you," she said, looking at me steadily.

"I know," I said and swung over the seat of the bike. A couple of people in the road were watching us. I pressed the starter and the engine roared into life. Ah-Leng came out and stood there, grinning in the shadowy doorway. I nodded at her as Carmen climbed aboard. I accelerated away, heading for Changi and the beach.

52

Things happened quite suddenly after this. Bron came back and stayed with Andy and I at St Heliers. It was a three-bedroomed house and Andy agreed we wouldn't charge her anything to stay with us. Andy was looking for a job on a yacht as an engineer and was in the process of organising his discharge. Things aboard Arakan were slowing down for everyone. We all knew we were pulling out of Singapore later in 1971 and I knew I had to arrange my discharge soon as well. I had a year left to serve in HM Forces and there was no way I was going to spend it in the UK. I knew we'd end up in Northern Ireland and that certainly wasn't on my agenda.

We were getting near the end of the year (1970) and things were going well. Andy had initialised his intention to leave the services and was looking forward to it. He had slowly been acquiring tools for his toolbox and had already asked me to take it back to the UK for him. I was making one up for myself. Things at the house were good and Bron fitted in well. We hardly saw her as by this time she had got herself some 'work'. She was well into the escort business and would entertain wealthy Chinese businessmen from time to time. One evening when she was at home, she was telling me about this particular businessman that she had dated a few times. He drove the latest Opal

Sports saloon and she said that I could borrow it for the weekend as long as I was very careful with it.

I approached the guys, and it was agreed that after a party that we were all going to on Friday night, we would use the car I had picked up from Bron and spend a relaxing Saturday at Kota Tingi waterfall in Malaysia. It was around midnight by the time we got back to St Heliers, a change of clothes and we all piled into the Opal. We needed to keep our passports with us as we were crossing the causeway into JB, and they sometimes carried out spot security checks. The roads were quiet, and we cruised through the border at JB. By the time we hit the beginning of the main Kuala Lumpur highway, it was nearly 03:00 a.m. I was driving as the car was my responsibility.

It was a powder blue Opal with a five-litre engine. This thing could motor. Andy was sitting next to me with Richard, Henry, and Thomas in the back. Tom had not long returned from the UK. He'd been doing part one of his Chartered Accountancy studies there. He'd stayed awhile at Mum's and had met Dee, Ken, and the girls. When he had arrived back at Singapore Airport he was in for a bit of a shock. The Singapore government under Lee Quan Yew were having a blitz on long hair for locals as it was associated with the drug and pop music culture. Tom was considered to have too long a hair style so before he could clear customs, he had a forced haircut. It was either that or back on the plane. When we saw him a few days later he looked like he had just come out of prison.

Beer was liberally being handed out as we made our way onto the jungle highway. At first, enthusiasm was high, and we were all laughing and joking. But gradually the chatter and joking quietened until I was the only one awake, driving in complete silence. We'd all been up since early Friday morning. Then, in the evening, we'd drunk a lot and eaten little. The chatter had kept me awake but now I was starting to feel drowsy. The road was a tarmac strip that ran almost in a straight line all the way to Kuala Lumpur. On either side of the road, for the most part, there were rubber plantations, and the trees came almost to the edge of the road. Villages were interspersed along the way, but these Kampongs were set back amongst the rubber trees.

From about 03:00 a.m. onwards, the rubber tappers themselves started to make their way to their various places of work. They either walked along the side of the road or were on push-bikes.

I was aware of them and, since we had started on this highway out of Jahore, I'd not seen another vehicle at all. As my headlights pierced the darkness, I could see the tappers making their way along the sides of the road. They all mostly carried their tiffin boxes with their lunch in, as well as the long handled parangs that were used for cutting or 'tapping' the rubber trees. Now and again, two or three push-bikes would appear out of the darkness. It seemed we were all heading in the same direction. I turned the aircon up and directed it into my face. It worked for a while but then I could feel my eyes getting heavy. The hum of the engine and tyres on the road surface had an almost hypnotic effect. My head started to nod forward, and it would suddenly wake me up. Fortunately, it was a pretty straight road. I was thinking about Anita and how difficult it was to get to see her. Then Carmen popped up in my head and I felt a sudden guilt, as I knew I was falling under her spell. She was intoxicating and I knew I needed to see a lot more of her. I also knew I couldn't tell Anita about her. I was in something of a dilemma. I had feelings for both, but one was almost inaccessible while the other was pretty much available. At this stage I realised that it wouldn't be difficult to juggle between the two. If I was careful, I could manage it. Because I had been so intimate with Anita, I couldn't just end it with her. I think she would have been devastated, especially after all the shit I'd been through with her brother-in-law. But on the other hand, no such barriers existed with Carmen as they did with Anita.

All this was going through my mind as I drove through the night in a kind of hypnotic trance. At some point I think I must have really nodded off. I felt the car swerve and I suddenly woke up. The road had started to curve, and the camber had changed as I neared the edge, towards a drainage ditch. The headlights suddenly picked up a couple of bikes being pushed along as two locals walked beside them. I panicked and suddenly pulled back to the centre of the road but not before clipping one of the bikes. In my rear view, I saw both bikes disappear into the drainage ditch and heard the shouts. *Fuck, don't stop, just keep driving*, I thought, remembering the tales we'd heard when we were convoy driving along this route. If you hit anyone, don't stop, keep going. They will kill you if you get out of your vehicle. I followed the turn of the road and put my foot down. Once it straightened out, we were doing around eighty miles per hour and I was driving in the middle of the road. The sweat was pouring off me. I shouldn't have thought there was much damage done. I had just clipped the bike, but it had certainly woken me up. None of the others had been disturbed and even my few swerving car moves hadn't aroused anyone.

Another hour and it was still very dark. The trees had gone from this section of road and what little I could see, was fields with tall rushes. Because of the heavy rains of the monsoons, sections of the road were quite severely pot holed. Staying in the middle of the road was the best place as long as nothing was coming from the other direction. The miles sped by, and I started to relax a bit more now that the tappers were no longer on the road. A faint change in the level of darkness told me dawn wasn't too far away and I noticed it was getting towards 04:30 a.m. It was fortunate I had stayed in the middle of the road because I was just about to nod off once again (and in fact, I think I had) when, for a split second, the road noise of the wheels on the tarmac suddenly went. The engine raced as I still had my foot on the accelerator. When I snapped awake the car was still aiming in the right direction, but we were momentarily airborne. We had just met an army 'Baily Bridge' and where the road met the wooden sleepers of the bridge road, there was a slight lip. The car was going too fast when we hit this lip and the vehicle just took off. Fortunately, we were within the width of the single-track bridge with its green, metal sides. As the car came back to earth, we hit the wooden sleepers with all four wheels. The noise was tremendous, the planks rattled and thumped and the engine growled. We were all off the seats as the vehicle thumped down on the springs. Shit, we'd just passed through the eye of the needle, stayed on the bridge, and made it across to the tarmac road the other side. I managed to slow down and stop the car, still in the middle of the road.

"Morning lads," I said, laughing.

"Are we there yet?" a voice croaked from the back seat.

I leaned forwards and put my head on the steering wheel.

Andy sleepily sat up in the front passenger seat. "You alright?" he asked, yawning.

"Yeah," I said, leaning back and taking a deep breath. "Getting a bit peckish, is all."

I needed a coffee, badly. Fortune would have it that we were not that far from Kota Tinggi and the roadsides were starting to show the ubiquitous small coffee houses. Most were still not yet set up but because the tappers started early, there were a few open. I continued on until I found a quiet one that had just opened. I pulled off the road and parked up.

"Breakfast lads, come on, wake up," I said.

We all sat around a metal table eating Nasi Lemak and drinking strong coffee in glasses. It was wonderful although I still had a bit of a tremble from the adrenaline rush of the near misses. I told them about the Bailey Bridge but not the tapper bike incident. Much later, during a lunch break on Arakan, I mentioned it to Andy. He was nonplussed. The car was fine and, although a bit muddy, there wasn't a mark on it. I had been very lucky. Later that day, when we had reached the waterfall, we all changed into our shorts and jumped into the deep rock pool. At the rear of the pool, the waterfall thundered down into it. Some brave souls went under it, but it was too strong a force of water for me to attempt it.

Around this time, my relationship with Carmen blossomed. We started dating a lot more seriously and I got to meet the rest of her family. There were a lot of them. There were five girls and three boys. The father was a Filipino and Mummy was a Cantonese speaking Vietnamese. Many of the family were musicians and good ones, too. The father had played violin in a National Orchestra and the eldest brother, Luis, had his own band. The father had had a stroke at some point and no longer able to play the violin. The large bass that was located in the front room belonged to Edward, whose family nickname was Toto. Mummy was a great character and, although fierce and very strict, we hit it off. She certainly ran a tight ship. Carmen's father Paul was not so keen on me, but I took little notice; Mummy was the power in that house.

Carmen's eldest sister was called Mona and she was married to an English lecturer-cum-author called Gregory Nalpon. They had two children, Zero and Jacinta. I would get to know them much later in life. One of her other sisters, Cecilia, was a stewardess working for Garuda Airlines and was seriously going with a lad called Harry Tay. Harry and I became close mates. I became very fond of Cecilia, and she was always supportive of me. Estrellita (Lina), Carmen's younger sister, I think was still at school then but about to leave. She was in her mid-teens. We never hit it off in those times and, for some reason, I found it difficult to get used to her. However, many years later we became good friends.

It was important to me to keep Mummy on side, and it was good when I was over at her house. She was always very serious and spent most of the time at the treadle Singer sewing machine or at the kitchen cooking range out the back. She cooked a fantastic curry, a Malaysian beef Rendang, and sometimes I would watch her cook, fascinated with the ways and methods of Asian cooking.

The cooking range was a large gas cooker that looked more like an Aga in a partially open area where there was also a sink and a large wooden table in the middle. Further along from this was an open yard with a clothes line. A narrow, shallow gutter ran down the centre of this area. To the left was a small outhouse that had an outside 'dunny' and a shower/wash stall. This had a large, open forty-gallon drum in it that was kept full of fresh water. A plastic saucepan apparatus was hung on a hook. The idea was that you stood in this stall area, closed the wooden door that never came to a full height, and sluiced yourself down. It was the next best thing to a shower. It all sounds pretty basic, and I guess it was, but it worked well, and I did later use it a few times.

Carmen had a job on the telephone exchange of the Mandarin Hotel down on Collyer Key. We sometimes met up for lunch there and had dim-sum in the mall which was then quite new. Meanwhile, things on Arakan were winding down and we were still working around Malaysia, dropping off equipment and such. Just before Christmas, Andy found the job he was looking for. It was on a private yacht called the Mia Mia that was heading for the UK via South Africa. I was pleased for him but felt sad that he was going. He organised his discharge and left Arakan. He was still with me at St Heliers Avenue but that, too, would soon come to an end.

We had our two cats – William and Sooty – and we both knew that we would have to do something about them. For a while, we put it all on hold and sorted ourselves out. I would set in motion my discharge, go back to the UK, and wait for Andy. We had some good plans. His yacht was sailing in January '71 and would eventually arrive in the UK around Sept/Oct '71. That suited me fine. I would be home before him which gave me time to save some money. We both wanted to live in Singapore, so that meant leaving UK together to come back out. However, we were going to do it by road. We would both buy new motorbikes in the UK, kit them out, and make our way across Europe over the Bosporus and pick up a boat to India. From there, we'd travel across the Thai/Malay border and make our way down Malaysia to Singapore. It was an adventure we were both looking forward to.

I wrote my discharge request and set it in motion. Meanwhile, Andy was tidying things up and getting himself organised for his move to the yacht. Not long after he had his gear aboard, he invited me for a look around. It was certainly a good piece of kit, and the engine didn't look to be too difficult to maintain. He had a nice cabin, and he was well satisfied with the set up. I saw some of his fellow Filipino crew members but didn't converse with them. Andy was a quiet lad who kept pretty much to himself and was a competent engineer with loads of common sense. He would be okay on this yacht.

A week before his departure, we made the decision to have William and Sooty put to sleep. Both cats were only friendly and tuned-in to the both of us. If anyone else approached them, they would go for them, and we didn't want them to live as strays or be mistreated. It was an awful moment for us, but we were with them both when they went. It felt very much like the closing of a door for me. Something had changed in my life, and it may sound strange to say that it hinged on something like the two cats, but everything felt different after that.

I couldn't get time off to see Andy sail, so we said our goodbyes at the house. We were both excited about the prospects ahead and looking forward to our new lives and adventures to come. However, fate had a different play on things. Andy had sold his bike and I was in the process of getting rid of mine. When the taxi came to take him to the yacht, I felt a lump in my throat. We'd spent many good times together, on and off the LCTs and were as close as brothers. As we hugged and he got in the taxi, we promised to see each other again soon.

After Andy left on his yacht, I kept the house in St Heliers Avenue on for a while and still had Bron staying with me. She too was missing him, but we supported each other well. Without Andy and the cats, I just wanted to move on. Bron found a place with a friend for a while but because her relationship with Jeffrey Jellah was difficult, she had decided to go back home to the UK. Things were changing rapidly. I decided to move back aboard Arakan until I too left for the UK.

Eventually, my discharge approval came through and I was due to fly home to get it sorted. I was to fly on 6th June. I made a point to see Anita and explain my plans and told her that Andy and I would, hopefully, be back towards the end of the year. She wasn't happy about the time frame but there was little I could do. She knew I'd been seeing Carmen 'on occasion' and it didn't go down well. But because of her circumstances, she knew something like this could happen.

Meanwhile, things with Carmen were going well. Although I wasn't totally committed to any serious relationship, we did see a lot of each other. She knew about Anita but not how close we were. I was being an idiot about it, thinking I could manage both girls, especially as Anita had restrictions imposed on her. I took advantage of that situation, but it would come back to bite me badly in the future. I behaved stupidly in those days but life in Singapore, in those times, was every young hot-blooded male's dream. I certainly didn't realise what was coming. I was also getting the proverbial feet under the table with Carmen and her family. I was well accepted by all of them with the exception of Carmen's father. I didn't like him, and he didn't like me, but I couldn't put my finger on why at the time. I also became very friendly with Carmen's sister's boyfriend, Harry. We became quite good mates.

Harry was from a 'Baba' family. This means a Chinese/Malay mix. His family lived in a small, residential estate downtown. He had two sisters and I got on well with them all. His father had been a well-known boxing enthusiast and had run a small gym. He was well known and respected by all and, as I later found out, by the Singapore underworld as well. Every now and again Harry and I would meet up for a beer and we'd go back to his place for a curry made by his mum.

Carmen was upset that I was leaving but knew it had to happen that way. She said she would wait for me and write when I was home. I'd told Mum about her, and she was keen to see a picture. Life aboard Arakan was getting busy as the British Forces were preparing to leave the Far East. My time aboard the LCTs was drawing to a close and I was now getting impatient to leave the services. I knew I would miss the boats quite a lot. I loved the Ts and being part of the crew, it was just all the Army bullshit that went with it that I objected to.

I had forwarded most of my stuff ahead of me, including Andy's toolbox along with mine. An army Land Rover picked me up from the ship and took me to Changi airbase where I boarded a BOAC Comet back to the UK. As we drove away from the dockside and Arakan, I felt a fear for the future and a sadness too at leaving the services and the LCTs. So much of my growing up and impressionable life had been during training and whilst serving on these ships and the camaraderie of the crews was second to none. I would miss it a lot, and even to this day, I can still feel that loss.

53

Being back in the UK was a massive wakeup call on many levels. The weather wasn't brilliant, which meant that the temperature was below the average for this time of year. It was June '71, heading into summer and I was freezing. I was also back in Gosport at St Georges Barracks while I awaited my discharge. Nothing is straight forward in the services and the red tape was stunning. Still, the outcome was what I had been waiting for. I'd arrived back in the UK on 7th June '71 only to be told that it would take a couple of months. So, I had to do some shore-side duties, mostly helping out in the workshops. I'd popped home to see Mum and explained the situation to her. She was glad to have me home, but I knew she was worried about me. After summer I would be out of a job, so I needed to get something temporary until Andy arrived back. It was a good opportunity to save some money, but I still had to give Mum some housekeeping money so getting some kind of work was necessary.

I went across to the NAAFI Club in Pompey a few times but didn't see anyone I knew. The girls had all been drafted to various units and most of the lads Tom and I knew were off doing other things on different ships. I was killing time waiting for my discharge notification to come through. There were moments when I stood by the harbour wall and watched the Ts come and go. Also, on the ferry over from Gosport to Pompey, you could see them in the Gunwharf. A couple of times I had popped on board for a chat. It was during this uncomfortable time, that I wondered if I had done the right thing. I knew I would miss the lads and the camaraderie that was always present during life aboard the ships. I did get a letter from the MOD offering me a two-stripe corporal rank with the opportunity to go on a course for my sergeant stripes. It was tempting but the pull of Singapore was too strong, so I turned it down. Besides, I didn't quite trust them to keep to their word.

On 10th August '71, I was ordered to attend the adjutant's office at Gosport barracks. Major Armstrong was in his office when I marched in. My discharge had at last come through. We had a pleasant chat and once again I was asked if I wanted to change my mind. They were offering the second stripe with an almost certain guarantee of the third stripe and, I have to say, it was tempting. I was missing life aboard the Ts but the adventure that was looming with Andy, the thrill of the long drive across Europe, then the Baltic states, on into Asia and then to Singapore, far out-weighed staying in the services. Little did I know that fate had other plans.

At some time during our conversation, a strong shaft of sunlight came through the high-level window behind him and struck the little red book that was on his desk. This was my discharge book, and I took that to be something of a sign. He flipped it open, and I was invited to go through it with him. As this progressed, we chatted about things, and he eventually asked me what my future intentions were. I explained about going back to the Far East to live and work. He just nodded and at the last page in the little red book, he picked up his pen and signed the page. Picking up a rubber stamp, he brought this down in a sort of act of finality and closed the book. Dust motes floated in the shaft of sunlight and we both sat there, saying nothing for a moment. He pushed his chair back and stood, holding his hand out. I stood and shook his hand and then saluted. It was my last formal act in the military. He said my book would be posted on to me at home and wished me luck for the future. I nodded, turned, and walked out, feeling the emotive power of the moment as I closed his office door and made my way out of the gloomy interior of this aged building and into the August sunshine. I felt a massive relief that it was done but also, if I was to be honest, a little fear too. I'd known very little else except military life for most of those early years and I suddenly felt a little cast adrift.

My next job was to hand in my uniform and what remained of my kit to the QM over at the barracks. I packed what I had left into a large, green kitbag, changed into jeans and jacket and, with a last look back at the made bed where I had been staying in St George's barracks, and the now empty metal locker, pulled the large door to the room quietly shut behind me. Then I walked out onto the veranda and down the steps to the QM's store to hand the kit back in. Ten years had passed. This was the end of that particular chapter and now it was all about what was ahead of me. I began to feel the tingling of excitement, tinged, I have to say, with an amount of fear. Over the years of my military service, I had learned to suppress fear and think on a positive level. Sitting on the train heading home, I looked out the window and as the scenery slid past, I wondered where the next ten years would take me.

There are times when certain moments stay with you forever and these are not always the ones of earth-shattering importance. When I walked away from the major's office, if I was to be really honest, I felt quite sad. I was walking out of the military for good; an establishment I had set my heart and mind on, more or less ever since I had left school. Images of my service time flashed through my mind, the ups and downs, the good and bad, the faces of friends, the places visited and lived in. It was a collage of all of these, and it made me swallow hard. I had no regrets at getting out now as I felt I had outgrown the services and military life, but it did bring a sadness for the friends and ships I was walking away from.

If I had stayed, I'm sure it would have been significantly harder to leave and by then I would have been quite a bit older and not as prepared for life after the military. I had my own road to travel and my own mark to make on the planet, not one that was based on the direction the services and establishment wanted. Life, places, people, environments, all were changing around me, and I hoped that I would be up to meet the challenges that this next chapter would be throwing at me. As I came out of the room, I took a last look back at my neatly made bed with the locker beside it. I stood a moment with my hand on the doorknob, smiled to myself, gently closing the door behind me, and walked away.

Once home in Bishop's Stortford I sorted out my things in my bedroom and went downstairs to Mum's cup of tea she had just brewed. She was just bringing in some washing off the line in the back yard and was preparing to put another load in the washing machine, mostly of my bits. It was a really warm day, so we sat on the back step and chatted and drank tea. It was so good to be home and I felt like a massive weight had been lifted. I could tell that she was really pleased to have me home but at the same time, worried about what I was going to do next. There were letters waiting for me from Carmen, mostly expressing how much she missed me and a list of items she wanted me to bring back when I returned. I also had letters from Anita and Rachel Sequerah, a very close friend who also kept me up to date on what was happening with the 'Exclusive Club'. Mum knew I was waiting for Andy to arrive back. I explained to her that once he was back, we would set about making plans for our return to Singapore, overland. We were going to buy identical motorcycles, probably a Triumph and organise spares, etc. to take with us, as well as planning our route.

I don't think Mum was particularly impressed about what Andy and I had planned. It was a long trip, but our love of bikes and adventure was something neither of us could ignore. Both Jo and Di were home, and the place was a bit neat, not to put a too finer point on it. But Mum loved having us all around. During the day, both girls were working so it was pretty quiet. I hadn't thought about getting a job because I knew I wouldn't be around that long. However, I was an extra mouth to feed so I did think about doing some odd work. In my infinite wisdom, I decided to do some painting and decorating work and Mum said she knew of someone that needed the interior of their house doing. However, I struggled with the stripping the wallpaper bit and, with the best of intentions, I was doing a terrible job. Needless to say, I didn't last and so decided to shelve my attempts at DIY.

It was near the end of August that I received a letter that was to change everything. It was from Andy's brother John, informing me that Andy had been killed.

At the end of July, Andy's yacht had reached Rodrigues Island, about three hundred and fifty miles east of Mauritius, in the Indian ocean. On 1st August, he was supposedly with a friend in a small dinghy just off the island. The friend was diving and left Andy in the dinghy. He decided to row nearer to a coral reef. He'd also mentioned that he intended visiting an English family who lived on Rodrigues Island. The chap that had been diving went back to the anchored yacht, leaving Andy to it. By teatime, however, when Andy hadn't returned, the crew notified the local police. The crew looked for him, but nothing was found until the following day when the overturned dinghy was discovered in a lagoon, along with his body.

Andy was a good boat handler and had done a lot of dinghy sailing. However, I knew he couldn't swim – a serious failing.

I was stunned and shocked. I sat on the couch in Mum's front room just looking out the front window, trying to put together in my head this sudden turn of events. It was an overcast day and clouds were scudding across the sky whilst birds aloft were struggling to maintain a course in the high winds trying to gain shelter in the branches of nearby trees. I likened my feelings at that moment to the birds. I'd suddenly lost my rudder and was adrift, unable to achieve any direction at all.

I knew Andy couldn't swim but he was a good dinghy handler and certainly wasn't someone prone to panic. John's letter had further gone on to say that his parents couldn't afford to have him flown home, so he had been buried on the island

A couple of years later there was to be an odd and coincidental turn of events that led me to believe that foul play could not be ruled out. Meanwhile, back home, I was at a loss as to what I was going to do.

Andy's demise changed the course of my life. It changed everything, but not my dream of returning to Singapore.

I had been using some of my savings to pay Mum but now I knew I had to get work until I could return to Singapore. My mind hadn't changed; I was going back there to live and work but now it was to be by air, and I would have to rethink about work out there.

Mum was as shocked about Andy as I was, but she had a much more practical and level approach. I was really down, and my mind was working overtime. I kept thinking about when we were living together in Serangoon Gardens, how we used to laugh at our two cats' antics, the trips to Malaysia on the bikes, the excitement of returning from the UK overland by bike, Bron's laughter with us over dinner, and his closeness to Sandy. It was a mental compilation of times spent in each other's company, especially just tinkering with the bikes and sultry evenings sitting on the porch drinking iced beer and chatting.

I shut myself away in my room and had a good cry into my pillow. A few hours later, Mum came up with a cup of tea and sat on the bed with me. She knew I was going through a host of feelings but feeling sorry for myself wasn't going to help. We talked about Singapore for a bit, but she was more concerned about here and now. She knew I had to throw myself into work and wandering about the house with my chin on the floor wasn't in the plans. The next day she got me the local newspaper and suggested I look through it for some work.

Both Anita and Carmen were corresponding at the time, so I wrote and told them about Andy. They were shocked and worried for me, but I said that I still intended returning to Singapore. I was still struggling to get my head around the turn of events and became more determined than ever to return to Singapore as soon as I was able. I have this tendency to overthink things, so it was more important than ever to get myself into a job as soon as possible.

As it happened, we used to get our milk delivered daily by Unigate and the milkman mentioned that the Co-op was looking for milkmen. I applied and got the job. It was mostly for some local outlying areas. The money wasn't too bad, but I had to start early. I was up at 04:00 a.m. to be at the Cold Storage by four thirty. This was about seven minutes' drive or twenty if walking. The depot was off the Dunmow Road, so it wasn't that far. Because most of my round was outlying areas, they had given me a bright yellow van. The rear of the van was open, and it was this that had to be loaded from the cold storage refrigerators. It was the time of year when the early mornings were starting to get really cold so hauling crates of milk and loading them on the van certainly got you warmed up. My sister Dinah had a Vauxhall Viva and sometimes I'd borrow that and drive to the cold storage. All the crates of milk that were mine had been loaded in a section of the walk-in refrigerator that was for my round, overnight. There was a sack-barrow that I could use to get them out of the fridge and move them over to the van, or 'float' as it was sometimes called. I had a book marked up with my various rounds requirements and I would therefore load the float in the order I would be delivering them. By the time I was able to get underway from the storage depot, I could make my first delivery at around 05:30 a.m.

There certainly was a learning curve in this job. It was mainly about learning the round as to who wanted what. At first, it was from the round book that I had to follow and for sure, I made a few mistakes. Not being sure of the round meant that it was taking me a lot longer to get through it and I wasn't finishing until around twelve to twelve thirty. Then I had to get back to the depot, unload the crates, and leave a note for any changes that were required.

But learning the round was not the biggest problem. The main issue was the piece of 'tack' they called a van; it was crap. The clutch turned out to be the main problem. It was so stiff that you almost had to stand on the pedal with both feet to get it in. After a couple of weeks of this I was starting to get problems with my left knee. I took the van round to my brother-in –law who was a motor mechanic and asked him to just check the pedal out and see if I was making a fuss over nothing. He was horrified when he tried it, so I got in touch with the Co-op and told them it needed fixing. They said they had a man at the cold storage depot that carried out running maintenance on the vans and they would get him to look at it. When I returned to the depot at the end of the round, I found the chap and told him. He said he'd sort it.

This was a seven-day job and at the weekends I had to collect the money from the customers. Most of the money I collected on Saturday and finished off collecting on Sunday. It was this part of being a milkman that was a whole new ballgame, something I'd never encountered before.

The old boy at the depot had told me that he had fixed the clutch and that he didn't know what I was making a fuss about. Well, whatever he did hadn't made any difference and I struggled on for a while longer. Meanwhile, I was getting to know the round and what people required without having to keep referring to the book. It was starting into autumn and one Sunday, one of the parents on a council estate asked me if one of their sons could help me out at weekends. I agreed. He was a scruffy little bugger with plenty of cheek with it, but he was useful. He got to learn from the book and although it was only at weekends, he was quite good fun to have around, and it helped the round go quicker.

One late September Sunday, along a quiet side road near Stanstead, the street was lined with massive horse-chestnut trees, and it was that time of the year when the branches were heavily laden with conkers. So, I parked the van under these trees and myself and the young lad both stood on the roof of the van and collected conkers. It was great fun, and we had a laugh doing it, even though I was late finishing the round.

The biggest problem with the job was collecting the money. There were some people that came up with all sorts of excuses to get out of paying. The main one was that I hadn't delivered their milk on certain days or that it must have been stolen. However, I used to tick the book by each address for every day that I delivered milk to them so that I knew I had certainly made the delivery. Others used make excuses for each week until their bill started to creep up. People would come up with the most amazing reasons to not pay. Usually, it was that they didn't have any change, couldn't find the cheque book, hubby hadn't left the money, they'd had an emergency expense… the list was endless and ninety percent of it was bullshit. In the end I'd notify the

Co-op who would then contact the customer. If they still tried to delay payment, I would stop delivering to them.

Then there were the OAPs, living on their own, who often never spoke to anyone from one end of the week to the other. They would often invite me in for a cuppa and chat about how hard times were. There were a group of railway cottages in Stanstead that were owned by a Trust for elderly people. These folk mostly lived on their own with the average age being around eighty. I never made it a habit to go into their homes, but one particular old lady always insisted that I come in and she would present me with a slice of Victoria sponge cake and a cup of tea. I was about three-quarters of my way through the round by this time and had already dropped the young lad off at his estate which was nearby. Her lounge was cluttered with knick-knacks and framed pictures. Her husband had passed away some years previously and she pointed him out in the photographs. He had been in the RAF and had flown in Bomber Command on the Lancs. She had also been in the WRAF as a chauffeur with the admin staff. He had been one of the few flight engineers to survive the demands of Bomber Command. There were lots of photos of them together in uniform. When she found out I was not long out of the services, it encouraged her to chat. She really was a dear old thing and I found it quite sad that she now lived alone, surrounded by all those pictures and memories.

One particular house that I had to collect from was not a good payer. On one Sunday morning I was without my little helper and decided I would need to get as many collections done as I could. I had already visited several houses and was doing well in collecting the money. It was around mid-morning when I knocked on this house. After a few minutes, the door opened and in front of me was a middle-aged lady with a very see-through negligée on. To make matters worse, it was open at the front. I stood there stunned for a moment then quickly looked down at my collection book. She owed about three weeks money and when I told her how much it was, she just stared at me. Then she asked me to come in for a moment while she tried to find her purse. I told her I was in a bit of a hurry as I was running late and suggested I leave it until next week. She just looked at me for a moment then shut the door. I breathed an enormous sigh of relief and practically dived across the road to the van.

Apparently, it was not uncommon to encounter this sort of thing and I could only conclude that people were more hard-up than I thought. There was certainly no shortage of incidents. Meanwhile, the milk van had still not had the clutch fixed and after repeated requests, I'd had about enough.

One sunny, Saturday morning, I had reached the village of Stanstead near the railway station. I still had about half a float of milk left to deliver. I parked up in a nice sunny spot and walked to a telephone box and rang the Co-op. I told them that I just couldn't drive it any longer, particularly as my knee was giving me a lot of pain. I told them that I had had enough, the keys were under the seat, and it still had half a load of milk on it, awaiting delivery. I then hung up and got the next train back to Stortford.

I actually thought that they would fire me, but they rang home later and said they would sort something out and would I continue tomorrow. It really all depended on what they did to the van. When I went in early the next morning there was a nearly new vehicle waiting for me. I loaded it up and found that it was a joy to drive after the previous piece of junk.

It was now approaching winter, and the cold weather was starting to settle in. I was communicating regularly with Singapore and both Carmen and Anita. I was saving hard to get some money together, but it was always good to hear from them and I was looking forward to going back out there. I never had a job lined up, but I felt confident I could get something.

Jo was home and we were sharing a bedroom. Mum's place was a two-bedroomed house, so Di slept with Mum in a large double bed and Jo, and I had two single beds in the rear bedroom. Because I had to get up early, I was always in bed before Jo, so that wasn't a problem. Jo had recently managed to get a job as a nanny to the American ambassador in Thessaloniki, Greece. She was really excited about it and would be going there in the New Year. That would make it a bit easier for me, but I knew that Mum was not quite so keen. Especially as I would be leaving for Singapore as well not long after Jo went.

As the weather turned, it started to get really cold. I was still keeping friends with the nurses at the Herts & Essex where Mum worked and every now and again, there would be a party. The nurses that I stayed friendly with were Susie, Sylvia, and Gene. Susie was married and from Trinidad, where her husband lived, Sylvia was single and an Indian from Guiana, and Gene was from Barbados. They were a good crowd and we all got on well together.

One Sunday morning it was particularly cold. We'd had snow for the past few days, and it was freezing. The round was going well, and I was keeping warm. I had the heater up full in the cab and although the roads were icy, they were manageable as long as you were careful. Just West of Stanstead was a large housing estate, and this was my next area of deliveries. I drove up this side road that curved into this estate. The roads were pretty clear of snow and just a little icy. I came around the blind bend into the estate and there, parked in the middle of the road was a Unigate, three-wheeler float. In micro-seconds I took in the scene. The Unigate milkman was over the road, leaning against a doorway, chatting to one of his customers. I knew that if I hit the brakes my vehicle would slide badly on the icy road. So, I took the only course of action I could think of which was to squeeze past the side of the float.

Now these three-wheeler vehicles had a small cab at the rounded front and an open back which, like mine, held all the crates of milk. Around the three sides of this back section was a rounded, wooded part that acted as a sort of buffer. To get past him I had to squeeze alongside, between his vehicle and the kerb. I knew it would be tight, but I had little choice but to go for it as I was still moving forward. Now, the flat-bed part of my vehicle was fractionally lower than his. As I went past, mine just caught under this wooden part of his. It didn't do any damage to either vehicle except that it tilted his float sufficiently to off-load all his crates of milk onto the other side of the road. The sound of smashing glass was made more impressive as it was about 08:00 a.m. Sunday morning and very quiet.

I pulled up just past the rear of his float and sat a moment to catch my breath. What an idiot, to park up, on a blind bend, in the middle of an icy road. I got out the cab and wandered back. He was still standing with his customer, and both had their mouths open. I took in all the smashed bottles of milk that was now freezing as it ran across the road. I walked around to the front of his float and on his grimy windscreen I wrote *Co-Op 1 – Unigate 0*. As I walked back to my vehicle, I called up to him, "You're a frigging idiot," got in my cab, and drove on to deliver my milk.

When I'd completed all the deliveries and drove back to leave the estate, he had parked over to one side and was sweeping up the glass into the gutter. As I went past, he started yelling something, but I just waved and drove on. When I had completed my round, off-loaded all the empties and crates, and arrived home, Mum had a message for me to ring the Co-Op on Monday. When I did and explained what had happened, they seemed satisfied with that. I never did hear anything more.

The winter wore on and I was getting used to getting out early and completing the round in pretty good time. Since being back from the Far East it had taken me awhile to adjust to the need to wear additional clothing. As the weeks of my return turned into months, wearing scarves and gloves and a decent, warm jacket became quite a pleasant thing to do. Coming back to Mum's into a warm, cosy front room had its merits. The frosty mornings that nipped at your ears or the crunch of frozen snow underfoot had a lot going for them and every now and again, Jack Frost turned the bare trees into a world of nature's artistic canvas. The dark mornings with the declining moon glinting off a snow packed field, accompanied by a glittering box of stars, sometimes made you just stand and stare at the magical wonder of it. It was a far cry from the humid heat and polluted air of Singapore but there were moments when I truly did miss the heat and the smells of street cooked spices and the constant cry of hawkers. I missed the girls too but not the pressure that the two of them put me under, even if it was for the most part self-inflicted.

It was on one of these cold, crispy mornings when my sister Jo thought it would be 'fun' to come on the round with me. She was a bit grumpy to start with as it was early and bitterly cold. But it wasn't long before I had her delivering the required pints to the various houses and we started having a laugh about it. Just off the Stanstead high street was a row of bungalows. There were some roadworks on this street and to get past them and park-up I found it easier to go part up on the pavement. One particular bungalow was having some building work carried out in the front garden and parked just inside this was a small, mobile cement mixer. I'd parked up on the pavement near this house whilst we delivered the milk. It was freezing and it had been snowing overnight, so much of it had settled. We'd both been joking about something when we got in the cab to move off. Well, I had to reverse a bit to get back down onto the road. In doing so, I decided to reverse part way into the drive of the bungalow where the cement mixer was. In the semi-darkness I had misjudged it and as I was reversing, I knocked into the round drum of the cement mixer. Over it went with a bang. Being the early hours of Sunday morning, the noise seemed rather loud in the quiet of the cold, early dawn.

"Oops," I said. Well, that set Jo off and she went into fits of giggles. "Come on," I said, "You're going to have to help me set it upright."

We jumped out and stood looking at it and I stole a look around to see if any lights suddenly came on in the bungalow. Thankfully, all remained still and quiet. Because Jo was laughing so much, she was worse than useless, so I ended up having to struggle with it myself. There was absolutely no way I could manage it.

"Oh, fuck it," I said, standing in the snow panting. "Let's leave it."

We both stood there for a moment, looking about to see if any curtains in windows moved or lights came on, but all was quiet. We hurried back into the warmth of the cab, and I drove off. We never did hear any more about that.

One of the perks of being a milkman, and there weren't many, was bringing home the odd pint of Jersey Gold-Top, great in coffee and on cereal, and also the odd pint carton of double cream. I loved cream and every now and again would open a carton and drink some. We always had cream in the fridge at home now and Mum used it on puddings and the like.

One morning after I had finished the round and was back home, I went to the refrigerator and took out a pint carton of cream. As habit would have it, I gave it a good shake, believing it to be unopened. That was a big mistake! On the vigorous upswing of my shaking action, the foil lid flew off and almost the whole container of double cream, shot out. Well, it went absolutely everywhere. It was quite a small kitchen, so not only was I covered in it but so were the walls, appliances, and floor. I must have yelped because the next thing Mum came running in and stood there in horror, taking in the scene. Boy was she mad! She really went off on one and was furious. Jo must have wondered what the commotion was and came down to investigate. When she saw me standing there, covered in cream, dripping off my glasses, nose, and chin, she absolutely fell about. Of course, that started me off and we both ended up in hysterics. Mum was not at all amused which seemed to make it all the funnier. Needless to say, we both turned-to and helped her clean the place up.

That was a bit of a benchmark for me as I stopped drinking cream in such quantities. However, many years later I paid the price for my indulgence with cream as I developed cholecystitis, an inflammation of the gallbladder. If I was to even nibble at a cream cake, I would regret it, with severe pain in my right side. I kept away from any cream for a long time, but it took many years to right itself. It wasn't until I was in my late fifties that I could perhaps eat a cream cake without doubling over in pain. Pigging-out on cream and Gold Top milk was never a good idea.

Christmas was approaching and I knew that this was a time when milkmen could get some good tips. I remembered helping my uncle Les out on his rounds when he worked for the Express Dairies in Fulham and Chelsea. He always got good tips and was never shy to ask the customer for one at this time of year.

"A little Christmas tip for the milkman, Madam?" he would say. Keeping this in mind, I decided I would do the same thing. Some of the customers I delivered to were quite wealthy if the houses and cars were anything to go by. At the other extreme, there were also the other end of the spectrum with the old folks who lived in Alms Houses.

The response to tips was poor – either I never had the magic that Les had, or I was in a particularly mean area. One place I did hold out a bit of hope for was a section of wealthy houses in Stanstead. When I went to collect my weekly bill, I asked a particular customer, "Christmas box for the milkman?" in a sort of cap in hand approach, standing a little to one side to remind him of the Bentley and Porsche parked outside. He fumbled in his pocket for a moment and pulled out a handful of coins and notes.

"Here you are," he said, handing over a one-pound coin and as I looked down at it, he quickly closed the door. I stood there for a moment then pushed the coin back into his letterbox. Sod it, I couldn't be bothered with prats like that. The elderly lady I would often chat to in the Alms Houses gave me a five-pound note. Over the whole round, it was noticeable that it was the lesser well-off that gave the most tips. A sad fact of a milkman's lot.

That was a particularly bad winter and, as we got deeper into it, everything froze. I remember delivering a couple of pints to one house and in my haste, slipped on some ice I hadn't noticed. As I went down, the milk bottles I was holding smashed against the step and my wrist. It didn't bleed so I carried on delivering. Once I'd warmed up inside the cab, I looked down at my arm and it was bleeding profusely from a deep gash. I had to make an additional stop at the Herts & Essex A&E department and get it dressed.

I stayed at the job of milkman for another two weeks, after which I pulled the plug. I knew I would be going back to Singapore in the New Year, and we were now well into December. There were a few parties starting at the nurses' home at the Herts & Essex and they would have clashed with the job. Carol P. was now going seriously with a lad called Chris and I avoided seeing her where I could although that wasn't easy. We still felt for each other but as I wasn't staying in the

UK it wouldn't have been fair to reconnect too strongly again. Susie, Gene, and Sylvia were always around and when the parties were in swing, it was these nurses I hung around with. I was just glad to say goodbye to the Co-Op.

I had developed a healthy respect for milkmen and although, over the years, milk deliveries to the doorstep seem to be a thing of the past, it still happens. Living in Balsham, we have milk delivered to us every other day from a local dairy and it works well for us. I know that it would be cheaper from the supermarket, but I'm disinclined to give up the milkman. These days, milkmen deliver more than just milk, including veg and fruit and even firewood. We have salt delivered monthly for the water softener and these 25kg bags are not light. I wouldn't be doing a milkman's job these days. Although, they don't come collecting money at the door anymore, it's all done online. We still leave a tip, every Christmas for them, in an envelope under the empties.

The remaining days of that year seemed to coalesce into a blur of winter. Even Christmas seemed to be a down-played affair with the usual round of parties at the Herts & Essex and the girls that I knew so well. Christmas Day at Dee's was the annual run of family present giving with Mum and Dee making a huge dinner with all the trimmings and Di and Jo playing with the girls (Debs and Sarah). I was drinking beer with Ken and trying not to listen too hard to his tales of how good the war years were. My Aunt Alice was staying at Mum's and was with us that day. The outside temps had dropped to around -5°C, but it hadn't snowed. By late afternoon we were all full of turkey and Christmas pud and were laying around trying not too hard to fall asleep whilst Ken played a few of his old LPs. One particular moment that evening, I remember getting a raging headache, probably from the drink and the central heating. No one seemed to have any paracetamol; so, Alice offered me a couple of her Codeines and like a twit, I took them. Combined with alcohol, I think I nearly exploded. My blood pressure must have gone through the roof. I had to go out in the cold and walk about a bit to cool off. Mum went ballistic when she found out. Poor Alice got a mouthful from one of my sisters and I got it for being a plonker and taking them in the first place.

My mind was on other things and getting my head around going back to Singapore was making me anxious. I didn't want Mum to worry too much, and I made the case that I felt confident about getting work out there. Of course, the reality was that I wasn't confident at all and didn't know what the hell I was going to do. I missed Singapore life and of course, the girls, Anita, and Carmen. Carmen's family were just as important to me as Carmen, and I really wanted to fit in with them and the way of life there. But I was a long way off from that. It was difficult to explain all this to Mum and my sisters, although I think Jo had an idea and Di was always looking at the sensible approach. I was frightened, truth be told, of the unknown and of failure but I couldn't let anyone at home know that. I always think that Mum really knew but didn't let on. She would have been far happier if I had stayed in the UK and got a decent job of work there. But I felt unqualified by standards required over here and my apprenticeship and subsequent military time appeared not to count for much. I believe these days that would not be the case but in those times with inflation at a thirty-year high and the Conservatives under Ted Heath struggling, things were not too good. The Northern Ireland troubles were getting out of hand and had now spread to the mainland. It was, indeed, a difficult time in Britain and, with all that happening, I felt that moving to the Far East to seek my fortune was the best-case scenario.

Little was I to know the events that were in store…

Thank you for reading 'A Journey Through Dreamtime'. Volume Two will be available very soon, where you'll be able to read about the rest of my adventures in the Far East and beyond.

In memory of a good friend - Andy C. Mortimer

In memory of another good mate, Neil 'Brummy' Lawrence.

NOTES

Chapter 2

1. This scheme was the result of an agreement between the British and Australian governments. It started in 1945 and ended in 1972. It was an attempt to populate the Australian territories, and between 1950 and 1960 around one million people took this on. By 1969 these figures were down to around eighty thousand per year. The condition was that you had to stay there for at least two years. Like my parents, many were disillusioned and, in fact, around twenty-five percent of all immigrants returned to the UK. It was to cost around £120 for the return passage.

Chapter 43

1. There is a twist to this tale that was unexpected. Recently, my niece Debbie, from Canada, whose mum is my sister Delia, visited her for a week to see how she is. Dee is now in her eighties and is suffering a bit from dementia but still living in the same house in Stortford. While visiting with her, Debs asked me how the book was going. As I mentioned about Sandy, she said, "Oh, that's funny, Fred (her husband) and I were looking at that movie just recently." I was stunned. She said that he was stood outside the church as we came out and took the movie of all of us. How was that for a coincidence?

Printed in Great Britain
by Amazon